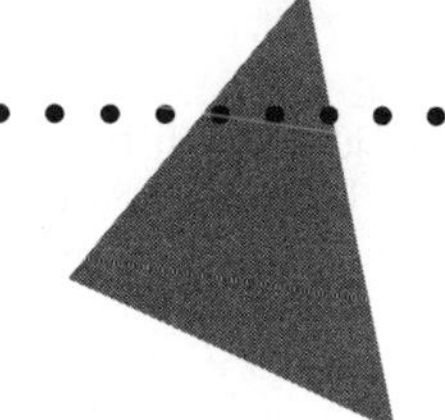

The Lotus Notes® Idea Book

Jeff Kovel, Kent Quirk, and Jay Gabin

Addison-Wesley Publishing Company

Reading, Massachusetts • Menlo Park, California • New York
Don Mills, Ontario • Wokingham, England • Amsterdam
Bonn • Sydney • Singapore • Tokyo • Madrid • San Juan
Paris • Seoul • Milan • Mexico City • Taipei

Many of the designations used by manufacturers and sellers to distinguish their products are claimed as trademarks. Where those designations appear in this book, and Addison-Wesley was aware of a trademark claim, the designations have been printed in initial capital letters or all capital letters.

The authors and publisher have taken care in preparation of this book, but make no expressed or implied warranty of any kind and assume no responsibility for errors or omissions. No liability is assumed for incidental or consequential damages in connection with or arising out of the use of the information or programs contained herein.

Library of Congress Cataloging-in-Publication Data

Kovel, Jeff.
    The Lotus notes idea book / Jeff Kovel, Kent Quirk, and Jay Gabin.
      p. cm.
    Includes index.
    ISBN 0-201-40787-6
    1. Lotus Notes for Windows.   2. Business—Computer programs.
  3. Database management—Computer programs.   4. Application software.
  5. Computer software—Development   I. Quirk, Kent.   II. Gabin,
Jay.   III. Title.
    HF5548.4.L692K68   1996
650'.0285'46—dc20   95–44807
                                                     CIP

Sponsoring Editor: Kathleen Tibbetts
Project Manager: Sarah Weaver
Production Coordinator: Erin Sweeney
Cover design: David High
Text design: Kim Arney
Set in 10 point Sabon by Pure Imaging

2 3 4 5 6 7 8 9 MA 0100999897
Second printing, June 1997

Addison-Wesley books are available for bulk purchases by corporations, institutions, and other organizations. For more information please contact the Corporate, Government, and Special Sales Department at (800) 238-9682.

Find us on the World-Wide Web at:
http://www.aw.com/devpress/

To Kim, who kept me working, and to Lincoln and Morgan, who kept me from working too much.

—Kent

To Pat Palmer, whose kind words I found so encouraging during the writing of this book.

—Jay

Contents

Part V Intercompany Applications   333

Index   379

Acknowledgments

Many thanks to all of the people who helped us during the creation of this book. In particular, we'd like to thank those who gave us advice, information, and encouragement. In alphabetical order, they include:

Laura Albert, Jimmy Becker, Michael Bertrand, Joanne Buckholz, Candace Clemens, Paula Daley, Adam Duboff, Paul Edwards, Patrick Fetterman, Luis Genao, Marc Griseta, Marni Hoyle, Pam Hurley, Melissa Leffler, Dave Kimball, Alison Kuryla, Cindy Null, Chuck Olsen, Suzanne Pahr, Lisa Petrucci, Art Quirk, Chris Quirk, Jennifer Schmidt, Diana Sykes, and Joseph Tutrone.

Special thanks to Kathleen Tibbets, Erin Sweeney, and their compatriots at Addison-Wesley who kept us firmly pointed on the right path. If this book hangs together, it was they who provided the glue.

Introduction

I Know I Need Notes, But I Don't Know Why

The genesis of this book can be traced to a dilemma faced by the CIO (Chief Information Officer) of a Fortune 500 corporation. This CIO was confused about Lotus Notes. For many months, his employees had been arguing that the company needed Notes. When asked to justify this claim, the employees provided vague and inconclusive arguments like: "We'll be left behind if we don't"; "Notes will help us communicate"; "Notes is the best groupware application available today"; "Notes can automate our work flows." The CIO grouped these arguments under the heading "I know I need Notes, but I don't know why."

According to our CIO, corporate computing was about providing reports—sales, expenses, income, and inventories. The company already had e-mail—why did it need Notes? Notes was costly—it would require new hardware, software, training, support, and consulting. Where was the return on the investment? What arguments could be produced to justify the purchase to management? Finally, after months of discussions, the CIO attended a Notes symposium conducted by Lotus Development Corporation. Rather than focus on the features or capabilities of Notes, this symposium reviewed a small number of successful Notes applications. By seeing how Notes had been used to solve business problems, the CIO began to see through the haze surrounding Notes. As the demonstration progressed, it became clearer and clearer what Notes was, how it fit into the corporate computing environment, and how his organization could benefit from its implementation.

This story is typical. Notes is an application development environment with powerful capabilities, many of which are unique to Notes. The breadth and depth of tools available can be overwhelming to the uninitiated. This book is intended to help readers get their hands on Notes. Each chapter reviews a different application. It took a demonstration of relevant applications for the CIO to understand the power of Notes, and we believe this is true for other people as well. By introducing the reader to a number of successful Notes applications, we hope that the reader will come to a better understanding of Notes and the role it can play in helping organizations communicate more effectively. For the newcomer to Notes, reading about these applications provides insight about what Notes is and how it can be used. For the manager of a Notes environment, this book provides examples of useful Notes applications and helpful Notes companion products. The Notes application developer will be able to see how other developers have solved similar business and technical problems. Each of these audiences will probably use this book a little differently. The newcomer to Notes will want to read the first few chapters sequentially. The Notes manager or application developer will probably want to use the book as a reference, reading chapters selectively.

The conclusion to our story is that, after the Lotus conference, the CIO approved a pilot Notes program. The pilot phase lasted a few months during which time standards were established, applications were developed, and personnel trained. At the conclusion of the pilot, the company began a global rollout of Notes to all employees. This rollout is continuing to this day.

WHAT IS NOTES?

Notes is a client/server groupware application that provides powerful tools to help organizations share information more effectively. Simple enough, right? While none of these terms exactly defines Notes, each is an important component of Notes and needs to be understood in that regard. Let's look at each one individually.

First of all, there is the client/server aspect of Notes. The *client* portion of Notes runs exclusively in graphical environments including Windows, OS/2, MacOS, and a number of versions of Unix. The client provides a very simple interface to create, edit, view, and delete *documents* (the basic unit of storage in a Notes database). In addition, it provides users with the ability to create and send e-mail messages and tools to develop new Notes applications.

Databases can be stored either locally on the user's workstation or on a server. Databases stored on a server can be shared among all users with access to that server. Access requires some type of connection to the server, which can be a LAN or a telephone line and a modem. The fact that users can connect to their server by modem is part of the package's strong support for mobile users.

Servers are typically powerful computers with large hard disks. The Notes server software runs under OS/2, Windows NT, Novell NLM, and a number of versions of Unix. Once a database has been copied to a server, that database can be *replicated* to other servers. Replication is a process whereby two databases can be synchronized according to an administrator-defined schedule. Let's say your company replicates a sales discussion database between your Chicago and New York servers. If this replication occurs hourly, messages posted in either New York or Chicago will show up on the other server within one hour.

The next term in our description, *groupware*, generally refers to applications offering at least one of the following features: e-mail, group scheduling, electronic forms, work flow, and discussion databases. While Notes provides some level of support for all these features, many of them require add-on applications (Lotus calls these add-on applications "companion products"). For example, while it is possible to create a Notes application that allows users to share their schedules, Notes does not inherently provide strong support for group scheduling. This is largely because Notes does not offer a calendar view of data stored in a Notes database, and it is difficult to support the queries that are typical of group scheduling applications (e.g., "Is Jane free for a meeting tomorrow at 3:00 PM? Is there a room with a whiteboard free in my building?"). There are, however, a number of companion products, such as Lotus Organizer, that work in conjunction with Notes to provide group scheduling capabilities.

A number of features in Notes set it apart from other groupware applications. Notes has the most robust security of any groupware application on the market today. This built-in security is very popular with large companies (and should be taken seriously by small companies as well). In addition, Notes provides tools to help distributed offices and workers share information with one another almost as if they were located in the main office. Having been through a number of releases, Notes is more mature than most of its competitors. As a result, Notes consulting services are readily available, new companion products are announced every day, and many companies offer services around Notes. Finally, Notes supports many different computer platforms. These characteristics really set Notes apart from the other groupware applications on the market.

The last part of our starting description of Notes involves the "powerful tools to help organizations share information more effectively." In each version of Notes, new tools have been added to make managing information easier. In the first version, users could look at a list of all the documents in a database. This feature was named views. In subsequent versions, Lotus implemented a full-text search engine. This tool allows users to perform lightning-fast queries locating all occurrences of a text string in a database. This tool is indispensable for locating relevant information in a large database. Lotus also provided a macro language (much enhanced in V4) to allow developers real flexibility in creating applications. Lotus has also provided tools to get data from other environments. These tools include robust support for OLE (object linking and embedding) and formulas that can retrieve data from other applications.

SO WHY IS NOTES SO GREAT?

Notes is a powerful platform for developing applications to share information. While it is difficult to pick a definitive list of useful Notes features, here are some of the leading choices:

Feature	Description
Multiplatform support	The client version of Notes runs on Windows, OS/2, MacOS, and Unix. The server version runs on Windows, Windows NT, OS/2, Novell, and Unix.
Easy to use	End users only need to learn a few menu commands to begin contributing and receiving information in Notes.
Industry standard	Notes is in use at thousands of companies around the globe.
Mature	Notes is a mature product, having been through a number of releases. As a result, it is reasonably stable and feature-rich, in comparison with other groupware applications.
Robust security	Notes security is based on the RSA security model, which is one of the most advanced and comprehensive security models available in computing.
Published API	Lotus provides programmers with Visual Basic, C, and C++ tools which allow them to build their own custom applications around Notes.

WHO USES NOTES?

Notes has been deployed in just about every industry imaginable. Up until recently, Notes was a very expensive piece of software that could be purchased only in large quantities. This restricted its market to the largest corporations. Recently, the price has moved significantly lower, and the product can be purchased one license at a time. This trend has been complemented by an increasingly skilled training and consulting community, all of which have lowered the barrier to entry for new organizations considering Notes. Early adopters of Notes tended to be forward-thinking companies looking for tools to change the way they did business. Some examples are provided in the following paragraphs.

One of the first organizations to adopt Notes was PriceWaterhouse. PriceWaterhouse is a large accounting and consulting company. They felt that deploying Notes would provide them with a significant advantage over their competitors. In Notes, they could share information about projects and clients. A user in New York could post a question in a discussion database and that question would be read and responded to by thousands of other users around the world in a matter of hours. In the succeeding years, many other consulting organizations agreed with the logic of PriceWaterhouse's decision and also purchased Notes.

Other early adopters of Notes included high-technology companies. These companies have a number of things in common with the consulting organizations: they are quick to adopt new technologies and tend to do most of their work in teams. These qualities allowed them to integrate Notes into their businesses rapidly. High-technology companies commonly use Notes to provide their partners and customers with information on their products, or to provide product support.

A number of government organizations (both within and outside of the United States) have deployed Notes to help them share information. Notes was selected over other packages because of its advanced security model, the inclusion of electronic mail, and ease of use. Among other applications, Notes has been integrated into the process of accumulating data and disseminating research.

Notes is in use in every industry imaginable. Large installations of Notes exist in pharmaceuticals, banking, consumer products, insurance, and automotive companies, to name a few. As you go through the applications described in this book, you will start to understand why they have all selected Notes, and what business problems they believe Notes solves.

I Guess I Need Notes, and I Still Don't Know Why. . .

If you have reached this point in the book and still aren't clear about what Notes is or how it might help your organization, you're not alone. Notes is a mature, powerful, feature-rich application development environment. It can take years to familiarize yourself with all the features included in the product. However, by reviewing the applications discussed in this book, we believe you will come to a clear understanding of what Notes is capable of and how Notes might be used in your organization.

PART 1

Using Notes for the First Time

Moving Notes into a company is a big decision. Notes is not just a desktop application that can be installed on one computer for a trial. In order to determine whether Notes is going to meet the needs of any given site, it has to be installed for at least a small group and given enough time to take root.

When an organization first installs Notes, it tends to follow one of two paths. One path involves a carefully planned pilot project, such as the one that was run at Chipcom (see "A Notes Pilot"). This path is usually taken by larger companies with a strong Information Systems group, who tend to proceed cautiously before adopting a new technology, but have enough resources to handle the training and support of a formal pilot project.

The other path involves a more free-form approach, installing Notes Mail and perhaps a couple of basic Discussion databases. On this path, people approach Notes at their own pace. Some will experiment with Notes Mail; others will read the Help database. This path is more likely to be followed by smaller organizations with a less formal structure.

Whichever path is chosen, the Notes applications discussed in this part of the book will play a key role.

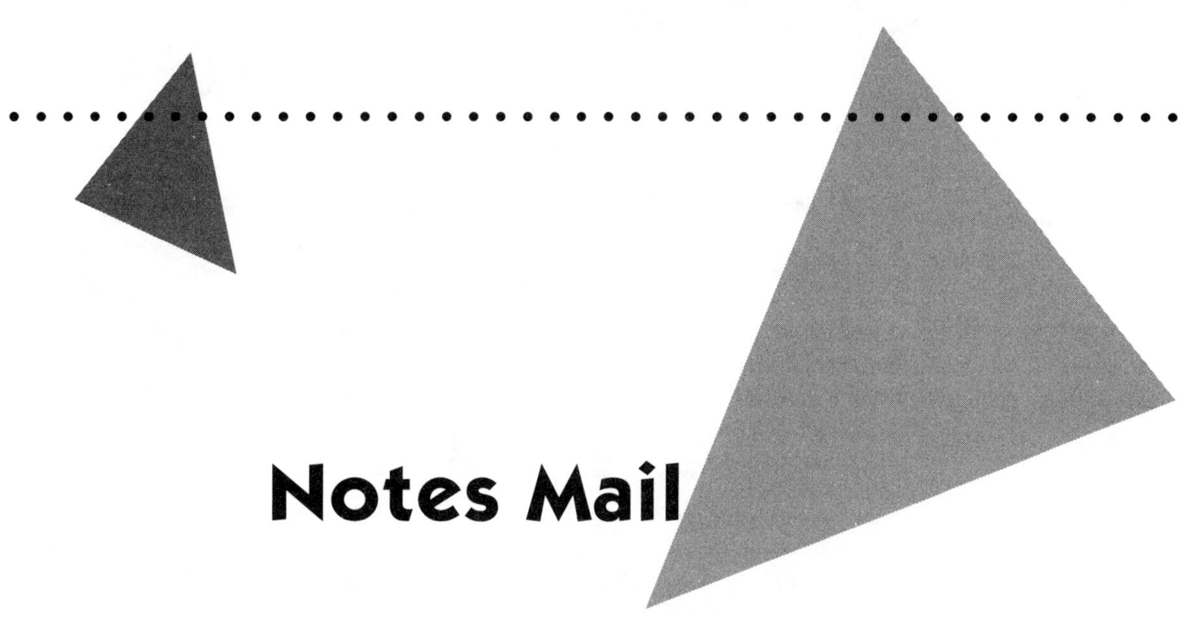

Notes Mail

Lotus Notes includes, as part of the product, a remarkably powerful electronic mail (e-mail) system. For companies needing only electronic mail, Notes is usually not an option, because even the least expensive Notes licenses cost about twice as much per user as a more traditional electronic mail product. But in situations where a company is already installing Notes on every desktop (or nearly every desktop), Notes Mail can have many benefits, in part because it integrates so well with other Notes applications.

Kimberley Foard is the system administrator for a hypothetical growing accounting firm. Her company has installed Notes for both e-mail and larger groupware applications. She has to train the general staff on Notes and plans to use e-mail as the way to introduce many of the basic concepts behind Notes.

The first thing she needs to talk about is the standard Notes environment. Starting Notes brings up the Notes Workspace. Like any Windows program, the Notes window has window borders and a menu. Like every Lotus program and many programs from other vendors, Notes also has an icon bar across the top and a status bar across the bottom.

In the center of the screen are several pages of what looks like folders or tabs. A Notes user can label each of the six page tabs individually. The pages are used to separate the user's Workspace into different groups of applications.

On each of the pages, the user can place *tiles* corresponding to applications. These tiles all have an icon and a title; they can also indicate the server and the number of unread messages in the application. The icons can be arranged by simply dragging them around the Workspace—even to other pages on the Workspace. Double-clicking on an icon opens the selected application for further work.

The Notes Workspace

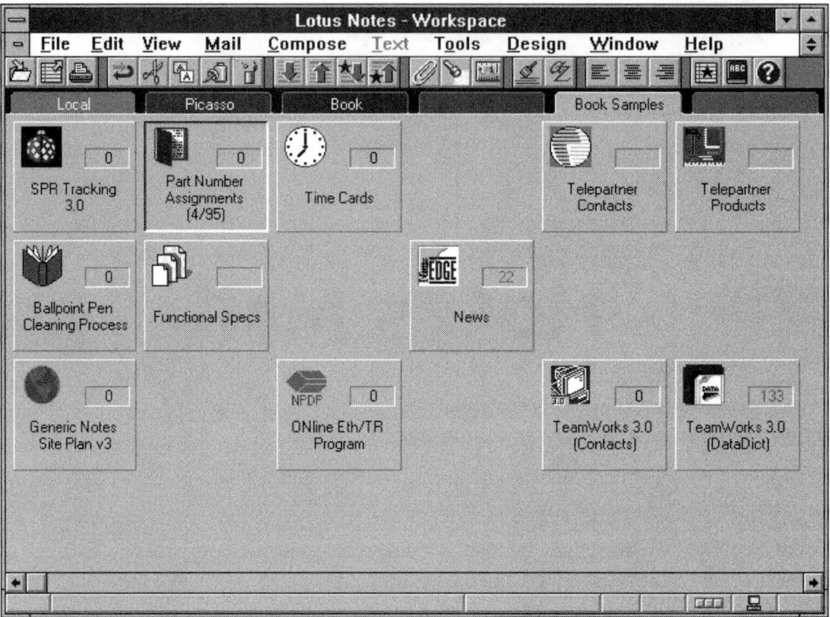

Kimberley decides that she will ask the students in the class to double-click the e-mail icon. Since Notes puts e-mail on every user's Workspace, she knows that everyone there will have a copy available. E-mail is also a good application for demonstrating some of the key features in Notes.

Opening the e-mail application opens up a Notes *view*. A view is a list of the documents in a database, arranged in some useful fashion. Each line of the view corresponds to a single document. A view can be organized in a wide variety of ways—sorted alphabetically, by date, or even categorized so that related documents get grouped together.

Any one Notes database can have many views. Most databases will have somewhere between three and ten different views, depending on the complexity and uses of the database. In a Mail database, one of the most useful views is the All by Category view.

In this view, the mail is first organized into categories, which are assigned by the person who owns the mailbox. Unassigned mail is grouped under the heading (Not Categorized), which makes it easy to find new mail, since new mail is uncategorized and this category shows up last. Within each category, the mail is sorted by date, newest at the bottom. So to see the latest messages, one can simply press Ctrl+End to get to the bottom of the view.

All by Category view in the Mail database

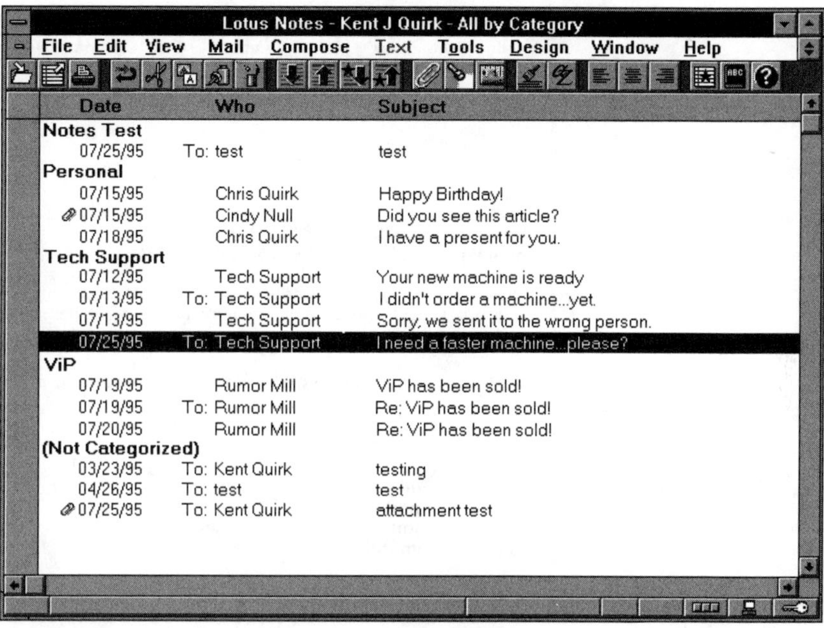

There are other views to choose from on the View menu. The Mail database comes with eight different views, and Kimberley decides to address them individually:

▶ All by Category sorts all messages, first by category and then by date.

▶ All by Date sorts all messages in the database by date. This is useful when looking for a particular message from a particular time.

▶ All by Person organizes received messages by the name of the sender and sent messages by the name of the recipient. This groups all correspondence to and from a single person together.

▶ All by Size sorts the documents by size. This is especially useful when one is trying to reduce the size of a mail file that's been accumulating messages for a bit too long.

▶ Attachments shows only those documents that have attachments. An *attachment* is an electronic file that has been, in essence, paper-clipped to the e-mail message. For example, to send along a copy of a spreadsheet so that the recipient can work on it, one can attach it to a Mail message. The Attachment view is sorted by date and shows not only the subject of the message, but also the number of attachments and their filenames.

A memo form being filled out

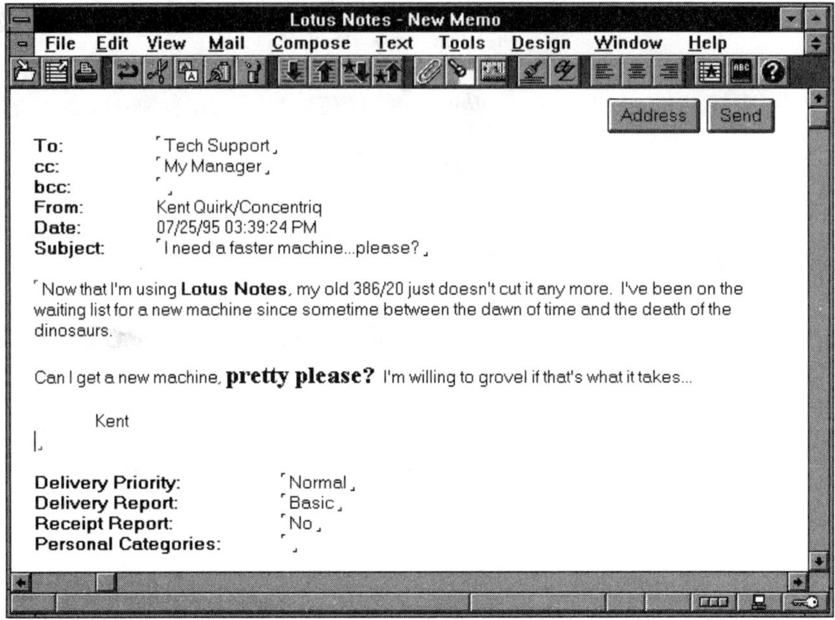

▶ Drafts by Category, Received by Category, and Sent by Category views all show a categorized view, but include only a subset of the full database. *Drafts* are documents that have not yet been mailed. Normally, sent and received documents are mixed together in the All by. . .views, but these views allow them to be separated.

At this point, Kimberley's whole class will have seen what views are, how to change views, and the range of views available in the Mail database. She can now move on to the act of creating and sending a Mail message.

NOTES, TAKE A MEMO

To compose a message, select Memo from the Compose menu. This opens up a blank mail form. Notes indicates the empty locations (fields) in the form with a pair of brackets. Filling in these fields is pretty easy. The To: field indicates the recipient; it is possible to send mail to more than one person at a time by separating the names with commas.

The cc: field sends an electronic "carbon copy" to other people to whom you want to send this message. The bcc: field sends a blind carbon copy—the other recipients don't see the contents of the bcc: field.

Note that the From: and Date: fields are automatically filled in. The From: field is filled in with the user name, and the Date: field by the current date. Neither field is editable. Notes does not permit users to mail anonymous or forged messages.

The Subject: line is the text that will show up in the view. It's intended to be a one-liner that briefly describes the content of the message. The body of the message is in a different, unlabeled field. This field is what Notes calls a *Rich Text* field. While the other fields are restricted to using the font, size, and color chosen by the database designer, a Rich Text field can use any graphic attributes at all, such as boldface, or a different size, color, or font.

Delivery Priority: field can be set to accelerate the delivery of mail in certain cases. The Delivery Report: field controls whether a reply is mailed to the sender when the message is delivered (or on delivery failures); a Receipt Report is sent when the message is actually read by the recipient.

When the message is completed, the user can press Esc, and Notes will present a dialog box with four options, each with a checkbox:

- ▶ **Save** saves the message in the sender's mail database.
- ▶ **Mail** mails the message to the recipient.
- ▶ **Sign** marks the message with an electronic "signature" that verifies who sent it, according to the Notes security system.
- ▶ **Encrypt** encodes the message so that only the recipient will be able to read it.

There are other kinds of forms that can be mailed. The standard Mail database includes the normal memo and reply forms for sending mail back to the author, and a special form for a phone memo (the equivalent of the pink "While you were out" forms used for taking messages).

Besides practicing filling in forms and navigating around them, Kimberley also expects to demonstrate the Sign, Encrypt, and Receipt Report features in the class. She can have the students send mail to one another and see these features work from both sides.

RECEIVING MAIL

Notes is set up to check for mail every so often (normally every 15 minutes, but that can be changed). When mail has arrived, Notes plays a little tune. New (unread) mail is indicated by a star in the left column, and the entire line of text in the view turns red. Double-clicking on a document opens it for reading.

There are a couple of ways to categorize Mail documents so that they show up in the view as categorized. The easiest way is to click the Categorize button while reading the message. This presents a small dialog box with a list of all existing categories, plus a place to add a new one. To categorize from the view level (useful for categorizing many documents at once), select the documents by clicking in the left margin of the view. When all needed documents are selected, choose Categorize from the Tools menu; the same dialog box pops up.

At this point, Kimberley has just about run out of time, but there are still a couple of features she should mention, in large part because these features give great benefit to a Notes installation.

Most electronic mail systems have the ability to forward a Mail message to another user. Notes can also do this, but it also can forward any document in any Notes database. Furthermore, instead of forwarding the contents of a document, it may be more useful to forward only a link to the other document. A *doclink* lets the recipient click on a small icon and read the actual document in the context of the database it came from. While these may not seem like big advantages early in the life of a Notes installation, these features become ever more powerful as the company matures in its use of Notes.

Kimberley is ready to teach her class. Besides being a powerful Notes application in its own right, Notes Mail is proving to be a good introduction to the entire Notes product.

FACT SHEET

Notes Mail

Purpose: Electronic mail communications between Notes users.

Application Origin: Standard Notes application, installed automatically with Notes.

Application Development Time: None.

Typical Size: 3–5 MB. Some users prefer to use Mail as a filing system, and let their mail files grow to 30 MB and more. Many organizations limit users to a maximum of 10 MB.

Forms: The basic form is the memo; there are also forms for replying to the author of a memo, replying to everyone named in the memo, and for taking phone messages.

Views: There are several views for seeing all documents in the database. The categorized view shows the messages organized by categories (assigned by the database user). There are also views sorted by person and by date, as well as other categorized views that show only draft, sent, or received memos.

The Help Database

Help in Notes

Like many computer programs, Notes has a built-in help system. Notes help is stored in a Notes database. This is different from most applications, which store help in a special file format defined by the operating environment. For example, most Windows applications store help information in a file that can be read by the Windows Help program. When you press F1, the Windows Help program runs and loads the help file for the application. The Windows Help program offers a consistent interface for help across most Windows applications. Unfortunately (or fortunately depending on your choice of operating system), Notes runs in a number of different operating environments, including Windows, OS/2, MacOS, and Unix. Rather than develop a unique help system for each operating environment, Lotus decided to store Notes Help in a Notes database. This has allowed the Notes developers to create a help system that is consistent across all platforms.

Starting with Help

In addition to generic help, Notes offers users *context-sensitive help*. Rather than just leaving the user at the top of a list of topics, context-sensitive help provides information that is directly related to the user's current activities. For example, when you have the File–New Database dialog open on your screen in Notes, you probably need help with creating a new database. Context-sensitive help is available at any time in Notes by pressing the Help key (F1 on PCs).

To see the Help database, run Notes. Notes starts you in the Notes Workspace (with your folders and database icons). Press the Help key (F1 on PCs) to bring up a document that provides information about the Notes Workspace. This is an example of context-sensitive help. If you open a view and press the Help key, Notes provides help about using views. If you open a document and press the Help key, Notes provides help about moving around in a document. If you are editing a document and press Help, Notes provides help on creating, updating, and saving documents.

Let's take a closer look at the Notes Workspace Help screen. The first thing we notice are a number of words surrounded by boxes (if you have a color monitor, the boxes are probably green). These boxes indicate that *pop-up help* is available on this topic. Pop-up boxes can be activated by holding down the left mouse button while the mouse pointer is inside the green border. Pop-up help is typically provided to define relevant key words or phrases that are important to understanding the current help document.

In addition to pop-up boxes, the Notes Workspace Help screen is interspersed with small rectangular gray boxes. These are Notes *doclinks*, links to other documents. Double-clicking on a doclink brings up another document. The developers of the Help database use doclinks to refer the reader to another document in the Help database that provides more information on a

Context-sensitive help on creating, saving, and editing Notes Documents

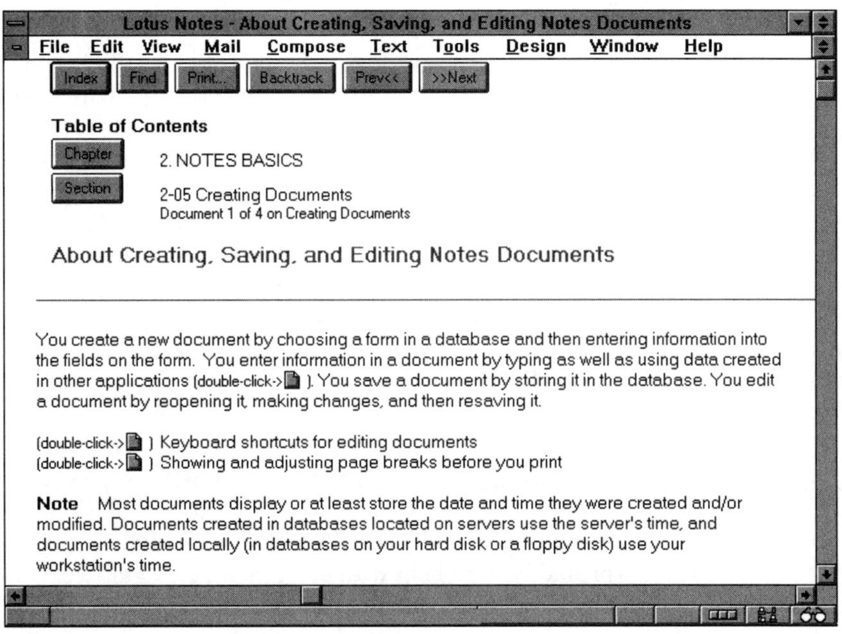

particular topic. Doclinks and pop-up help allow the user to collect information quickly on important topics related to the help search.

While context-sensitive help is easy to use, there are a number of drawbacks to its implementation in Notes. First, Notes is not particularly good at guessing the context of your request for help. If the information you are looking for is very specific (e.g., "What is the shortcut keystroke to switch to Edit mode when a document is highlighted in a view?" Answer: Ctrl + E), it is unlikely Notes will provide the right Help document. Second, the tools Notes provides to navigate context-sensitive help are weak. There is no way to search the Help database and the user cannot navigate to the index of all Help documents.

THE HELP DATABASE

There are alternatives to context-sensitive help in Notes. You read earlier that Notes Help is stored in a Notes database. Thus, by opening the Help database directly, you can use the Notes document management tools (including views and full-text search) to identify the Help documents you need. The Notes Help database can be opened in two ways: you can double-click the icon on your desktop, or you can use the Help menu. The choices in the middle of the Help menu will (with one exception) open various views in the Help database. Each menu choice in the Help menu is described in the following table:

Option	Action	Sample Usage
Table of Contents	Opens the Help database to the Table of Contents view. This view lists all documents in the Help database by chapter.	You are looking for general information about a particular topic, such as Notes security.
Keyboard	Opens a document from the Help database describing how various keystrokes can be used to perform actions in Notes.	You want to figure out how to move to the top of a view.
Messages	Opens the messages view of the Help database. This view lists a number of error messages that Notes might present to the end user.	You have received an error message in Notes that you don't understand.

(continued)

Option	Action	Sample Usage
@Functions	Opens a view of @functions in the Help database. Each @function has a corresponding document describing the arguments it accepts and what it returns. This information is critical for application developers.	You are developing a private view or a macro and you don't know how to use a particular function.
Index	Opens the Index view of the Help database. The Index view is a list of categories in the Help database. Double-clicking on a category lists all documents with information relevant to that category.	You know the exact topic you are looking for and want all documents with information on this topic. In this case, you might want to consider full-text search, discussed later in this chapter.

If you open the Help database directly, you will find one additional view: Release Notes. This view shows one document that provides general information on the Release Notes database, which contains information on your particular version of Notes and might contain other information that Lotus did not have time to include in other documentation.

Let's take a look at the Help database itself. Select Table of Contents from the Help menu. This brings up a view in the help database that is arranged like the chapters in a book—documents are organized into chapters and sections. This is a good place to learn about Notes. For the purposes of this exercise, we are going to open the document titled "What Is Notes?"

One of the first things you notice in the document are the buttons across the top of the form. These buttons are there to help you navigate through the documents in the Help database. They are particularly useful when you want to navigate through documents in a particular view (e.g., when you want to

Table of Contents view in the Help database

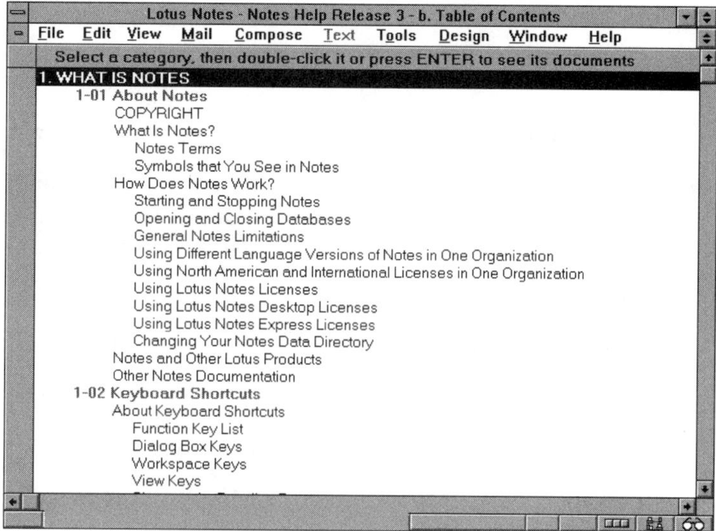

"What Is Notes?" from the Help database

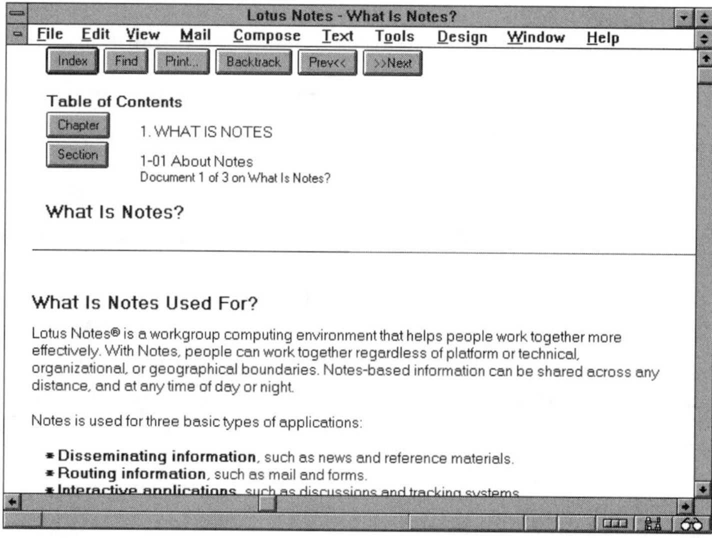

read all the documents in a chapter sequentially). The functions of each button are described in the following list:

Button	Purpose
Index	Opens up the Index view of the Help database.
Find	Opens the text search bar. The text search function can be used to find a string in the database or in a particular document quickly.
Print . . .	Prints the open document.
Backtrack	If you have been opening a number of Help documents at once (e.g., you open one then open a doclink to another), this button returns you to the prior document.
Prev<<	Moves to the preceding document in the open view.
>>Next	Moves to the next document in the open view.
Chapter	Opens the Table of Contents view and highlights the chapter named to the right of the button.
Section	Opens the Table of Contents view and highlights the section named to the right of the button.

In addition to buttons, each document in the Help database can have doclinks and pop-ups. These provide additional background information.

The Notes Help database is the same across platforms. As a result, Notes Help often contains platform-dependent information. This type of information is preceded by a small rectangle containing the name of the platform for which the information is relevant (e.g., WIN, PM, APPLE). For examples of platform-dependent information, look through the Table of Contents for documents related to using the keyboard. The Macintosh and PC keyboards are different, and some actions require different keystrokes depending on the platform.

HELP AND FULL-TEXT SEARCH

The last, and perhaps most important, tool to help you get information from the Help database is *full-text search*. Full-text search allows you to search all the documents in the Help database and pick out those with relevant information. If your initial search returns too many documents, you can refine the search to get the exact information you need.

Get back to the Table of Contents view in the Help database. Across the top of the screen you see the full-text-search bar (if you don't, you might want to contact your administrator about getting the database's full-text index updated). You type a query in the text entry box (for example, "replication") and click on Search. This returns all documents in the database with information on "replication." The documents are no longer ordered by chapters and sections; they are now ordered by *relevance* to your search criteria. *Relevance* in a full-text search refers to the number of times your search string appeared in the searched document. Documents with the largest number of appearances are put at the top of the view. These are the most relevant documents. Documents with the least number of appearances are put at the bottom and are the least relevant. A bar along the left side of the screen shows how the documents ranked—the darker the bar (it is usually black at the top), the more relevant the document.

You open the first document returned by the search. As you open it, Notes puts boxes around every occurrence of the word "replication." This allows you to quickly move from the first occurrence of the word to the next (press Ctrl+Shift+Plus to move forward one occurrence and Ctrl+Shift+Minus to move backward). The Notes full-text search allows you to pinpoint immediately the documents and sections of documents with relevant information in your hunt for help.

THE REST OF THE HELP MENU

When a database is open or highlighted, the two menu choices About and Using become available. These menu choices are followed by the title of the active database. Selecting the About menu choice brings up the About page for the active database. This is a page, typically completed by the application developer, that provides background information on the application. It might include the developer's name, a manager's name, the purpose of the database, and intended audience. This document is also displayed the first time you open a database. Selecting the Using option brings up the Using page for the active application. The Using page typically provides information on the structure and use of the database. This might include descriptions of forms, views, and macros, identifying any special features, application workflows, and so on. These documents are valuable sources of information to get help with a particular Notes application.

Finally, at the bottom of the Help menu are two other menu choices: Release Notes and About Notes. Selecting Release Notes automatically opens the Release Notes database. This database contains information specific to the release of Notes you are using. The last choice, About Notes, provides information on the version number, copyright notice, and release date for the software.

CONCLUSIONS

It is worth your while to spend time familiarizing yourself with the Help database and some of the other help functions provided in Notes. The Help database has answers to many of the most common Notes related questions. You might want to print out some sections of particular interest to you, such as, full-text search. Using help effectively not only enhances your understanding of Notes, it allows you to use Notes in a more efficient and creative manner.

The Discussion Database

The Discussion database is the most useful, versatile, and popular of all Notes applications. It implements all of the basic features of Notes shared databases, is easy to learn and use, and is general enough to be applied to a great variety of needs. Because it is a simple database, it is often the first database a group uses when learning Notes.

Eric Fleming is in charge of getting his group up on Notes. He's set up a server and installed Notes on a few people's computers. He's given everyone a little training on how to start Notes, how to access their Mail databases on the server, and how to send and receive Notes Mail. Now Eric is ready to take the next step in exploring Notes' capabilities: group discussions.

DISCUSSION DATABASES VERSUS NOTES MAIL

With Notes Mail, each person has his or her own database. If someone wants to create a message that several others see, that person addresses the mail to each recipient. The message shows up in each recipient's mailbox.

If someone who receives the message wants, in turn, to reply to the sender and all the others who got the message, she mails a reply to all of these people, and this new message shows up in everyone's mailbox.

If the discussion continues for long, pretty soon each person's mailbox is littered with all of the messages. There are several disadvantages to this scenario:

▶ It wastes disk space. There will be as many copies of each message as there are people participating in the discussion.

▶ It is unstructured. The messages comprising a discussion (sometimes called a *thread*) are likely intermixed with other mail messages, making it difficult for a user to see all of the messages comprising a discussion at once.

▶ When there are multiple discussion threads going on at the same time, it gets even harder to look back and see all the messages for a particular discussion.

▶ Users who habitually delete old mail will often find that they receive a new message in a discussion, and they no longer have the previous messages that provide the context for the new message.

For these reasons, Notes comes with a template called Discussion, which can be used to create Discussion databases. These databases support multiple, ongoing discussions by multiple people, avoiding the disadvantages of plain e-mail.

SETTING UP A DISCUSSION DATABASE

The Discussion template is possibly the template used most often by Notes databases—it is easy to construct, is easy to use, and facilitates basic group communication.

Eric decides to create a Discussion database to let his group get used to Notes and get them accustomed to interacting with others in a Notes database. He starts Notes, tells it (from the File menu) to create a new database (on the server so all can access it) from the Discussion template, and realizes he must give the database a title. Eric decides to use the database as a mutual-support database for Notes itself, so members of his group can discuss Notes, ask questions, answer questions, and help each other become proficient in its use.

After entering the title of the new database as "Using Notes," Eric clicks the OK button. Notes creates the database and puts an icon on his Workspace. The database is now ready to support group discussion about how to use Notes. (Eric might want to modify the database's access control list, which controls which people have what level of access.) He decides to use the database a little on his own, to understand how it works and help others get started. He can also "seed" the database by putting in some starting documents to get discussion going.

Eric begins by double-clicking the icon to open the database. He finds he is in the view called Main View, which is empty because there are no documents in the database. Once there are documents, this view will show the topics sorted by date, with the responses indented below each topic. The other views in the database, By Author and By Category, also show topics and responses in this fashion, and provide different ways to access the documents in the database. For an explanation of Notes views, see the sidebar "Views: What Are They?"

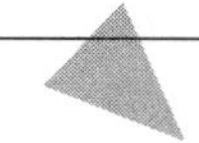

Views: What Are They?

Notes *databases* are collections of documents. In order to see lists of documents that are in a database, Notes provides *views*. A view is a list of some or all of the documents in a database. Views also provide access to the documents in a database—to get to a document, one opens a view, finds the documents listed in the view, and double-clicks its listing (each document is listed as a line in the view).

A database may have one or many views, and the views available in a database are listed in the View menu. The views that appear in this menu are created by the database designer.

Multiple views will exist in a single database in order to provide different types of listings, or sortings, of the documents in the database. For example, one view might show all of the authors who have put documents in the database and, under each author, the list of documents they have created. Another view might show all of the documents in the database sorted by date, so that the most recent documents appear at the bottom (or perhaps at the top in a reverse sort).

Views can be used to limit the number of documents displayed to provide meaningful lists of certain documents. For example, a database tracking action items might contain a view called Late Action Items, which displays a list of only those action items that are late.

A powerful feature of Notes is the *private view,* which lets users create their own views of public databases. Only the user who creates a private view has access to that view. This feature is powerful because it lets users tailor the way they access a database in ways that make them most efficient.

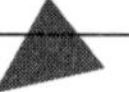

Now that Eric is accessing the database, his next step is to create the first document. This document will be the start of a discussion—one of many that will soon be taking place inside the database. New discussions are started by creating documents based on the Main Topic form. From the Compose menu, Eric chooses Main Topic. Notes produces a blank Main Topic document. The Author field is already filled in with his name. He can now specify the discussion topic by typing in the Subject field. To kick off the first discussion, he enters "What are your first impressions of Notes?" This subject will appear in the views of the database so users know what the document/discussion is about.

Next Eric might decide to provide a category for the discussion. At first, the database doesn't have any categories defined, so he creates a new one by entering "General Comments." Then, when users access the By Category view, they will see a category called General Comments, with this new document listed under that category.

Having specified the subject and category, Eric can now type the meat of the document itself. This is entered in the Rich Text body field in the middle of the document. Because this field is a Rich Text field, he can use different font sizes and colors, as well as pasting in pictures and file attachments. For now, Eric simply enters a couple of sentences, like, "To get used to responding to other's documents, create a Response document to this one containing your first impressions of Notes!" When he has finished typing, he saves and closes the document.

In the Main View, Eric now sees his document listed, including its title "What are your first impressions of Notes?" which was entered as the document's subject. He decides to take his own advice and respond to this document. To do so, he chooses Response from the Compose menu. This Response document allows him to participate in an existing discussion instead of creating a whole new one. He enters his first impressions by typing, "I'm really enjoying using Lotus Notes. While I am finding it takes a little getting used to, I think it will be extremely valuable to me and to our organization." He also gives it a subject of "I like it!" and then saves and closes the document.

Now in the view, below the first document, Eric can see this new document. Since it is a Response document, it is indented. This lets him scan the view and see which discussions are taking place, and then see the list of responses that comprise each particular discussion. (In the By Author view, responses are not indented, but they are noted as being responses.)

Before sending mail to his group urging them to use the database, Eric explores one more element of the database: the Response to Response form. This form lets him respond to other people's responses, as opposed to the Response form, which is used to respond to Main Topics. In the Main view, a Response to Response document is nested one indent deeper than a Response document. For example, if someone wants to comment on Eric's first-impression document (perhaps to simply say, "Me too!"), they can use the Response to Response form. If they want to give their own first impressions in response to Eric's Main Topic requesting first impressions, they use the Response form.

Getting Others Involved

At this point, Eric has created a Discussion database to be used by his group to discuss their use of Notes, and he's created two documents—a Main Topic and a Response. He is ready to have the group participate in the database, and so he sends out mail asking people to access the database. To help get the ball rolling, Eric calls Susan Alston on the phone and asks her to respond to his query about first impressions and create her own discussion topic.

Susan opens the database in the Main View and sees Eric's Main Topic asking about first impressions. She creates a response titled "It's awesome!" and types her impressions before saving the document. The view now displays

Eric's Main Topic asking for first impressions, and two Response documents (both indented below the main topic) containing Eric's and Susan's impressions.

Susan then begins a new discussion designed to elicit ideas on how the team can use Notes. She creates a Main Topic with the subject "Let's get some ideas for using Notes", and in the body of the document she writes, "Enter your ideas for things we can do with Notes as Response documents. We can comment on each other's ideas using the Response to Response documents." She saves the document.

Moments later, Larry Dazzi accesses the database and sees the two discussions that have begun: one on first impressions and one on ideas for using Notes. He enters his impressions of Notes as a response to Eric's Main Topic, and then he creates a Response to Susan's discussion topic about ideas for using Notes. In his response, he creates a subject of "Let's track the office football pool with it," and in the body of the document he describes how he would use Responses and Response to Responses to coordinate the pool.

A few minutes later Susan opens the database to see if anyone has put in any ideas in response to her discussion topic. She sees Larry's idea about using it to track the football pool. She immediately creates a Response to Response document to Larry's document in which she comments "But we all know betting on football is illegal. Bad idea!" This document will appear indented below Larry's, signifying that it is not an idea for using Notes but a comment on Larry's idea. The Main View looks more active now.

The Main View in the Using Notes database after some discussion

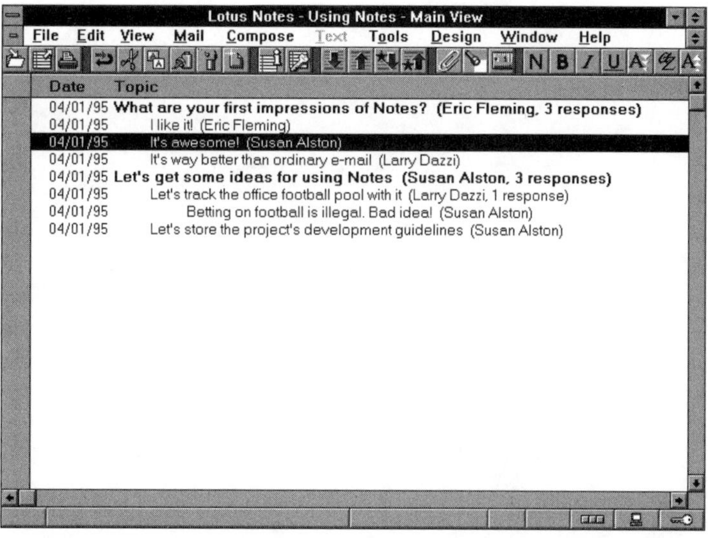

From Eric's office, he periodically checks in and sees that the Discussion database is taking off. His group is now well on its way to effectively using Notes as a means to support group communication.

FACT SHEET

The Discussion Database

Purpose: To support a group of people having multiple, ongoing discussions. The database organizes each discussion by grouping the documents together and indenting responses.

Application Origin: Derived from the Discussion template bundled with Notes.

Application Development Time: A few minutes—no custom development.

Typical Size: 1-10 MB (100–1000 documents)

Typical Use: The Discussion database is so general and so widely used, that there is no "typical" use. It can be used for anything from brainstorming and casual data collection to report publishing and critical documentation.

Forms: The Main Topic form is used to begin a discussion or thread. The Response form is used to participate in a discussion by responding directly to the Main Topic. The Response to Response form supports commenting on others' Responses to the Main Topic of discussion.

Views: The Main View, the default view of the database, displays Main Topics in date order. The By Category view provides a listing of discussion topics by category, where the categories are created on the fly by users entering discussion topics. The By Author view provides a listing of documents grouped by who created the document.

Getting Familiar with the Name & Address Book

Beginners soon get comfortable using Notes Mail for sending and receiving electronic messages, replicating mail to a laptop, and using other basics. At this point it makes sense to explore a special Notes database called the *Name & Address Book,* or *N&A Book* for short.

The N&A Book is where most of the miscellaneous administrative information is stored. There is one on every server and every client (personal workstation), and NAMES.NSF is always its filename. On a server, the N&A Book stores things like people known to the server, groups of people (used for security and group mailings), other servers, replication schedules, mail routing information, and more. On a client, the N&A Book stores much of the same information, but it is generally used a little differently.

Remote Clients

Notes is a client/server product. The *servers* are computers that typically support 50–100 simultaneous users as they read and send mail, access databases, and do other Notes tasks. The workstations, or personal computers, used to access the servers are referred to as the *clients*.

Clients are said to be either *local* or *remote*, depending on how they access the server. If the workstation is connected to the server via a local area network (LAN), it is said to be a *local client*. If the workstation is connected to the server via a modem, it is generally referred to as a *remote client*.

A remote client is characterized by its lack of a high-speed, permanently available connection to the server. This is often the case with people who travel a lot and use Notes on a notebook computer. It is also usually the case with people using Notes from home. Even at the office, people might occasionally use a modem to connect to the server instead of having access to the server via a LAN.

The lack of a high-speed, permanently available connection to the server requires a remote client to use Notes a little differently than a local client. These differences are mainly in two areas: *replicating* databases instead of simply opening them, and using *workstation-based mail*.

Replicating databases from the server is the preferred method of accessing a database by a remote client because it improves the performance of Notes. Here's how it works: the user chooses the database(s) to replicate and tells Notes to replicate. (Replication is initiated from the "Tools" menu. When Tools * Replication is chosen, the Replication Options dialog box is displayed, including the option to send workstation-based mail.) While Notes is replicating, the user can do other things like access other databases that have already been replicated, compose mail, take a shower, or get a cup of coffee. After Notes replicates, the user can access the database locally and have great performance, since no data is traveling over the modem (a relatively low-speed link compared to a LAN).

Workstation-based mail combines the use of replication, as just described, with a "store-and-forward" mechanism for sending mail. For reading mail, instead of accessing a mail file on the server, the user replicates her mail to her local workstation and then reads the mail. For the same reasons as replicating, this provides optimal performance for a remote client. When sending mail, a client setup for workstation-based mail will hold each mail message that is sent until explicitly told to send the mail to the server. That is, when a remote client composes and sends a piece of mail, Notes actually saves the outbound mail in a local database called MAIL.BOX. This improves performance because the user doesn't have to wait for the mail message to travel over the modem. Later, when she chooses, the user tells Notes to send her composed mail messages to the server (that option is on the Tools menu). Again, the user can go do other things while the mail is being transferred.

This special method for remote clients to access the server for databases and mail is a key feature of Notes. It ensures that Notes is easy and efficient to use whether a client is connected to the server via a LAN, or is a remote client, dialing into the server over a modem.

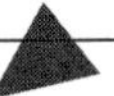

ON THE SERVER

Judith Luby, or Judy for short, is a beginning user ready to become familiar with the N&A Book. She starts by examining the N&A Book on her server.

To start her exploration of the N&A Book, Judy finds the icon for the server's N&A Book on her Workspace or by using the menus to access the server and locate its N&A Book. Once open, she pulls down the View menu

A Person document in the Name & Address Book database

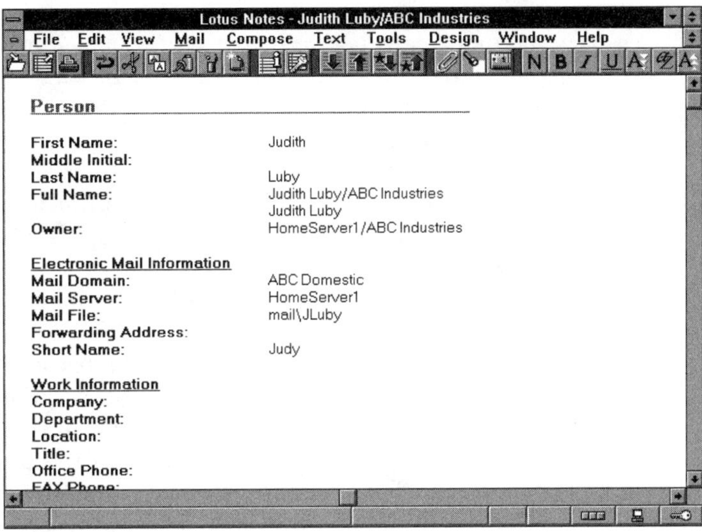

and sees a variety of things: people, groups, servers, connections, and so on. She selects the People view.

Judy now sees the list of people that her server knows about, who appear when she selects the Address button when composing mail. She recognizes many of these people as her co-workers, with whom she's already been exchanging mail. She scrolls down (or types the first letter of her last name) to find her own Person document and opens it.

Aha! It contains all of the information the server knows about her. Judy sees her name broken into first, middle, and last, as well as her Notes full name (which would include her organization identifiers, like Judy Luby/ABC Industries). She also sees e-mail–related information like the database that stores her e-mail on the server.

A little further down, Judy sees work and personal information, like address, phone number, and fax number. This is the first customization she'll do. She enters her work information and the personal information she's comfortable giving out to her co-workers. Now, co-workers can get Judy's phone number if they need it by looking up her Person document. She takes a few minutes and looks at some of the Person documents of others. (In some cases, Notes administrators change the ACL (access control list) on the N&A Book, which might prevent one from doing some of these things in a particular Notes installation.)

Returning to her Person document, Judy looks back up at the top where it lists e-mail information. She sees a field called Short Name, which can contain a nickname to make it easier for others to send her mail. Since everyone around the office calls her Judy, she writes herself a note to ask her administrator to put "Judy" into the Short Name field. That way people can send her mail by addressing it simply to Judy.

Scanning down her Person document, Judy sees a field called Photograph. Wow! Cool! She promises herself to bring in a picture of herself and scan it in so she can include it in her Person document, thinking how useful (or at least neat) it would be to be able to see people's photos and be able to match them with the faces she sees around the office.

After she spends a moment of contemplating how to use a drawing package to paint a mustache on her boss's photograph in his Person document (which, by the way, she can't actually do—Notes security will prevent it) Judy comes back to Notes. She closes her Person document and goes back to the View menu, where she spots a view called Groups. She chooses it.

The Groups view shows Judy all of the groups that have been defined on her server. These groups contain lists of people, servers, and often other groups. They are used in two main ways: security and mail. When used for security reasons, groups can be listed anywhere a person or server would be listed (e.g., a database access control list), therefore making it easier to administer access to databases, documents, servers, and so on. This is especially useful when the same list would have to be entered several times, as in the case where the same group of people need access to several databases.

The other use is for mailing lists. When Judy addresses a Notes Mail message, she can address it to a group, and Notes will send the message to every person in the group. If there are other groups embedded in the group, Notes will *expand* them—finding all of the people in those groups as well (and in the groups within those groups, and so on). This way, she can send a mail message to a whole group of people with one address.

Judy scans down the list of groups and sees that there is a group called "Project Alpha Team Members." Since she is working on project Alpha, she opens the group document and (surprise!) sees a list of all of her team members. Now she realizes that she can send mail to everyone on the team simply by addressing mail to Project Alpha Team Members instead of listing each person. What a time saver!

Judy quickly thinks of several groups she'd like, and so she goes to the Compose menu, but she finds she can't create a Group document on the server's N&A Book. In general, Judy and others won't be able to put documents into the server's N&A Book because it is so critical to the administration and security of the server. She is limited to editing certain things in her Person document and to using the N&A Book as a reader. Does this mean Judy can't create her own groups? Read on!

ON A PERSONAL WORKSTATION: THE CLIENT

Judy closes the server's N&A Book and turns her attention to the N&A Book located locally on her client. Again she finds the icon or uses the menus to open the NAMES.NSF database on her machine. Since it is based on the same template as the server's N&A Book, the views and forms are identical. Judy immediately recognizes the People and Groups views, as well as the Group form that she was unable to compose on the server.

Why does Judy have a version of the N&A Book on her local machine? For two reasons: First, it is a place where she can create new documents. She was not able to create new documents on the server's N&A Book for administration and security reasons. She is free to do anything she wants (including accidentally delete things) to her own N&A Book. Second, the Notes client running on Judy's local machine uses this N&A Book for many of the same things that her server uses it for—especially for connection and authentication purposes.

Since Judy can create a Group document in her local N&A Book, she chooses Group from the Compose menu and instantly sees a blank Group document. She enters a group name of "The lunch crowd," and then enters the half-dozen people she regularly eats lunch with in the Members field. Now Judy can send mail to these people by addressing the mail to The lunch crowd. She saves the document and immediately sends mail to the group, inviting them to get together for lunch and to discuss the exciting things she's been doing with Notes N&A Books. Judy's lunch crowd will not be able to similarly send mail to each other by addressing mail to "The lunch crowd" until they also create this group in each of their local N&A Books. If only Judy's Notes administrator were in her lunch crowd, she might talk him into putting the group in the server's N&A Book. Oh well. (She might send the administrator an e-mail requesting the group anyway. . .)

The next thing Judy thinks about is Person documents. She goes to the People view in her local N&A Book, and sees that there is nobody listed. Another way to make mail more convenient when she is working offline is to create Person documents in her local N&A Book. Judy may have noticed that Notes includes a couple of features to make addressing mail easier. One is the pop-up window that displays a list of people and groups she can select from. Another is the way Notes looks up names, expands them when it recognizes them, and lets her know when it doesn't. These are great features, but they don't work so well when she is not connected to her server, because the features are looking up information in the server's N&A Book.

Here is another way Judy's local N&A Book is useful. She can create Person documents (and groups, as we saw before) for people she commonly sends mail to. When she is offline, Notes' address-lookup functions can still use her local N&A Book. She decides to try it out by creating a person document for

Harrison Neederbaum, whom she'd like to be able to address mail to as Harry. In the Person document, Judy enters Harry's name information and e-mail information, including a short name of "Harry." Now she can send mail to "Harry" and get Notes to expand it automatically for her into his full name by pressing F9.

Since it's almost time for that lunch she invited her friends to, Judy takes a quick peek at a couple of the other things in her N&A Book before calling it quits. She notices a couple of views in particular—Connections and Cross-certificates. *Connection documents* are used by clients and servers to determine which other machines they know how to connect to. Judy can create Connection documents in her N&A Book to list the various servers she dials into. In each document, she can list the phone number Notes should use. *Cross-certificates* are used when Judy needs to access a server to which her ID alone won't grant her access. When this happens, her administrator will create a Cross-certificate and put it in the server's N&A Book. For Judy to access the other server, she needs to copy this Cross-certificate document from her normal server's N&A Book and paste it into her local one. This is necessary because when she tries to "authenticate" on the other server, her server isn't involved, so she needs to have the required information in her local version.

By customizing her Person document on the server and creating new Person and Group documents in her local N&A Book, Judy is starting to use Notes like a pro. Later chapters will go into more detail about Connection documents, replication, security, and other places where the N&A Book plays a role.

▼ FACT SHEET

Name and Address Book

Purpose: Standard Notes database used for administration, mail, security, and other purposes.

Application Origin: Created directly from the built-in Notes N&A Book template.

Application Development Time: Not applicable.

Typical Size: On a server, 10–200 MB, depending on the number of Notes users. On a client, 200K–1 MB, depending on the user's customization.

Typical Use: On a server, server administration. On a client, making mail addressing easier and storing Cross-certificates.

Forms: Connection records, Domain documents, Group documents, Person documents, Mail-in Database documents, Program documents, Server documents, Statistics and Event documents, Cross-certificates.

Views: One for each type of form.

Managing Personal Information

Lotus Notes is typically used in a group context. People in the same group or department will access a common database, and people in different groups, departments, and even companies will collaborate through shared databases. There is a definite learning curve with Notes, and once a user has become experienced in it, it makes sense to use Notes wherever possible. One such area where Notes can be extremely useful is in storing individual information, both work-related and personal.

Steve Quinn is fairly new to Notes. He's got the hang of accessing databases, using Notes Mail, and replicating databases from servers to his personal workstation (desktop PC, home PC, and notebook). He's now ready to venture forth and create his own, personal Notes database. Steve will use it to store all variety of things, including "to-do" items, project notes, word processing documents, spreadsheets, and even some personal notes.

The simplest type of database to use is the Discussion database. Since this database is easy to use and extremely flexible in the types of data it can store, Steve starts by creating his own discussion database. He does this by choosing New Database from the File menu, selecting the Discussion template, and giving the new database a name. He decides to call it My Notes. Notes creates the new database and creates an icon for it on his desktop.

The database opens with a Help window. Closing that window, he finds himself in the Main View of the database. The view is empty—Steve hasn't put anything in the database yet. Since the By Category view is more useful than the Main View, Steve switches to the By Category view. He is now ready to begin placing data in this new, personal database.

CLEANING UP THE OFFICE

The first thing Steve decides to do is use Notes to get rid of all of the little yellow pieces of paper all over his desk, computer, chair, and whatever else has a little spare room on it. These notes are mainly reminders of things he needs to do. So, he picks one up and decides to enter it in Notes. The piece of paper says "Review boss' memo and return by wednesday." (Steve isn't a grammar or spelling wizard.) He composes a new Main Topic to store this information.

The first field to fill out on the form is the Subject field. Steve enters "Review boss' memo and return by wednesday." The next field is the Category field. He presses Enter and sees that he currently has no categories defined. He defines a new one called To-Do. Finally, there is room in the note to store additional information (in the body of the note). Steve enters "Remember to avoid correcting her grammar—she hates that!" He saves the note and throws out the piece of paper.

Back in the By Category view, Steve now sees a category called To-Do, with the note about reviewing his boss's memo neatly listed and indented below the category label. He quickly grabs the other pieces of paper littering his office containing to-do items and enters them in a similar fashion. Now when Steve creates a new to-do item, after entering the subject and moving to the category field, he simply has to press *T* and Notes will fill in the category To-Do. In a few minutes his office is looking ten times cleaner, and his to-do items are neatly listed in the By Category view of his new database.

Before moving on to another type of data, Steve decides to take advantage of Notes' ability to track Response items with the items they are responses to. Since he's already skimmed his boss's memo, he decides to document his first impressions while they are still fresh in his mind. Steve highlights the item about reviewing his boss's memo and composes a Response document. In the Reply field he types "First impressions," and below in the body of the response he enters his thoughts. Steve saves the new document and returns to the By Category view. Now, indented below the item about reviewing his boss's memo, is a new line stating "First impressions." He sees how one can easily store information related to the to-do items.

PICKING UP SPEED

Already feeling like a Notes pro, Steve decides to try something a little more daring than To-Do documents. He decides to store his project notes and documents in his My Notes database. He thinks about how he tends to work on several projects at the same time. Each project can be a category, so Steve can group his notes and documents by their projects. Further, since documents can have more than one category, he can make a single document appear listed under more than one project.

The new Super-Widget project that Steve's been helping out on is really hot. He has got some ideas about new features for the Super-Widget that he hasn't gotten around to jotting down. Steve composes a new Main Topic and enters a subject of "New feature ideas for the super-widget." He creates a new category called Super-Widget, which he will use to group notes and documents related to the Super-Widget project. He then enters his thoughts in the Rich-Text field at the bottom of the note. He saves it and sees that it has been properly categorized in the view under the category Super-Widget.

Steve recalls that a few days ago, he received a Mail message containing the list of contacts working on the Super-Widget project. He left it in his mailbox, but now he's got an idea. He opens his mailbox and finds the mail. Steve opens it and copies the list of contacts to the Clipboard. He then closes the mail message and mailbox and returns to his My Notes database. Steve creates a new Main Topic and enters a subject of "Contact list for Super-Widget project." He selects Super-Widget as the category and then moves to the body field below. He pastes the contact list into the note and saves. Now in the By Category view, he sees both his ideas about features for the new Super-Widget and the project's contact list grouped neatly below the Super-Widget category.

Steve quickly creates notes for each of the other projects he is working on. He creates a note with things he needs to do for Project X. When he chooses a category for this note, he not only chooses Project X, but he also chooses To-Do. This way, Steve will be reminded of what he needs to do whether he is perusing his to-do items or the items grouped together for Project X. Even though the note will appear in both places, it is really the same note, which means he can edit it from either place in the view, and when he later accesses it from the other place the edits will be there.

WARP SPEED!

After an hour, Steve's database is really shaping up. He has categories defined for all of the projects he works on, as well as for his to-do items. He's entered various thoughts that have been on his mind, cleaned up all the loose pieces of paper with to-do and project notes, and transferred text from various Notes Mail messages into his database. The next step is storing other application documents, such as word processing documents, spreadsheets, and presentations. To do this, Steve will use *file attachments* and *object embedding*.

Since file attachments are most useful for files that one won't be editing often, the Microsoft Powerpoint presentation, which a co-worker just gave Steve on floppy disk, comes to his mind. This is a presentation that Steve's department gave recently about Project X, which he would like to keep a copy of. While he could create a directory for it on his hard disk, he knows that he runs the risk of never finding it again. So, Steve creates a new Main Topic with the subject "Bob Jones's Project X Presentation." He gives it a category of

Project X and moves to the body of the note. He types "Here is the presentation Bob Jones gave about Project X." He then uses the File menu's Attach option to attach the presentation file to the note. Steve selects the file from the dialog box, and Notes attaches the file to the note. An icon appears with the filename of the attachment. He saves the file. From now on, he will always be able to view the presentation by going into his My Notes database, going to the Project X category, and opening the note that says "Bob Jones's Project X Presentation." Since he knows he is much more likely to find it this way than by searching his hard disk directories, Steve spends half an hour attaching the various other miscellaneous files he has lying around.

While doing this, Steve invents a few new categories he finds useful for grouping information. He creates a category General Work Information where he stores, well, general information about work. For example, he just received a Notes Mail with an attached document containing instructions on filling out the new purchase orders. He copies the file attachment to the Clipboard and pastes it into a new document categorized under General Work Information.

Steve then explores the capabilities of *object embedding*. File attaching is fine for a document one doesn't expect to edit, but it is inconvenient for documents one is in the process of working on. To explore object embedding, Steve creates a note to contain a new document he's been meaning to start. In the note he enters a subject of "Instruction for installing a Widget-Plus." He categorizes it in the category Widget-Plus and then moves to the Rich Text field below. He intends to write the installation instructions in Microsoft Word instead of Notes, because not all people who need the instructions have Notes on their desktop. To create the document, Steve chooses Edit, Insert, Object and then selects Microsoft Word 6.0 Document. Word opens up and lets him create the document. He types a few introductory sentences and closes Word. He's now back in Notes and the Word document is stored as an *embedded object* in the note. Steve saves the note. From now on, he can edit the document by going to the By Category view, looking under Widget-Plus, and finding the document he just created. He can edit the document by double-clicking the embedded object, and his revisions will be stored back in Notes.

Realizing how much easier it will be to find his word processing documents, spreadsheets, and presentations using Notes than searching directory structures (is it /word/widplus/install or is it /widplus/word/install?!), Steve decides to make it even easier to find things he's stored in the database. He decides to index the database for full-text searches. He sets up the database for full-text searching, and in each of his Notes, he makes sure to include a sentence or two about what the note contains. For example, in the note about installation instructions for Widget-Plus, in addition to the embedded Word document Steve writes, "This is a Word document containing installation instructions for installing a Widget-Plus. These install instructions are based on

Personal Information Management

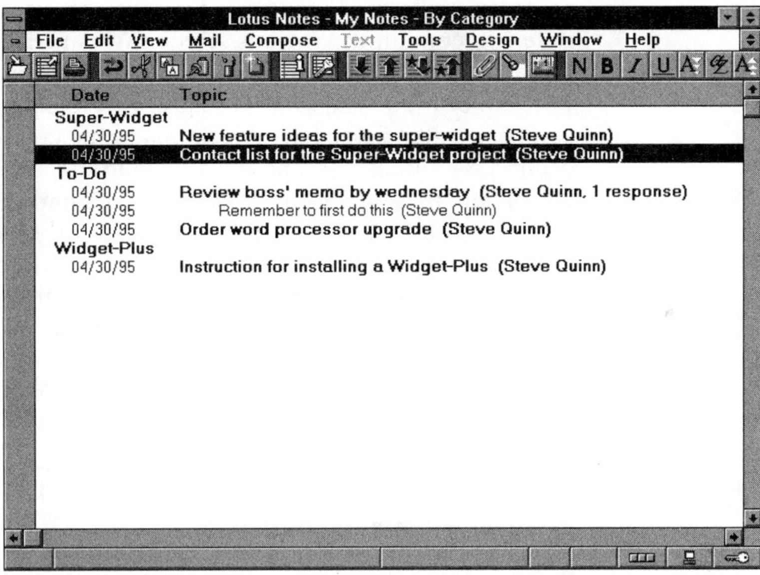

the instructions for installing an enhanced Widget and contain special instructions for avoiding the doohicky bug." Now Steve knows he'll be able to find this document simply by typing a keyword or two into the full-text-search bar. For example, if he remembers the instructions made special care to discuss the doohicky bug, he can easily find the document by simply typing "doohicky" into the full-text-search bar.

ON THE PERSONAL SIDE

After spending the rest of the day getting his work life under control by organizing his to-do items, general company information, project notes, word processing files, spreadsheets, and presentations, Steve decides to organize some of his personal stuff before calling it quits.

Steve realizes that he can create a category called Personal To-Do. Using this category, he creates some reminders about doctor appointments he should make, house chores he should do, and other things that have been on his mind. The Personal To-Do category will keep them separate from his work to-do items, so he will not be distracted by the personal items during work.

Steve then thinks about the miscellaneous files he has lying around. Some are screen savers scattered around his disk. Some are utilities and games. Some are jokes and cartoons. He creates another category called Personal Stuff to hold these things. He creates a Main Topic with a subject of Screen Savers, a category of Personal Stuff, and a sentence explaining that responses to this note will contain the various screen savers he is collecting. Steve can then create a response document for each screen saver and attach the screen saver. Now all of his screen savers are grouped together, and he didn't need a whole category called Screen Savers. Similarly, he created Main Topic documents to group his utilities and another to group his jokes and cartoons. By attaching or copying these things into Notes, Steve's hard disk becomes far less cluttered and he can actually find those little things that keep getting lost. Again, full-text indexing means that it is easy to find what he wants. For example, if Steve imports a document with jokes, then he can find that joke about corporations and bureaucracy by typing "corporations and bureaucracy" into the search bar. With his personal Notes database, he's now in position to be more efficient at work and at preparing his joke list for this evening's cocktail party!

FACT SHEET

Personal Information Database

Purpose: To organize personal information on a local workstation instead of, or in addition to, a stand-alone personal information manager.

Application Origin: Derived from the Discussion template.

Application Development Time: None.

Typical Size: 10–100 MB, depending on whether utilities and other large files are stored in the database.

Typical Use: To leverage users' Notes skills in organizing their individual work and information.

Forms: The forms of the Discussion template (Main Topic, Response, and Response to Response).

Views: The views of the Discussion template (Main View, By Author, and By Category).

A Notes Pilot

Paula Daley is a program manager at Chipcom Corporation, a company in Southborough, Massachusetts, that designs and develops computer networking equipment. Paula and other members of her department manage the development process for new products.

Chipcom develops projects using a group called a Project Management Team (PMT). A PMT is a cross-functional team of people from all of the groups concerned with the development of a new product, such as hardware engineering, software engineering, manufacturing, quality assurance, and marketing.

As Chipcom grew, it became clear that it was necessary to improve the communications between the members of a PMT. Paula and others within Chipcom wanted to be able to find a mechanism for communicating that fit somewhere in between having a meeting (and thereby forcing everyone to be in the same room at the same time) and communicating by e-mail, which seemed too unstructured for long-term use and storage of information. They felt that e-mail simply couldn't replace face-to-face contact between members of the team.

According to Paula, they also wanted to "provide a document repository for the teams to be able to have one-stop shopping for documents related to a project—ongoing status and project management information, as well as background documents like functional requirements, original product requirements, and test plans." They needed to be able to have all that information in one central location. Previously, individuals would each try to keep track of

---

the documents that they personally needed. No one person had a full set of all the project documents, no two people had the same set, and yet there was significant redundancy.

Paula had used Notes at a previous job and had a good idea of its capabilities. She felt that a groupware type of product could provide a central repository for all this information, and Notes seemed to be the only reasonable alternative. They looked into competitive products, but didn't find anything that could really meet their needs.

HIRING A CONSULTANT

Chipcom had not made any large-scale committment to Notes, though it was in place within one group. Since the corporate MIS group wasn't really in a position to make any kind of corporate committment to a product like Notes, it was decided to implement a pilot program on a limited scale. They agreed to design an eight-week trial, with a custom application that met their needs, that would be used by two PMTs. Because they felt they didn't have the internal experience to implement this pilot themselves, they hired a consulting firm, Connexus, to design the database and help them to implement the pilot program.

"I was in a position when I started this project to know what Notes could do for us, but I didn't know where to start," says Paula. "I didn't know how to go from 'Oh, let's use Notes to solve this problem' to actually having a working application. I didn't know what it would take to get to the point where we could actually deploy a pilot. These people (the consulting firm) were knowledgeable, not only about the technical issues of bringing up a Notes application but also the cultural, political, and other kinds of issues that come into play. So once we decided that we wanted to use outside help to get this rolling, they were pretty much a clear choice."

Paula and others worked closely with the consultants for about two months (not full time) to design and implement a database that met their needs. They held group design sessions with concerned people within the organization to make sure that everyone felt their needs were being met. They met with the teams who would be using the database to determine the requirements, and again to give feedback once the requirements were written.

DATABASE DESIGN

The database was designed around the way the PMTs were organized and the way they work on a project. In particular, Chipcom tried to model the database after the processes and the documents that are handled during a project.

Chipcom organizes its projects into *programs*—a program comprises a set of products that have something in common, such as a hardware platform.

There is one database per program. Within each program can be several projects; one person may work on one or more projects within a program.

Use of the database begins with the creation of a Project Team Summary document. This document serves as a "Who's Who" of the people on the team and the functions they serve. It also has a reference for the time and place of the team meeting, and a short synopsis of the project. The project team summaries are used as the basis document for all other documents in the system.

The next form is a Meeting Agenda form. It contains fields for the names of the attendees, the subject of the meeting, the time and place, and an agenda. To call a meeting, one composes a Meeting Agenda; it automatically defaults the attendees field to the names of the team members, and the time and place to that of the standard weekly meeting. Unfortunately for this Notes application, Chipcom uses Microsoft Mail for their mail system. Since it does not integrate well with Notes, the database cannot send mail automatically.

After the meeting is over, the person taking minutes can click the Create Minutes button on the Agenda form to create the minutes as a Response document to the agenda. A doclink to the agenda is automatically placed on the minutes form. Action Items are created as separate, individual responses to the meeting minutes. This way, each person can see a view of all Action Items and to whom they are assigned. Each Action Item has fields for the person assigned to handle it, the date by which it is due, and the status of the Action Item.

An Action Item

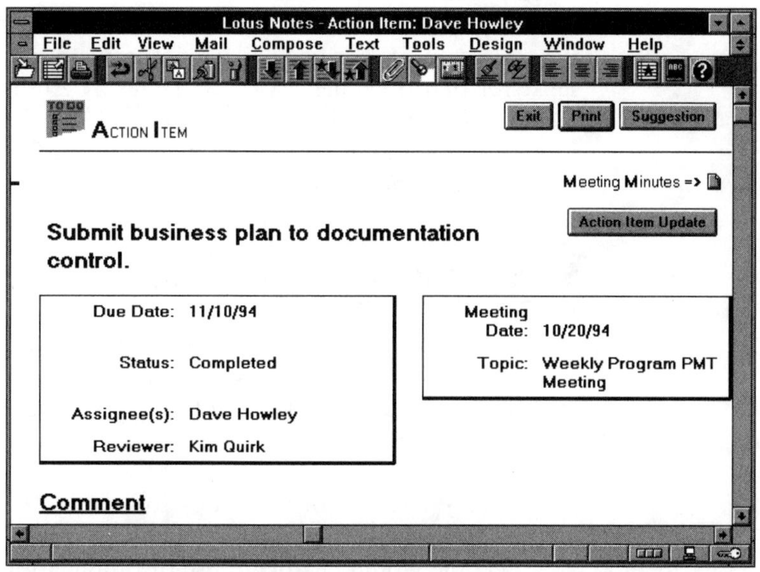

There is also a special Response document used for recording important decisions. This is generally reserved for key decisions that affect the course of the project, not routine, day-to-day ones.

The next set of documents has to do with documenting the project itself. There is a form used for storing project documents. It has fields to identify the particular project, the date and subject of the document, and the document type (business plan, documentation plan, sales forecast, etc.). One of the advantages of Notes for Chipcom is that these documents can be stored as Notes Rich Text fields, which means that they can be read on both Windows and Unix workstations. Chipcom has a large number of each.

Chipcom has also replaced the standard engineering notebooks with *conception memos*. When people have ideas for a project, they compose one of these memos. It is marked with a date and time stamp and cannot be edited. These documents are used to freeze an idea for future use in a patent application or other legal documentation. There is also a way for people to "witness" a document—to stamp it as something they read at a particular time and date.

People can respond to conception memos or any other document in the database with typical Notes Response forms. This allows comments and discussion to evolve within the database.

Finally, there is a place to create and store the monthly status reports that are passed on to upper management.

While this is a large number of forms for one database, it is exactly this range that makes this database successful. By successfully implementing both the paperwork and the processes of the existing PMTs, Paula and her team ensured the success of the database design.

Each of the major document types also has one or more views that show the collection of that particular document, organized in whatever ways make sense for that document type (By Date, By Author, or By Project). The Meetings views show all the meetings, along with all resulting documents from the meetings (minutes, action items, and decisions), by project and date. There are no views that show all documents.

STARTING THE PILOT PROGRAM

Two PMTs were selected for initial participation in the pilot program. One of them had been going for some time, while the other was fairly new. Paula took several steps to make sure that people would quickly be able to be productive using the new tools:

▶ Every member of the teams took a one-day training class on Notes in general, and this application in particular. She wanted to be sure that people would be able to use the application immediately.

The Meetings View

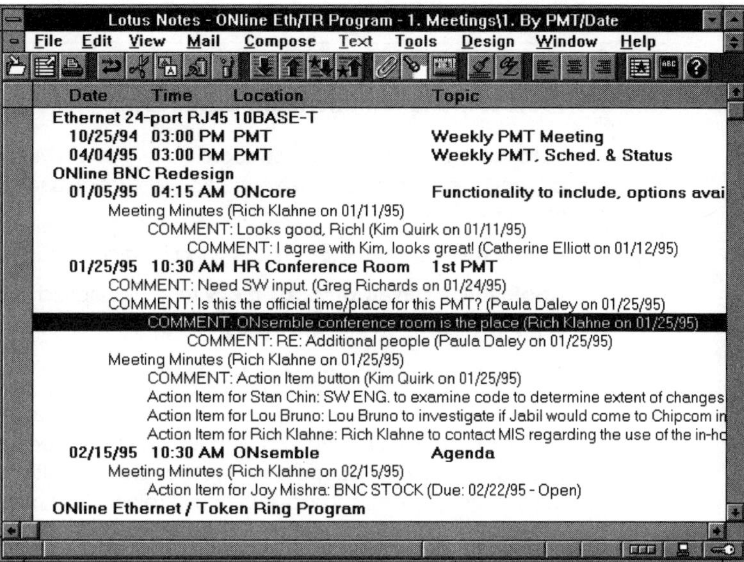

▶ During the weeks before the pilot began, Paula began populating the database with the actual minutes and documents from the PMT that was already running. This way people would find the database useful right from the start.

▶ Every form in the database had a Suggestion button; at any time, someone who felt they had a good idea about the database design or usage could click this button and submit a suggestion, which was immediately available to the database developer.

The pilot was scheduled to run six to eight weeks. During the pilot, several other PMTs were added to the program, and a few changes were made to the database design, based on suggestions from the users.

At the end of this time, Paula distributed a detailed questionnaire asking the participants to rate the project. In general, she said, she was very pleased with the quality of the evaluations she received—she said that people took the time to fill them out well. In general, the results were very positive.

Rollout of this application on a larger scale, however, presents some significant difficulties, since Notes is not currently available on every desktop at Chipcom. Rollout and deployment will require a significant investment of both money and personnel. However, the demand is high—there are several other teams that would very much like to have this application available. It is hoped that the application will soon be available to a wider constituency.

FACT SHEET

Project Management Team Database

Purpose: To facilitate project coordination by providing simple storage and access to all project documents. To increase staff collaboration and reduce meeting times by providing a forum for project-related discussions.

Application Origin: Custom-designed by a consultant.

Application Development Time: 2 months elapsed time.

Typical Size: 5–10 MB per program (consisting of multiple projects).

Typical Use: Project management.

Forms: A Project Team Summary document defines a project and its people. Meeting Agenda forms set up meetings, and act as a base document for recording meeting minutes. There will also be Action Items and Decisions resulting from these meetings. At any time, team members can compose various Project Documents, Status Reports, Schedules, and other key documents. There is a Discussion form for free-form comments.

Views: Each document type has one or more views that show its documents. The Meetings view shows the meeting agendas, minutes, and Action Items organized By Project or By Date.

PART 2

Small-Group Applications

The implementation of Notes in an organization often starts with a single pilot group or department testing the waters. These "small-group" applications
generally support from 5 to 50 people and are supported by one Notes server.
They include general Notes applications like Ad Hoc Discussion databases, as
well as highly customized applications like the TeamWorks Contact Management system.

Small-group applications are generally not the primary reason a company
decides to buy Notes, but they do provide a major portion of the real value of
Notes in practice. They also often provide a good way for a company to see
what Notes is all about. The applications described in this section are examples of how Notes can be used in a small-group setting. As these applications
prove themselves, companies typically raise their sights and target the more
advanced applications, which are described in later sections.

While the applications themselves run from the simple to the complex, they
are all focused on solving a straightforward business problem, so they're a
great place to start our exploration of what Notes can do.

Notes Site Planning Guide

Because Notes affects nearly every portion of a business, it's important to plan a rollout of a Notes system well. There are many decisions to be made while planning a rollout; if they're not made explicitly, they will be made by accident or haphazardly during the process. The planning process embraces a range of issues. It is necessary to create standards for everything, including the kinds of PCs and configurations that will be supported, the names and locations of servers, and levels of security. Tasks must be assigned, from handling the rollout all the way through support. Of course, to do the tasks requires personnel—how many of them are there and who will they be?

One must think carefully because once the rollout is underway, there are several decisions that can not easily be changed. For example, decisions about security and naming conventions are expensive to change once the applications are rolled out and installed.

InfoImage

InfoImage is a company based in Phoenix, Arizona, that specializes in project planning and enterprise deployment of applications, especially (but not exclusively) Notes applications. They have developed a Notes database they call the Notes Site Planning Guide. It is a database designed to help in the planning process for Notes applications.

Hundreds of big and little decisions must be made when a Notes rollout is underway. This Notes application helps to provide both a structure for addressing those decisions and a place to record them.

When InfoImage is consulting on a Notes rollout, they typically set up a one-day or two-day meeting with the key people in the client company. They use the discussion guide as a meeting agenda, and take the opportunities along the way to educate the staff on particular issues regarding Notes deployment. All the decisions made in the meeting are recorded by the Info-Image consultant. After a two-day turnaround to prepare the documentation, InfoImage delivers a pair of customized reports and a database detailing not only the decisions made, but including the justification behind those decisions.

There are two versions of the report, both of which come from the same Notes database. The first version is the full report, containing not only all the decisions, but all the justifications for them and salient points from the Notes documentation. It typically runs about 120 pages. The second version is the abridged version. It contains only the text of the decisions themselves, and is usually about 50 pages long. The abridged version tends to be used more often during the rollout.

The resulting report database is stored online in the Notes system, and is used as a live reference for standards, policies and procedures pertaining to the Notes installation. Since it's online, when decisions do change, they can be changed in the document so that the document can stay up to date.

VIEWS

When the database is delivered, it is essentially an online book. There are three major view categories: The Complete views shows every document in the system in its most complete form. The Abridged views show only those documents pertaining to the customer's decisions, and only the decision parts of those documents appear. The Editing view shows every document in the book, plus some others that act as instructions for editing the book itself. The Editing view also shows a bit more information about the documents themselves.

The Complete and Abridged views each have three versions. The Table of Contents view shows the document in outline form. The chapters and sections can be expanded or collapsed for a good view of the whole book. This view also displays some "empty" documents that serve to mark the start of a chapter. The Print view is set up for easy printing of the whole document (whether complete or abridged), and ignores "empty" documents. Finally, the Index view shows the documents categorized by the index field in each document, which is filled with a few keywords that characterize that particular section. While full-text search can take over this task, well-chosen keywords can make an index a pleasure to use.

The Complete\Table of Contents view

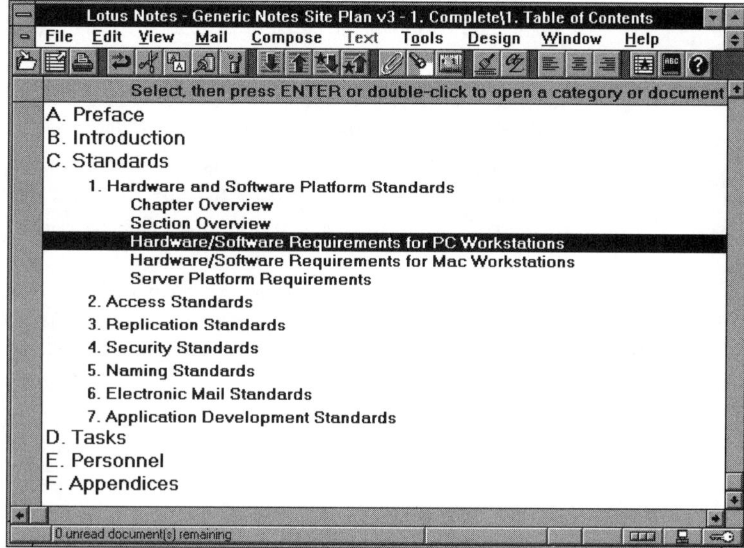

FORMS

There are a large number of quite similar forms in this database. They are designed to allow the resulting book to look good when printed. The book is organized into three levels—at the top level are chapters; beneath the chapters are sections; and under the sections are the individual Contents documents.

Chapters always start a new page in the book. They may be nothing more than a title, or they may contain a chapter introduction. This is reflected in the Forms menu by forms called Chapter with contents and Chapter without contents.

Sections also may or may not contain introductory text. Especially brief sections may not even cause the start of a new page. The section forms included are Section with contents, Section with FF and contents, and Section with FF and no contents (FF means form feed, or start a new page).

Finally come the Contents documents themselves. They too might or might not start a new page, so the forms are called Contents with FF and Contents with no FF. The same is true for the Appendix forms, which will always be sorted out to the end of the document. There is even a Cover form, which is basically a blank, free-form document.

COMMON FEATURES

All the forms have some common features that make this database especially nice to use. They all have a row of buttons, with commonly needed features. Prev and Next buttons move through the list of documents. Print makes it easy to print the current document. The Find button will invoke the Notes search utility (or the full-text search if it's been enabled for this database). The Index button opens the database to the Index view.

One of the especially nice features of this database is the fact that the buttons are found on both the top and the bottom of the forms, which means that they're almost always accessible when needed.

There is also a Comment button, which makes it easy to enter responses and comments on a document. This is useful as a document evolves—people who notice problems can flag them while they're still fresh.

The forms all have a Doc number, which is a numerical index. The documents are sorted according to this number. This gives ultimate control over the sequencing of the contents within a section and chapter.

Finally, there are checkboxes for which parts of the form will be included in the Abridged version. Every form includes not one, but two body fields. The

A Contents form in Edit mode

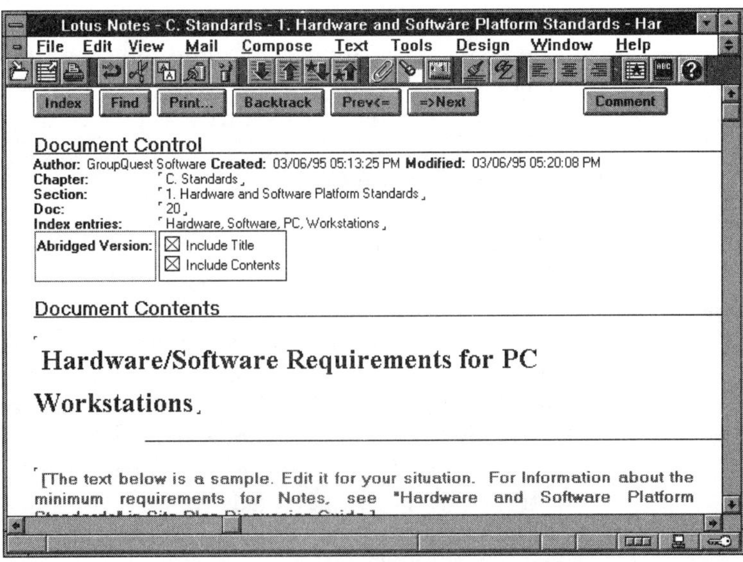

first of these never shows up in the Abridged version. The second only shows up if the checkbox marked Include Contents is checked. Checking the Include Title checkbox will also print the title as part of the Abridged version. The result is that one database can store both the complete and abridged versions in one document without rewriting the text.

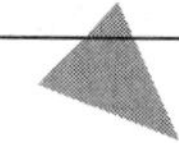

Hiding Information

It's not always desirable to show all of the information that is stored in any given Notes document. It is quite common, for example, to have explanatory text that is visible during the editing of a form, but not visible when the form is being printed or read. Notes makes this sort of thing easy with the Hide when controls.

Any individual paragraph in Notes can be hidden under different circumstances. Many databases, for example, suppress author names and edit history when a document is being printed.

The rollout database uses a more sophisticated hiding mechanism to handle the Complete and Abridged views. The views use a Form Formula, which is a way to tell Notes dynamically which form to use when displaying or printing a document. The Form Formula can make decisions based on the fields in the document and the operation being performed. In this case, the formula selects the form to use based on the settings of the Include checkboxes.

The Hide when part of the paragraph formatting dialog

Diana Sykes, who now works for InfoImage, used to be the director of large scale deployment and site planning for a major financial firm. She believes this product can make the difference between a successful and failed implementation of Notes. "I would have killed for this product back then," she said. She now uses this product in her own consulting as a consulting project planner and project manager for InfoImage. The product is also for sale in a stand alone form.

FACT SHEET

InfoImage Notes Site Planning Guide

Purpose: A database to assist in the planning and documentation of the rollout of a Notes installation.

Application Origin: InfoImage, 1661 East Camelback Road, Suite 265, Phoenix, AZ 85016. Phone: 602-234-6900, 800-489-9511.

Application Development Time: 2 days consulting, 2 days documentation time.

Typical Size: 2 MB.

Typical Use: Using this database as a template, participants discuss and record all necessary decisions for planning a Notes installation.

Forms: There are forms for Chapters, Sections, Contents, and Appendix documents, each of which has several versions. The different versions make it easier to produce a good-looking printed book.

Views: There are different views for a Complete version of the book, with all discussion and decisions, and an Abridged version, which only includes the decisions specific to that organization. There is also an Editing view used when assembling the book.

Supporting Ad-hoc Discussions

Notes is often used to implement a particular application. This may be a totally new application, or it may be a re-engineering of an existing application. In either case, these are usually applications which are developed to meet a particular need, and which are often accompanied by requirements, prototyping, testing, training, etc.

Yet Notes can also be used in another fashion. Sometimes people need a standard Notes discussion database to facilitate rapid group discussion. Kathy Welch is very familiar with the ways in which her company currently uses Notes, but at the moment she needs a discussion database created on her server, and she needs it *fast*.

THE EXISTING PROCESS

As a product manager at a high-tech company, Kathy knows that speed counts. She has found that since her company started using Notes, many processes have become faster. When a new product is starting up, she has a Requirements Discussion database created. When the product makes it to the field, it becomes a category in the Sales Discussion database used by the sales team. There are Notes databases being used to distribute company forms and policy documents, store sales presentations, and support a variety of other applications. Everyone is using Notes Mail for exchanging information and especially for sending files to each other (like spreadsheets and documents).

To support these applications, Kathy's company has staffed a whole department dedicated to supporting Notes. This department runs the Notes servers, develops Notes applications, and provides an interface to the rest of the company for implementing and maintaining Notes applications. The department has a standard process that is followed whenever a new Notes application is proposed. This process includes steps such as:

▶ Ensuring that an existing Notes application does not already meet the needs the new application is designed to address.

▶ Reviewing the application requirements to ensure that the application can be implemented with Notes.

▶ Evaluating the application for implementation issues: Will it run on one server or multiple servers? What are the replication scheduling needs of the application? How big will the application get?

▶ Developing a prototype with sample forms and views that can be used to ensure that the developers are building what is intended.

▶ Implementing the new application in a limited trial at first, evaluating the trial, and then rolling out the application in full.

This process has worked extremely well in ensuring that new Notes applications will succeed. The process also helps prevent the proliferation of many similar databases, and in turn this helps prevent *dead* databases, databases that are used for a little while and then sit idle for months or years.

THE NEED FOR A NEW PROCESS

Kathy appreciates this process, but at the moment she has a need to use Notes with others in her department to discuss an upcoming conference in which she plans to demo some of her products. Kathy is in charge of selecting the products to demo, picking the demo applications, and arranging for people to attend the conference to staff the demo tables. She wants to use Notes to discuss these issues and any others that are going to arise over the next few weeks before the conference. She doesn't need a fancy application—a simple Discussion database will do. She makes a call to her Notes support department to arrange for the database to be set up.

"Hello, this is John of the Notes Support department. How can I help you today?"

Kathy explains that she'd like a discussion database set up on her server as soon as possible.

"OK. The first step to getting a new Notes application up and running is for you to fill out an Application Description form. You can find it in the Notes database called New Notes Application Requests on the server. . ."

Kathy explains that she understands the standard process for implementing a new application, but that she doesn't want anything fancy. Just a Discussion database on her department's server, preferably set up by the end of the day.

"Umm. . . Well we're not really set up for that kind of thing. Let me transfer you to Beth Caro, my boss."

When Beth gets on the phone Kathy explains what she'd like to do. Beth says that her group receives many requests like this, and that their current process does not support it very well. She says that the Notes Support department has been thinking of implementing a new process specifically for this situation. She explains:

"We're calling these applications Ad-Hoc Discussion Databases. We'd like to make it easy for people to have a new discussion database created on one or more servers within four hours of the request. We want to track these databases carefully to ensure that they do not get too big. We want to ensure that these databases are around for a month or so and are then either deleted or converted to real supported Notes applications.

"We are thinking of adding a new type of request to our existing New Notes Application Request database in which people can request that an Ad-Hoc Discussion Database be created. Would you be willing to meet with us this morning to discuss what would go on such a form? We can use the meeting to gather information about your request to set up a discussion database. We'll set up the database for you this afternoon, and we'll also build the new form so the next person making this request can simply use the form."

Being a helpful sort of person and really wanting the discussion database up this afternoon, Kathy agrees to the meeting. At the meeting, various issues are discussed that help the Notes Support team develop their request form and help Kathy understand why the request form and process is necessary.

The first thing discussed is the general handling of the request form itself. There are already request forms in the database that people use to make an initial estimate of the scope of a new Notes application. The form is filled out and saved in the database. The Notes team scans the database for new forms on a daily basis, looking for new projects.

Since these Ad-Hoc Discussion databases are usually rush orders, the team decides to mail-enable the form. This way as soon as someone fills out a request for an Ad-Hoc Discussion database, mail will be sent to the Notes support team. The team decides to create a new group called Ad-Hoc Request Handlers to whom the form will be mailed. This will let the Notes Support team tune who receives the mail without touching the design of the form.

The discussion then turns to the data that users should complete in the request form. Some basic fields were identified right away. Requester would track the person making the request. This would also be the point of contact regarding the database, so the Notes Support department would know who to deal with when issues about the database arise. This person will be notified as soon as the database is on the server(s). Because phone calls are even faster than Notes Mail, another field for Requester's Phone Number is identified. Also, the date and time the request is made are also identified as fields on the request form.

Next the discussion turned to the data associated with the new database itself. Database Title is immediately identified as a field on the form. Then the issue of database location (servers and directories) comes up and things are suddenly not so obvious.

Kathy suggests letting the user simply specify the server or servers where the database should go and the directory where the database should go. The support team has some concerns with that:

▶ The directory structures on the servers are carefully laid out to support the standard Notes applications. They want these ad-hoc applications to be different so people don't confuse them with the more permanent applications. They argue for a directory to be added to each server called "Ad-Hoc Discussions" where all these databases would go. This sounds OK to Kathy, and has the advantage that requesters don't have to specify a directory for the database.

▶ There is a big difference between the database existing on one server and it existing on multiple servers. To replicate the database to multiple servers could entail more work and time delay than could fit in the four hour turn-around time they wish to achieve. It also involves the question of how often the database will replicate. Kathy suggests a compromise where the user specifies a main server for the database first. The support team will create the database on this main server right away so users can start using it.

▶ For multiple servers, the team suggests having a field on the form where the user can optionally list one or more additional servers to replicate the database to. If the user specifies additional servers, the form will have another field where the user can request a replication priority for the database. This will be implemented as a radio button offering the choices High, Medium, and Low. In the case where the database is to be replicated to additional servers, the Notes Support team will need to evaluate that part of the request and carefully ensure that the replication can be supported. The team does not commit to doing this within four hours. Everyone agrees that 48 hours is reasonable, since in the first 48 hours people will have access to the replica on the main server.

▶ The next issue discussed concerns the temporary nature of the databases. The Notes Support team does not want Ad-Hoc databases to exist for too long. They argue that after a couple of months, the database will either be idle (no one is using it), or it will be so active that it should be converted to a more permanent application. If the database is idle, it should be deleted, perhaps after being archived. If the database is active, it should be evaluated like any other permanent application, in terms of efficiency of design, replication requirements, access control list management, and so on. Therefore, it is decided to add a required field for Estimated Duration (in weeks), with a maximum of eight weeks. When the duration is almost up, the database will send mail to the Notes Support team and to the requester reminding them that the database is due for deletion/conversion.

▶ The final issue discussed is that of access control to the database. Who should be the manager of the database? A simple answer would be to make the requester the manager. Someone suggests not relying on that, since the person making the request might not know how to manage access control lists; for example, a secretary might make the request for others. Kathy suggests adding a field called Managers where the requester could list the people who should have manager access to the new database. The field could be optional; if it is unfilled, the Notes Support team would make the requester the manager. Also, all agree to make the default access level No Access, so that only people who are given access to the database by the databases manager(s) will be able to gain access.

The meeting ends with the Notes Support team knowing exactly how to implement the new Ad-Hoc Discussion Database Request Form, and Kathy being promised that her new database will be up in a few hours.

THE NEW PROCESS GOES PUBLIC

Kathy's new Discussion database is created that afternoon on her department's Note server in a new directory created for Ad-Hoc Discussion databases. A week later she receives an e-mail that went out to the entire company containing directions for requesting Ad-Hoc Discussion databases. Since the new form is on line and it just so happens that Kathy has a need for another discussion database, she starts Notes and opens the New Notes Application Requests database and composes a new Ad-Hoc Discussion Database Request form.

On the form Kathy asks for a database titled "Project X Discussion." She specifies her department's server as the database location. She specifies one of the members of her team as the manager of the database. She specifies a duration of 4 weeks since she just wants to get a quick snapshot of the department's ideas about Project X. She saves the form. Kathy notices that the bottom of her Notes window says that a mail message has been sent. She realizes this mail message is sent to the Notes Support team so they get immediate notification of her request.

Later that afternoon Kathy looks in the ADHOC directory on her server and she sees her new database Project X Discussion now exists. She sends mail to her department asking them to participate for a few weeks in a discussion about Project X. She is pleased that it was so easy to get an Ad-Hoc Discussion going.

Ad-Hoc Discussion Database Request form

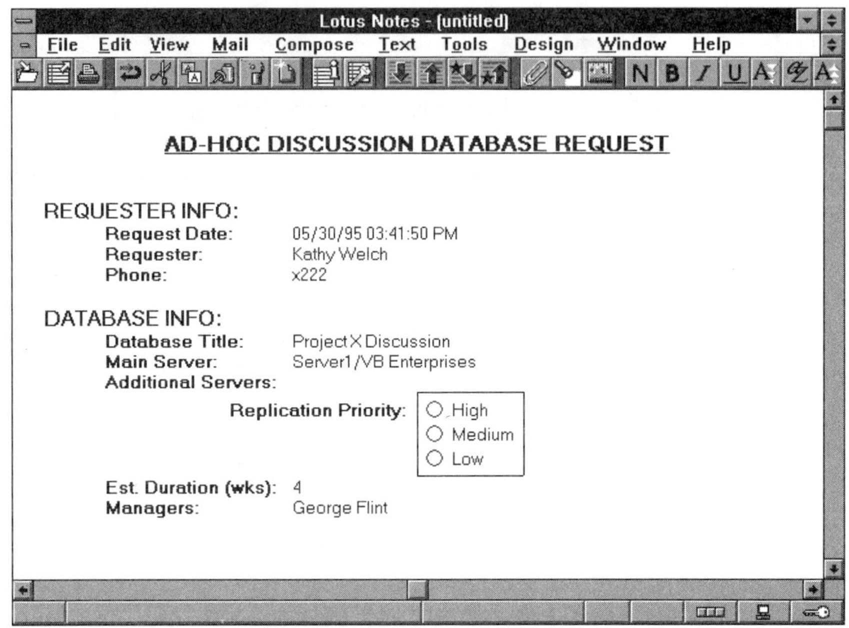

Three weeks later Kathy receives a mail message reminding her that in one week, the database is due for deletion. It's good that she was reminded, since she used the database heavily for a couple of weeks but then let it go. Kathy opens the database and sees that all of the fruitful discussion she expects to happen in that database has happened. She replicates a copy to her local PC as an archive and returns to the mail message she received about the database being due for deletion. She pushes a button in the mail labeled OK to delete, which sends a mail message to the Notes Support department saying it's all right for them to delete the database.

A couple of months later, Kathy receives an e-mail from the president of her company addressed to all employees. The mail describes the recent product announcements the company's main competitor just made. They have released a new product that competes very favorably with the company's main product, and they have priced it below what the company sells it for. The president asks that all employees participate in a two-week company-wide discussion about how the company might respond to this. The mail contains a list of servers that have a replica of the Discussion database, as well as the title, Competition Discussion, and the fact that it is in the ADHOC directory.

Kathy is interrupted by her phone ringing. On the phone is Beth from the Notes Support department. She has called to thank Kathy for her help in developing the Ad-Hoc Discussion Database Request form and the process to get Ad-Hoc Discussions going. She says the database Kathy just received mail about, the two-week competition discussion, was created in response to a request form received from the president's office. She says the form has been used quite a bit since they introduced it, and that it has made it efficient for her department to support this clear need for temporary Discussion databases.

▸ FACT SHEET

Ad-Hoc Discussion Database

Purpose: To support short-term collaboration quickly, without the need for lengthy custom development of any kind. A Request form in a Request database can be used to minimize the overhead associated with creating and managing the life cycle of Ad-Hoc Discussion databases.

Application Origin: Ad-Hoc Discussion databases are based on the Discussion template bundled with Notes. A Request form and Request database are custom developments.

Application Development Time: It takes no time to create an Ad-Hoc Discussion database from the bundled Discussion template. Creating an Ad-Hoc Discussion Database Request Form may take a few days to develop and test.

Typical Size: Typically small (1–5 MB)—it is a short-term database.

Typical Use: Short-term collaboration. Typically this is used by people comfortable with various Notes features, as opposed to a staff trained only in a particular Notes application.

Forms: The forms of the Discussion template: Main Topic, Response, and Response to Response. An Ad-Hoc Discussion Database Request form may be used for requesters to supply all necessary information about a new Ad-Hoc Discussion database to the Notes support staff.

Views: The views of the Discussion template: Main View, By Author, and By Category.

Constituent Correspondence Database

One of the primary responsibilities of U.S. congressmen is to represent their constituents in the Congress. As a result, senators and representatives devote many hours to reading and responding to constituent letters, e-mail, and telephone calls. These communications might be in response to a particular bill in Congress, a personal request from the constituent, or an issue about which the constituent feels strongly. The congressman has an obligation to respond to each and every constituent who contacts him (particularly if he wants to get reelected).

Louise Paloma is an operations analyst working for Senator Philip Stuart (not a real name). As such, one of her primary responsibilities is to write letters and make phone calls to constituents who have contacted the Senator. The Senator receives far too many requests to respond to each one personally. However, he ensures that he or one of his staff gets back to every constituent with a question or concern. The letters the Senator does respond to are few, and these are selected by his staff. The criteria used by the staff include the poignancy of the request, the relevance of the letter to current affairs, and a random sampling of letters received by the office.

Prior to working in the Senator's office, Louise had worked for another government agency where she had been trained in the use of a number of different computer software packages. She found that she had a certain facility with computers and has since taken it upon herself to learn a number of different software packages on her own. Louise saw that a number of different government agencies were using Notes and decided to learn about it. She obtained a (legitimate) copy from her network administrator, got a set of manuals, and began learning about Notes. Initially she focused on understanding the interface and the menus. She went through each of the sample applications included with Notes to get a better understanding of the product. Next, she began to copy the sample databases and change their designs to suit her own needs. She created a database for personal action items and meetings. One shortcoming of her experiences was that she never got the opportunity to use Notes on a server. This was unfortunate because most of the power of Notes comes from sharing information with other users. Nevertheless, she continued to develop applications for her own use. One application was designed to help her respond to constituent communications.

THE APPLICATION

The application had two forms: Main and Response. The Main form was used to capture information on the constituent and their correspondence with the Senator. Fields on the form included Constituent Name, Constituent Address, Constituent Zip Code, Type of Correspondence, Date of Correspondence, Topic of Correspondence, Bill/Issue, Position, Status, Original. The Response document included fields for Response Date, Response Type, and Response.

When Louise received a letter, e-mail, or phone call to respond to, she put the relevant information into her database. If the communication was an e-mail, she would put the text of the original e-mail in the field called Original. If it was a phone call or letter, she would reference the date and time of the phone call or the location where the letter was filed. In the address field she would put their e-mail or mailing address or, in the event the constituent had called the office, she would put their telephone number. In the Type field, she would pick from a keyword list including e-mail, Letter, Telephone Call, and Personal Visit. She used the Bill/Issue field to type in the Senate bill referenced by the constituent, or the issue raised by the constituent. The Position field could be used to categorize the constituent's position on an issue (for or against) quickly. The status field was a keyword list with values like Complete, Open, and Requires More Info.

To respond to a constituent, she created a Response form. The document would inherit some information from the original form like Constituent Name, Date of Correspondence, and Type of Correspondence. Louise would then fill in the fields for Response type (typically this would correspond to the same keyword list used in the Main form), Response Date (which is the date the response was actually sent to the constituent), and Response. The response itself might contain the actual text of a letter, or it might contain a description of how the response was provided to the constituent (e.g., telephone conversation covering these three issues). The Response form also included a button to update the status of the Main document (e.g., to close an open issue). Louise had even worked through how to print a letter directly from a Response document to the Senator's letterhead. This meant that she was keeping a record of all letters sent out in Notes.

THE OFFICE BUYS IN

Louise started showing other people in the office the application. As her application got larger, she began to use Full-text search to find similar correspondence sent to other constituents. She created views to see the Open issues. She also created views that categorized the documents by issue and created totals so she could see how many letters had been received on a particular issue. As its utility became obvious, other staff members expressed interest in getting access to the application. Louise suggested they contact their network administrator to ask him about getting a Notes server.

It turns out that the administrator had set up a Notes server in his office, which he was sharing with a number of people in different Congressional offices. They could actually reach this server through their network, and he said that the server had enough capacity to add the Senator's staff and the application without a problem. He suggested that in the long run, they might want to talk to the Senator about a more permanent solution (getting a server of their own).

The network administrator got Louise a valid Notes ID and provided her access to the server. She then copied the database to the server. The administrator provided Louise with IDs for each member of the office. Gradually, over a few weeks, Louise helped the rest of the staff install Notes and connect to the server.

Louise then organized an informal day of training for the office. During this training, she introduced the office to Notes, provided an overview of the Notes interface, and began teaching everyone how to use the application. In general, it is important to teach users general Notes skills outside of any particular application. This helps to ensure that the users are comfortable in Notes and can solve their own Notes-related problems. In Louise's case, she knew that she would be available in the office to answer questions, so she was more concerned with her officemates' understanding of the application, rather than Notes.

CONCRETE RESULTS

Over the next few months, more and more of the office started using Louise's Notes application exclusively to respond (or record responses) to constituents. As is so often the case, the office continued to find more and more uses for the data they were collecting. If the Senator had been particularly active in fighting a bill or getting a bill passed, the Senator's staff could look back through the records to find the constituents who had supported the Senator's position and send them a letter thanking them for their support and providing details of the Senator's involvement in the passage or rejection of the bill. The Senator began to use the database to help determine how his constituents felt about a particular issue.

The Senator also has plans to use the application around reelection time. From the database, he can quickly generate letters to his constituents updating

Main View in the Constituent Correspondence database

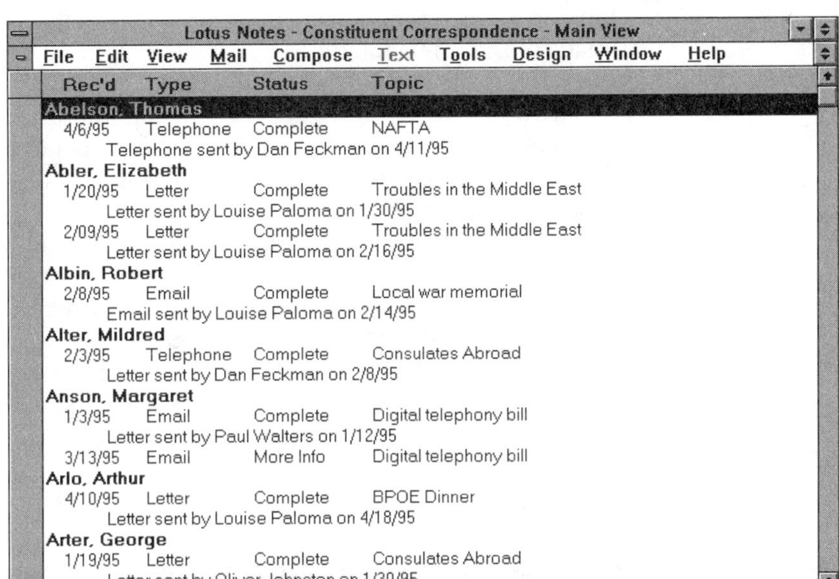

them on his position on a particular issue. The letter might appear quite personal. Constituents typically appreciate this type of gesture. The Senator used the Zip codes stored in the database to invite local townspeople to political rallies in their area. Finally, the database was used by the office to build up "histories" of various constituents. Some of the constituents would write to the Senator again and again on the same or similar topics. The database allowed them to track these communications and respond appropriately. It also allowed the office to identify the persistent, but reasonable, constituents and address their issues accordingly.

UNFINISHED BUSINESS

As with any application designed to help customers (or voters), Louise's application could be made far more sophisticated and provide much more leverage to the office. These capabilities need to be weighed against the costs of implementation of many of these features.

One of the simplest additions would be to include scanned images of all correspondence from constituents. In the event that a constituent sent a letter to the Senator, the letter would be filed, and the location of the letter would be recorded in the Notes document. It would be far more useful (particularly in looking at historical documents) to provide the office member with a scanned image of the original letter. This would help to ensure that all necessary information was included in the database.

The office has also considered creating another database to track pending legislation and current affairs. This database could be used to keep staff up to date on current issues, and to copy from the documents contained in this database to respond to constituents.

The office might also consider deploying an implementation of Phone Notes, a product from Lotus Development. Phone Notes allows people to access data stored in Notes documents from a telephone. The office could use Phone Notes to give constituents access to data stored in Notes databases. This might include the Senator's voting record on various bills, information on pending legislation, information on how to contact the Senator, or other information important to constituents.

▶ FACT SHEET

Constituent Correspondence Database

Purpose: To capture and maintain records of correspondence between the Senator, his staff, and constituents in the Senator's state.

Application Origin: Developed from Discussion template by a member of the Senator's staff.

Application Development Time: 1 man-week to complete a prototype.

Typical Size: Documents (excluding scanned images) are quite small; the office receives 100–200 letters each week. This yields 5,000–10,000 documents each year and a total database size of approximately 7–12 MB. Scanned images can increase the size dramatically.

Forms: Main and Response.

Views: Main View (By Constituent), By Author, By Date, By Zip Code, By Topic, and By Bill.

The Corporate Audit Application

The Ralphson Company is a large (hypothetical) multinational pharmaceuticals organization. Linda Emery works in the company's Audit department. The Audit department is responsible for auditing business units and projects to assess progress toward business objectives. The purpose of the audit is to identify deficiencies and allow management to address these deficiencies before they become significant problems. As an auditor, Linda spends much of her time on the road visiting the various business units for which she is responsible. Recently, the company began installing Lotus Notes. Notes' ability to support remote users, store unstructured information, and manipulate documents lends itself directly to the auditing process. As a result, the Audit department was targeted as one of the first to receive Notes. Linda, as one of the chief auditors, has been selected to oversee (dare we say audit?) the project.

The Audit department performs two types of audits: first, there are *routine audits*. Routine audits are performed at each business unit once every two years. The order in which business units are audited changes from year to year to ensure some level of surprise when the auditors arrive. The second type of audits are *requested audits*. Requested audits are conducted at the request of managers to assess the progress of a business unit or project against corporate standards. Requested audits are not necessarily an indication of significant problems. Sometimes managers request an audit simply to get a better understanding of a project's current status. In all audits, the division, business unit, or project being audited is referred to as the *client*.

The Audit process is highly structured. There are various pieces of critical information that need to be accumulated, interviews with key personnel that need to be conducted, and a summary report that needs to be circulated for review. The entire process of an audit can be conducted in a relatively short amount of time (assuming the business unit or project team has already prepared the required information). It is only the largest audits that require more than a week of time. During an audit, the auditor will typically be located on site with the business unit or project team being evaluated. This helps to ensure that the auditor has all necessary information as quickly as possible. The Auditor typically brings a portable computer and inputs information into the computer as it becomes available. The completed information is then compiled into a report, which is circulated to relevant management. Ralphson intends to use Notes to help auditors collect information on site, replicate the data back to the Auditing group's Notes server, and circulate the final report for approval.

DEFINING REQUIREMENTS

Linda works directly with Ellen Lapin, a computer consultant, on developing the requirements for the application. Initially, their meetings focus on helping Ellen understand the Auditing department's business and their existing work flows. Ellen starts to incorporate this information into a Requirements document describing the needs of the Auditing department. This includes not only an overview of the audit department's business processes, but a rough outline of how these work flows might be mapped to a Notes application.

While it would be desirable to store all audits in a central database, it is likely that the database would become unmanageably large after a short period. Version 3 of Notes limits the total size of a database to 1 gigabyte. While this is a significant amount of storage, the audit process typically involves a number of supporting documents that may be stored as file attachments, embedded graphics (like Excel spreadsheets or charts) or scanned-in images (like faxes or relevant paper documents). This rapidly adds up, and can exceed the 1 gigabyte limitation. Another argument against a single large database is the fact that most users will be operating remotely on laptop computers. It is undesirable for them to be carrying any more information than is absolutely necessary; both because of the limited storage available on laptops and the time it would take to replicate all of that data over a modem line. Since the audits need to be spread across databases, Linda and Ellen decide that the most logical division would be by business unit/project. Dividing the databases in this manner ensures that when an auditor goes to visit their client, they have the relevant historical information on that client. This division is better than having a separate database for each audit, as this would require the auditor to download a series of databases before departing for the client.

Ellen's document provides an overview of the process of completing an audit and the work flow involved in approving a completed audit. An auditor who departs for the client's site will need to take a copy of the Client database along. The Client database will contain all of the prior audits done on the business unit/project. This might serve to highlight areas of the client's business that warrant in-depth investigation or might simply be useful as a reference (e.g., reminding the auditor of the names of the managers in the business unit). The auditor will then begin the process of accumulating the necessary audit information. This information will be input directly into a Notes document in the database. There will be a main document that provides an overview of the current audit and a series of Response documents to capture various pieces of information collected throughout the audit. The forms listed include Audit, Compliance, Financials, Interviews, Audit Assessment, Comment, and Response. Audit will be the main document, describing the overall context of the Audit. Each of the other documents will be Responses to the Audit. Each main Audit document might have a number of Responses of the same type (for example, a number of interviews might have been conducted as part of an audit). The Compliance form will be used to evaluate the client's compliance with corporate policies and procedures. The Financial form reviews the client's financial goals and progress toward those goals (typically in the form of a written description and attached spreadsheet). The Interview form will be used by auditors to record interviews conducted as part of the audit process. The Audit Assessment form will be used to store the auditor's final report on the client. This document may either reference or incorporate elements of each of the other documents collected for the audit. The last two forms, Comment and Response, allow relevant personnel to participate in an electronic discussion on a particular client or audit. This will be particularly important in the event that an audit is rejected or some aspect of the audit is considered controversial. The views in the database are by Audit Date, Auditor (author), Audit Number (assigned by the auditing department), Assessment, and Discussion. The database will be full-text indexed so that auditors can find information quickly.

Finally, Ellen's document describes the approval process that each audit must go through before it can be considered complete. Once the auditor has collected all the information necessary for an Audit (and written the Audit Assessment), the Assessment will be sent by Notes Mail to each of the relevant managers. The manager who opens the Mail document will be presented with buttons to Approve or Reject the Assessment. In either case, the document is mailed back to the original Audit database. The manager who rejects an assessment is required to input the reasons prior to sending the message back to the database. This gives the auditor an opportunity to address the manager's concerns and resubmit the assessment for approval.

The rough draft of the requirements document is circulated to the auditing department. Linda has written a comprehensive document and gets a fair amount of comments as a result. Some of the comments point out inaccuracies in the discussion of the auditing work flow, and others make suggestions for changes to the design of the database.

BUILDING THE APPLICATION

The development of the database design proceeds quickly. Ellen starts with the Discussion template and builds the forms and views identified in the Requirements Definition document. To build the forms, Ellen relies on copies of paper audit forms provided by Linda. Where possible, she maps the paper forms directly to Notes design elements like checkboxes and keyword lists. Once this process is complete, Ellen builds the views for the database.

The most difficult development effort involves the logistics of the audit approval process. After an auditor completes the Audit Assessment form, he or she must click the Submit for Approval button. A copy of the form is then automatically sent out to the managers listed by the auditor. Prior to being sent, doclinks to the original Audit document are created and included at the top of the Audit Assessment. This allows the manager to double-click on the doclink to view the source documents that the auditor used to create the assessment. Once the manager has had an opportunity to review the assessment, he or she can click either the Approve or Reject button on the document. In either case, the document is mailed back to the original database.

Implementing this work flow is more difficult than it sounds. There are many logistical issues that need to be worked out to get the work flow to operate properly. Questions regarding the work flow abound, and design compromises are made out of necessity. The list of managers who need to approve each audit is different. There is no easy way to calculate this automatically. As a result, the auditor will need to provide a list of the managers to whom the document should be forwarded before submitting an audit for approval. Once a manager has approved the document, the document needs to find its way back to the Audit database from which it came. Notes can only mail documents to users or databases that have been registered in the company's Name and Address book. As a result, a record must be created in the Name and Address book before each database can be used. Finally, there is no easy way to make a document that is mailed to a database a response to a preexisting document. This makes it difficult (though not impossible) to construct a view that retains the relationships between documents. As an interim solution, Ellen creates a new view called Approvals, which just lists returned responses. A user of the database wishing to see the status of a particular audit must switch to this view to see the list of approvals or rejections. In the long run, this database is a good candidate for some level of API tools to fix such problems (see "Unfinished Business" later in this chapter).

DOING AN AUDIT

Linda is the first auditor to use the application. She takes her portable computer on the road and inputs information as it is collected. At the conclusion of the audit process, she submits her assessment for approval according to the work flow defined by Ellen. Her assessment is that the application takes care of many of the organizational issues that used to bog down the auditing process. In the past, much of the auditing time was taken up in the accumulation and organization of information. Putting the information into Notes helps her focus her efforts on the analysis of the information collected. Another benefit of Notes is that all of the documents related to a particular audit (whether electronic or paper) can be stored in the Notes database. Finally, the ability to perform full-text searches against the database allows auditors to identify relevant information in the database quickly.

Once Linda's initial evaluation of the application is complete, the application is deployed generally to other auditors. Some care needs to be taken in creating databases for all of the auditing department's clients. The team needs to ensure that appropriate access controls are placed on the databases as the information is typically quite sensitive.

Main View in the Corporate Audit

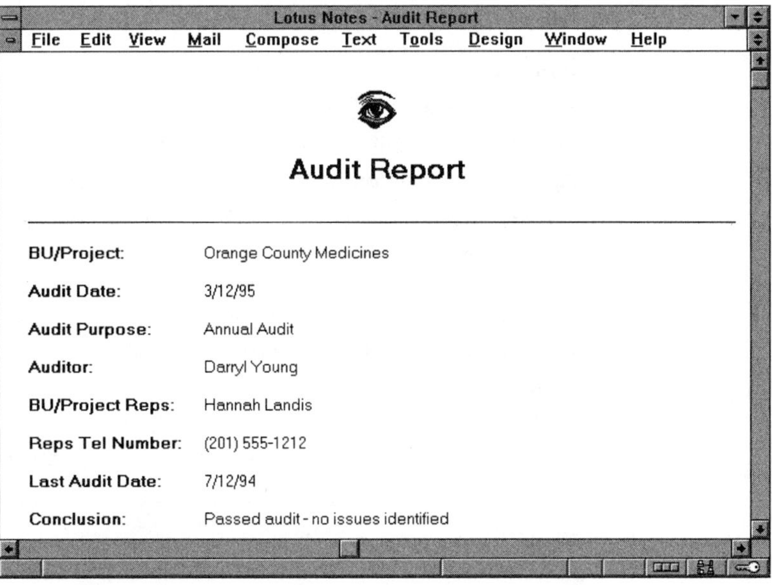

UNFINISHED BUSINESS

There are a number of improvements that might be made to Ralphson's auditing application. First of all, the approval process is inadequate. There are simple and complicated solutions to this problem. A simple solution would be to write an API to automatically populate the managers' names for approvals. This program would also take returning documents and make them Responses to the appropriate main Audit in the database. A more complicated solution would be to purchase one of the workflow-computing engines available for Notes and implement the approval work flow using one of these. These can be expensive to purchase and complicated to install and maintain.

Other possible improvements include integrating a forms package into the audit work flow. Forms packages allow companies to duplicate their paper forms in an electronic format exactly. This simplifies training and ensures that the forms comply with any legal requirements (which typically exist in regulated industries) governing the appearance of the form.

Another improvement to consider is to prepopulate information for the audit before the auditor visits the client. This might be automated (downloading the financial data from the company's accounting system) or manual (getting relevant personnel to answer questionnaires prior to the auditor's arrival).

FACT SHEET

Corporate Audit Application

Purpose: To capture audit information on projects and business units. For each business unit/project audited, a new database will be created.

Application Origin: Based on design of the Discussion template.

Application Development Time: 3 man-weeks of development.

Typical Size: Each database covers only a business unit or project. As a result, each database should not exceed 2–3 MB in size, unless there are many scanned images; then size could grow beyond the 1 GB limit.

Typical Use: An auditor takes the database to a business unit to be audited and uses the application to capture all relevant audit information.

Forms: Audit, Compliance, Financials, Interviews, Audit Assessment, Comment, and Response.

Views: By Audit Date, Auditor, Audit Number, Assessment, and Discussion.

Teamworks Contact Manager

Uptime Computer Solutions, Inc., is a California-based Lotus Notes Premium Partner dedicated to the ongoing development of highest quality software to improve and facilitate better communication and information delivery. "As Notes consultants, we often found that we were 'cleaning up' after other consultants," said Michael Bertrand, a consultant for Uptime. "They installed Notes and left without making sure that the company had integrated it into their operation. We also found that nearly everyone had some sort of contact management system and a desire to share that information across the team."

Since Uptime had people on staff who had experience training on various contact managers, they felt they could develop a Notes application that would be an easy-to-use introduction to Notes as well as a fully functional contact manager. The result is TeamWorks.

The TeamWorks contact management system is designed to allow extensive customization by the customer to meet the needs of the particular situation. To accomplish this, Uptime built a Data Dictionary, a Notes database that co-operates with the TeamWorks database to provide many customizations to the TeamWorks system.

THE DATA DICTIONARY

The Data Dictionary is the central reference for the TeamWorks product. It allows people who know little or nothing about Notes database design to customize the forms and prompts used in the system. Every time the user enters a keyword selection field in the database, the TeamWorks system looks in the Data Dictionary for the set of possible selections. Further, the Data Dictionary allows the user to determine not only the keywords in response to a prompt, but the text of the prompt itself.

The key form in the Data Dictionary is called a Keyword Definition. Certain keyword fields in the TeamWorks database look up their values in this database. For example, when creating an Action Item, one of the prompts is Action Item Type. The possible values in this field, such as Call—Follow up, and Information Request—Sales are taken from the Data Dictionary. This lets the local customer define the choices that are offered in these key fields.

THE WORK FLOW

Once the Data Dictionary has been filled out, the TeamWorks database is ready for use. Like many contact management systems, TeamWorks is built around a hierarchy of companies and contacts.

The first task for anyone using TeamWorks is to fill out a Company Profile form. The Company Profile contains the basic contact information for an organization—its name, address, and phone numbers, along with information on its relationship to other companies. In many cases, one company might have many different divisions, but ask that all billing information go to a central place. TeamWorks allows for this. A company can be marked as either a Headquarters Company or a Division. Later, other companies can be linked to the headquarters company to create a hierarchy of relationships among companies.

Once the relationships are established, buttons on the form will move up the hierarchy to the headquarters of a division or move down and get a list of divisions.

3-2-1 CONTACT

After the company record is complete, it is then possible to create a contact record for an individual employee. In order to make it easier to enter the data and to ensure that the contacts are created only while a company record is highlighted, the only way to create a contact record is to click the Compose Contact button from within Notes.

The contact records are straightforward—name, address, and phone numbers, plus a field for Additional Information. Having completed a contact record, it is now possible (by means of the buttons on the Contact form) to take other actions.

An Activity Report is created any time there is contact with a customer. Whether the customer calls support, meets with a salesperson, or gets called by one, an Activity Report is created. The Activity Report describes the activity (chosen from the list that has been entered in the Data Dictionary), the

The Contact Profile form and its buttons

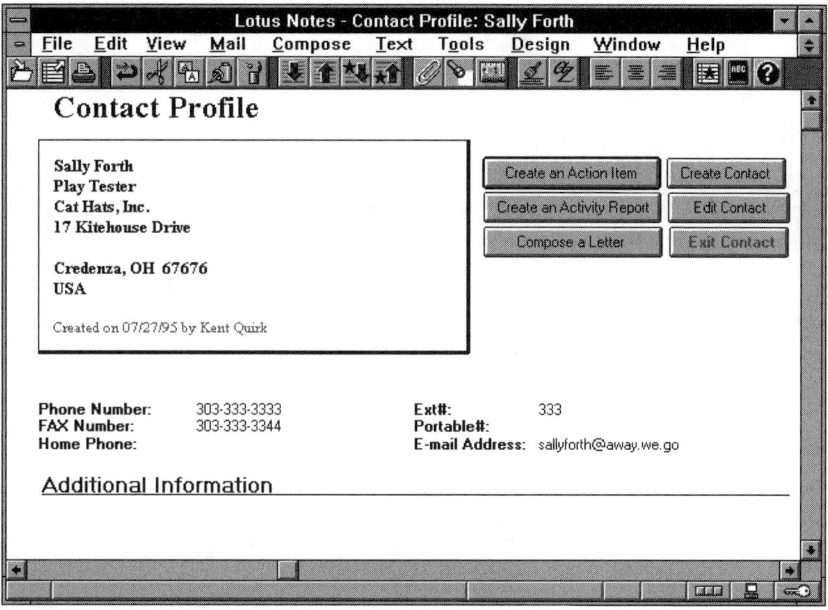

type or reason for the call, and includes a subject line for the view as well as a summary of the activity. There is also a set of fields for recording who was involved in the activity on both the customer side and the company side.

One or more Action Items for the company employees can be the result of an activity. These can include such items as a request to follow up with more information, making an appointment, or placing the customer in a tickler file to be called back in a few months. Each Action Item has three major sections.

The Description section includes the activity type (chosen from the Data Dictionary), a subject line (which shows up in the views), and a full description of the activity, a Rich Text field that can be used for description, pasting documents, or attaching files.

The Assignment section allows the Action Item to be assigned to a particular person. A salesperson might assign the Action Item to herself for later followup, assign it to the Mail Room for literature fulfillment, or assign it to Engineering for design work. An Action Item also requires a due date, by which time the action item should be completed. It is also possible to set up the system to automatically remind both the author of the action item and the person to whom it is assigned—it can even send the reminder a few days in advance.

An Action Item being filled out

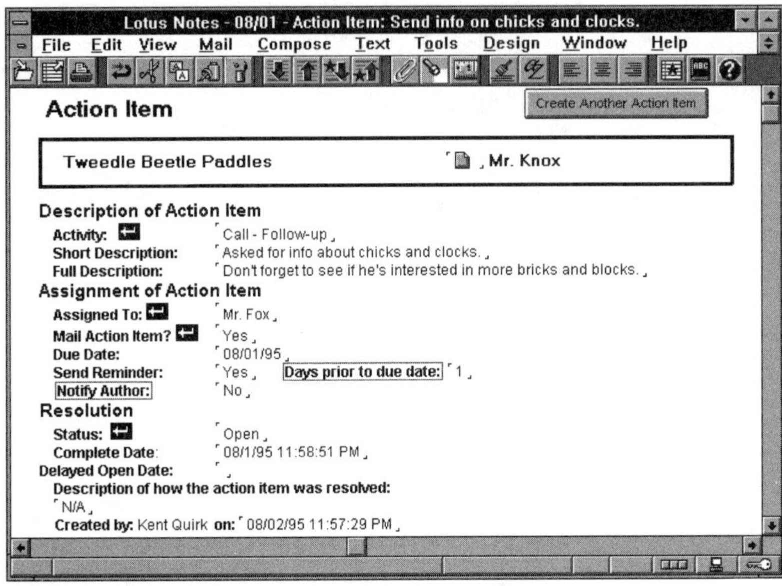

Every night, a Background Macro is run against this database. The macro checks every Action Item, looking for Action Items that are either overdue or within the range of the reminder date. The macro then automatically composes an e-mail to the appropriate people with the information about the action item. It also includes a doclink back to the original item.

In fact, pressing the button to compose an Action Item or an activity automatically pastes a doclink into the new item that points back to the original item. This way, the doclinks can be followed all the way back to the contact name that originated the action.

The last section on the form has to do with the Action Item Resolution. It starts with a status field that indicates the status of this action item. Possible values for status are Open (the initial value), Closed (the Action Item has been successfully resolved), On Hold (not resolved, but not ready to be acted upon), and Delayed Open (to be opened again at a certain future time).

If the Action Item is Closed, the date of closure is recorded. If it is to be delayed, there is a date field for filling in the date it should be reopened. The background macros will send a reminder at that time. Finally, there is another Rich Text field for further explanation of the status.

DON'T FORGET TO WRITE

The system includes the ability to write a letter to a contact easily, by pressing the button labeled Compose a Letter. This is a standard blank letter that has the author's name, company name, and the contact name and address pre-placed on the form. The author merely has to fill out the letter type and the subject, and write the body of the letter.

The Data Dictionary has information on different paper types for letters such as letterhead and blank. It also has information on the size of the letterhead. When the letter is composed for letterhead, the sender's address information will be omitted. For blank paper, it will be included. The system can accommodate several different letterheads.

VIEWS

The most commonly used view is the Company Full View. This shows a categorized list of companies, with each company broken down into its divisions and the contacts within each. Each contact has a list of all the Activities, Actions, and Letters that are associated with it.

The Company Full View

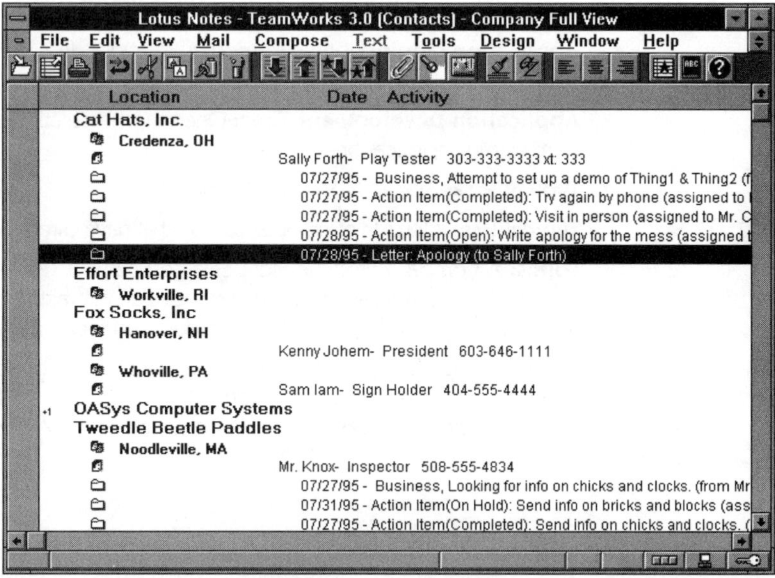

Because this view shows every document in the database, organized by company, it's an excellent view for getting an overview of the whole database. The other popular views are the Contact List views. These essentially act as the customer address book. They can be organized by last name, first name, or company name. The Contact List views show name, address, and phone number; the Phone List views show name, company, phone number, and title.

Other available views are the Action Item views of the To-Do list, available by Status or by Person. There is a view specifically corresponding to the To-Do list, which is the view showing only open Action Items, by Person.

The Activity Report views show the ongoing activity in the system. The Staff Report view shows a calendar of each person's past actions and future responsibilities.

Michael Bertrand says that Uptime's customers find this system to be very easy to use. "It acts as a central repository for all the customer contact information that used to be spread all over the company. It also acts as a simple introduction to Notes—customers tell me it makes Notes into a 'plug-and-play' application. Companies that are new to Notes can use this simple application; then they ask 'Where can we go now?' and they're ready for the next step."

◣ FACT SHEET

TeamWorks Contact Manager

Purpose: To act as an introductory Notes application and maintain a contact list combined with a tickler file for action items.

Application Origin: Uptime Computer Solutions, Inc., 2 North First St., Suite 512, San Jose, CA 95113. Tel: 408-280-0147.

Application Development Time: One week installation and training, plus conversion time from existing applications.

Typical Size: About 35 MB, 6000 contacts.

Typical Use: All parts of an organization that have direct contact with customers.

Forms: A Company Profile describes a company. A Contact form identifies a person within that company. An Activity Report describes an interaction with a customer; Action Items act as items on a To-Do list, complete with automatic reminders for past-due or upcoming items.

Views: The Company Full View shows all companies, contacts, and actions, sorted by company. The List views show contact information in different ways. There are also views showing different types of documents, such as the Activities reports.

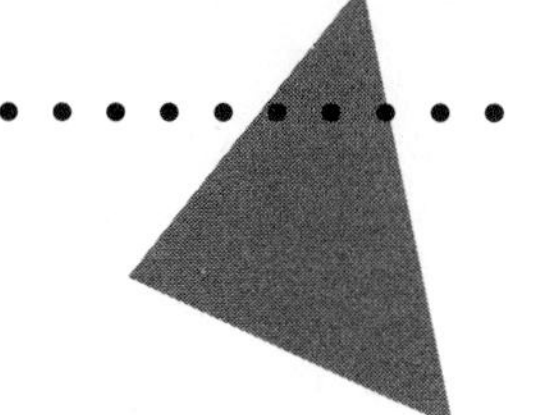

Managing Change Management

Sharon McKenzie works for CitizenSoft, a (hypothetical) multinational software company that is experiencing increased competition in all markets. In an effort to meet this competition, CitizenSoft has decided to reduce the amount of time necessary to develop new products and services. The company has been

The By Change Date in the Change Management database

Type	Description
March 11, 1995	
PC OS	Upgrade DOS
March 12, 1995	
Portable PCs	Install and distribute new laptop PCs
March 15, 1995	
Network	Upgrade file server hardware
Network	Upgrade network software
March 18, 1995	
Network	Upgrade TCP/IP on all OS/2 servers
March 21, 1995	
PC OS	Install Windows for Workgroups on Help Desk PCs
March 22, 1995	
PC Applications	Upgrade office application suite
March 23, 1995	
Network	Install new file servers
Network	Install network CD ROM jukebox
March 25, 1995	
Network	Upgrade remaining file server hardware
Unix	Install new Unix workstations
Mainframe	Install new mainframe connection
Unix	Add Mac users to NFS
March 29, 1995	
Network	Replace NFS on Unix servers
Network	Configure Internet gateway

identifying, evaluating, and implementing new technologies as rapidly as possible. Sharon's personnel have all received new PCs, with the latest operating system, office applications, and so on. To provide state-of-the art service to her customers, the company has installed a new PBX linked to her customer database. She has implemented modern RDBMs, an object-oriented development environment, and even Lotus Notes!

Unfortunately, the process of adopting these new technologies often has the side effect of destabilizing existing systems. Primarily, this is because changes are initiated before the planning phase has been completed. To combat this, CitizenSoft has hired a team of management consultants to help implement *change-management* procedures.

Change management is the practice of carefully planning changes prior to their implementation. The goal of the change-management processes is to identify how the changes will impact existing systems, the resources required to implement the changes, the steps required to implement the changes, and how the original systems can be restored, in the event that the new system doesn't work. By mapping all of these out, CitizenSoft should be able to implement changes quickly and efficiently while minimizing disruption to existing services.

While change-management practices can be applied to any department experiencing significant change, it is clearly well suited to organizations implementing new technologies. As a result, senior management has targeted the Computer Support department to improve the level of service provided by that organization to the rest of the company. Computer Support is responsible for all computer hardware and software including corporate LANs (local area networks—each office has its own LAN) and WANs (wide area networks—links between offices). This organization has experienced significant problems implementing new technologies. These issues have directly affected the organization's customers (end users). For example, Computer Support recently attempted to upgrade the operating system used on end user's workstations and found, after having upgraded a few dozen users, that there were certain incompatibilities between some of the company's standard applications and the new operating system. A number of users were unable to perform their work until the old version of the operating system was reinstalled. This type of situation seems to have become commonplace in the Computer Support department. Sharon, as a member of that department, has been selected to work with the management consultants to help implement the change management practices.

WORKING WITH THE CONSULTANTS

The process begins with meetings—lots of them. Sharon and other members of the Computer Support department provide data on every aspect of existing systems to the consultants. The goal is to identify the systems the organization supports, the procedures that support those systems, and the likely changes in the near future. During these discussions it becomes clear that a number of the support procedures are neither complete nor documented. The interviews take a couple of weeks to complete. At the end of this period, the consultants give a presentation to the group's management on their findings. This is an opportunity for the department to agree or disagree with their findings. Clarifications are made, and the consultants revise their documentation.

During the next phase, Sharon works with the consultants to identify a proper tool to support the change-management procedures being defined. The final application should be compatible with existing systems; should be able to integrate easily with Help Desk systems (the Help Desk will have to speak to the irate customers when changes go awry—see the chapter entitled "Help Desk"); and be efficient at handling large amounts of unstructured data (text). Finally, as the application is being designed to meet an evolving set of requirements, it is critical that the application be easy to modify. At this point, it is clear to Sharon that Notes is probably the appropriate environment in which to develop this application. When the consultants learn that prototypes can be developed and revised in a matter of hours, agreement is reached that Notes is a reasonable selection for a development environment. Sharon volunteers to build the prototype herself.

Sharon spends time attempting to define the requirements for the application. This requires a thorough understanding on her part of exactly what procedures will be implemented for change management. Once Sharon feels she has an understanding of the general principles, she suggests creating three forms for a prototype. The forms are Change Request, Comments, and Resolutions. Sharon also suggests some basic views: By Change Date, By Implementation Date, By System Affected, and By Author. This will give the prototype the critical features necessary to actually start working with sample data. Finally, in an effort to develop an overall timetable to implement the Change Management database and procedures, Sharon provides the consultants with her estimate of the total amount of time it will take to develop the application.

Starting Development

This application will have one Main document (Change Request) and two Response documents (Comments and Resolutions). Sharon decides to use the Discussion template provided with Notes as the basis for her application. She creates a new database from the template, and renames the forms to match her form names. As the Discussion template has fewer forms than her change-management application, she makes an extra copy of a form and renames it as the remaining form. These forms will serve as placeholders until she has time to update their contents.

In designing a database, it is easiest to complete the forms before developing views. If the forms change significantly, the views become outdated and must be updated to reflect the changes to the forms. As a result, she begins work on the main document of the database, the Change Request form.

The purpose of the Change Request form is to capture all information related to a given change. While filling out this form can be time consuming and tedious, this type of information is critical to ensure that changes are well understood and can be implemented easily. Other members of the organization will be able to make comments on a Change Request using the Comments form. Once all comments have been incorporated into the change (or discarded as irrelevant), the Change Request will be reviewed by a Change Approval Team comprised of representatives from the different organizations within computer support (e.g., LAN Support and Applications Support).

Sharon has identified a number of fields that will be added to the form:

Field Name	Purpose
Author	Name of original author of document
ChangeNumber	A unique number generated when the form is created to identify the change request
Descrip	Brief description of change
ChangeType	Categorization of the change type: focuses on system affected (network, mainframe, or operating system)
ResourcesRequired	Resources necessary to implement the change
ChangePreRecs	List of steps that must be complete prior to implementing change
ChangePlan	Overview of plan for change
InstallationPlan	Description of steps to "install" change
Testing	Description of testing done to confirm change will work
TestPlan	Steps necessary to test the installed change
EducationPlan	Means of communicating change to relevant parties
Downtime	Downtime that will result from this change
TimeToImplement	Time necessary to implement the change

Field Name	Purpose
BackoutPlan	Plan to restore system to its prior state, in the event the change cannot be implemented
DocumentationChanges	Changes to system documentation
AssignedTo	Responsible party
HelpDeskInfo	Help the Help Desk support users with questions or problems
MeetingDate	Date of meeting to review change request

Sharon's goal at this point is to get as many of the fields as possible added to the form as quickly as possible. In Notes, you can always go back later to change the appearance or order of fields on a form. Once the fields have been added to the form, she saves it and starts work on the other forms.

The Comments form will allow users to make comments on filed change requests. This form will inherit the change number and description fields of the original Change Request form and provide a field for authors to input their comments on the request. Once this is complete, she begins work on the final form, Resolutions. This form will capture the results of Change Approval Meetings. A particular change may be accepted or rejected. In either case, there is a field to allow a text description of any specific terms of the acceptance or rejection—an acceptance might require certain amendments to the change request (e.g., this change must be done at night on a weekend). Similarly, a change might be rejected because the request is incomplete or perhaps inappropriate at this time (e.g., a request discussing a change that has not been thoroughly tested). Once the forms are complete, Sharon develops the views identified earlier. The database is now in shape to review with the consultants. She schedules a meeting to review the prototype. The entire development process has taken about a week.

The meeting to review the prototype takes two hours. During that time, she reviews the forms and views in depth. Some of the changes, like fonts and arrangement of fields can be made during the meeting. For others, such as new views to help manage pending changes, she takes notes and agrees to make the changes in the next few days.

Once the changes have been made, she adds a rudimentary access control list to the database, identifying each of the management consultants as editors of the database, Sharon's department (input as a group entry in the ACL) as authors, and herself as manager. Next, she posts the database to her department's

The By Change Type view in the Change Management database

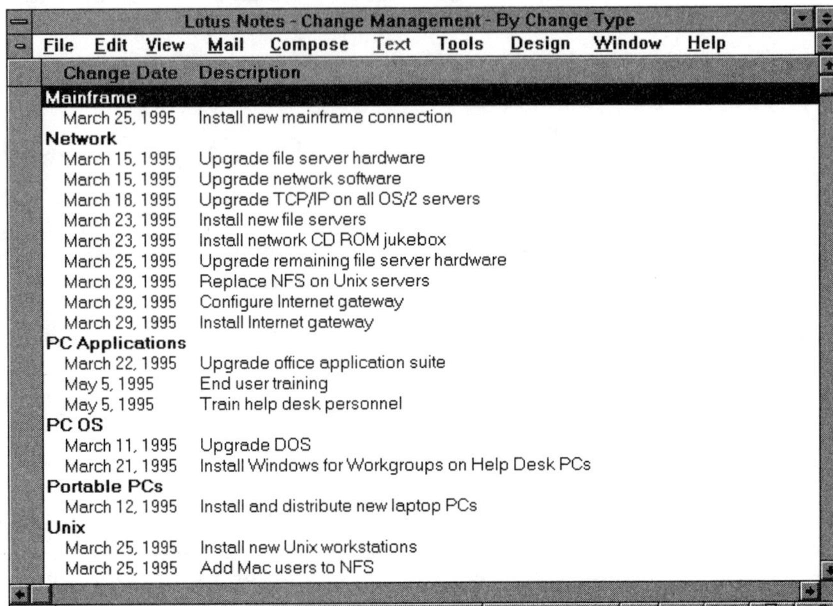

Notes server and sends her department an e-mail indicating that the database has been posted to the server for comment. She carefully emphasizes that it is there for evaluation only. The consultants take a few days to familiarize themselves with the application and discuss exactly how the application can be integrated into their change-management procedures.

A TEST CASE

The best way of testing an application (or set of procedures) is to take some real-life examples (provided by the eventual end users of the application) and run these examples through the application. Sharon is aware that the network group is going to upgrade the hardware on one of her company's file servers in the next few weeks and suggests this to the consultants as a reasonable test for the application. In this case, while the data will be input into the application, the process will not rely on the application. The change will occur according to schedules and plans, regardless of the information collected in the database.

The team of consultants meet with the LAN team to provide an overview of the new change-management procedures. As a group, they begin to go through each field of the Change Request form to create a change request. During this process, the LAN team begins to understand the process and how it relates to them. They provide practical input on additional fields that might be useful, suggest ways they could use this information to help manage their own projects more effectively, and provide insights as to what kind of information should be included in the Help and About documents for the database (see the sidebar "Database Help").

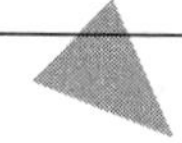

Database Help

An application designer may include a number of different types of online help in a Notes application. First, the application designer has two documents, one called Help About and the other called Help Using (accessible under the Help menu when an application is open). These documents provide an opportunity for the developer to describe the background, use, and administration of the application. The documents can include text and/or graphics. Typically, application designers use the Help About document to provide an overview of any policies or procedures related to the application. These might include how the access control list was set, when backups are performed, and confidentiality of the data. Other key pieces of information that may be included here are the names of some of the people responsible for the application (the database developer and the database manager) and a brief history of the inception and evolution of the database over time.

The Help Using document is used to describe the forms and views in the database. This provides the developer with an opportunity to describe the purpose of each of the design elements in the database and identify any subtleties that might not be apparent in the operation of the database. The reader should be aware that the amount of information included in these documents is directly related to the standards an organization observes relating to documenting applications and the thoroughness of the database manager and developer.

Notes also allows an application developer to provide *field-level help*. Field-level help is a single line of text that appears at the bottom of the Notes screen when a user moves to a particular field of a document he or she is editing. Field-level help typically complements text prompts on the form (the form might say "Topic" next to the field, while the field-level help might say "Enter a brief description of this document"). Field-level help can provide clarification of the type or format of data expected for a field.

Developers and end users can add pop-up boxes to text or graphics. When a pop-up exists, the text or graphic which the pop-up has been associated with will be surrounded by a green border. When a user clicks within the border, a pop-up box containing text written by the creator of the pop-up will appear. Developers can use pop-ups to provide a longer help description than can be provided with field-level help. End users can use pop-up boxes around text in a document to clarify a point.

Finally, developers and end users can place buttons in a form or document. These buttons, when clicked can provide an end user with a text message and ask the end user to click OK to continue. This can be used in cases where it is important to grab the user's attention.

The Change Request form forces the LAN team to think about measures of quality they might not have otherwise considered. The form requires them to provide an estimate of total down time and a backout plan. The team must identify the exact steps necessary to implement the change, as well as how they will restore the old server in the event the change does not work (e.g., some component of the new hardware fails). All of this process forces them to consider the process more carefully than they had. At the end of the meeting, Sharon has a completed form.

Other users in the department now have a week to comment on the proposed change. Different users make comments on the proposal, some asking for clarifications, some asking for more information, and others simply criticizing. Of particu-

A completed Change Request in the change management database

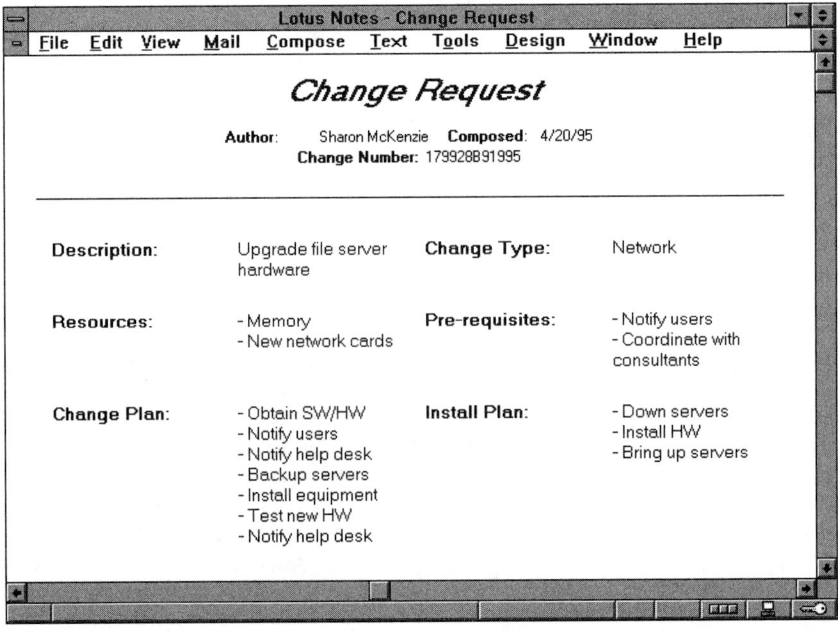

Change Request

Author: Sharon McKenzie   **Composed:** 4/20/95
Change Number: 179928B91995

Description:	Upgrade file server hardware	**Change Type:**	Network
Resources:	- Memory - New network cards	**Pre-requisites:**	- Notify users - Coordinate with consultants
Change Plan:	- Obtain SW/HW - Notify users - Notify help desk - Backup servers - Install equipment - Test new HW - Notify help desk	**Install Plan:**	- Down servers - Install HW - Bring up servers

lar importance are comments from the Help Desk team. They are the closest thing to an internal spokesperson for the end users who will be affected by this change. As a result, they provide a good indicator of how changes will be received. In this case, it is generally agreed that the impact on end users should be minimal.

In addition to filling in a form in the database, the management consultants work with the computer support department's management to implement the review and approval procedures recommended by their organization. Once the form is completed and comments have been made, a meeting of the Change Approval Team is held to review the pending change. A meeting agenda is created identifying all change requests to be considered at the meeting (in this case, only the LAN group's change request). When the meeting is finally held, there is significant criticism of the change request, and the change is ultimately rejected. The rejection is meant to send a message to members of the department that the change-management process is to be taken seriously and to ensure that the first change listed in the database is a good example of how other change requests should be completed. The rejection is recorded in a Resolutions form. At this point, if the change-management procedures were actually in effect, the LAN group would not be allowed to implement their change and would have to file a new change request (incorporating any changes suggested by the Change Approval Team) to perform the change.

Sharon and the management consultants repeat these steps working with other teams in her department. After two more such change requests, most of the department has been directly involved in at least one complete change request process, and the changes to the application are becoming less frequent. Soon thereafter the application is declared in production and placed on a server. Management then issues a statement that requires all changes that might affect services to use the change-management process.

UNFINISHED BUSINESS

While Sharon's department, her managers, and the consultants are pleased with the resulting application, she is aware of certain changes that could be made to the application to improve its functionality. These changes are not critical to the core functionality of the application, or they would have been incorporated already. When she has more time, perhaps she will revisit the application and incorporate some of these features. Some of them include the following:

> ▶ Approval workflow. It is possible in Notes to send a document sequentially through a number of individuals for approval. It is conceivable that some of the Change Requests might not require a full meeting of the Change Approval Team, but could be approved electronically without discussion. This feature was not implemented because identifying which users in each part of the department actually issue approvals, as well as how to handle vacations and sick leave, is extremely difficult. In

addition, it was recognized by a number of people that the face-to-face meetings of the Change Approval Team provide value by allowing different department members an opportunity to exchange information. This has value which an electronic approval process would not.

▶ An Amendment form. Currently, if a change request is changed from its original format, the author of the request will need to update the original document to reflect the changes. This process could be relegated to another form, perhaps called Amendment, which would capture the original change request and highlight the amendment. This would provide a simple history with the original document preserved and the amendment showing the approved version. Unfortunately, Notes cannot inherit Rich Text into a Response document, and a number of the critical fields of the original Change Request form are Rich Text fields.

▶ Implement version control. Notes provides a simple mechanism that saves edited documents as new documents. Typically, the original document is saved as a response to the new document. This is called *document versioning*. It is not actual *version control* (which seeks to ensure that somewhere there is always a "correct" version of a document that users can obtain), but it can help an organization maintain a record of the changes that have been made to a particular Change Request form. This would also allow the organization to capture original documents and amendments.

FACT SHEET

Change Management Database

Purpose: To help the company's Computer Support department monitor and implement changes to systems while minimizing the impact on existing customers.

Application Origin: Developed from the Discussion Template provided with Notes. The developer changed the content of existing forms and added new forms to meet application needs.

Application Development Time: 36 hours over $1\frac{1}{2}$ months for application development.

Typical Size: About 10 MB per 6-month period.

Typical Use: The computer support organization decides to upgrade the standard operating system in use on all desktop PCs. A Change Request is filed by the responsible member of the support organization. The Change Request describes which steps are to be taken, by whom; which systems will be impacted; how the group will restore the systems to their original state in the event of disaster; and contingency plans. The Notes database allows other individuals to comment on or even amend the Change Request. The final request is reviewed by the group and approved or rejected. Instituting these practices should help the organization provide a consistent, high quality of service to its customers across the company.

Forms: Change Request, Comments, and Resolution.

Views: By Author, By Change Date, By Implementation Date, By Change Type, By Request Number, and Resolutions.

Using a Sales Discussion Database

Providing a means for geographically dispersed sales forces to stay in touch is a classic application of Lotus Notes. It is often the first use of Notes beyond simple e-mail that a salesperson is likely to encounter. In this chapter we follow Joan Hale as she is introduced to a Sales Discussion database, and see how it becomes part of her daily life.

Joan is a saleswoman for a fast-growing company. Until recently, the sales force numbered around 50, and communications among the salespeople and between sales and headquarters was manageable, if barely. Once a month at the big sales meeting Joan would get together with her fellow salespeople to discuss new clients, sales strategies, ideas for new products and product enhancements, and so on. The sales managers would get together every now and then with marketing and development people at headquarters to relate this information and to bring new information out to the field.

All of that seems to be changing. The sales force now numbers around 100, and, in another year, looks like it will double again. The sales region is spreading out geographically, and more and more salespeople live too far to make monthly meetings feasible. It is clear that when the firm goes national, some new ways of working will be required.

ENTER NOTES

That probably explains why Joan's sales manager gave her a notebook computer recently and sent her to a course in using Notes. At the course, she learned how to connect to a server, how to send and receive Notes Mail, how to replicate a server-based database to her notebook so she only has to connect to the server once a day or so, and the other basic Notes skills. She returned from the course ready and eager to put Notes to work. The following scenario describes Joan's introduction to Notes and the Sales Discussion database.

Joan's regional sales manager calls her to a meeting with the other salespeople in her region. At the meeting the manager gives Joan a floppy with her user ID on it. She also gets instructions on how to connect to the server she has been assigned to. Finally, the manager demonstrates the first application the salespeople will be using: the Sales Discussion database.

WHAT IS THE SALES DISCUSSION DATABASE?

The Sales Discussion database, the manager explains, will be the focal point for communication among salespeople and between the sales force and headquarters. The Notes development team has built an application based on the Discussion template, with new forms and views tailored to supporting the sales force. Since Joan and her colleagues learned how to use Discussion databases at the course, the manager proceeds to describe the way in which it will be used in this particular application:

"Since this will be your first use of Notes, we have made very few modifications to the standard Discussion database that comes with Notes. In general, the database will consist of information stored in Main Topic documents—created either by you or by folks at headquarters. You will compose Response documents with comments, questions, and issues about this information. You will compose Response to Response documents to comment on each other's comments.

"The standard views of the Discussion template have been retained: By Author, By Category, and Main View. These views will always contain the entire contents of the database, albeit displayed in different forms. In addition to these standard views, a few new views have been provided. These views display subsets of the data in various ways. For example, in the view New Topics, Main View displays only those topics that have been created in the past month. Two other views, New Topics–By Author and New Topics–By Category, similarly display topics created in the past month, categorized by author or by category.

"The Notes developers added one new feature to the Main Topic form: a subcategory field. All views have an extra column added to categorize these subcategories within each category. The use of these extra fields will become clear as you begin to use the application.

"The database has been primed with some starter documents. These documents establish a beginning set of categories and subcategories and provide an example of how we expect the application will be used. In particular, main categories have been created to support the following types of discussion items: clients, products, and general.

"The Clients category is used to group discussion threads related to particular clients. Each client's name will be entered in the subcategory field. Therefore, to find discussion about a particular client, open the view By Category and scroll until you see Clients in the left column. The documents directly below will be organized by the client they relate to, and the clients' names will be indented under Client. Scroll until you see the client's name you are interested in. The documents directly below will be the discussion threads you are looking for.

"The Products category is used in a similar fashion to group discussion threads related to the various products we sell. Each product's name will be entered in the subcategory field. This way, in categorized views you can scroll until you find Product in the left column and then scroll until you see the particular product you are interested in indented below.

"Finally, the General category is used to group all other discussion, such as discussion of general sales strategies, events at headquarters, conferences, and courses of interest.

"That should be enough to get you going. Begin using the database immediately. We have built one new form, the Comments on This Database form. Use it to provide feedback and suggestions on the application itself. The form is mail-enabled, and will send mail to the people supporting the application. Good luck!"

On Her Own for the First Time

At her first opportunity, Joan dials into the server and replicates the Sales Discussion database to her notebook. She disconnects and opens the database in the By Category view.

The view must be set to open in the collapsed state, where only categories (no documents) are displayed, since what Joan sees is three rows of information: the three main categories created by the application developers. The view simply lists Clients, Products, and General. Joan double-clicks on Clients and the category expands. She sees several screens full of information appear, one row per client her firm supplies. She finds her best client, HLI Distributors, and expands that subcategory. She sees one document listed.

Joan opens this document and sees a brief note from the application developers. It reads simply, "This document was created to establish this client as a subcategory in the client's category. Create main topics with the category Clients and subcategory HLI Distributors to create discussion threads about this client." Getting the idea, Joan decides to do just that. From the compose menu she chooses the Main Topic form.

Joan types as a subject, "HLI would prefer we bill them bi-weekly. . ." She enters a category of Client and subcategory of HLI Distributors. In the body of the document she describes why HLI would prefer bi-weekly billing. She asks if others have had this request made of them and saves the document.

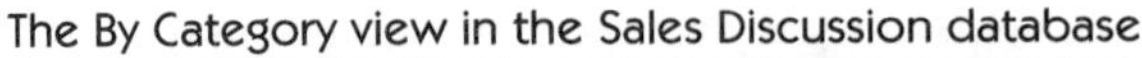

The By Category view in the Sales Discussion database

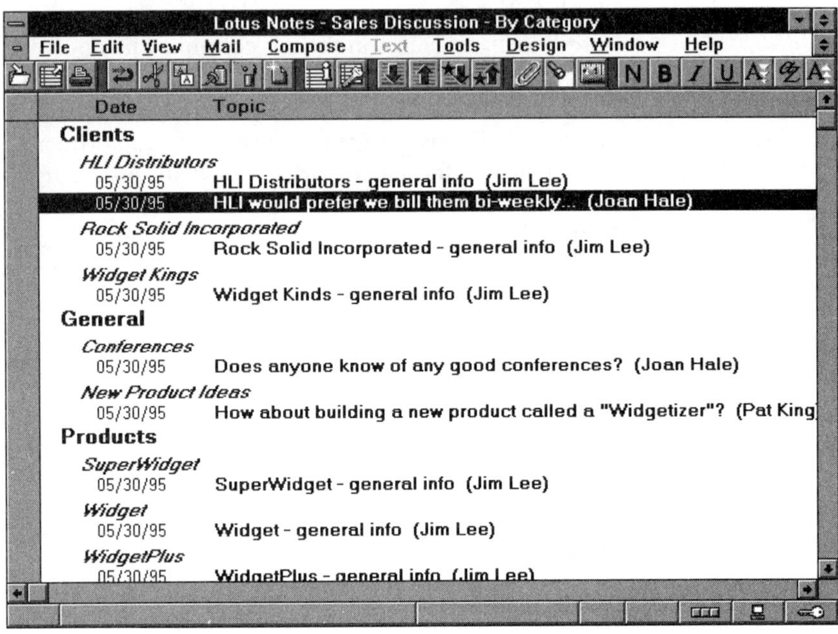

Joan spends some more time exploring the database, entering other ideas and issues she has on her mind. In the Products category, she enters some of her ideas for product enhancements. In the General area she asks if anyone knows of any good conferences coming up. When she has finished, Joan replicates with the server to upload her additions to the database.

The next day Joan replicates the database again to get whatever new information people have added to the database. She sees there has been quite a lot of activity in the Products category. Salespeople from various regions have entered many ideas for enhancements to the existing products and for entirely new products they think would sell. Seeing their ideas sparks Joan into thinking of some more ideas of her own. One person has added a document suggesting a new product, a "widgitizer," which some of Joan's clients have expressed interest in. She responds to this by adding her own document. Joan lists the clients she knows would be interested in a widgitizer, the reasons they want it, and any other ideas she can think of. Joan is excited because normally she wouldn't think of writing a proposal for the idea—it just wasn't that high on her priority list. But since someone proposed the idea in the Sales Discussion database, she took a minute to respond. If enough others express interest. . .

VALUE OVER TIME

As the months go by the information in the Sales Discussion database becomes more valuable. Everyone is contributing and interacting, and it happens on a daily basis instead of once a month at the old face-to-face meetings. People at headquarters are also interacting in the database. They are especially interested in the new product ideas and product enhancement ideas. Joan has seen her friend Jack Tripp from development participating, and decides to give him a call. When she gets him on the phone she asks him what development thinks of the Sales Discussion database. He enthusiastically tells her, "It's been a very efficient way of gathering specifics on changes we should be making to our product line. I like being able to get information directly from the field without having it filtered by half a dozen people in between. It's very valuable to see who is asking for particular features, and to be able to ask questions up front about the specifics of why features are desired, not just what features are desired. Sometimes we in development can solve a customer's problem immediately by providing their salesperson with tips on using our existing products. This can save the time and expense of going through a whole product/feature planning and development cycle. Other times, we can ask for input from the salespeople as to how a new product or feature would be used to help us make it better.

"For example, I saw that you were one of the people supporting the idea of building a widgitizer. A colleague of mine had mentioned an idea like that a few months ago over lunch, but never got around to fleshing out the idea. Now, with the input he's been getting in the Sales Discussion database, he has been working out some of the design details and interacting a lot with salespeople (through the database) to help refine the idea. If marketing doesn't pick up on the idea by monitoring the discussion, he's planning on writing the proposal himself. This never would have happened if he hadn't been engaged in discussion by the Notes application."

Joan hangs up and contemplates the way Notes has become part of her daily work life. As she thinks of new product ideas, she simply enters them into her notebook computer, and once she replicates them everyone has access to them. When Joan needs to find another salesperson to talk to about handling a client issue, she scans the database for topics related to her issue. When she finds them, she can see who the author was and can call or simply create a response in the database and wait for others to respond. The General category has been a great source of information about conferences, classes, seminars, and other events and has had all sorts of miscellaneous conversations among the salespeople about serious and not-so-serious things. Joan finds that the database has not only made her more effective, but has given her a sense of connection with more fellow salespeople than she's had before. As each new salesperson that joins the force discovers the database, Joan meets them online immediately, instead of at the monthly meetings if they're in her region, or worse at the even less frequent cross-regional meetings.

FACT SHEET

Sales Discussion Database

Purpose: To facilitate communications among members of a sales force, and between the sales force and other divisions (e.g., marketing and development).

Application Origin: Based on the Discussion template bundled with Notes with some minor customizations.

Application Development Time: 2 weeks to design, develop, and test the application.

Typical Size: 10–200 MB depending on size of sales force, number of clients and products, and so on.

Typical Use: Used by companies with a large and/or geographically dispersed sales force. Very helpful for facilitating communications without face-to-face meetings.

Forms: The standard Discussion database forms (Main Topic, Response, and Response to Response) exist with the addition of a subcategory field. A Comments on this Database form exists for sending comments, suggestions, and feedback to the database support staff.

Views: The standard Discussion database views (Main View, By Author, and By Category) and versions of each of those showing only the documents added in the last month.

Managing Employee Resumes

Archonix is a large (hypothetical) multinational consulting organization that provides management and computer consulting services to companies around the globe. Traditionally, large companies have great difficulty identifying skilled resources to meet the needs of a project. Size and geographic distribution must be overcome to match skills with needs. This is no less true for Archonix than any other organization. Typically, the project team leader in Switzerland has no way of knowing that there is a person in the company's New York office who just completed a similar project. To combat this problem, Archonix decided to develop a Notes database to help it match project needs with consultants' skills and experience. There are a number of reasons Archonix decided to use Notes for their application. Notes provides tools to manage documents and share information among users in geographically distributed locations. Notes security can be configured to allow each employee the right to maintain his own data without being able to edit other employees' information. This database will be integrated into a set of Notes applications, designed by Archonix, to provide managers with information on projects being conducted around the globe.

For this application to be successful, managers across the company will need to know that they can rely on the database for information that is accurate and up to date. As a result, it will be critical to ensure that the data collected meets the needs of management, that the database is kept continually up to date, and that the application makes the data readily accessible.

Main View in Resume database is By Location

```
                 Lotus Notes - Resume Tracking - By Location
 File   Edit   View   Mail   Compose   Text   Tools   Design   Window   Help
      Name                        Telephone
 Boston
     Candice Allenton              (212) 555-1212
     James Genao                   (212) 555-1212
     Michael Grant                 (212) 555-1212
     William Harlow                (212) 555-1212
     Anne Teller                   (212) 555-1212
 Chicago
     Frank Branson                 (212) 555-1212
     Howard Brenner                (212) 555-1212
     Julius Cortes                 (212) 555-1212
     James Lapham                  (212) 555-1212
 New York
     Brad Jessup                   (212) 555-1212
     Elizabeth Kim                 (212) 555-1212
     Tom Kim                       (212) 555-1212
     Susanna Kinnock               (212) 555-1212
     Phillip Marcellus             (212) 555-1212
     Irene Miller                  (212) 555-1212
     Caroline Stanger              (212) 555-1212
     Paula Tutrone                 (212) 555-1212
     Elaine Womack                 (212) 555-1212
 San Francisco
     Francis Ellerton              (212) 555-1212
     James Su                      (212) 555-1212
```

To ensure the success of this application, senior management has assigned
John Bergman, an up-and-coming executive, to *sponsor* the database. As
sponsor, John will be required to perform a number of activities:

▶ Work with managers to define the required content of the database.
▶ Work with developers to build a prototype.
▶ Ensure that the application meets corporate standards and integrates
  easily with other similar management applications.
▶ Review the prototype with managers.
▶ Deploy the application to a target department.
▶ Populate the database with complete, up-to-date, accurate information.
▶ Deploy the application to other departments.
▶ Set up procedures that ensure that the data is maintained over time.

John's first action is to schedule a meeting with a team of relevant managers
and a developer, Karen Saugerties. The team of managers was selected based
on their familiarity with Archonix project management needs and Notes.
Karen Saugerties was selected because she had helped define the corporation's
standards for Notes application development. One of the benefits of Karen's

involvement is that she can help ensure that the prototype and application will conform to company standards.

At the meeting, John presents the high-level requirements from management and a rough estimate of the timetables involved. This is followed by a discussion of exactly which information should be captured in the database, and how this information relates to data currently being maintained by the human resources group. The application will include (at a minimum) the following pieces of information for each consultant: a current resume, the employee's home office and telephone number, a list of the employee's relevant job skills, and a list of the person's recent project experiences.

Karen, the application developer, guides the discussion to ensure that the requirements being developed can be implemented in Notes. She also identifies some major project milestones and expected delivery dates. These are developed based on her understanding of the application, her prior experiences with Notes development, and other commitments. The first milestone is to complete a prototype of the application. The application will have a main document, called Employee Profile, and will not need any Response documents. The prototype will need views of the documents by employee name, skills set, and location. Karen estimates that the prototype will take a few hours to develop. Given current work loads, it will be a week before the prototype will be finished.

John sends out an e-mail to people in the human resources department requesting up-to-date resumes in an electronic format. Eventually, after some persistence, John collects about 20 resumes. This is a good number for the prototype—it provides close to a full screen of information for each view. John also collects the information necessary to fill in the rest of the employee profile form for each person. This includes the location of the employee, their skill sets, and relevant project experiences. John realizes that skills need to be categorized to be useful. As a result, Karen has put in two fields to capture skill set information—a category field where skills are broadly grouped (e.g., Accounting, Advertising, Computer Hardware, Computer Software, and Management), and a text field for a more specific description of the person's skills. The existence of this second text description makes full-text searching the application more reasonable so that users of the database will be able to refine searches based on skills set. John ensures that all the resumes can be easily cut and pasted into Notes and provides this sample data to the developer for inclusion in the prototype.

While Karen is creating the prototype, John focuses on defining the application's security requirements, deployment schedule, and database maintenance procedures. John is also trying to identify a department for initial deployment. The department needs to be relatively large (a few dozen people) and, preferably, should span geographic locations. It is critical that the department already have Notes up and running, have a defined need for this sort of tool, and have users with at least a rudimentary understanding of the product. John narrows

Names categorized by skills (By Industry view) in the Resume database

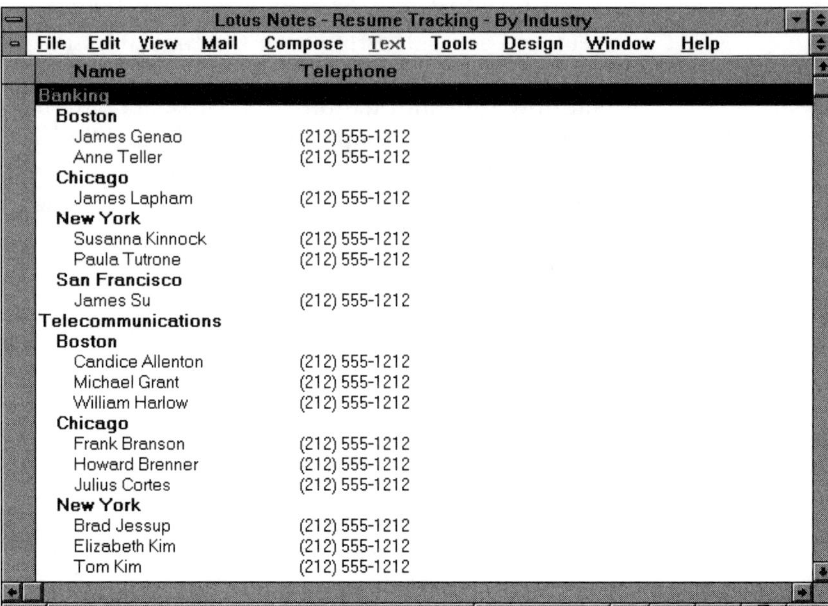

down his list and decides to take the list back to the managers for a final decision. Once the first department has been deployed (and the data is complete for that department), John will deploy the application to other departments in a defined order. It will be important to ensure that the same criteria applied to the first office are applied to subsequent offices as well. John decides to work with the managers to define the deployment schedule.

John spends a lot of time pondering the issue of maintaining the database over time. The sheer magnitude of the effort requires that employees be responsible for maintaining their own data. To that end, it becomes clear that senior management must stand behind this application and send a message to junior people that maintaining this data is a critical job responsibility. Furthermore, management must use the database as a resource when looking for people to fill a particular job. John resolves to ask senior management for just such a commitment.

Karen creates the prototype application and populates the database with the resumes John provides. The prototype is now ready to be reviewed by the managers. John schedules a second meeting and shows them the forms and views in the prototype. John demonstrates a full-text search showing how one can use the view to identify a category of skills and full-text search to identify particular individuals who might meet project needs.

The managers comment on the arrangement of data on the forms, the organization of the views, and the formatting of the data. Their input is duly noted by the developer. The developer agrees to complete the changes in the next few days and ready the application for the initial deployment.

John reviews the deployment plan and asks for management's input regarding an appropriate target department for initial usage. They suggest the company's post-sales support team. This group is responsible for working with customers to ensure that installed products are operating correctly. To that end, they frequently need to identify appropriate resources to solve problems. In addition, they have had Notes distributed among a number of sales offices for a few months. This seems to make them good candidates for the initial deployment, and a schedule is set. It is decided that the initial deployment, will last one month. During this time, the target department will be responsible for populating the database with the data on their employees and for providing feedback on the application.

The managers also decide on a deployment plan for the remaining departments. One department per month will be brought on until most of the company is using the application. While the application will be deployed company-wide, it is clear that some departments (e.g., shipping) might not need direct access to the database. Finally, the group decides that senior management should commit to the application and fund persons to help the first department populate the database. This is done to help ensure that the database is well received in its initial deployment. Finally, managers from the target department agree to communicate the action items to relevant personnel in the department.

John arranges a meeting with senior management. He demonstrates the database, provides them with an outline of the deployment plan, and asks for resources to populate the database and a statement to all employees identifying its importance to ongoing operations. Management agrees to provide staff from the human resources department to help with collecting data for the initial deployment and asks John to propose a statement concerning the application for general distribution. John writes it up and submits it to senior management. The statement is released in a mail message to all indicating that this database is considered one of the company's critical work items and that every employee is expected to provide the necessary input to maintain the data. John hopes that this statement (and his diligent efforts) will be enough to keep the data accurate and up to date over time.

The developer comes back to John with the "final" changes to the application. As with most Notes databases, changes are relatively easy to implement, and minor changes will need to be made to maximize the useful life of the database. Luckily, the design and purpose of this application are simple enough to make it unlikely to require major changes over time. John sets the database ACL so that he, servers, and administrators are Managers and end users are Authors (who cannot create new documents). John contacts his company's central Notes administration staff and requests that they post the database to the hub server. Once the database is posted, the regional administrators (located in each office) will be able to replicate the database to their local servers. John calls the administrators in the regional offices who support the target department and requests that they replicate the database as soon as possible.

Over the course of the next month, human resources staff work with the department team members to create or update resumes and populate the database. By the end of the month, 80 percent of the data for the department is complete. The deployment continues, incorporating more and more offices. As the amount of data in the database increases, usage by managers increases too. John frequently receives reports indicating data is inaccurate or incomplete, but these are to be expected. By far the majority of the data is up to date and proving useful. Finally, senior management, recognizing John's capabilities and accomplishments, commends him highly, granting him that coveted corner office and a key to the executive washroom.

FACT SHEET

Resume Database

Purpose: To provide a resource for managers to find personnel with specific skills to meet project needs.

Application Origin: Developed from scratch by the company's Notes developers.

Application Development Time: 6 hours over 3 weeks for application development; ongoing to maintain the data.

Typical Size: 2.9 MB for 500 documents (one document per employee).

Typical Use: To manage resumes and lists of skills for all employees of the company.

Forms: The Employee Profile form is the only form in the database. This form provides a field to input resume information, the employee's home office and telephone number, a list of the employee's relevant job skills, and a list of the employee's recent project experience.

Views: By Person, By Industry, By Location, and By Project.

Hotel Management Tools: The Sales Management Application

Adam Duboff manages a chain of five Marriott Residence Inns in the New England area. The Residence Inns are "extended-stay" hotels, intended for people who have to stay five or more days in one place. Unlike a traditional hotel, the rooms have a small, equipped kitchen and a living room area.

Marketing this kind of hotel is different than marketing for more traditional hotels. The Residence Inn caters to very specific market segments— training programs, special projects, corporate relocations, hirings, and layoffs. Attracting these key customers requires applying a lot of effort to building relationships. This, in turn, requires the company and its salespeople to know who are the key sources of economic activity in an area, and what kinds of projects are going on. Maintaining a good set of contacts is crucial.

While each property is managed as an independent unit, the whole organization also has to be coordinated over a large area. It's a challenge to regional management to stay on top of the issues and trends in each property. It's necessary to forecast occupancy rates, make judgments on which business to pursue, and still stay on top of current committed reservations.

Before they acquired Notes, Residence Inns used a weekly reporting system and held a lot of meetings to keep up to date on the current status. They had experimented with customized database application development and looked into both sales contact managers and some of the applications designed for the hotel industry, but hadn't had much success with any of them. They wanted someting less structured than the databases and more customized than a contact manager. They felt that Notes' Rich Text capabilities and its customizable, form-oriented user interface would fit their needs well.

INN-FORMATION AT YOUR FINGERTIPS

The Sales Management database has many forms, organized in a way similar to other contact managers. However, it has many specialized customizations for the hospitality industry. The key principle of this system is to provide an audit trail of every customer contact by the sales team. This helps the sales-people by providing them with all the information they need to do the job well, and helps management by giving them continuous access to the most current information about the state of the business.

The database revolves around the Client Info form. Each individual contact gets a form that includes company name, industry, address, overview, and market segment (a categorized field used to organize the type of industry or contact, such as training, project, relocation).

The entire database is set up to inherit information from a form being pointed to when a new form is composed. This makes it easy to add new contacts within an existing company by pointing to someone already at that company. All the useful information is copied into the new document, saving quite a bit of typing.

A Client Information form

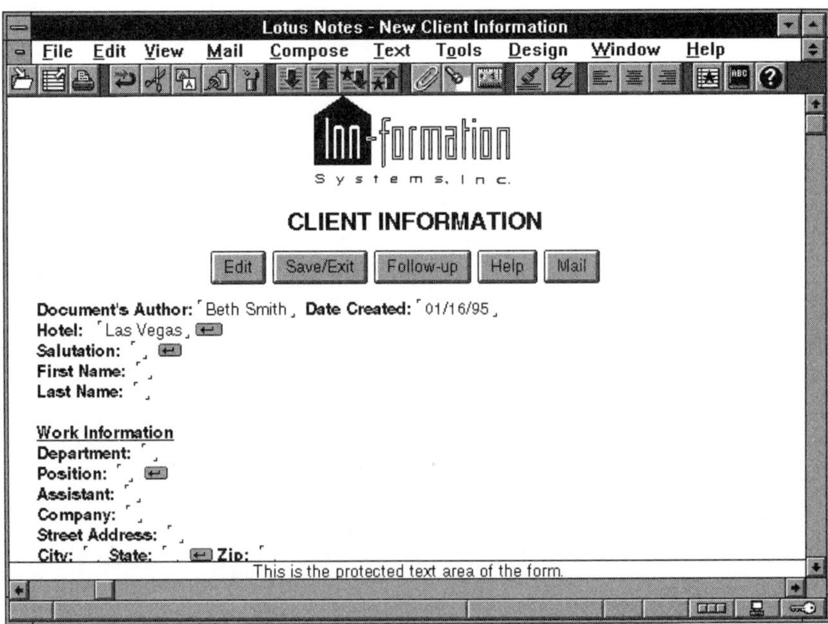

Every time a customer is called, a Call Summary form is filled out (by pointing to the contact record before composing this form, the call information is automatically included). This form is used for taking notes on a call and making a permanent record of the contacts.

When a customer talks about a plan for future use of the hotel, a Tentative Reservation form is filled out. This form tracks the number of rooms requested, the number of days for which they'll be needed, and the rate quoted. The results of this form are used to forecast occupancy rates. This form also tracks the ongoing status of this tentative reservation. If, through the ongoing efforts of the salesperson, the tentative reservation becomes definite, that's valuable business, and the status field is changed to Definite. If the business is lost, this is valuable competitive and sales information, and the status field is changed to Lost. As Adam Dubroff put it, "If you're not losing business, maybe you're not trying hard enough, and you may be unaware of competitive business situations."

There is also a Definite Reservation form that is used when the sale is originated by a customer calling in to place a reservation.

Displacement analysis is the process of calculating the relative value of two different pieces of business, each competing for use of the same hotel space. For example, if one customer wants to rent 8 rooms for 30 nights at $80 per night, and another customer wants 10 rooms for 21 nights at $90 per night, which is the better business? The Sales Management database has a Displacement Analysis form that helps to compare potential new business against other tentative sales and also provides a place for the user to record a justification of the decision that was made.

The database also contains a custom letter form, which is basically a blank letter, preaddressed to the customer; the text of the letter can be filled in and stored within the Notes database.

The Pre-call Planning form walks the user through the analysis of a planned call to a customer. This is especially useful to newer salespeople, but it also has value as part of the audit trail for a customer.

Finally, there is a Notes and Comments form that is used for general discussion within the database, either for free-form comments on a customer, or just for discussion between salespeople.

VIEWS

The Residence Inn managers have created several views that give the salespeople lots of information in different forms. A view by Sales Team shows how the entire team is performing, breaking down the occupancy forecast on a monthly basis and showing both booked and tentative reservations.

There is also a view by Call Plan. Every form has a button marked Followup. Pressing this button stores a followup date with the form. The call plan views sort the information by this followup date, showing calls that should be made today.

It is also possible to get a History of Activities, documents created by date or by the particular document type. This is useful for management to see the performance of a salesperson, or for the sales reps themselves to keep track of their own performance and customers.

The view by Market Dollars also adds the "loss" component—the dollar value of the tentative business that went elsewhere. This lets managers know what the competitors are doing and also gives a sense of the size of the entire market.

There are also some views designed to make it easy to export the contact information to a mailing list, sorted by company, by industry, or by market segment.

Management and the sales team use these views differently. The sales team members set up a screen with open views first on their personal call plan, and then other views for reference on the team performance and forecast bookings. They can then use these to track their daily efforts.

The sales management team focuses on people's work habits. They have at their fingertips the call plans and history of calls for individual salespeople and can use these tools to work on personal motivation.

At the regional office, they have instant access to the performance of the entire chain of properties. They see all information at the control center, and they get it in a timely fashion. They used to have to wait for weekly performance reports, but now they have continuous access to current information, organized in any way that might be useful.

THE BENEFITS

Inn-formation Systems has recognized and documented the value of this system to their business. They feel that they have better management knowledge of the general state of the business, and in particular, it has moved their sales meetings to an entirely different level. "We don't need meetings to discover where we're at," says Adam Duboff. "We already know. Our focus now is on planning, and then improving those plans. Everything else we *already* know."

He also feels that it vastly improves the sales team management. "There are no excuses anymore for poor performance, and the mutual admiration society disappears. The only valid excuse is 'I haven't put it in yet,' and that grows thin after a while."

Inn-formation Systems feels that they are able to train people measurably faster than other Residence Inns in the Marriott system. Because all the information is online, and there is no obscure paper filing system, their new sales representatives can be productive within a few weeks, rather than a few months. It also affects the retention of people; when people go to participate

Sales By Current Year and Next Year

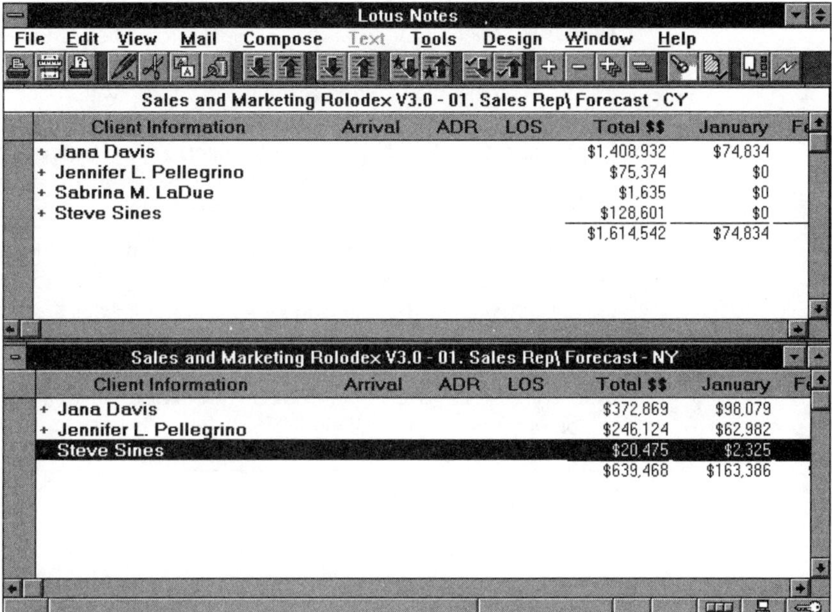

in national programs (such as training sessions), they realize how far advanced their system is compared to those at other properties. Salespeople like being part of an organization like that. Finally, it saves time. People can spend more time on client activity and less time storing, cataloging, and reporting on information.

Adam Duboff feels that "On balance, we've consistently performed among the top properties in the Marriott system, and we've stayed there even through some tough economic times in New England. We had a recession here, but fortunately we didn't have to participate in it—in fact, we've shown steady growth. I can't say it's the tools that did it—the people using the tools made it happen."

▸ FACT SHEET

Sales Management Database

Purpose: To record and track performance of the sales efforts for a hotel property.

Application Origin: Inn-formation Systems, Inc., P.O. Box 3477, Telluride, CO 81435. Phone: 800-243-2434, Fax: 970-728-6367, E-mail: adam@snownet.com

Typical Use: The sales team records contact information and tasks and uses the system for planning and executing the sales effort. Management can use it to track sales, predict occupancy rates, and monitor the performance of the sales team.

Forms: The Client Info form records client information. The Call Summary form is used every time a client is contacted. A Tentative Reservation form is used to record prospects, and has a status field that marks whether the tentative reservation becomes definite or is lost. A Definite Reservation form is used for reservations that are not the result of a direct sales effort. The Displacement Analysis form is used to compare two business opportunities. The Custom Letter form records mailings to clients, and the Notes and Comments form is used for free-form discussion. A Pre-Call Planning form is used to structure information before calling a client.

Views: The Sales Team view shows the performance of the entire team in dollars, breaking down the occupancy forecast on a monthly basis and showing both booked and tentative reservations. The Call Plan views show the sales team a schedule of who should be called when. The History of Activities shows actual calls by date for individuals and is useful for monitoring performance. The Market Dollars view shows the total sales, as well as lost sales for a given time period. The Export views are designed to allow the exporting of information to a mailing list.

The Meeting Minutes/Action Items Database

Effective communication is one of the keys to sound project management. As a tool that helps organizations share information, Notes can play a crucial role in helping project team members communicate. For example, Notes can help project team members share databases of project deliverables, project documents, schedules and project plans, hours worked on a project, and meeting minutes and action items.

Al Braddock is part of the technical support group for Frontage, a large (hypothetical) consumer products company. He is responsible for developing Notes databases for his company, and for maintaining templates for commonly used applications. Over time, he has developed a number of templates for project management in Notes, including the Meeting Minutes/Action Items database.

The purpose of this database is to track two aspects of project management—meeting minutes and action items. Capturing meeting minutes allows team members (and outsiders) to catch up quickly on project activities and serves as a record of agreements reached during meetings. *Action items* are project tasks that are assigned to an individual or a small number of individuals. Action items are frequently developed and assigned during project meetings. The Meeting Minutes/Action Items template is typically combined with other project management databases to meet the needs of a particular project. For example, smaller projects might lump all project information sharing into one database. Other projects might want to capture each item separately. Finally, some project managers have their own combinations of databases to support their project management needs.

ORIGIN

Early in Frontage's Notes deployment, forward-thinking project managers perceived the potential benefits of using Notes to help share information among project team members. These managers asked Al's group to create databases to support their project management activities. Al was chosen to help them develop these applications. The Meeting Minutes/Action Items database was one of the first databases developed by Frontage. It has been enhanced over time, but retains the same basic forms and views as in its initial incarnation. The database is now a design template replicated throughout Frontage to ensure that refinements to the design are reflected in each of the specific Meeting Minutes/Action Items databases in use. It is important to understand that design templates are primarily good for simple revisions to existing designs, rather than dramatic changes. This stems from the fact that as more data gets added to databases, people come to rely on the structure of the database. If significant changes are made (e.g., deleting a form that was used to create many documents), this could undermine their ability to use the database.

The initial design of the database was derived from the Discussion database template. As is often the case in Notes, starting with an existing design can be easier than starting from scratch. Templates provide a foundation of basic design elements (like forms and views) and preexisting relationships (Main document and Responses) that are common to many applications and can simplify the process of creating new applications.

The development process started in JADs (Joint Application Design meetings) with the relevant project managers. Prior to the first meeting, Al created sample forms for Meeting Minutes and Action Items. Al brought a computer to the JADs both to show the forms and to actually do some redesign during the meetings. The JADs were run by a co-worker to ensure that Al would have time to redesign the forms during the meeting. A number of suggestions were made during the meeting. For the meeting minutes, it was suggested that it might be useful to provide additional forms to capture meeting dates and meeting agendas. For action items, it was determined that at least one additional form should be created to allow employees a response form to indicate how a particular action item was completed (or why it was not). In the end, Al changed the Meeting Minutes form to allow a field for meeting agenda, and created the additional Action Items form. At the end of this process, the database contained the following forms:

▶ Action Item: Project team members use this form to record and assign an action item arising either from a meeting or some other project activity. Once completed, the form is mailed to the person(s) responsible for completing the action item.

▶ Resolution: This form is used by project team members to record the completion of an action item, or the reasons an action item was not completed in the time originally allotted. In either case it provides the author with an area to input additional information about the action item.

▶ Meeting Minutes: Once a meeting is scheduled, a form is created containing the meeting date and an agenda for that date. Once the meeting has been held, the author opens the same document to record the minutes of that meeting.

This is a general description of how the forms in the application might be used, however, in practice, each organization uses the database differently. For example, some groups require their team members to provide detailed information in the Resolution form on how project action items are completed. They feel that recording this information provides other team members with a record of how the project has progressed toward its overall objectives. Different groups have different definitions of the term "meeting." On some projects, the only meetings recorded are formal weekly project review meetings. On other projects it is considered important to record any meeting between two or more people related to project activities. Each organization makes its own policy decision about how information should be recorded.

The views in the database are quite straightforward. In the case of meetings, the views can be used to scan upcoming meetings or review prior meetings. In the case of action items, users can use views to look for open or closed action items. The primary views are listed below:

View	Description
All By Date	Meeting minutes and action items listed in chronological order.
Meeting Minutes By Date	Meeting minutes listed in chronological order.
Action Items By Date	Action items listed in chronological order.
Action Items By Assignee	Action items listed by person(s) responsible for completing action items.

The All by date view in the Meeting Minutes/Action Items database

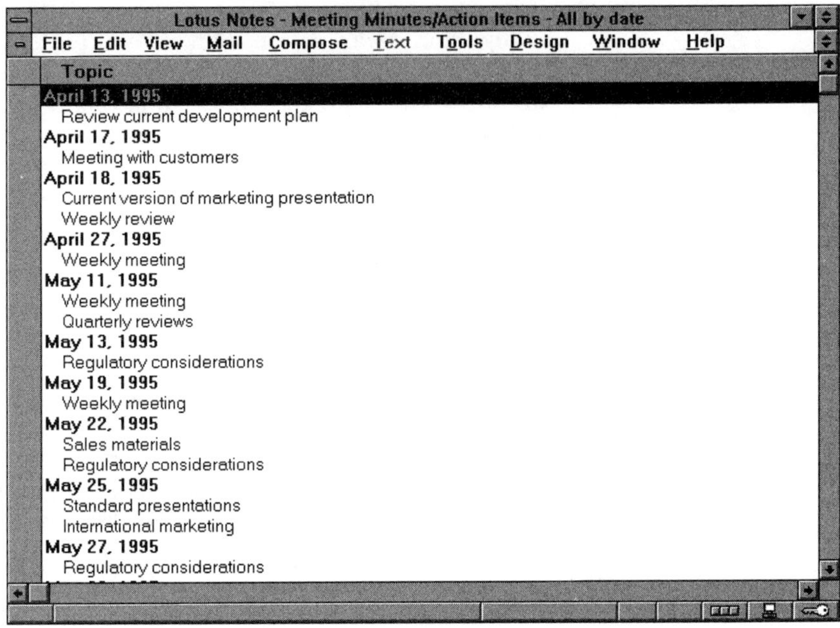

USING THE APPLICATION

Recently, Al was asked to come in and help a new project manager implement the project management databases for one of her projects. The first step was to talk to the project manager about how she would like to use Notes and the project management applications to support project-related activities. Al scheduled a meeting to discuss these issues.

Prior to the meeting, Al created a copy of the Meeting Minutes/Action Items database on the project manager's server and added a new Meeting Minutes document to the database. In this document, Al fills in the meeting time, date, location, the attendees (Al and the project manager), and a brief agenda. Al updates the access control list on the database (setting the default access to author) and renames the database to reflect the project's name.

During the meeting, Al introduces the application to the manager, demonstrating all forms and views. As the meeting progresses, Al records the proceeding in the Meeting Minutes form created for the meeting. This allows the project manager an opportunity to see an example of how the form can be used. In addition, a number of action items are generated, which are captured in Action Items forms. This requires Al to fill a general description of the ac-

A completed Meeting Minutes form

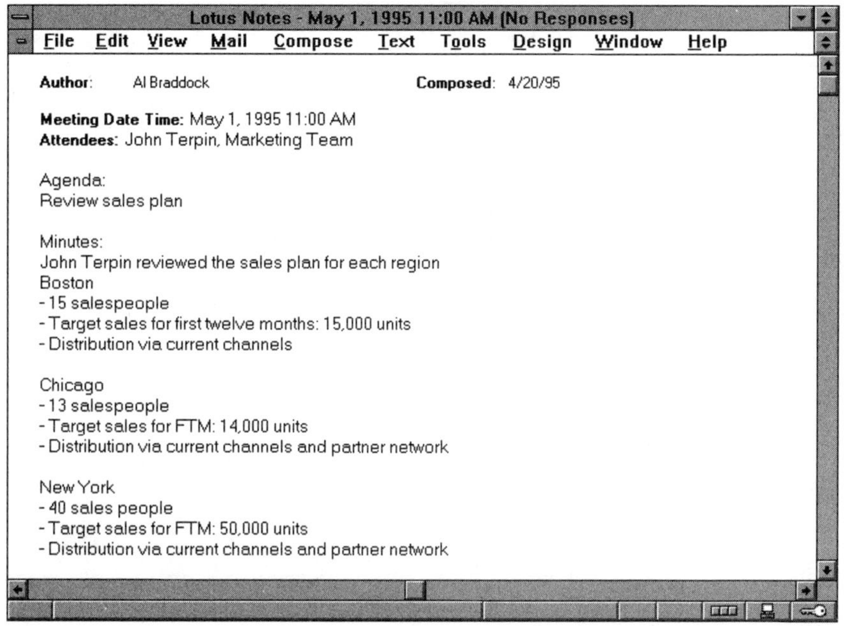

tion item, a detailed description of the action item, an Assigned To field (in this case containing Al's name), and an expected completion date. Upon completing the form, it is saved in the database and sent to Al via Notes Mail. Finally, Al creates a response to one of the Action Items showing how a project team member can complete the form. In this case, Al closes his action item briefly describing how the action item was completed and the date of completion. While assignees cannot edit the original action item, they can create an interim response that indicates why the original action item was not completed according to its original definition.

One of the problems with Notes is that it is not an essential tool. Unlike a spreadsheet, without which certain types of financial analysis would be impossible, it is possible to work without using Notes. In this situation, Notes can help project team members keep informed about ongoing project activities and play a significant role in project management. For Notes to play this role, the applications must suit the needs of the project team, and the project manager must advocate its use. As a result, part of Al's goal in this meeting is to persuade the project manager of the value of the Meeting Minutes/Action Items database and ensure that she will push her project team members to use this tool.

A completed Action Item

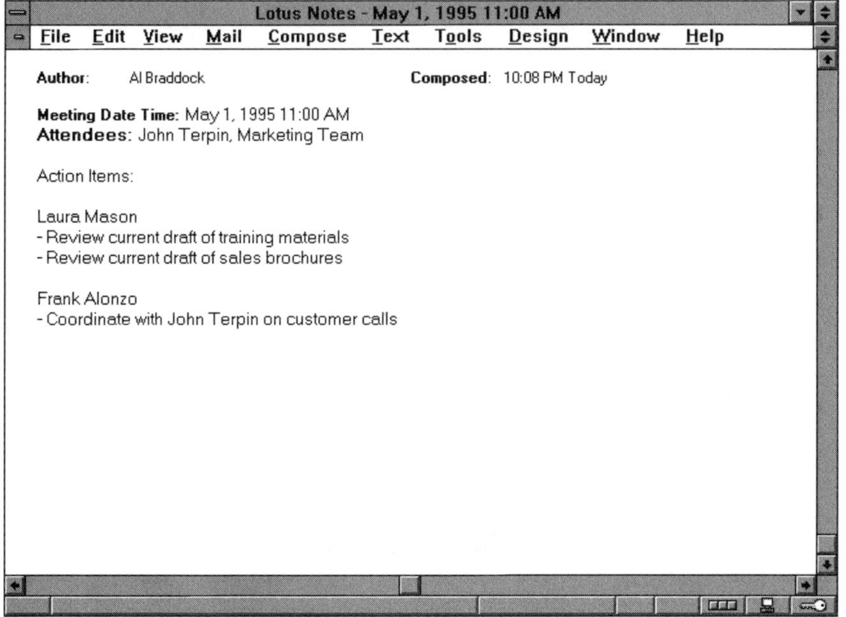

UNFINISHED BUSINESS

There are a number of tools that might be used to complement the Meeting Minutes/Action Items database. Here are two examples:

▶ Group Scheduling: There are a number of products on the market (e.g., Lotus) that enable group scheduling in conjunction with Notes. These applications allow a project team member to schedule a meeting by checking other people's schedules that are stored online. If the program finds an open time shared by a list of attendees, it sends an e-mail to each attendee asking if they can attend the meeting. This simplifies scheduling significantly. Many packages offer options that allow the program to schedule a room with proper facilities (e.g., a whiteboard or an overhead projector) as well.

▶ Pager Gateway: Depending on the nature of the action items, some may be time-critical. For these action items, it might make sense to page the individual assigned to ensure that they know they are now responsible for completing this action item. In Al's case, this can be accomplished by enabling a *pager gateway* on Al's Notes network. Generally, the pager gateway receives Mail messages (which are addressed to a pager number) and sends the text to the person's pager.

FACT SHEET

Meeting Minutes/Action Items Database

Purpose: To provide a group with a shared repository of upcoming meetings, meeting minutes for past meetings, and action items arising from meetings.

Application Origin: Derived from the Discussion database template.

Application Development Time: Approximately 10 hours over a few weeks.

Typical Size: Meeting minutes and action items are typically very small; occasionally there are electronic attachments to meeting minutes; after a few months, this database has 200 documents and is approximately 3.5 MB in size.

Typical Use: To save the information a group shares related to meeting minutes and action items

Forms: Action Items, Meeting Minutes, Response

Views: All by date, Meeting minutes by date, Action items by date, Action items by assignee

Request for Proposal

Jake Eller is a manager in the sales department of New York Cement (NYC, a hypothetical company), which provides cement to construction sites in the New York area. Jake's position puts him in touch with lots of problems. His people spend a high percentage of their time on the road, and the company's computer systems are not designed to support the mobile user. Communication between salespeople is infrequent. Salespeople in the same office can go months without seeing one another. It is common for a salesperson in the field to expend significant effort in solving a problem that another sales person has already solved for another customer. Notes is in use in Jake's company and is slowly being deployed to the sales force. Jake knows that Notes has the power to solve these problems.

Jake's salespeople are frequently asked to respond to Requests for Proposals (or RFPs) from customers. RFPs are requested by customers to evaluate how NYC's products might solve a problem or set of problems faced by their organization. Companies might request an RFP for a number of reasons. Some companies are looking for more information on a particular product or service. Others want to collect information from companies with similar products to use in a competitive evaluation. Still others are looking to learn more about a technology, product, or service. Whether the customer is sincerely interested in purchasing a product or just out kicking tires, the salespeople need to respond to each RFP as a serious sales prospect.

Unfortunately, responding to an RFP can be a time-consuming affair. It is common for companies to develop their own variations on common questions that require tailored (rather than canned) responses. Some companies include highly specific requirements that are unique to their environment which must be addressed. Frequently these types of RFPs require input from a number of different organizations to complete (e.g., sales, engineering, and manufacturing). Finally, each RFP is organized differently, and this organization must be followed in the response. All of these factors make responding to an RFP a potentially time-consuming affair.

Each year, NYC responds to around a hundred RFPs. Under the current process, each salesperson receives (or is assigned) an RFP, writes the response (bringing together the appropriate personnel to answer all of the client's questions), and stores the RFP in his files. As a result, each salesperson's ability to reference prior work is only as good as his own files, or the files of anyone he happens to ask for help on an RFP. It strikes Jake that Notes would be a superb way of collecting and sharing RFPs among salespeople.

Writing an RFP

While NYC has Notes developers, Jake knows that they are overwhelmed with work and not accepting new projects without the blessing of their managers. He also know that their managers have so many people asking for applications that they are less than sympathetic to new requests. As a result, Jake decides to identify a consulting organization from outside the company to help design and build this application. As a means of evaluating different organizations, Jake decides to write an RFP.

Jake's first objective is to identify some basic requirements for the system. Jake received a one-day introduction to Notes a few months ago, and has been using the Discussion database and Notes Mail since that time. Using this knowledge, he decides to list critical features the application will need to have. This will be used as source material for his RFP.

- ▶ It must support up to 200 documents of 50 pages each per year.
- ▶ The RFPs must be stored in a word processor format.
- ▶ It must allow full-text searching of all RFPs.
- ▶ Each RFP must be assigned a unique RFP number for reference (don't know how this will be used, but might as well put it in).
- ▶ Each RFP must capture whether the RFP resulted in work.
- ▶ Views must sort documents by customer, author, product, sales person, date, and RFP number.

In writing an RFP, it is critical to provide the recipient of the RFP with all the information necessary to write a proposal that directly addresses his needs. To that end, Jake provides background information on NYC, NYC's Notes environment, the due date for responses to the RFP, target delivery dates for the application, expected documentation of the application, and his department's anticipated training needs. Jake adds to the requirements listed above, "and add a list of questions the consulting organization must answer." These include questions about rates, total project costs, expected start dates, estimated duration, proposed deployment plan, issues related to importing existing RFPs, other similar projects the organization has completed, resumes of personnel who might be assigned to this project, and references from other customers. The entire RFP is about two pages in length.

He sends the RFP out to a number of Notes consulting organizations in the New York area. Phone calls are made and meetings are scheduled to provide the interested consulting firms an opportunity to get more information and understand the requirements more completely. A few weeks after the initial RFP is sent out, responses start to arrive. The responses vary dramatically in length (largely depending on the amount of information each company provides about itself or its projects), but the descriptions of the application and project are generally a few pages in length. The total cost of the project ranges from a low estimate of around $10,000 to a high estimate of around $50,000. The low estimate is by a relatively small and inexperienced consulting organization who is looking to move into Notes consulting. The high estimate includes lots of business consulting to help Jake's group rethink its existing processes. Neither of these sounds like the right organization or proposal to fill Jake's needs. He starts to look at the middle group of proposals. He looks for organizations who have a "methodology." This implies that the organization has done a lot of this type of consulting and knows how to structure a project. He checks some of the references provided in the proposals. This also helps to separate the experienced organizations from the inexperienced ones. Finally, Jake talks to people in his computer support group. They have worked with a number of these consulting organizations and help Jake to make the final selection.

BUILDING THE APPLICATION

Once the contract has been signed, the consultants arrive for a kickoff meeting. During this meeting, Jake introduces the relevant persons from his team, identifies project roles and responsibilities, provides additional background information on the current RFP process, and gives the consultants some sample RFP documents. The consultants identify the project's phases (with titles like Requirements Definition, Development, Testing, and Deployment); expected project deliverables, and project milestones. One consultant has been assigned full time to the project. The expected project duration is around three weeks. All of this is documented by the consulting company and given to Jake as a simple project plan for developing the application. A meeting is scheduled for the following week, when the consultant expects to demonstrate a prototype of the application.

During the intervening week, the consultant builds the prototype application. The application has a single form, which captures the following pieces of information: customer name, author, creation date, product information (this includes product name, model, and year), the customer's sales person, RFP due date, a body field, and RFP number.

The body field (the name "body" is commonly applied to the primary Rich Text field in a form) is used to store the response to the RFP. Users can either type or scan the text of the RFP, embed the word processing document as an object, or attach a copy of a word processing document containing the RFP.

The RFP number is a unique number assigned to each document. The formula combines the year, month, day, hour (using a 24-hour clock), minute, and author's initials into a single string like "9910061107JS" for a document created by John Smith on October 6, 1999 at 11:07. While this scheme is somewhat cumbersome, it is simple to understand and highly likely to be unique. The RFP number offers a consistent way of identifying and tracking individual RFPs.

The application has views that sort RFPs by customer, author, product, salesperson, date and RFP number.

The prototype is reviewed in the team meeting. Much of the meeting focuses on how the RFPs will be stored in the Notes database. This decision

View by Customer in the RFP database

View by Salesperson in the RFP database

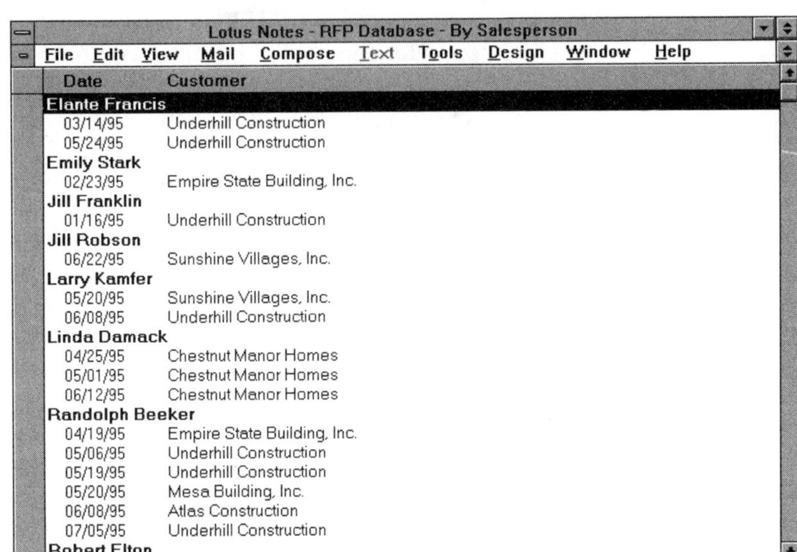

might affect how proposals are written and might also affect the usefulness of the completed application. The discussion focuses on four options:

▶ Write the proposals in a word processor and paste them into Notes as text.
▶ Write the proposals in a word processor and embed them as objects into Notes.
▶ Write the proposals in a word processor and attach the completed files to the Notes document.
▶ Write the proposals in Notes.

There are pros and cons to each approach. Options 1, 2, and 3 allow the salespeople to follow their current style guidelines and procedures for responding to RFPs. Option 4 would require the team to give up some of their style sheets and word processing features, but would be a simpler process (as the additional steps required in 1, 2, and 3 to get the data into Notes would not be required). A key consideration in all discussions is usability. Options 1, 2, and 4 have the disadvantage of storing the entire text of the proposal in the body of the Notes document. Unlike word processing programs, Notes reads the entire text of a document into memory. This makes opening and closing the documents slow, particularly considering the size of most RFPs. Unfortunately, option 3 has the significant disadvantage that full-text search will not work on file attachments. As a result, only the other fields such as Author, and Project, would be available for full-text searching. The ability to search the text of the RFPs was perceived as one of the significant benefits of storing and managing the documents in Notes.

After much discussion, option 2 is selected as the appropriate way of getting the RFPs into Notes. This method requires authors to paste their word processing documents into Notes as objects once the file is complete. If they need to edit the document afterward, they double-click on the object in Notes (which automatically runs the word processor and loads the file), and save their changes back to the object stored in the document. In addition, large documents load slowly. However, this option supports full-text searching, which was considered an essential feature by the group.

The consultant incorporates the changes into the application and documents the new procedures for contributing RFPs into the application. This document also includes complete descriptions of the forms and views in the database, and will serve as a "tutorial" for new users of the database. These descriptions are incorporated into the Help documents for the database. The consultant then populates the database with the last few months' worth of RFPs. This is generally agreed to be enough documents to make the database usable for salespeople. Finally, the consultant works with NYC's Notes administrators to get the application loaded onto the appropriate Notes servers (the database is replicated to a number of servers to reach all salespeople).

Over the next few months, Jake gets consistent feedback from his salespeople. The ability to share RFPs and search for specific pieces of information had reduced the total time necessary to write a response to an RFP and increased the quality of the final deliverable.

UNFINISHED BUSINESS

As with any application, there is always room for improvement. For this particular application, one area that was not investigated was the option of using document scanning and optical character recognition (OCR) as a source for the application. Scanners are devices which can take a "picture" of a paper document and store it in electronic format. OCR tries to recognize the letters and words in a scanned document. With a good OCR program, a user could perform a full-text search against scanned documents. Without a good OCR program, the computer looks at the scanned documents as pictures rather than words.

A number of companies (including Lotus) have provided companion products for Notes that scan images and OCR them. This process might be useful for the RFP application as a means of reading hardcopy documents for which no electronic document exists (for example, when the person who wrote the document has left the company). In addition, some company's RFPs actually require the respondent to complete their RFP form. Unfortunately, this requires that the respondent type the information onto the form that they provide. As a result, these RFPs will not exist in electronic format. These documents also would be candidates for scanning and OCR.

Finally, the process defined for creating RFPs was less than optimal. It would be interesting to investigate tools to streamline the RFP process. NYC might look at Visual Basic or other programming tools to get the data from the word processor into Notes. This might reduce this process to simply clicking on an icon. Alternatively, the organization could examine ways of moving the entire proposal writing process into Notes. It might even make sense to bring in the original consulting team for a short project to identify and propose appropriate alternatives to the existing process.

◢ FACT SHEET

Request for Proposal Database

Purpose: To capture RFPs and ensure these RFPs are available to other salespeople to serve as source material for their own RFPs.

Application Origin: Developed from scratch by consultants.

Application Development Time: 2 man-weeks to complete a prototype.

Typical Size: RFPs can be many pages each; at NYC, each year's worth of RFPs is approximately 20 MB of data.

Typical Use: A corporation submits an RFP to NYC for response. The database is searched to identify prior similar RFPs. NYC salespeople then coordinate with other departments at NYC to complete the RFP. The new RFP is also saved in the database.

Forms: RFP and Comment.

Views: By Customer, By Author, By Product, By Sales Person, By Date, and By RFP Number.

The Project Management Database

C.J. Niven is a development manager for All-Night Software, a hypothetical software development company. She's in charge of the development team for a new software product. Reporting to her is a development team of designers, developers, quality testers, and writers of documentation. Besides keeping senior management updated, she also has the responsibility to work closely with the marketing staff and the manufacturing department.

At the beginning of the project, C.J. needs to find a way to communicate lots of information about the developing product efficiently to the team. Types of information include the following:

- ▶ Design specifications: It's critical to distribute these as widely as possible so as to catch errors and problems early. However, they also need to be changed often. Electronic distribution is really the only solution.
- ▶ Development, testing, and documentation status by component: This information is critical for tracking the progress of the project.
- ▶ Customer feedback and results of usability testing: This will help accelerate product evolution and keep team members aware of how the actual product is doing with real users.
- ▶ Concerns expressed by team members: An active feedback forum can keep small problems from becoming large ones.

Notes is perfect as a tool for storing all this information together where it can be managed, while at the same time allowing it to be retrieved in meaningful ways.

DESIGNING THE DATABASE

On a really large project, C.J. might want to break this up into a set of related databases. For example, she might build a Project Specification database, a separate database for bug tracking and QA testing, and a Discussion database for usability testing. However, for smaller projects there is benefit to be gained from keeping the information all in one place. This project is small enough to do just that.

The Component Specification Form

The database revolves around the project specification. Most of the information in the database will concern the specifications and remarks about them. The Component Specification form describes a single component of the project (e.g., a product feature or module of software code).

The form starts out with a title for the component (this is used as the title of the document in views and when printing). The components are also organized into major component groups (for example, all the components of the print module are grouped under Printing).

Next come the form names of all of the people who are responsible for this component; they are known as *owners*. C.J. has organized these by creating a separate field for each major group in the organization: design, development, testing, and documentation. If more than one person is involved for a given group, she uses multiple values in the single field.

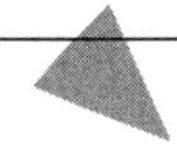

Multivalued Fields and Other Oddities

Sometimes it's difficult to figure out where to file a document. Imagine a message to a manager asking for a meeting between the Human Resources director, the manager, and a problem employee. Should this be filed in the HR folder, the Meetings folder, or the one marked with the employee's name? In some electronic mail products, it would be necessary to choose only one. In Notes, it is possible to put the mail in all three folders, because they're not really folders, they're categories.

In the standard Notes Mail database, there is a single field called Categories. To categorize mail, all that happens is that this field gets a particular value, such as HR. What's fun and interesting is that it is possible to put multiple values in a single field. In the categorized view of the database, this mail message will be listed under each category, although they're all the same message.

Nearly any field in Notes (except a Rich Text field) can have multiple values. They can be used to keep track of a list of dates (the edit dates of a document, for example), the set of people allowed to approve a purchase order, or a series of data values over time. However, the most frequent use is in a categorized field where the item might fit multiple categories. Some examples include folders in a Mail database, the people responsible for maintaining a particular document, the recipients of a Mail message, or the states in which a lawyer is licensed to practice.

Notes has explicit support for multivalued and categorized fields in several ways:

▶ Keyword fields allow the designer of a form to specify keywords as checkboxes, where it is possible to check more than one box. The result is a field with multiple values, one for each keyword.

▶ The Categorize command on the Tools menu will assign values to a field called Categories, if the view is sorted by that field. This is why so many Notes databases use a field by that name.

▶ There are special functions in the macro language to deal with categorized and multivalued fields.

▶ If a view is categorized, Notes will show the same document under all the categories that apply, even though the document only occurs once in a database.

Notes also has a different special value for a field, called @Unavailable. If a field's value is equal to @Unavailable, that means that the field has no value. It's not zero, or blank—it simply has no value at all.

These strange ways of treating data may be a bit confusing, but they're well suited to dealing with the kinds of information usually found in the real world, and they're some of the big strengths of Notes.

Next to the Owner field for each group is the status of the component for that group. For example, the documentation group will assign its own status values marking the state of the documentation for that component. Status values for the development group include the following:

▶ Placeholder: For new documents that haven't yet been fleshed out.
▶ In Design: Rough concept in place, still needs design work.
▶ Design Complete: Design work done, ready to be coded.
▶ Design Changes Needed: Request by some other department for more work.
▶ In Development: Development has begun.
▶ Ready for Testing: Development work is believed to be complete.
▶ Development Changes Needed: Request for more development work (bugs or additional features needed).
▶ In Testing: QA department is testing.
▶ Testing Complete: The component has passed its tests.
▶ Obsolete: Mark obsolete components instead of deleting them; often, old information is valuable as part of the project history.

A Component Specification form being filled out

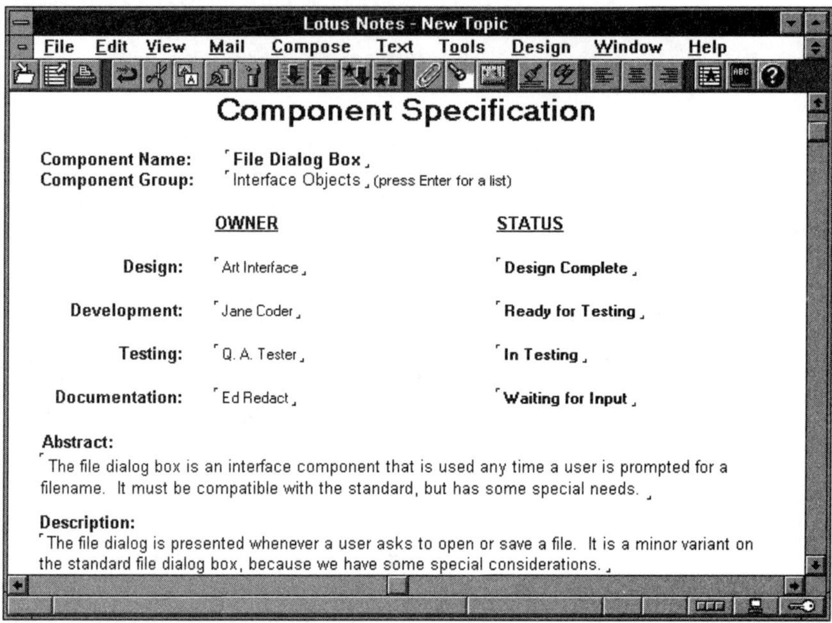

The Component Specification form also includes an *abstract,* which is a one-paragraph summary of the component's behavior. This abstract is useful for people who are skimming the database looking for certain information. It can also be used for printing a broad overview of the entire product in only a few pages. Of course, there is also a detailed specification for the component.

This may seem like a lot of fields, but a database like this is used by many different people in many different ways. The large number of fields allows for the creation of views that meet the needs of the various constituencies on the team.

There are also other forms in this database:

▶ A Document form, which is a notes Main Document form used for storing documents or discussing issues that don't pertain to any particular component. It includes a status field about the document (Open Issue, Closed, Reference, or Obsolete).

▶ A Question form, created as a response to a Component Specification form. This has a field identifying the group to whom the question is aimed. This is a formal way for the different groups and team members to ask questions of one another.

▶ A Response to Response form, used for more general commentary and for responses to the Issues and questions.

These forms are the basis for a whole set of useful views:

▶ The By Component views show all the components stored in the database. There are Component views sorted by Component Group (this is good for general browsing of the database), or by Status (useful for management to view the status of the product development). Normally, these views show the Component documents along with any applicable question or comment forms, but there is also a view that shows components only, which is good to see the current state of the product design.

▶ The By Owner views are a suite of views showing the documents by development owner, testing owner, and so on. This is useful for individual contributors to find the components that they're responsible for.

▶ By Status views show the state of the project on a number of different axes. The All documents by development status is usually used by management to see the overall state of development. There are also subviews showing only documents with a particular status value. For example, the Ready for Testing view shows a test team member the documents that have reached the ready status but have not yet been tested.

▶ The Issues by Status view allows someone to examine the open (or closed) issues on a project without needing to see the components as well.

The nice thing about the Notes View capability is that if someone needs a special view—a different slice of the information in the database—it's very easy to create it, even after the database has been up and running for some time.

Using the Database

Once C.J. got the database designed, she needed to roll it out to the team in a way that would ensure its success. So she called the managers together and demonstrated it to them. While there was initially some grumbling at the thought of all that data entry, once she showed them the wide range of views available all objections were cast aside. She asked for their help in populating it so that the database would be useful from the start.

The marketing manager agreed to move the product's marketing requirements documents into the database and use them as a framework for filling in the component specification documents. The design manager volunteered to take some of the early product specifications and use them as a source to populate the database. Documents that she knows will be needed, but doesn't have the source for yet, will be marked Placeholder. Other teams will create some open issues documents and a few reference documents with their own plans for the project.

Over the next couple of weeks, the management team took on these tasks, and involved some of the more positive team members in the early work. Once the rumors got around the team that something new was coming, it was time to roll it out. C.J. called the team together and announced the existence of the database.

She told them that this database exists to provide them (and her) with a single point of reference for the project as it moves forward. She impressed upon them that she was making a firm committment to Notes as the place to put the information. "As far as I'm concerned," she said, "if it's not in there, it doesn't exist."

The design team was thrilled to have a place where anyone can look for the latest version of a design. The development group was less excited, because it felt like too much formality. They had lots of concerns about how they were going to document the design changes that happened during the development process. But after a while, most of them realized that it wasn't a one-way street. They didn't just consume design information from the database, they had also been given a means for giving their own input into the design of the product, which is a very empowering thing. It also gave them a tool for checking on the testing status of their components.

THE BUSY TIME

As the project got into the busiest stages, some of the managers began to complain that they were getting obsolete information on status from the database. A little investigation showed that so many components were being worked on simultaneously that the people responsible were having a hard time keeping the Status documents up to date. So C.J. created a couple of macros so that people could select several documents at once and run a single macro to update them all. She also fine-tuned some of the views to help people find their own information more quickly in the database. And at a team meeting, C.J. and the other managers reaffirmed their committment to using Notes as a status tracking method, and emphasized the importance of keeping the documents up to date.

At the end of the project, Notes became a valuable tool for watching the status of the various components change on a daily basis. It let management easily identify hot issues and reassign team members to help out on the most difficult pieces. Marketing used it as a way to identify and stay up to date on key features for the product rollout. When the project finally shipped successfully, C.J. used the the database as part of the project post-mortem in evaluating what was done well and what needed work the next time around. They all agreed that using Notes was one of the many things that worked well.

FACT SHEET

Project Management Discussion

Purpose: Provides a forum for storing status and discussions about an ongoing project. Allows team members and management to communicate with one another and with other organizations within the company about these issues.

Application Origin: Custom-designed to meet the project needs, starting with standard discussion database.

Application Development Time: Two days to one week.

Typical Size: 1–10 MB, depending on the discussion.

Typical Use: Used by a project team as a repository for project specifications. Users can track status of the various project elements, as well as carry on discussions about them during the project.

Forms: The Component Specification form is used to document one component, subsystem, or other small piece of the project. The Document form is used for storing documents that are not tied to one particular component, such as general specifications, customer feedback, or marketing documents. The Question/Comment form is a Response to either of these main forms above, and the Response to Response form continues the discussion.

Views: By Component (by group or by status) is useful for general browsing of the database or for status tracking. Components Only shows the current state of the design, leaving off all questions—good for printing a design summary. By Owner is useful for individual contributors to find the components that they're responsible for. By Status can mean all documents, or only documents with a particular status—useful for people to track the particular components they need to work on next. Issues by status is used examine the open (or closed) issues on a project without needing to see the components as well.

Accounting, Notes, and the Sales Force

Red Bank Furniture (RBF) manufactures high-quality office furniture that they sell to corporations around North America. The (fictional) company has about 3,000 employees and a sales force of 200. The sales force is spread across the United States and focuses on developing large corporate accounts. The sales force is divided into regions. There are offices located in each region, with regional managers to oversee the salespeople. The sales force spends most of its time on the road. While people in regional offices might see one another a few times a month, the salespeople rarely see people from outside their region. To address the requirements of this distributed team of people, RBF has purchased and deployed Lotus Notes.

Notes was selected because of its robust support for distributed users, the simplicity of its interface, and the relative ease with which applications can be created and modified. A variety of applications were developed for the salespeople: databases of product information, discussion databases with other salespeople, lead-tracking databases, and partner discussion databases. While this has addressed the majority of the needs of the salespeople, there are a number of other activities that have been identified that could help the salespeople do their jobs better. These additional areas include order entry, order fulfillment, and close monitoring of customer ordering patterns.

The current process for entering orders is for the salesperson to take down on paper all relevant information for a particular order. This form is then taken back to the regional office, where it is typed into the company's accounting system by an administrative assistant for processing. The accounting system then oversees the process (such as forwarding the order to the shipping area) until the order is received by the customer. Unfortunately, the only way the salesperson can get information on the status of the order is to consult the

Sales Order by Author View in the Customer Sales Order Database

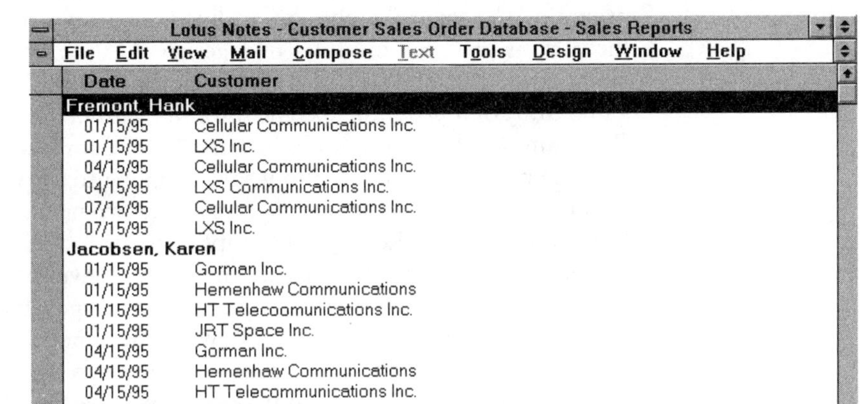

company's mainframe-based accounting system. Few of the sales force have been trained to use the accounting system (let alone the mainframe) and, as the accounting system offers weak support to distributed users, their only access point is the administrative assistant who types the orders.

John Repartier works in RBF's Information Systems (IS) department. John managed the rollout of Notes in the organization. John has been examining this problem for a while, and realized that there is a potential solution: some level of integration between Notes and their accounting system. John has two people working for him who should be able to help him complete this project—Susan Paxton, a C developer with significant experience with the Notes API, and Larry Jenkins, one of the caretakers of the mainframe system, who has written a number of tools to get reports out of the accounting system. John speaks with senior management to get buy-in for his idea and then broadly outlines how his solution will work.

At their first meeting, they take the work John has done and divide it up among themselves. The division of labor is fairly straightforward: John will oversee the project, manage coordinating activities, arrange meetings, and so on. Susan will develop a program using the Notes API to get information from Notes and put information back into Notes. Larry will take the output of Susan's program and generate requests to the mainframe accounting system. He will also address the issue of responses and how these should be handed back to Susan's program. The team sketches an outline that defines the scope of work and how the various program modules fit together. At the end of the meeting, each team member is assigned the task of filling in the outline. The objective is to develop a first draft of a program specification that can be reviewed with the sales force. The team decides to use a Notes Discussion database to capture their ideas. In the long run, they hope to allow salespeople into the database to allow them to comment directly on various aspects of the program.

Each person on the team develops a list of program modules and functions that will be necessary to provide the defined level of functionality for the application. For the purposes of this draft of the specification, it is adequate simply to provide a paragraph overview of the function and a list of the inputs, processing, and outputs the program will perform. John's responsibilities include designing the Notes database that will be the "front end" for the application, putting together a presentation for the sales force, and defining what the desired inputs and outputs are for the program. In the first iteration of the program, the Notes database will have just two forms for salespeople to fill in: Sales Order and Get Order Status. The application will also have a report form which will be used to store reports generated by the accounting system, but this form will be read-only for the sales force. The database will be called the Customer Sales Order Database. John is also responsible for putting together the presentation that will be given to key members of the sales force to describe the functioning of the application.

To get two programs to communicate, developers must identify a common language through which Larry's and Susan's programs can exchange data. In this case, Larry and Susan have elected to use ASCII text. Both of them have preexisting tools that they can adapt for this program. Susan will write two different programs: one to write data from a request form to ASCII, and a second to take reports produced by Larry's programs and read these into John's Notes database. Larry will write a program to post requests to the accounting system and a second to write responses to disk. Susan and Larry will also define some rudimentary tools to log program activities (all log activities will be stored in a Notes database) and mechanisms to handle processing errors. The form in the Notes database will be written to ensure that salespeople complete all required information to submit a request. In the event a request is submitted which Larry's program still cannot process, Larry's program will generate an error, that Susan's program will post back to the original request. Finally, Larry's program will pass a request ID number (generated by the accounting system) back to Susan's program. This request ID will be added to the original sales order and used to get information on the progress of the order.

The completed programs will allow RBF salespeople to submit sales orders on behalf of their customers into a Notes database. Sales orders placed in this database will be automatically submitted to the RBF accounting system for processing. Once an order has been submitted, the salesperson can get updates on where the order is in processing by creating another request. Finally, the sales person will receive reports on a regular basis (initially quarterly), showing each of their client's purchases for that quarter.

MEETING THE SALES FORCE

Once the initial specification and John's presentation are completed, the team sets up meetings with key salespeople from each region. From the list of key contacts, they identify a smaller number who can make themselves available for a meeting at the headquarters. It is John's objective to engage as many people as possible, but not to let the process of arranging meetings impede progress toward the project's ultimate objectives.

John's presentation is tailored to its audience—it focuses on how the application will help salespeople do their jobs more effectively, rather than any of the more technical details concerning how it functions. His objective in the meeting is to get the attendees to buy-in and feedback on what additions to the program might be useful. John reviews the present version of the Customer Sales Order Database and provides charts showing current and amended work processes. This gives the attending salespeople the opportunity to see the forms and views they will use to submit and track orders, and review client purchasing. John takes the attendees through the various forms and views, and shows the group some completed documents to demonstrate how the database will eventually look.

The reaction of the salespeople is positive. The comment is made that information is one of the keys to a successful sales process, and this system will give them access to significantly more information than before. The salespeople provide suggestions for additional views in the database, including viewing documents by region and by quarter. John observes that one of the benefits of Notes is the ease with which applications can be updated to reflect changing needs. During the meeting, a rough timetable is defined, and Larry and Susan agree to complete the design specifications and submit it to the salespeople for review. As the salespeople are not particularly technical, this review is not expected to provide real suggestions for changes and is being done more to ensure that no problems or issues are overlooked in the design of the application.

DEVELOPING THE APPLICATION

The following week, Larry and Susan submit their completed design specifications. As expected, there is little feedback from the sales force, and Susan and Larry move directly into development. Susan has the more complicated of the

Completed Sales Order form

Lotus Notes - Sales Order

File   Edit   View   Mail   Compose   Text   Tools   Design   Window   Help

RBF Sales Order

Customer Name: Cellular Communications, Inc.
Customer Account #: 883-161-327
Sales Rep: Hank Fremont

	Model	Quantity	Price
1)	99-2330-9012	3	$1,200
2)	99-3891-0052	1	$380
3)	99-4268-0014	1	$160
4)			
5)			

two development assignments. The mainframe and the accounting system are fairly mature, and there are many tools that can be adapted to submit orders and retrieve reports. While Susan has tools that allow her to read Notes databases, she needs to format the output for Larry's program. Mainframe reports continue to assume a constant-space (monospace) font. When these same reports are placed in an environment with proportional spacing, columns and rows are confused. For the first iteration of the program, Susan will import the reports using a Courier font. This font ensures that the original format of the report is preserved, but at the expense of readability (columns frequently go off the screen to the right) and aesthetic appearance (Courier is not the most appealing font). Susan's piece takes approximately two weeks of full-time work to complete.

Larry's development process is primarily an integration effort—integrating pieces of code and programs in use for other applications. His entire development time is under one week (about four days).

Both programs will be run on an OS/2 server running Notes server software and software necessary to access the company's mainframe computer. John's database is replicated to this server, as well as all the other servers across the United States. Susan's API reads requests in this database and writes them to an ASCII file. Larry's program reads the ASCII file and creates requests that are submitted to the mainframe. Larry's program also reads responses from the mainframe and writes them as ASCII files to the server's hard disk.

After about three weeks of development, the application is stable and complete enough to begin initial testing. John opens the Notes database to a number of salespeople located in different regions. Initially, they are expected to provide bogus sales orders, which are not submitted to the mainframe. Once the salespeople have gotten comfortable with the application, Larry's piece is turned on, and the requests are actually submitted to the accounting system. For the first month, the local administrative assistant who used to be responsible for typing in the orders verifies the accuracy and completeness of the submitted requests. Once this period is finished, the application is rolled out for general consumption.

Unfinished Business

While the application addresses the needs of the sales community, there are many enhancements and additions that can be made to the program. The reports the application currently produces are quite narrowly defined. One enhancement would be to provide salespeople with the opportunity to request a variety of reports generated on the fly. This would enable them to request relevant information from the accounting system as needed. Perhaps more important, *triggers* could be added to the application. Triggers, like *agents*, are programs that perform an action when certain criteria are met. An example of a trigger might be that if a customer's order has not been fulfilled in a certain amount of time, a mail message is generated to the salesperson in charge. Triggers could also be written to send a mail message if a regular customer stops ordering or misses one of their orders.

Fact Sheet

Sales Order Database

Purpose: To provide salespeople with a simpler, more direct mechanism to access data stored in the corporate accounting system.

Application Origin: Involves a Notes database, API programming (done in C), and tools to access data stored on the corporate mainframe.

Application Development Time: Approximately 3 man-months.

Typical Size: Database varies depending on requests and archiving policy; generally 10–20 MB.

Typical Use: Salesperson in the field completes a sales order in Notes for a particular customer's purchase; order is posted by API to mainframe system; salesperson can get status of order and customer account through database.

Forms: Sales Order, Get Order Status, and Report.

Views: By Company, By Order, By Report, By Date, and By Author.

Attracting Customers with a Networked Kiosk Application

The retail music business—tapes and CDs—is highly competitive. Attracting customers can take more than just a decent location and a reasonable selection. It can take even more than just the best price. Especially when targeting the younger crowd, other differentiators can come into play.

Skip Nelson, president of JAG Music (a hypothetical retailer), is looking for something special. He wants something distinctive for his stores that no other store has. While his chain of music stores numbers 20 at the moment, he has big plans to expand a lot further.

Skip calls in consultants who pitch various ideas to him. The one that has caught his imagination is a *networked kiosk application,* where his customers can interact with each other, no matter which store they frequent.

NOT JUST A KIOSK

Linda Flax is an information management consultant specializing in the music industry. She has been meeting with Skip to discuss various ideas for attracting the younger crowd to his stores. At her present meeting, she is discussing kiosks.

"Skip, a kiosk is one of those computers we put in a fancy display case that your customers can use. They typically provide general information about the business they are supporting. In your case, we could provide information about JAG Music, about the latest CDs that have come in and that are going to come in, about the hottest artists, and that kind of thing. We can place a touch screen on it so users won't be daunted by the keyboard.

"Further, we can put speakers in the kiosk so it can play music, video clips with sound, and all that. We can make use of the latest multimedia to really wow the customers—especially the kids."

Skip has seen kiosks, and in the past has not been impressed. "I've seen those things in malls and such. They're usually not so hot. They provide a couple of pieces of information, but the information is usually so dry. And the touch screens are so limiting. I've seen these kids using computers, and they're not daunted by keyboards."

Linda thinks and hits upon an idea. "Skip, here's an idea which might take more resources than it's worth, but listen. What if we let your customers enter their own information into the kiosk—reviews of songs and CDs, information about bands they like, questions about their favorite artists. Then we let other customers see and respond to this stuff. Then, and here's the wild part, we network the kiosks from all your stores together so people are interacting with customers from all over."

Skip thinks about that. This kind of application where people interact with each other could be really good. Skip knows how popular the Internet is becoming, and he knows how computer-savvy many of the younger customers are. He also knows that no other store has anything even close. He asks Linda to come up with a plan with time and schedule estimates. He doesn't know if the application will work, but if it's not too expensive, it just might be worth taking a shot.

THE TECHNOLOGY BEHIND THE NETWORKED KIOSK

Back in her office, Linda thinks about the networked kiosk application. A basic kiosk application is a pretty standard job. Multimedia PC, cabinet, some special software to keep the thing running, and a CD-ROM drive where the custom software is stored. Updates are a snap—just send out a new CD-ROM.

But a networked kiosk—that's another story. How will the kiosks communicate? With each other? With a central server? Modems? Protocols? BBS systems? Dedicated lines? Linda decides to call a meeting of some of the other consultants at her firm to discuss possibilities and to form a team to put together a proposal.

The meeting covers a great variety of topics. The first is that of response time between stores. When someone in one store enters a review, how long can it take before the review appears at the other stores? The first suggestion is 24 hours, since a customer would probably not come in the store again until the next day. But then someone suggests that the next time a customer comes in, the goal would be that the person would be able to see responses to what he or she wrote. In that case, what a user enters in one store should appear in the others within a couple of hours. That way others can respond and have their responses get back to the original store in time for the first person to see them. They need a technology that will copy information between the stores every couple of hours.

The next topic they discuss is whether people at the store can be involved in initiating the send/receive process to update the kiosk. This idea is met by a resounding NO! Not only should the kiosks be 99 percent stand-alone, it is argued, but the requirement that they synch up every couple of hours would be very difficult to follow. The team decides the entire operation must be fully automated from the store's point of view.

Someone then suggests using e-mail as a way of moving the data between kiosks. The kiosks could automatically dial an e-mail service every hour and broadcast their new additions to the other kiosks, and at the same time download what the other kiosks have recently sent.

At this point Lou Mulligan suggests using Notes as the networking infrastructure as well as for the overall data storage. He explains that Notes clients can be set to automatically dial in every hour and synch up with a server-based database. The kiosks could store their information in Notes databases and then replicate their changes up to the server. During this replication, they would receive changes that were uploaded by the other kiosks. This way, they could use Notes to handle the data storage and networking issues, and use Notes replication to keep all of the information from the various kiosks in synch.

Linda asks Lou if he thinks the average customer is going to be able to figure out how to use Lotus Notes. Skip replies, "Certainly not. We are going to have to build custom software to run in the kiosks to interact with the customers anyway. We will build a user interface that makes it easy to use, and that uses Notes to store the data. The customers would never know Notes was being used."

Linda then asks about the servers. "Notes requires servers, right? Who would run the servers? Where would they be located? How many would they need? What does it cost?"

Lou says he can answer some of these questions, but others will need some study. He explains that JAG Music would probably want to set up a small computer room where they could locate a server. They would need some phone lines, perhaps just two or three to start and then more as they expand. They will want to hire someone to run the Notes server and to also keep an eye on the application to make sure it is behaving well. Since this is not a static application, it will require ongoing attention and maintenance.

This triggers discussion about censorship. If anyone can walk up and type anything they want, some people may abuse it—causing possible legal ramifications for JAG Music. Linda thinks this is an excellent point and suggests that a lawyer be consulted by the team she is forming to put together the proposal.

Some more discussion follows, and the general feeling is that Notes combined with a custom front end is the right technology for the job. Linda forms a small team to put together a proposal and a quick prototype of the kiosk user interface.

Exploring Current and Future Capabilities

A few weeks later, Linda is back in Skip's office discussing the proposal. She has brought Lou Mulligan with her to demonstrate the prototype and to answer technical questions. They explain to Skip the proposal for setting up a computer room with a Notes server and a couple of phone lines. They explain the overall cost, and the fact that there is ongoing administration and maintenance for this system, not just a one-time setup like with a more standard kiosk application. They also explain about the possible legal hassles if people misuse the application.

Skip thinks the idea is hot, and is not concerned with the cost of maintaining a server. He asks if Linda's team can handle staffing the application and server maintenance position for the first six months. This way, if the project doesn't work out he minimizes his hassle tearing it down. Linda has no problem with that.

Skip understands the legal concern. He agrees to bring in his own lawyers to evaluate the proposal before they move on it. He of course will also need to consult with his stores, but he's confident they will buy into the project.

Skip then wants to explore what will happen if the application really takes off? What if he triples his number of stores? Can the application handle the load? In what other directions might JAG Music be able to take the application?

Linda prompts Lou to discuss capacity and growth. He explains, "The current single server model will probably support 25 or 30 stores. The real trick is the number of simultaneous connections to the server that can be supported. Each connection requires a phone line and a modem connected to the server, and they ordinarily don't like to put more than eight on a server. If the chain grew to 75 stores, they might put in two or even three servers. They would also start looking at alternate communications solutions to the individual phone lines that they will start with."

Linda explains that for applications above a certain size, her firm refers clients to other firms specializing in running Notes networks. She says there are various options for JAG Music in that case, including building expertise in-house, hiring firms to run the network in-house, and even outsourcing the entire application to a Notes service provider. She explains that several companies such as AT&T, Compuserve, and WorldCom are offering Notes outsourcing arrangements where they house and run the entire Notes server and access complex.

Skip approves of the growth options and the plan to start with a small computer room and a single server. He then wants to discuss another idea he had for the application if it takes off. He asks Linda if the application can grow to support individual users connecting to it from their homes? He explains that if his customers like using the computer application, they might like to connect from home. Then he could get into the electronic commerce arena by selling CDs via computer.

Linda and Lou chat back and forth for a minute, and Lou explains that this is definitely possible, but would need to be carefully thought out. "The technology supports that type of application very well. Users could run a variation of the same software running in the kiosks. The Notes servers would support the same dial-in connections that the kiosks use. But there a couple of challenges.

"One challenge is capacity. If the service really took off, then potentially thousands of users, instead of dozens of kiosks, could be dialing into the servers. This would require a very serious Notes installation. At this point you would probably want to contact one of the Notes service providers we mentioned.

"The next challenge is cost. Every one of your kiosks will need a copy of Notes on it. Because we are using the very basic functionality of Notes, we have specified using the Express version of Notes to minimize cost. This is presently around $50 per copy. This is not an issue with a few dozen kiosks, but this could be prohibitive to a general consumer market. We would need to explore ways to reduce this cost, at least for the user. One possibility would be for JAG Music to subsidize the cost.

"Because of these challenges, we might want to consider other alternatives if you get to the point of wanting users to have the ability to use your application from home. An obvious alternative is to look at World-Wide Web (WWW) technology. An increasing number of users have access to the Web from home. If you decide to support this market, we can look at building a Web interface to the application. There are already products coming out that link Notes to the Web, so this should be quite feasible."

Skip is satisfied that the technology has adequate growth possibilities. He asks to view the prototype that Linda and Lou brought. With great pride, Lou brings the kiosk application up on his notebook computer.

"Here is the main screen of the kiosk. After 30 seconds or so of inactivity, it will always return to this screen. At the moment, we have not added the fancy graphics and video, since we wanted to demonstrate the user interaction capabilities. You see we have several areas the user can enter, including the CD Room, the Press Release Room, the Upcoming Concerts Room, and the Local Bands Room. All of these areas have been enabled for customer interaction. For example, let's enter the CD Room.

"Here we see a list of artists, as well as a link to a searchable index. If we choose the artist ProtoBand, we now see a list of their CDs. Notice that each screen has a button labeled Your Place (we haven't found a great name for this yet) where users can go to give reviews and read what others have written. When I choose the ProtoBand CD called ProtoDisk, we see the list of tracks on this CD. I can highlight the first track, ProtoLove, and click the Your Place button. The user interaction window opens.

"This is where users can see what others have written and where they can write their own ideas. In the top part of the window, we see the list of topics that others have written, including original ideas and comments on those ideas. The user can click on any one to read it. Then you see the options to create a new idea or respond to the highlighted one. Here I will create a new idea where I express my opinion of the track."

Linda takes over from Lou. "This prototype gives the general idea of how the kiosk application would work. Of course, we will be adding graphics, sound effects, music clips, video clips, and so on. It will be a flashy, interesting application. If you want to proceed on the project, we can prototype that aspect next. The important thing is does this capture your idea? Is this what you're looking for?"

Skip thinks the prototype is great, and that it perfectly captures the general idea of letting users interact with each other. Skip, Linda, and Lou discuss various ways of making the application a little friendlier, and he looks forward to seeing the next prototype. The idea is taking form, and he hopes to have the kiosks installed within three months. Linda and Lou think that is reasonable for a first trial.

Viewing and writing opinions in the Kiosk application prototype

 **FACT SHEET**

Networked Kiosk Application

Purpose: To provide a unique service to customers of a retail music store chain by letting them interact with each other via an electronic kiosk.

Application Origin: Custom developed.

Application Development Time: Approximately 1 month of prototyping, and 3 months to trial, given a small, experienced development team. Ongoing development as the trial grows to full deployment expected through the next 6 months.

Typical Size: 20–30 MB to store user messages and basic artist/CD data. More if Notes is used to store the additional music clips, video clips, and so on.

Typical Use: Used by chains of music stores to link customers together as a way of providing additional incentive to visit their stores.

Forms: The underlying data storage mechanism is based on standard Discussion databases, so all Notes clients can access it. The Discussion database forms are used.

Views: Not applicable, since a custom user interface is used.

PART 3

Applications That Connect Groups

The value of Notes increases with the number of users. Therefore it is natural that "islands" of Notes users start to link together to form larger user communities. By taking advantage of Notes replication and security features, the new larger user community can implement applications like the Electronic Parts Library used at Natural MicroSystems, where evolving information can be shared among several departments in the company.

These applications that connect groups are where we start to see how Notes can transform the way an organization works. Instead of being a tool used to improve on existing business processes, Notes supports new ways of interacting and collaborating. Businesses that learn to take advantage of these possibilities can be rewarded with substantially lower costs or other competitive advantages.

The applications in this section provide examples of how using Notes to connect groups can benefit an organization. These applications can be stepping stones to the larger company-wide and inter-company applications described later.

Facilitating an Interdepartmental Project Discussion

The deployment of Notes in a company often proceeds in phases. In the early phases, individual groups and departments will use Notes for their own particular needs. When the groups begin interconnecting their Notes servers, users will make use of Notes Mail as an efficient way of transmitting messages and files. In the later phases, the groups will make use of Notes replication to share applications between groups and departments. Gil Lawrence has been with his company since they began deploying Notes, and is about to nudge his company beyond simple Notes Mail for bringing departments together.

As the head of product management at a no-longer-so-small company, Gil has seen the value that Notes provides by facilitating communication among the staff in his department. He remembers when he was the whole department, and most of his communication needs were served by the daily meetings with his partners. Then, as Gil took on staff to form the product management department, he brought in Notes so his department could communicate on their various projects as efficiently as possible. Other departments grew in the company—development, marketing, production, and more—and these departments also have used Notes.

In the past, the departments have run "islands" of Notes users, where each department has its own server, and the users in a department interact primarily with other users in the department. The servers are interconnected so everyone can exchange e-mail, but that's about the extent of the use of Notes in aiding interdepartmental activities. Since it was Gil who first brought Notes into the company, it's not surprising that it's he who decides to pioneer the next use of Notes in his company—the Interdepartmental Project Discussion application.

A GREAT IDEA IS BORN

The idea comes to Gil as he thinks about how quickly the company has grown, and how the warning signs of bureaucracy are already showing. He's noticed an ugly upward trend in the number of meetings scheduled and memos produced, with a corresponding increase in time to market. He decides that his next project will use Notes to facilitate the communication between departments, and to reduce meetings, memos, and general inefficiencies.

As his test case, Gil picks a new project idea that has been kicking around his department a little, but has not been discussed with the company at large. The idea is for a whole new product line that could leverage the technology his company specializes in, but opens up new markets. There are a million questions about whether the company has the technical expertise, competitive information, staff resources, and so on to support the project. Ordinarily Gil would call a meeting. . .but not this time! He's seen Notes used in his own department to help incubate an idea and then take it through successful execution, and he decides to try the same thing here, on a grander scale.

Gil fires up Notes and creates a new database from the Discussion template, and names it Project X, which is the name his department has been using when discussing the new project. The database opens up and he switches to the view By Category.

Gil knows the importance of seeding a Notes database with the type of information he expects to see, so he quickly creates some placeholder documents to establish some categories.

First, Gil creates a document with a category Product Features. In the document he describes a few of the ideas that have been kicking around his department. He then asks some leading questions such as, "Do we know how to build these features?" and, "How would we market these products?"

Next Gil creates a document with a category Development Strategies. In this document he asks for ideas on how the products could be developed, and what existing company assets could be creatively reused in the development of the new products.

He continues by creating a document with a category Target Markets in which he describes the markets his department has been thinking they could sell into. He asks questions such as, "How will we sell into this market?" and, "What other markets might these products sell in?"

Gil continues creating categories and asking leading questions. He purposefully phrases the questions to engage the different departments. He challenges development to think of ways to implement the features. He challenges marketing to think of where the products might sell. He challenges sales, production, and facilities to contribute their own expertise to the project. By doing this, Gil maximizes the chances of getting various departments involved.

Not wanting to wait any longer, Gil composes a Notes Mail message and addresses it to his department's Notes administrator, Ed Reid. He requests that the new database be placed on the server, and that appropriate ACLs be set so that all members of all departments have Author access. He also requests that the database be immediately replicated to the other departments' servers. He then file attaches the database he created, and sends the mail.

HELPING IT GROW

Having set the deployment of the application in motion, Gil grabs a quick lunch and heads off to his one o'clock meeting. It happens to be a Project X meeting, and so he takes some time to tell everyone about the database. A couple of folks make presentations, and so Gil asks them to put the presentations into the Project X database (which should be available on the server by the time the meeting is over). He also asks the person taking meeting minutes to publish them in the Project X database. While a couple of people grumble (as they always do when asked to break routine) Gil has his reasons, and he is the boss.

One of Gil's reasons is to get his department immediately involved in the Project X database, which, in turn, will help ensure the critical mass of users that is so important to the success of a Notes database. While this is important, even more important is the inclusion of information from Gil's department that other departments will find valuable. Gil knows that people in other departments will love to see the presentations and meeting minutes from the product management Project X meetings. They have had little access to this information, since they are too busy in their own meetings to attend his! Since this holds equally true in the other direction, Gil hopes to set an example so that he can see other departments' presentations and meeting minutes in the Project X database.

The next day Gil checks on the status of the database. It is indeed on the server. He replicates the database to get any new activity into his local copy on his personal workstation. Gil is pleased to see a new category called Meeting Presentations & Notes, in which the presentations and meeting minutes from the previous afternoon's meeting now reside. He sees that the presentations are file attachments, and the files were created using a presentation graphics package that, fortunately, his company standardized on. This way, all users will be able to view the presentations by double-clicking their icons and selecting "launch" from the dialog box that appears, which will run the appropriate presentation graphics program with the attached presentation loaded.

Project X database viewed By Category

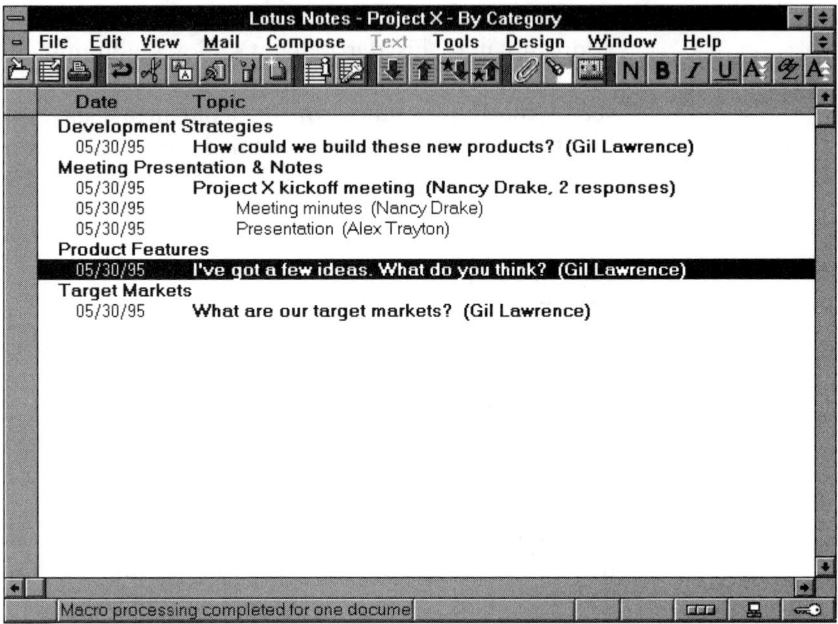

Gil's PC plays it's mail tune, and so he checks his Notes Mail. There is a response from Ed saying that the database has been replicated to all departments and is ready for action. He now thinks about how to involve the other departments. How will people know it's there? How will people know to use it?

Gil considers sending out a *shotgun* message—a mail to every user in the company. But then he decides that the mail runs the risk of being ignored—most people receiving it won't recognize Gil as someone whose mail they should care about (online life is hard!). Therefore, he decides to send mail to the other department heads and follow up with phone calls.

In the mail, Gil briefly describes Project X and how he wishes to use the Project X database to involve all departments in discussing the idea. Knowing that people are often willing to click an icon, but unwilling to search menus, Gil makes it easy for the department heads to open the database by providing a doclink to a document in the database. This way, the heads can read the mail and double-click the doclink to get the database onto their workspaces. He sends the mail, and then waits an hour or two to make sure it has been received.

Gil then makes phone calls to each department head. He explains that he has sent mail about the Project X database and he asks them to find it and double-click the doclink. Gil takes them through some of the documents and categories in the database, and answers any questions and fears they have about using the database for discussion instead of the standard set of meetings, memos, and so on. He encounters some resistance, but nothing substantial—everyone agrees it is a fine idea.

On the phone, Gil asks each department head to send mail to their department explaining the database and urging them to participate. Coming from their department head, the mail has a good chance of being read. The department head can forward the mail Gil sent, so that everyone receives the doclink to help them get to the database.

THE IDEA TAKES OFF

As the next couple of days go by, Gil closely monitors the activity of the Project X database. As members from the other departments enter some ideas and comment on others, he provides gentle encouragement by participating as well. Some users will be glad to see their ideas being responded to at all, and will be glad to continue. Some users will be impressed that Gil is personally participating and will use the database for that reason alone. Whatever the individual reasons are, Gil is glad to see people using the database, and glad to see the types of things being discussed increasing from the few ideas he initially created to all manner of topics.

Pretty soon Gil sees that the brainstorming/initial-idea phase of discussion seems to be slowing down. The database now contains a fairly complete catalog of ideas for features and markets, along with numerous advantages and disadvantages of each option. He calls a meeting of the decision-makers who quickly agree on the set of features and markets to be targeted. The outcome of this meeting is entered into the database and discussion immediately begins to focus not on what to do, but on how.

Development immediately begins asking pointed questions about how particular features should behave, and whether it is OK if they behave a little differently. Everyone immediately wants to know the schedule and resource constraints. Human resources even posts a few resumes of candidates they feel would be useful on Project X. Sales begins having meetings on how to sell the new products; which existing clients will be interested; and how to get new clients. These discussions go in the database so marketing and development can plan accordingly. The ball is really rolling.

THE PROJECT MATURES

Every time Gil opens the Project X database and sees the new documents, he feels proud that he has applied Notes to a new situation and it has been a complete success. Yet he notices that the database has been getting quite crowded, and that people are making suggestions about modifications to the database. It seems that every department wants to change the database to be more aligned with how they work. Finally, he notices that the departments are creating their own databases to support Project X. Development is creating a Requirements/Design database, Sales is creating a Sales Discussion database, and so on.

As the weeks go on, there is less and less discussion in the Project X Discussion database, but Gil knows this is because each department is using Notes in their own best way to get the job done. The Project X database is still used, and will continue to be used through the new products' lifecycles, but as the development of Project X is now well underway, Gil's thoughts turn to the next challenge. Project Y?

◣ FACT SHEET

Project X Discussion Database

Purpose: To support multiple departments in a company working together to achieve a common purpose.

Application Origin: Derived from the Discussion template bundled with Notes.

Application Development Time: A few minutes.

Typical Size: 1–100 MB, depending on the size of the company and the complexity of the project being discussed.

Typical Use: An Interdepartmental Project Discussion database is typically used in a medium or large company, where improved communication between departments is desired.

Forms: The standard forms in the Notes Discussion template: Main Topic, Response, and Response to Response.

Views: The standard views in the Notes Discussion template: Main View, By Author, and By Category.

The Time-Card Tracking Database

Why don't more companies track their employees' use of time with Notes, instead of with paper time sheets or time cards? It seems like an obvious Notes application. Everyone needs to use it, the information is stored in a central place, it needs security, and so forth. The answer seems to be that it's hard to do it well.

Anyone considering implementing such an application needs to think carefully about balancing the needs of security and ease of use. Natural Microsystems seems to have created such a balance, and has developed a system for tracking time-card information that has proven to be successful in practice.

Natural MicroSystems (NMS), based in Natick, Massachusetts, is the leading provider of open platforms for the integration of telephones and computers. NMS has an international list of clients that purchase their technology to build a wide variety of computerized telephone systems, from voice mail products to telephone systems to automated calling computers.

Many companies that do research and development need to keep track of the hours their employees spend on particular projects. Some companies keep track mainly for cost and quality metrics. But for companies that do consulting and third-party development work—especially those that work for the government—keeping track of hours is essential. These companies have to account for every hour billed to their customers.

The NMS Time Cards system comprises three databases. One database, called Time Card Codes, is used to store reference information for the accounting codes. The New Project form stores a project name along with a numeric

---

accounting code and the person responsible for the product. The form also has a couple of category fields. The Corporate category is used for general categories such as Overhead, Development, or Support. The Engineering category is used for finer detail in the engineering department, and is usually the name of a product or product line.

The second reference database, called User Codes, is basically just a cross-reference between employee names and employee numbers.

Each database has a specific view that is used by the Time Cards system to look up code information. One of the views, Names vs. codes, has a list of the User Code documents, showing name and accounting code for each. This is used to look up the code from the user name. The other view, called ByCode, shows accounting codes sorted numerically with the description for each.

A third database called Time Cards is the one that actually stores the time-card information. There is a single form in this database, called a Time Card. The Time Card form is used to store all of the information for a single week's time tracking.

Because people normally fill out time cards only for themselves, many fields in the form are automatically filled in, though they can be overridden in special circumstances. At the top of the form is the name of the person filling it

A Time Card form being filled out

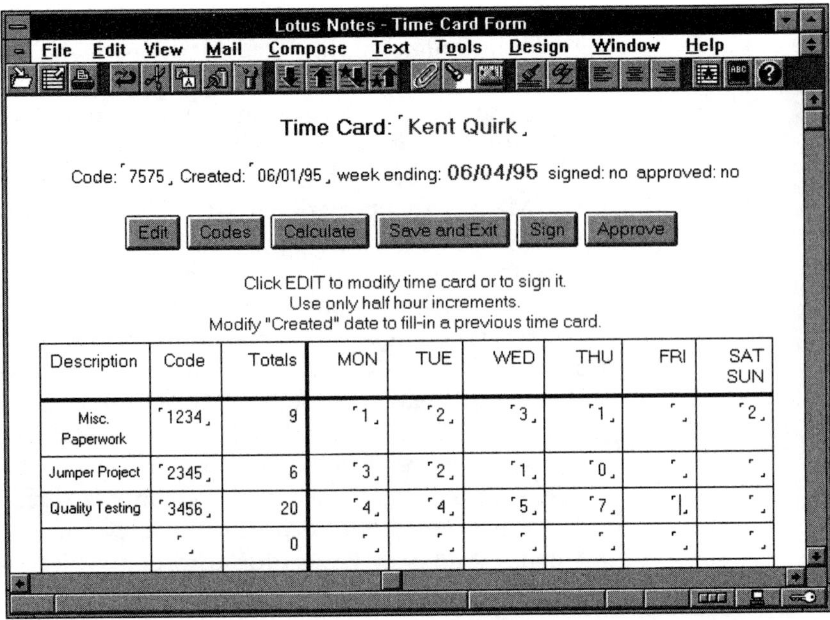

Description	Code	Totals	MON	TUE	WED	THU	FRI	SAT SUN
Misc. Paperwork	1234	9	1	2	3	1		2
Jumper Project	2345	6	3	2	1	0		
Quality Testing	3456	20	4	4	5	7	1	
		0						

out. The accounting code (Code) is automatically looked up in the User Code database. The creation date is filled in with the current date and the date of the Sunday that ends the week.

The time card is arranged with each day of the week in a separate column. Each row corresponds to a single accounting code, for a project, client, or task. Filling in the accounting code automatically looks up the code in the codes database and fills in the description line. If the code doesn't exist, the user sees an error message. Totals, by accounting code as well as by day, are calculated on demand. There is also a comments field for explanations of unusual events.

There is a set of buttons on the form for common tasks. The Codes button opens the database of project codes to make it easy to look them up. The Edit, Save and Exit, and Calculate buttons are there simply to make it easier to use the form.

There are two other buttons on the form. One of them "signs" the form. Signing a form indicates that the form is completed and correct.

Typically, employees will fill out the form periodically during the week, opening it from time to time to fill in their work hours. Once the form is complete, clicking the Sign button will mark it as finished and save the form.

The engineering supervisor will check the form, and click the Approve button to complete the form. This is for use only by the engineering supervisor; code under the button will prevent anyone but him from approving the form.

End users of the system have but a single view available called Time Cards (private). This view makes use of a special feature in Notes called Private on First Use. This view limits the documents visible to a particular user to only those documents he or she created. This provides some measure of privacy, though not security.

View Types

There are three distinct types of views in Notes.

Shared views are views potentially available to all users of the database (as long as they have the right security level). The view index is also stored with the database on the server. These views have the advantage that the information is stored in one place for all users. Also, the indexing process (which can take a long time) doesn't have to be performed for every user individually. However, shared views can only be created by someone with Designer or Manager privilege. Also, a shared view cannot use any formula that would cause the view to be different for each user. For example, it is not possible to have a shared view that shows individuals only their own documents.

Private views can be created by any user. Both the view and the view index are stored locally, on the end user's machine. This means that the view is reindexed for every user, which can be time consuming. It is also impossible to make a Private view into a Shared view, and it's not easy to give a copy of a

Private view to someone else. Private views can, however, be customized to each individual user.

Shared, Private on First Use views are basically private views that are stored on the database. However, when a user selects a view like this, it becomes a Private view. This is a way of creating customized views that can easily be shared.

IN PRACTICE

In use, the database has proved quite successful. Before its existence, NMS used a manual time-card system. Pam Hurley, manager of this database at NMS, said that one of the biggest benefits of the Notes system is that it does the math automatically. "The old system was notorious for incorrect math, and people would often use incorrect accounting codes. That has mostly been eliminated now."

One view, called the By Week view, was designed for use by the accounting department. For each week, it shows the employee name and ID number for all of the time cards that were filled out, the total hours for each, and the total hours for each of the project codes for that user.

It's a busy screen, but that one view contains all of the information needed by the person who's entering the data into the accounting system.

There is also a By Person view, showing the same information (total hours and hours per project) broken down by week. It is sometimes useful when the HR department needs to check the status for a particular employee.

Though it would be possible to create views by project that would do such things as show total hours spent on a particular project, NMS has not done much more than experiment with these kinds of views. Their accounting system already does a pretty good job at this kind of query, and since the real purpose of this database was simply to make entering time cards easier and more accurate, it has been deemed a success.

POSSIBLE IMPROVEMENTS

This database could be improved in both ease of use and security in a number of relatively simple ways.

First, the Codes field could allow selection from a list of preexisting codes and their explanations, generated by a lookup into the codes database. This would eliminate the need for the Codes button. On the other hand, the list of codes is quite long, and the large query might slow data entry down noticeably. Since most users know most of their own project codes by heart, and the codes are confirmed by lookup of their descriptions after entry, this really isn't that much of a problem.

Security could be greatly improved with the following special features:

▶ Sign the form with a Notes encrypted signature.
▶ Remove the originator from the list of allowed editors, once the form has been approved by a supervisor (this would prevent a form from being edited after it has been submitted).
▶ Use sections to cordon off the approval portion.
▶ Use sections to prevent anyone but the originator or someone with the approvals role from seeing the data.
▶ Use a *role,* which is a way to assign special privileges, to allow approvals by more than one person.
▶ Use a role to prevent most users from creating private views.

As NMS grows, and as their knowledge and use of Notes expands, they might find these features more attractive. They might also be interested in creating and using more views, such as a view by project.

◤ Fact Sheet

Natural Microsystems Time Cards Tracking

Purpose: To track information on the time employees spend on different projects.

Application Origin: Custom-developed.

Application Development Time: 1 month.

Typical Size: 6 MB, 1000 records.

Typical Use: Individual employees enter time-card information on a daily or weekly basis. Once completed, the time cards are approved by the engineering manager, and the data can be collected.

Forms: The Time Card form is used to enter the information for one week's worth of data.

Views: Individuals can only view their own documents. The engineering manager and human resources people can view all the documents, and have a couple of densely packed views designed to show summary information for the entire engineering department at a glance.

Server Tracking Database

Palace Company supplies auto parts to United States and European auto makers. The (hypothetical) company is based in Milwaukee, Wisconsin, and has 22,000 employees worldwide. The company has manufacturing plants throughout the United States and a number of locations in Europe. Sales offices are primarily located near automobile manufacturing plants.

Frank Terrif manages the company's global network. He is responsible for file servers, print servers, network routers, and so on around the world. About six months ago, the company purchased a number of expensive high-end servers from a reputable manufacturer. These servers were intended to be used as file servers in large offices, supporting a few hundred users per server. From the time they bought the servers until the time they got rid of them, Frank's staff had nothing but problems with the machines. Initially, the computers seemed to crash more often than other brands of similarly configured computers. Software compatibility became a major issue—the server used a proprietary video display card that was difficult to get working. Frequently, the computers would lock up entirely. When Frank contacted the manufacturer, he was told that there were a number of sites that were up and running without a problem. The problems with Frank's computers must be related to the configuration of the machines. Frank assigned some of his people to work directly with the manufacturer's customer support personnel to try to resolve these issues. None of this seemed to help. In fact, the problems seemed to get worse. Up time for the servers was measured in hours rather than weeks or months. Some users complained that the servers seemed to be unavailable more often than they were available. Two months later, the manufacturer announced publicly that certain key components of the servers were prone to failure, and it would upgrade these for free. Frank's machines got the up-

plications. The Help Desk has access to a much broader array of information than Frank's group and might spot patterns in equipment failures that go beyond Frank's servers. The database might be tightly integrated into a Change Management application. The database is already capturing change information, and there might be a reason to link the application to the Change Management system. This would ensure that information is not repeated between the two applications.

FACT SHEET

Server-Tracking Database

Purpose: To help an organization track problems, solutions, and changes made to servers.

Application Origin: Modified from another similar database.

Application Development Time: 1 man-week.

Typical Size: Size will vary, depending on the number of computers included and the size of configuration files added to the database; typically the database will remain under 10 MB.

Typical Use: Company begins having problems with a particular brand or model of server. Administrators use the database to provide feedback to manufacturer and monitor the effectiveness of proposed solutions.

Forms: Computer, Problem Report, Solution, Change, and Outage.

Views: By Computer, By Status, By Serial Number, By Changes, By Outages, By Date, and By Author.

The Bug Tracking Database

Software has bugs. Some people prefer to call them defects, problems, or SPRs (software problem reports), but the colloquial term is bugs. During the development portion of a new software product, the new software typically has a lot of bugs. Jerry Parkinson is the manager of the Quality Assurance (QA) group for a hypothetical software product that's currently under development. For a product on the scale of the one his company is building (about a dozen developers working for a year), he can expect his QA team to find and diagnose roughly 1,000 bugs in the system during the development cycle. When the company was small, the QA process was relatively informal, and in fact much of the time the QA was done by the programmers themselves. Now, the company has grown, and it's becoming necessary to install a formal bug-tracking system. There are several such systems on the market specifically aimed at defect management, but since Jerry's company uses Notes since extensively, they opt to use Notes.

Jerry considers what the system needs to be able to do. Basically, it needs to keep a running list of all bugs found in the software. For each bug, he needs to track:

- ▶ The current status of the bug: new, open, pending retest, or closed
- ▶ The personnel involved with the bug: who wrote it, who is responsible for fixing it, who will retest it
- ▶ Which component or product area is affected by this bug
- ▶ The bug severity: how serious the failure is, ranked from 1 (crashes the system) to 5 (cosmetic)
- ▶ The bug priority: how important it is that this be fixed, ranked from 1 (must be fixed ASAP) to 4 (candidate for not being fixed)

▶ Once the bug has been closed, the reason for closure: for example, fixed, duplicate of another bug, could not reproduce, or product feature, etc.

QA testers need to be able to see all the bugs in their area and the status of each. They need the ability to enter and store detailed information on how to reproduce a bug. They need to see which bugs have been fixed and need to have the fixes verified. And they need to be able to close bugs that have been fixed (as well as bugs that are duplicates or not reproducible).

Developers need to know which bugs are assigned to them to be fixed. They need to be able to mark a bug as fixed (pending retest by the QA person responsible).

Managers need to be able to track the current state of the product. They would also like to be able to see a history (preferably graphical) of the trends in the system (number of open bugs, bug close rate, and bug find rate).

The system as described can easily be implemented in Notes, with one important exception. While Notes is good at showing everyone the current status of everything, it doesn't track history well. A database that attempts to track the history of each document would quickly get huge and difficult to manage.

After discussing it with other managers in the development organization, Jerry decides that he can provide the limited amount of historical data needed by building a couple of special-purpose tools, and that the advantages of using Notes (a common tool already available and known to everyone in the organization) overcome the disadvantage just described.

THE DATABASE DESIGN

The key elements of the database he builds are a single main Bug Report form, enough views to meet everyone's needs, and some careful work with the database ACL (access control list).

The Bug Report form is fairly complex. In order for the various organizations involved to have the information they need, the form needs to have a lot of individual fields. Following are some of the important ones:

▶ Names of all the responsible team members: The authors of the original bug report, the QA person responsible, and the development person responsible. The form also tracks every person who edits it.
▶ All the important dates for the bug report: The date the report was originally entered, the date it was first marked open, and the date it was closed.
▶ Component or product area: The name of the portion of the product in which the bug was found. This field is useful for showing the bugs broken down by product area. It helps in planning the workload during the closing stages of the project.

▶ Status: A keyword field used to track the status of the bug. It has possible values of New (the bug has been entered, but has not been verified by QA), Open (has been verified), Pending Retest (the development team believes it has been fixed), Closed (has been fixed and verified, or closed for other reasons).

▶ Priority, a field that can be used to set the priority of the individual bugs: 1 (fix immediately), 2 (fix ASAP), 3 (fix when convenient), or 4 (fix only if there's nothing else to do).

▶ Severity, indicates the level of inconvenience the bug causes the user: 1 (crashes system); 2 (halts program or erroneous results); 3 (causes failure, no workaround); or 4 (causes failure, workaround available); 5 (minor annoyance, does not affect work, or request for enhancement).

▶ Title: A short (one-line) description of the bug that can fit into the Notes view.

▶ Description: A long description, possibly including screen shots or file attachments, that describes in detail what the bug is.

▶ Reproduce instructions: A detailed description of how to cause the bug. This is split into a separate field from the description because it does a better job of reminding people to include this vital information.

▶ Close description: A detailed description of the development effort required to close the bug.

▶ Close reason: if the bug has been closed, indicates why: Fixed, Not reproducible (the instructions were insufficient to be able to recreate the bug), Feature (it's not a bug, the product is supposed to work that way), No Plan To Fix (it may be a bug, but it's so obscure or difficult to fix that it will never be fixed), or Fix Next Release (this will not be addressed until the next release of the product).

Having built a bug reporting form, Jerry then creates views for the different team members to use. Depending on their ole in the project, different people need the information to be accessible in different ways.

The individual members of the QA team need to be able to see the bugs organized by QA owner, so they can find the bugs they're responsible for tracking. They also need to see bugs sorted by status so they can verify new bugs and retest the bugs that have been fixed.

The developers need a view showing open bugs by development owner and priority; this helps programmers to plan their work. They also need to see bugs by product area and status, so they can see what's coming based on New and Pending Retest.

Managers have to assign the owner fields for development and testing, so they need a view showing bugs that have not yet been assigned. They also need to see totals by product area, of the number of bugs at each status level. A view by status organized by severity shows the general state of the system being developed—if the number of high-severity bugs is low, the system is getting

A view categorized by bug (SPR) state

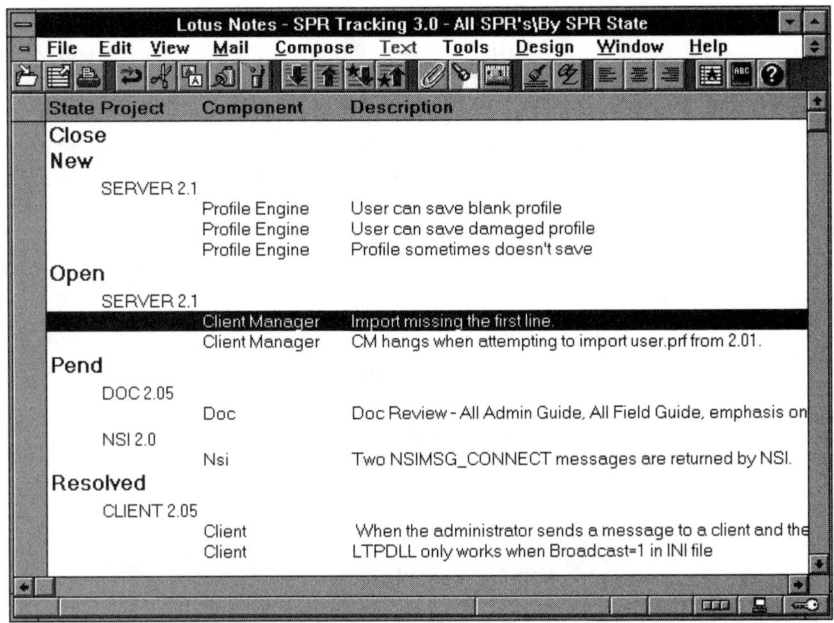

fairly stable. A view by status organized by priority helps to plan workload. A view of developers and close dates can show who is being the most productive in fixing bugs; the same view for testers can show who's finding the most bugs.

Jerry even makes some strides toward tracking historical data by clever use of date information. He creates a view showing, for each week of the project, the total number of bugs opened, total number closed, and the difference between the two. When the close rate begins to stay higher than the open rate, it's probably getting close to the end of the project.

His next problem is trying to ensure that people have only the access levels they need to get their work done. QA people and developers need to be able to enter bugs, correct them, and make changes to the status fields, so both teams need Editor access to the database. While it would be possible to be much more stringent about the form design, for example, allowing people access to only certain fields, Jerry feels he's better off trusting the people involved not to abuse the privilege of editor access. He does take the precaution of preventing anyone else from being able to delete bugs from the system. He also makes sure that each form tracks the user's name and time every time it's edited.

Other members of the team have to be able to enter bugs, but they don't need to be able to edit them. Jerry gives them Author status, and again removes the ability to delete a form. Managers have Designer access. This will allow them to edit documents, delete them if necessary, and even create new views if they feel the need.

Jerry and the other managers roll out the database to the team. While a few people grumble about the additional workload, many others breathe a sigh of relief that there will finally be a more formal method of bug tracking. Pretty quickly, several of the QA people make suggestions about the design of the forms and views. While there are no major changes, several minor ones are made that make the forms a bit easier to use and understand, or add additional information to the views. Upon request, Jerry also creates macros that let people change the status of several documents at once to Open or Pending Retest.

While there are more bugs in the system than Jerry would like, at least he has a way of keeping track of them now. The team is communicating better about detecting and fixing bugs, and the managers have a better handle on the real state of the project.

◀ FACT SHEET

Bug Tracking Database

Purpose: To track the defects (bugs) found in a software product under development.

Application Origin: Original design.

Application Development Time: 1 week

Typical Size: Can grow to 10–20 MB, depending on number of bugs to be tracked.

Typical Use: Entire team can enter bugs into the system. QA department verifies them and opens them (sets status to "Open") if they're verifiable, or closes them if there are problems. Development fixes them, sets status to Pending Retest. QA verifies the fix and closes the bug. If the bug was not fixed, it's reopened. A wide range of views allows the various participants easy access to the information they care about.

Forms: Only one; a Bug Report form with many fields to help build the views.

Views: Many views; specific views appropriate for QA (By Status, By QA owner); development (By Status, By Developer, By Component); and management (By Date, Open Bugs, Bugs Closed This Week).

The Specification Archives Database

Learningways, a Massachusetts-based division of Davidson and Associates, is a developer of interactive multimedia curricula and other educational software, primarily for school use. Learningways works with educational publishers to produce multimedia software that integrates content and tools and fosters active learning. Their customers are the publishers of textbooks for use in primary and secondary schools. Learningways has been using Notes since mid-1993. Chuck Olson, president, knows a lot about Notes, since he used to work at Lotus. It's his feeling that "working in an entrepreneurial environment requires collaboration with many clients and vendors. Coordination of work is particularly difficult, and workgroup technologies like Notes are critical to allowing us to compete."

At any given time, they might be working on more than a half-dozen projects for different customers. One of Learningways' competitive advantages is their System—they have a fairly standard software architecture that allows them to build high-quality educational materials without reinventing the entire environment every time. This is good for Learningways, because it lets them take advantage of the synergy between products developed for different customers—a feature useful to one customer might well be useful to another. It's good for their customers because they get the benefit of more engineering at a lower cost.

Specification Archives developed by Learningways, a division of Davidson & Associates, Inc. All rights to the Specification Archives are the property of Learningways.

WHAT CAN BE SHARED?

The kinds of things that can be shared between projects are such items as:

- ▶ Interface ideas. A product designer might come up with a snappy new way to display information or a clever way of navigating around the user interface of a product.
- ▶ Interface components. In a system design like the one Learningways uses, there might be interface tools or components that can be packaged for reuse by other product groups.
- ▶ Data file formats. In software development, data file formats can be a nightmare to design and maintain. If someone does a good job of building one, it only makes sense to try and leverage it.

The problem is that everyone is so busy, it might be hard to give synergy a chance to happen. In a typical software development environment, most people are assigned to particular projects, and stay assigned to them for the duration of each project. If people on different projects don't talk to one another about the right features at the right time, opportunities for reuse of ideas, components, and interfaces may be lost.

To help ease the burden of communication, Learningways built a Notes database called Specification Archives. It's a fairly simple design, which was a good idea in this case. The general purpose was, first, to facilitate the process of writing functional specifications for Learningways products, without unnecessarily adding to the workload. The second purpose was to provide an up-to-date reference source of existing functionality for the rest of the organization and selected clients.

When this database was first created, Learningways already had many specifications for products, mostly stored in Microsoft Word for Macintosh documents. The idea was to provide comprehensiveness without creating an enormous maintenance and upkeep burden for designers. A full-fledged specification on the system (combining all the features in the existing specs) would be over 250 pages long and would be time consuming to manage and keep current.

Learningways decided that a better approach would be a database with a feature list that simply pointed to the pertinent information. All the major features in the system would be listed and cross-referenced to the specifications. This way, if the information changed (e.g., a new feature added), all that would need updating would be the reference (for example, changing a page number). The specifications would also be stored, but instead of moving them into the database as native Notes documents, they would be stored as attachments.

FORMS

The form design of this system is very straightforward. There are two forms. One is used for storing the specifications themselves. It contains only summary information about the specification, such as the spec name, the author, the date, and a list of updates to the spec. The spec is stored as an attached Word document.

The other form is for storing an individual feature description, with a pointer to the correct location in the spec. It has almost exactly the same layout as the spec document, except that it also contains a page number reference to the specification.

Because Learningways develops educational software, at least half of their computers are Macintoshes, while the rest are PCs. The specifications were written in Microsoft Word—some for the Mac, some for the PC. The Learningways designers composed a "spec" document in the Notes database for each of the Word specifications they had created. To minimize people's problems with reading the documents, they chose to store each specification in both PC and Mac forms in the Notes database. One of the items they made sure to include in each of these documents was a list of the key contributors to the specification, so that people with questions would know whom to address.

They then went through the specifications and, for each major feature, composed a "feature" document with a cross reference to the spec. The cross-reference included the spec name, page number, and a Notes doclink to the particular spec document.

Doclinks

A *Doclink* is a feature of Notes that can be extremely useful. It lets you create a "link" to another Notes document in any database. Someone reading your document can click on the link and be taken right to the reference. A doclink looks like this:

A doclink as found in the Notes Help database.

These are some typical uses for doclinks:

▶ From a Table of Contents document, each line in the table of contents can have a doclink to the document it references.

▶ When referencing an original document, especially in an e-mail about the document, it's useful to use a doclink pointing back to the original. This lets the reader see things in context. Note, however, that you can't put a doclink back to an original in your own mail file—the person you're sending the mail to won't have access to your mail file.

▶ Anytime you quote from a document, it's handy to be able to connect a doclink to the original.

▶ When you need to reference information from a different database, such as a name and address in a customer database. Rather than copying the original information, use a doclink. This way, if the customer changes an address or phone number, the referenced information won't become obsolete.

Doclinks work even in a remote environment, because they reference a database's replication ID. This means that any replica of the database can be used to resolve a doclink, no matter which server it's on.

To create a doclink, first find the document you want to reference. Highlight it in the view, or open it. Then choose Make Doclink from the Edit menu. This creates a doclink and stores it on your computer's Clipboard. You can now paste it into a document.

VIEWS

There are three views in the Specification Archives database:

▶ Master Specs: A repository of all the existing functional specs. Each spec is stored as a Microsoft Word attachment in both Mac and PC versions. The PC versions are identified by their .DOC filename extensions.

▶ Feature List, Alphabetical: An alphabetical listing of all the existing core features and key concepts. The actual specifications themselves are not shown in this view. This view is useful for browsing the features available or contemplated.

▶ Feature List, By Category: Identical to previous view, but grouped by category.

A view of the Feature index, sorted By Category.

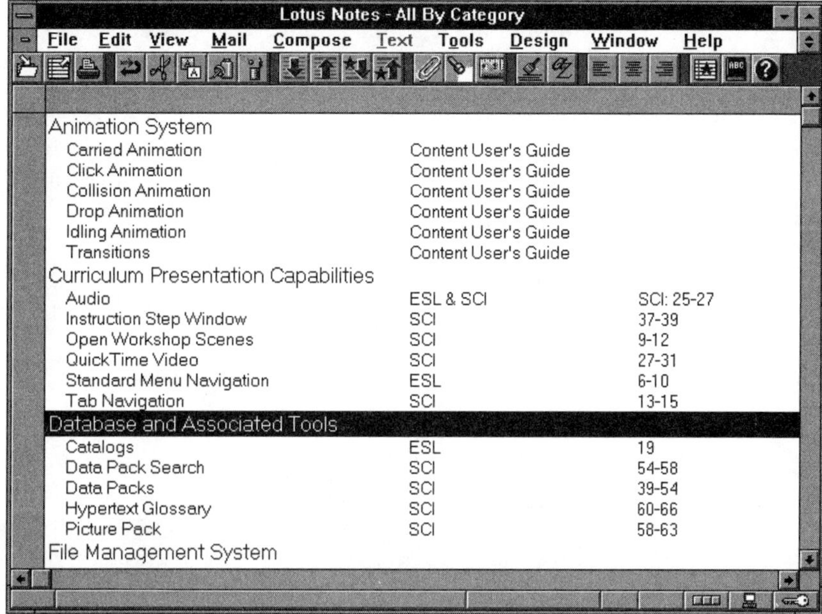

THE DATABASE IN USE

The database has generally been a success, though it's turned out to be harder than they would like to keep the specs up to date. Storing large attachments, particularly on the Macintosh, is a bit of a performance problem. These specification files contain a large number of graphics and can sometimes take more than two minutes to attach and detach. This means that people are not likely to detach a specification unless they need it badly, and minor edits become annoyingly difficult. The database is therefore not as useful for a reference tool as it could be.

Learningways could make the database more productive and useful by moving the documents from Microsoft Word into native Notes format. While this conversion might be somewhat difficult initially, it needs to be done only once. It would probably be easiest to create a rule that anyone modifying a specification should move it into Notes at the same time. The specs would then move over time without becoming a major burden on any one person.

This kind of conversion would mean that people could use the database as an online reference tool, rather than following the current practice of printing out specifications and keeping a private copy. It would make editing the specifications much simpler, since changes could be made directly within Notes. Furthermore, the Notes full-text searching could be used to make the database better suited for searching and cross-referencing.

◢ FACT SHEET

Specification Archives Database

Purpose: This database has two purposes: to help facilitate the process of writing functional specs for designers; and to serve as an up-to-date reference source of existing product functionality for everyone in the company.

Application Origin: Custom developed internally by Learningways.

Application Development Time: 2 days.

Typical Size: 20–30 MB, 200 documents.

Typical Use: The database stores all of the company specifications. While Learningways stores the specifications as file attachments, it would be better and more useful to store them as Notes documents directly. It also stores a cross-referenced feature list. The feature list references the specification and page number of all specs that contain that feature.

Forms: The Spec form stores the specifications themselves as attachments, with information on the author, subject, and date. The Feature form is used to store a cross-reference to each major feature, with the feature's name, date, category, and page numbers.

Views: There are three views in this database: Master Specs is an alphabetically sorted repository of all existing functional specs. Feature List, Alphabetical is an alphabetical listing of all the existing core features and key concepts. Feature List, By Category shows the core features and key concepts, grouped by category.

The Soft Toolbox

Nathan Goodrich is a software developer heading up a software tools group within Vapor Productions, a hypothetical large software development company. The job of Nathan's organization is to build tools that will help others within the company build commercial software. These tools have included a wide range of items, such as small utilities that help developers to automate their work more easily, a software problem-reporting (bug tracking) system developed in Notes (see "The Bug Tracking Database"), and libraries of functions that help developers to test systems and track down bugs.

The biggest problem Nathan has is that there isn't much teamwork in his organization. The projects in this group are small enough that most developers have their own independent projects. They don't get much of a chance to talk together, so they don't share code or ideas. The last straw happened recently when he discovered two different developers working on basically the same set of subroutines—while their projects were independent, they accessed the same database.

There Must Be a Better Way

Since all of Nathan's clients and his team are all using Notes, he decided to implement a software request-and-delivery system using Notes. He called it the Soft Toolbox.

The Soft Toolbox is comprised of two integrated systems. The first is simply a storage platform for all the tools that Nathan's group has developed. The second is a work request system that allows Nathan to prioritize and manage the work.

The storage platform is very simple. Nathan started with a standard Notes Discussion database, and modified the Main Topic form to a Toolbox Item. First, he added several fields. The Developers field is a list of the names of the people who built a tool; they can be approached if more information is needed. Platform describes the operating environment for a tool, such as DOS, Windows, or Notes. The Keywords field is a multivalued keyword field that classifies a tool by categories, and Abstract includes a brief description of a tool's purpose.

Someone filling out a Toolbox Item form includes the fields above, and types the title of the tool on the subject line. The body of the form contains the tool documentation (either directly posted into Notes or attached as a document) and the attached executable file for the tool itself.

There are several Toolbox views, by Platform, by Keyword, by Author, and by Subject. This range of views makes it easy for people to find tools in a variety of ways.

Nathan hoped that posting their tool group's output would help people to visualize the kind of work that they do, as well as provide a repository that would allow anyone to retrieve an existing tool without having to hunt down the original author. He left the standard Response and Response to Response forms in place, in case people wanted to comment on the database or the tools in it. He also encouraged people who develop their own tools, such as editor macros, to add them to the Toolbox as well.

Of course, many people will look in this database and fail to find a tool that meets their needs. They needed to have a way to request that a tool be developed, so Nathan also created a Tool Request form.

This form has a subject, a date, and the identification of the platform for which the tool is being requested. There are two date fields: Date Required and Date Desired. Nathan originally only had the former, but found that people would err too much on the side of caution and specify a date earlier than they really needed. With both dates to fill out, they are more honest about their real needs (although he jokes that he ought to just set both fields to "yesterday" and leave it at that).

There is also a Priority field, with values of "Low—it would make life easier if we had this," "High—we need this, but we would somehow get by if we didn't have it," and "Urgent—we have no alternatives to this." Nathan found that putting the extended descriptions in the field made people more honest about choosing a priority.

The description field starts out as blank, but there are different questions to be asked, depending on the type of request being built, so the form has buttons labeled Utility Request, Notes Application Request, and Library Request. These buttons insert appropriate questions into the description field.

Finally, the form asks for the name, phone number, and e-mail address of the user so that the tools group can get more information if needed.

The Tool Request form of the Soft Toolbox

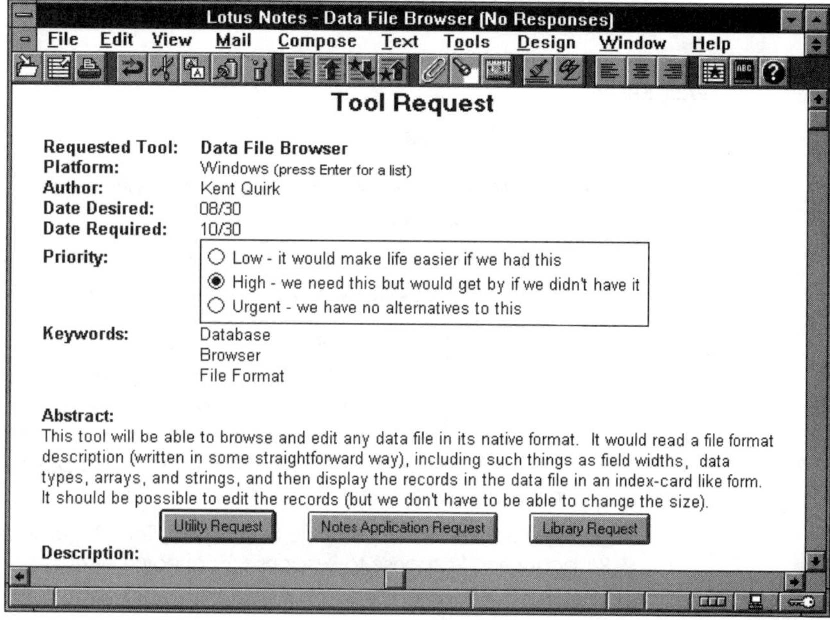

Once the form has been filled out and stored in the database, there is a section that can be edited only by the Tools group. It contains a Status field with values of New, Needs Information, Pending, In Development, Not Accepted, and Completed. There is a Projected Completion date field, and the name of the developer to which the project has been assigned.

After seeing a request, the tools group evaluates it and sets the status field appropriately. This will often initiate a discussion in the database between the person or team making the request and the tools group. The standard Response and Response to Response forms facilitate the discussion of the requests right in the database. Occasionally representatives of other groups will chime in and add their own commentary and feature requests to a topic under discussion. By encouraging discussion and improvement, Nathan's group can develop tools that are useful to a wider audience.

The Requests views show all requests by Date, by Platform, by Author, and by Status.

Since the creation of the Soft Toolbox, Nathan's group has run much more smoothly. The group's clients can easily find out the status of pending projects. The publicly posted requests have led to the development of better products, because the ideas and specifications are refined before being committed to code. Also, the group's visibility within the organization has improved, because the size and quality of the group's output is now much more obvious.

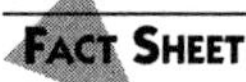

FACT SHEET

The Soft Toolbox

Purpose: Management of work requests for a software service organization and distribution of the resulting products.

Application Origin: Modified from the standard Notes Discussion database.

Application Development Time: 1 day, plus continuous improvement.

Typical Size: 10–50 MB (mostly the file attachments).

Typical Use: Customers make requests to have software developed. Members of the tools group and the customers themselves discuss the requests online and come to agreement. The status of the development effort is tracked in the database, and the resulting software is posted in the database for public use. The software posted includes software developed within the organization, macros, and custom tools.

Forms: Toolbox Item for storage of software, Tool Request for requesting the development, Response and Response to Response for ongoing discussion.

Views: Toolbox views show the Toolbox Item forms. There are views sorted By Platform, By Keyword, By Author, and By Subject. The Request Views Show The Tool Request Forms, By Platform, By Status, By Author, and By Subject.

Sales Order Entry and Tracking: The Contact Database

Telepartner International, founded in 1985, is a leading developer of high-performance software products for remote and mobile computing. Telepartner offers a range of wired and wireless connectivity products for communicating between large computers (mainframes and midrange computers) and PCs or workstations. Telepartner's products include Packet/PC™ for SNA/asynchronous connectivity and Synchrony, a managed-software-distribution product. They are a pioneer in the wireless communications industry, where they optimize wireless performance with data compression.

Telepartner has a very large product line for a company its size. It supports over 500 configurations of its various products; the variations are the support for different communications protocols and configurations. As the product mix grew, the paper-based ordering system, which was never all that easy to use from the start, grew ever more complex and error-prone. An attempt to deal with the increase in errors evolved into a complex approvals process, where everyone from the sales manager to the shipping department had to sign off on the sales order before it could be allowed to go through. Since this was an entirely paper-based system, the paper could get lost almost anywhere in the process.

LOOKING AT NOTES

It was clear something had to be done. Dave Kimball, President of Telepartner, instructed his staff to consider Notes as a way of addressing this problem. "We had been automating several of our other processes, and we always chose solutions that seemed appropriate for the particular need, but none of them

"

would talk to each other. We were always writing special utilities to bring things together. It seemed that Notes offered us most of the abilities we wanted to have, and we could get out of the business of writing conversion programs. Notes did force a few compromises on us—it wasn't the absolute best solution for the application, but it puts it all together."

They hired a consultant to help them build the Notes application.

THE PRODUCT DATABASE

The first problem that needed to be tackled was their list of products. They built a Product Information database for storing that list. Telepartner's database is a bit more complex than the average product list because Telepartner's product mix is more complex. They have arranged it into a hierarchy.

The first level of detail is the basic product family. The next level of detail is the type. This is a finer-level description of the area within the product family. Finally, there is a model number. This determines the general class of features available in the product, such as the communications protocol or software version number. All of this data is eventually summarized in a Telepartner part number, which is a long product code that completely specifies all these options. There is also a Description field, which is useful when reading the parts list and as a confirmation of the product ordered (since the description is included on the order form).

There is (surprisingly) only one view in this database. It is categorized by product line. Each product shows a product ID, the model number, and a description. Telepartner is considering adding a view that will help people to understand the logic behind the model number designations, but it hasn't been completely implemented yet. They could probably also benefit from adding some views that show products and prices, for rapid reference.

Had Telepartner implemented only this database, the system could have been called a success. The salespeople now had at their fingertips a complete reference for all Telepartner product numbers. Furthermore, updates to the product mix were instantly available. All a salesperson had to do is replicate the database to have a complete and up-to-date reference to all product information, including prices.

THE CUSTOMER DATABASE

The next step to implementing an order-entry system is to implement a contact manager, or at the very least a customer database. In order to provide an adequate amount of structure for handling the orders, Telepartner created a multilevel contact database. There are two levels of forms in the system. The first level is used to store the information corresponding to a particular facility of a corporation or entity. Telepartner calls it a Location Profile. The Location Profile contains fields with the corporate name, the name of the parent company (if any), and the mailing and business addresses of that location. It also contains some information about the facility's accounting department and some basic data about the networking environment in use at that site.

The next level of entry in the system is a Contact, or individual working at this particular location. It is composed as a Response to the Location Profile. In fact, the only way to create one is to press a button labeled Compose Contact from within the Location Profile form. The Contact form contains all the information about a single person, including title, phone number, e-mail address, and the Telepartner products that interest he or she the most.

The views in this database fall into two classes—by Location and by Contact. The Location views show each major business location with all of the contacts at each location. These can be sorted by company name, by the name of the Telepartner account executive, or by status (whether the customer is a distributor or end user). The contact views show only the contacts themselves, leaving out the location information. These views can be sorted by company name, account executive, or contact name (as in a traditional address book).

Telepartner uses this database not as a contact database, where every contact a salesperson makes gets entered, but only as a customer database. Only those who show enough interest to accept an evaluation unit or purchase a product will get entered into this database.

The customer database with sample customers

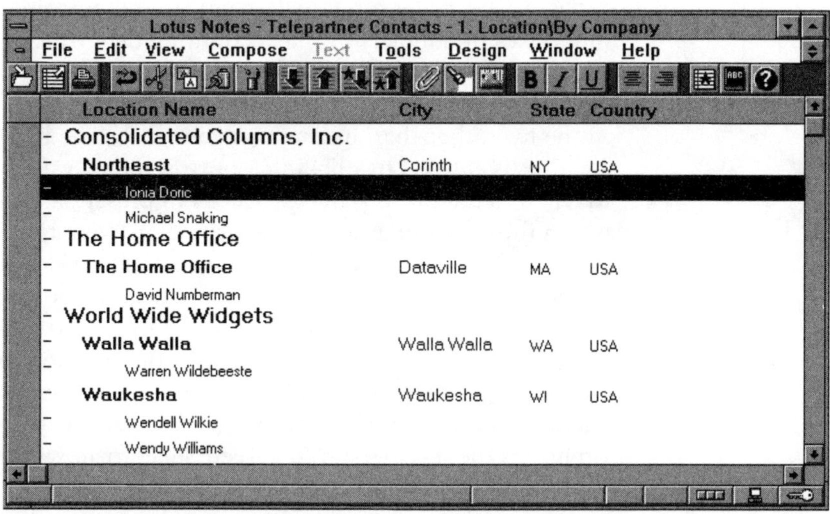

THE SALES ORDER DATABASE

Having successfully attacked the problems of the customer list and the product list, Telepartner was ready to move on to actually automating the sales order process. However, they first had to address the issue of basic process reengineering. The error-prone nature of their paper-based process had caused them to develop a rather cumbersome set of procedures that had to be followed in order to handle an order.

These procedures needed reevaluation, and the entire order process had to be carefully examined within the context of a Notes solution. Jeff Lee, Sales Director for Telepartner, said, "I can't emphasize enough how important it is to get the eventual end users of a system involved at the early stages. Being the sales department, there was no shortage of opinions around here. They're not always in agreement, but it's very important to take the aggregate set of opinions and implement that. Our first pass was a little rough because the salespeople weren't involved. However, it turned out to be very easy to fix—out of 33 problems we identified after the first round, the consultant was able to fix 30 of them in one day."

The result of this process reengineering cut out several of the required approvals from the sales process and streamlined several other parts as well. The final system is built around a single Sales Order form in the Sales Order database. At the top of the form is found the Ship To and Bill To information for the company placing the order. These items both come from the existing customer database—they are handled as automatic lookups.

The next portion of the form has to do with Telepartner's internal sales management functions. It identifies the salesperson involved, whether or not this is a new order, and such items as the customer purchase order number and names of contacts in the accounting department.

The next section has to do with what is actually being ordered. Because of the desire to have a form that automatically totals and looks up information on the fly, rather than having someone fill in the blanks in a table, each line of the form is entered by clicking a button that says Select A Product. The macro attached to the button then proceeds to present a series of prompts to the user, asking for such things as the item to be ordered, the quantity required, and the price (which defaults to the list price in the price list). The results are then pasted into a table that is stored on the Notes form. All the line items are placed into the correct locations on the form and automatically totaled.

Some of Telepartner's products are complex combinations of hardware and software, and need more information than can fit on their basic order form. There is a button on the form marked Compose Tech Sheet. Clicking this button brings the salesperson to a Tech Sheet form where they can fill out detailed technical information for those products that require it. This includes such items as network protocols, hardware interfaces, disk space, etc.

The last thing to be entered to complete the order is the customer's request for the means of shipment. At this point the salesperson has two choices. One is to save the form as a draft, which lets the order be put away temporarily pending further changes. The other is to submit the order for approval and further processing.

When the form is submitted, it's automatically saved in a database and marked with a status called Awaiting Sales Director Approval. An e-mail is automatically composed and mailed to the sales director saying that the order exists and asking him to approve it. He can then open the document, go to the section marked Sales Director Approval, and click a button marked either Reject or Approve. This changes the status in the document to Awaiting Accounting Approval and sends mail to the accounting department. Accounting then goes through the same process. Once accounting has approved the form, it's ready for shipment and gets mailed to the shipping department. They also have a chance to reject the order if there is insufficient technical information to complete it.

If anyone along the way rejects the order, the order gets set to a status of Re-routed to Account Executive for changes. The rejector must specify the

The Approval section of the Order form

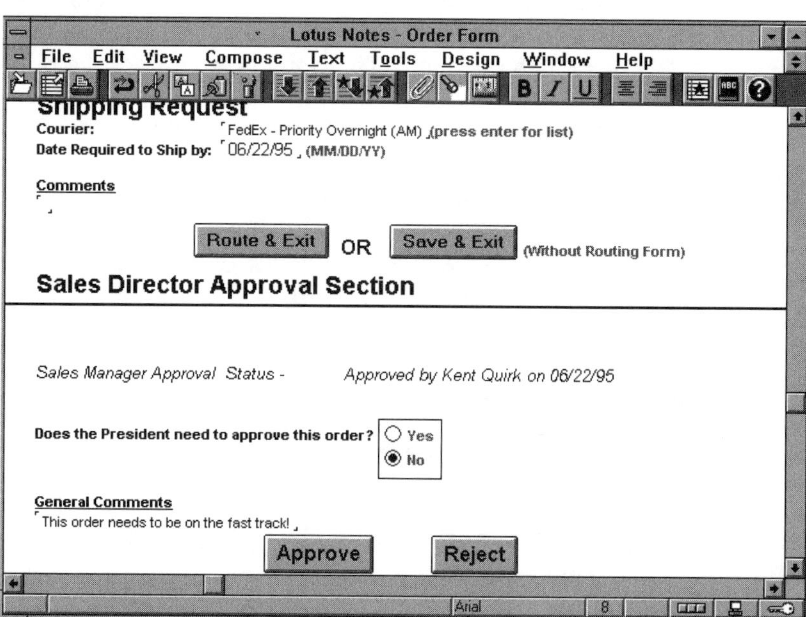

reason in a comments field. After the changes have been made, it is returned to the status from which it was rejected.

The database also supports entry of orders for temporary use of evaluation equipment. Because of the complexity of its product base, Telepartner often lends or rents equipment to its customers for product evaluation. Under their old paper-based system, it was very easy to lose customers in the evaluation process by not following up on the evaluations or by leaving the unit there longer than necessary. In the same database as the order-entry system, they also created an evaluation-entry system. The process of creating an evaluation order is nearly identical to that for a sales order. However, there are special fields for the length of the evaluation, as well as special status values for recording whether the evaluation was a success (resulted in an order) or not.

There are many views in this database. One of the most popular views shows the orders categorized by status, with totals at the view level for the total dollars at each status level. This particular view is especially appreciated by the sales and accounting departments, who can track total sales, as well as sales in process. The sales manager often uses a view showing orders sorted by salesperson, so that they can see individual account executive's sales by status, as well as a total dollar volume. There are also views by Date, by Company, and by Product, all of which let different constituencies get the information they need to do their jobs effectively. The same set of views exists for the evaluation orders. Finally, there is a view called Company Files that shows all orders or evaluations to any given company, showing the status of each.

There are a few problems with the system. One particular problem has to do with the implementation of the entry of the Bill To and Ship To portions of the order form. It currently requires that the company name be entered three times. This gets to be a bit tedious, and it annoys the users. It will be fixed in a future release of the form.

In general, the system is far easier to use than the old paper-based system; it also provides better data for tracking ongoing status of orders. They have had fewer errors caused by missing information, such as incorrect pricing or shipping the wrong configurations of equipment. Overall, people are very pleased with the results.

◣ **FACT SHEET**

Telepartner's Sales Order System

Purpose: To automate the entry, tracking, and storage of sales and evaluation orders for Telepartner's products.

Application Origin: Telepartner paid a consultant to do the development.

Application Development Time: Approximately 6 weeks.

Typical Size: 50 MB per year, with Telepartner's volume of sales.

Typical Use: The application has three major pieces:

▶ The Products database stores the complete list of Telepartner products, configurations, and prices.

▶ The Customer database stores the list of Telepartner customers and serious prospects.

▶ The Sales Order database actually tracks the orders, and uses the other two databases for lookup of reference information.

Forms: The Product form stores all the information about a particular Telepartner product, and is stored in the products database. The Location form tracks a particular customer facility. The Contact form stores data about the individuals who work at that facility. These are stored in the customer database. The Sales Order form and Evaluation Order form manage the entire order-entry process. The Sales Order form is manipulated by a series of people as it moves through the system.

Views: The product database has only one view: a summary of all the products organized by product line. The customer database has a variety of views, broken down into two categories, the Location view which shows companies and the contacts within them, while the Contact view shows only the contact information.

The Competitive Intelligence Database

Craddock Heavy Industries manufactures machinery for use in the construction and manufacturing industries in the United States. The (hypothetical) company has been in business for almost 100 years and was at one time unchallenged in its field. Over the last two decades, Craddock has seen a gradual erosion in its share of the market. This has been brought on primarily as a result of two forces—increased competition from abroad and restructured, more competitive domestic manufacturers. The company has been through years of turmoil while attempting to find a management team that can respond to these challenges. The current management team has determined a number of strategic objectives to help the company regain its once-preeminent position, including massive internal restructuring, a renewed emphasis on understanding the company's customers, and increased understanding of its competitors.

It is clear that Craddock Industries needs to begin the process of collecting *competitive intelligence*. Competitive intelligence is any information that Craddock can reference that gives it a better idea of its competitors' sales, marketing, or development plans. This information can be gathered at trade shows, through the mail, via the Internet, or from published periodicals. Accumulating and organizing this information are the keys to providing management with a clear understanding of their competition.

Craddock has deployed Notes in a number of different areas. All of the key managers who might be consumers of the competitive intelligence are already Notes users. As a result, the decision is made to attempt to gather—in complete or abstract form—documents for a Notes database that will allow these managers to keep tabs on the competition. The company decides to use two librarians from the Public Relations group, Jack Limpick and Fran Estapa, to manage the collecting and inputting of the information. Ira Keough, the company's primary developer of Notes applications, will build the application and help the librarians get started inputting the information. Ira will work directly with Liz Marcusa, a Vice President, to ensure that the developed application meets management's needs.

DEFINING REQUIREMENTS

The first step in any development project is to define the customer's requirements for the application. Ira sets up an initial meeting with Liz, Jack, and Fran to help identify a preliminary list of requirements. At the meeting, Ira focuses on understanding the inputs to the application (including what expected sources of information will be needed), outputs from the application (how management expects to use this information), and any special requirements (full-text search is essential).

Liz makes the point that the information contained in the database will be from a variety of different sources, such as periodicals, marketing/sales materials, and word of mouth. Jack points out that many of the periodicals are available from electronic newswires to which the company currently subscribes. Liz indicates that the major source of marketing/sales materials are from trade shows. This information will need to be scanned in to make it available in the database. Ira suggests that this might cause as many problems as it solves. First of all, to allow the information to be fully text-searchable, it will need to be run against an optical character recognition program. These programs are less than 100% accurate, and with the fancy fonts and pictures that appear in sales and marketing materials, much of the text will be lost. As a result, a compromise is reached where the first page will be scanned in, an abstract will be typed in by one of the librarians, and the document itself will be filed in the library.

After the meeting, Ira writes up a document summarizing the requirements he heard expressed in the meeting. This document is circulated to the team for review. Ira's document outlines a variety of views, and a small number of forms. Based on Liz's input, it seems likely that each view will list all documents. The proposed views are as follows: By Company, By Industry, By Region, By Product, By Sales, And By Author. Liz comments that the list is a good place to start, but is likely to change over time as processes become more institutionalized.

There will be three forms to start: Company Information, Document, and Comment. The Company Information form will be used to provide basic information on the company, like location, industry, size, and corporate officers. The Document form will be used to store articles from periodicals or newswires, and analyses including annual report information, and marketing and sales materials. Each of these different sources of information will be recorded in the document in a field called Source Type. The Comment form will be used by business people looking to provide some personal insight or information on a topic. Jack points out that comments might be Responses to other documents in the database ("One of my customers has purchased one of these products and it hasn't worked right yet."), or might be made outside the context of existing documents ("I called Larry yesterday and he says AcmeCo is coming out with a new killer product this quarter.").

BUILDING THE APPLICATION

Incorporating the other team members' comments, Ira starts development of the application. Ira's strategy is to develop the first version of the application quickly in an effort to get additional feedback from its users, and also to validate that the proposed input mechanisms (particularly in the case of the newsfeeds and scanned images) are practicable.

Ira starts the development process from a blank database. While many developers start with a preexisting template, Ira typically feels more comfortable building from scratch. In this manner, he can be assured that there are no surprises lurking behind a button or formula that he didn't write himself. First Ira creates the Company Information form. This form has a number of fields that will be used to organize the documents in views (e.g., location, industry, size, and products). The other two documents, Document and Comment, will be Response documents and will inherit the company name from the Company Information document. By keeping these other documents as Response documents, the organization of views is ensured, even if some of the corporate information (such as location) changes. Next, Ira builds the Comment form. This is a simple form containing the company name of the competitor, the topic, and the comment itself. The form is written as a Response document so that the document can be attached to existing documents. The purpose of the Comment form will be to comment on existing material. The database is not currently envisioned as a place for discussion. As a result, the Comment form is the only mechanism for users to input information into the system. Next, he creates the Document form. The Document form provides people (generally assumed to be the librarians) with the opportunity to put in articles, analyses, and reports related to the company in question. The form provides the author with a place to input the type of source material (e.g., newspaper article or annual report), a checkbox to indicate whether the information is an abstract or a complete document, an Agent field to input the name of the person who provided the document in the first place, and the body field to contain the document itself. Finally, Ira builds basic versions of the application's views. These versions display the documents sorted in the expected sorting order, but lack some of the finer points of view design such as appropriate categories, fonts, and colors.

Once this is complete, Ira populates the database with a number of sample documents and puts the database up on his local Notes server. Ira then asks each team member to provide him with feedback. In general, the reception is positive, and Ira makes some suggested changes and fine-tunes the database. This last step includes experimenting with fonts and colors, getting a flashy icon for the database, and putting in small bitmaps on each form. Once this is complete, Ira sends out a note indicating that Jack and Fran can begin the process of adding documents to the database.

LOADING THE DATA

Liz provides Jack and Fran with drawers full of files that she has kept in her desk. Out of these files, Jack and Fran decide that only a few documents are actually worth scanning—much of the material is outdated, and there are many empty folders that clearly contained something at one point. They scan in the chosen documents and input abstracts for the rest. In addition, they allocate a large section of their library space to store materials related to this project. They file each of Liz's papers in drawers organized by company name.

Craddock has just installed LN:DI—a Lotus application to help the company integrate scanned images into Notes. Documents are scanned into the database and run through the OCR program automatically. This allows users of the application to perform full-text searches against scanned documents stored in the database (insofar as the OCR process accurately recognizes words). There are many document imaging systems available in the market. LN:DI, like many of its competitors, offers companies the option of saving scanned images to CD-ROM. Storing the images to CD-ROM is beneficial in that once written, the information is basically permanent, and CD-ROMs are significantly less expensive than a similar amount of hard disk space. While there are other more powerful imaging solutions available, Craddock selected LN:DI because of its high level of integration with Lotus Notes. Jack and Fran scan the documents into the Notes database using LN:DI. For now, all documents will be stored on the server's hard disk—if the database becomes particularly large in the future, they will consider moving the scanned images to CD-ROM. The entire process of filing the documents, writing the abstracts, and scanning the images takes about two weeks. Liz's files covered about 20 companies and many years of information.

Jack and Fran have also started working on an automated method of getting newswire information incorporated into the application. Craddock currently subscribes to a number of different newsfeeds, many of which offer Notes-based services. In the short run, Jack and Fran decide to evaluate a number of different services in an effort to identify those which most closely match their needs. As Notes is not a real-time system, most services offer some level of prescreening before the data is shipped out. This attempts to ensure that the data sent out is directly relevant to the client's needs. After some discussion, Jack and Fran conclude that the key criteria in evaluating the different offerings will be the number of sources of data available, ease of integration into the application, and the flexibility and power of the company's prescreening engine. As a short-term solution, Jack and Fran get a subset of data from one of the vendors for evaluation purposes and use this to populate the database.

DEPLOYING THE APPLICATION

Once the preliminary data has been input, the application is ready for deployment. Ira updates the ACL to allow access to the relevant management personnel, and an e-mail is sent out to those personnel with a link to the database. Jack and Fran continue to input information from other managers' files and settle on two different newsfeeds to populate the databases. The two newsfeeds differ, in that one provides articles from daily newspapers and magazines, while the other focuses on research-oriented periodicals. The process of accumulating information is slow, due to the manual nature of so many of the procurement and input processes. Eventually, the application becomes perceived as an essential business resource by management.

View by Company in the Competitive Intelligence database

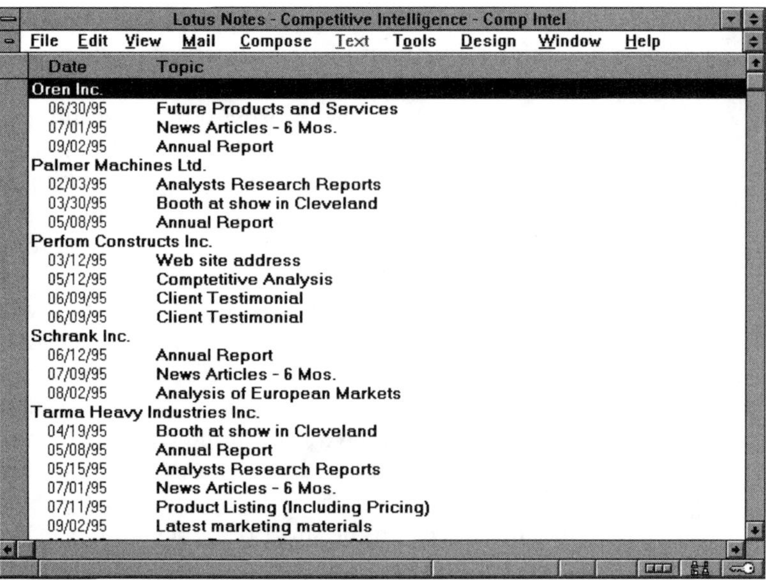

Unfinished Business

There are many other sources of information that might be included in the application. Of particular interest are World Wide Web sites that offer electronic copies of company brochures and announcements. This is a ripe source for inclusion in the Notes database. Other areas for expansion include trade show announcements, company annual reports, and product evaluations. All of these might help Craddock understand its competition and significant market trends better.

Fact Sheet

Competitive Intelligence Database

Purpose: To collect information regarding the company's chief competitors.

Application Origin: Started from scratch.

Application Development Time: 3 man-weeks.

Typical Size: Varies depending on the amount of scanned information. Scanned images can take a few hundred kilobytes to store. As a result, databases can grow rapidly.

Typical Use: Sales, marketing, and senior management contribute information about competitors' products, plans, and pricing which can help the company define strategy in these areas.

Forms: Company Information, Document, and Comment.

Views: By Company, By Industry, By Region, By Product, By Sales, and By Author.

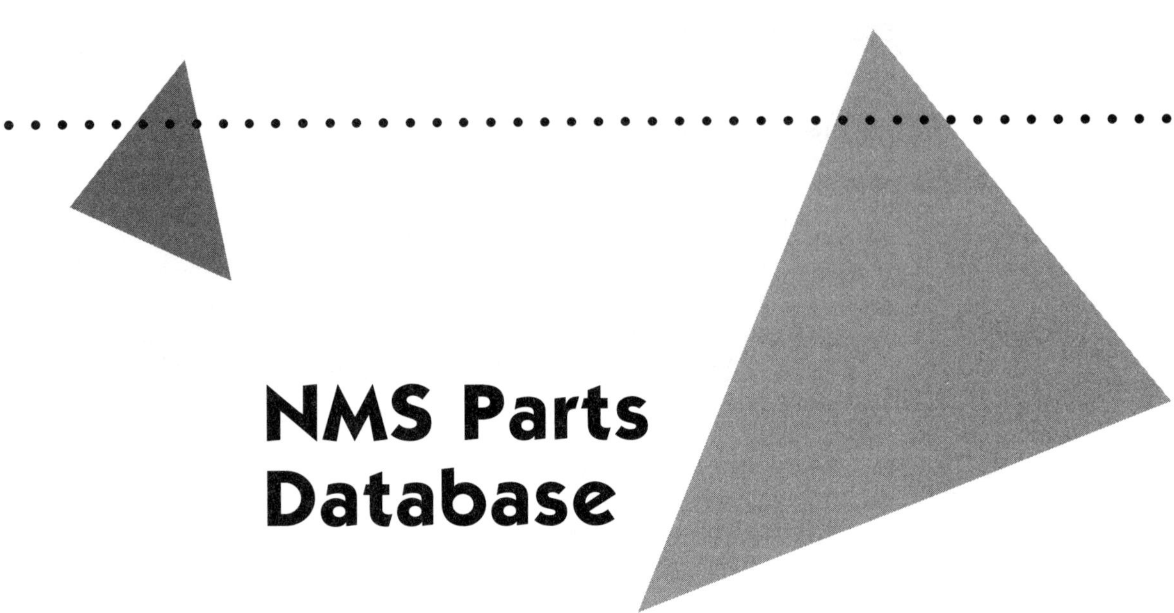

NMS Parts Database

Natural MicroSystems (NMS), based in Natick, Massachusetts, is the leading provider of open platforms for the integration of telephones and computers. NMS has an international list of clients that purchase their technology to build a wide variety of computerized telephone systems, from voice-mail products to telephone systems to automated calling computers.

Like any company producing electronic equipment, Natural MicroSystems has a standard list of electronic parts. Of the millions of components available from various vendors around the world, NMS uses only a couple of thousand in its own equipment. It's a lot of effort to keep track of the parts that are used.

THE LIFE CYCLE OF A COMPONENT

During the design phase of a new product, a circuit design engineer chooses the components that will be used to create a product. Many of these are already standard parts used in other products. But some will be new parts never before built into an NMS product.

When a new part is used it must first be assigned a unique part number specific to NMS. It's not possible to use the manufacturer's part number, because the manufacturers change. The market for electronic components is highly competitive, and equivalent components are often available from many manu-

---

Screen shots courtesy of Natural MicroSystems Corp., Natick, MA.

facturers. In specifying a part, an engineer will try to find two or three equivalent parts from manufacturers.

After the product is ready to be manufactured, the purchasing agent examines the parts list, tries to find more vendors for the part, and then places an order for them. The receiving department checks to make sure that the parts received are the ones that were ordered. Finally, the manufacturing department (or an offsite manufacturer) will place the parts into the product.

During this process, the part is placed on a list of standard components. Engineers will consult this list during the design process in an attempt to use already-approved components in new designs. Purchasing uses the list as the basis for buying parts. Receiving and manufacturing departments use it as a reference to make sure they're handling the right part.

In a paper-based system, such as the one that NMS was using before 1995, this parts list can grow quite unwieldy. With multiple copies, each copy having several thousand pages of reference material, it is easy for the lists used in different groups to get out of synchronization. NMS has found a way to do the job in Notes.

THE PARTS DATABASE

Components can also be assembled at a higher level than a single part—they can be a circuit board or subassembly, a manual, a diskette, or even a whole product. These items also go into the corporate parts list.

The Parts database NMS built uses a single form for each part type—component, assembly, diskette, manual, product, and so on. Each form is tailored to prompt for the specific information needed to handle that type of part.

The Component form is the most sophisticated. Creating a new Component form, or a new part form of any type, triggers a lookup into the existing Parts database. A new component number is automatically created in the proper sequence. This can be overridden if a specific part number is desired.

Normally, an engineer creates a new Component document during the design phase of a new product. When filling out this form, the engineer will first enter a description of the component.

The Component form has fields for specific features common to many different types of components. For example, passive electronic parts usually have a value (the measurement of the part's primary attribute, such as electrical resistance). Electronic rating, size, tolerance, and composition are all important for various types of components, so they have their own fields. Since these are typically standard items for given classes of parts, NMS has used keyword fields here to make selection of these elements faster and more consistent.

The Type field is a two-part field—the first part specifies the particular mounting style of component—whether it is intended to be inserted into a hole in the circuit board (THRU-HOLE) or mounted on the surface (SMD). The

A Component form being filled out

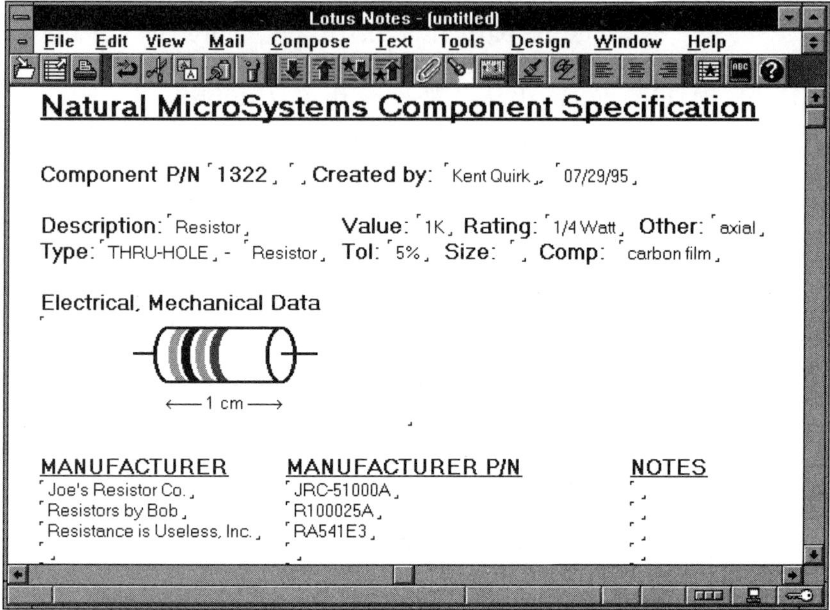

second part defines the particular component type, such as Resistor, Capacitor, or Integrated Circuit. There are some 50 component types in a keyword list.

In the first version of this database, the field marked Electrical, Mechanical Data was a simple text field. But in a paper parts list, the part description is often just a photocopy of a page from the component catalog. So the field became a Notes Rich Text field. It is often filled with scanned images from the vendors' component catalogs.

SCANNING THE GLOBE

Anytime someone starts talking about adding lots of scanned images to a database, the big worry becomes the size of the database. NMS was concerned about this, and first made sure to install the database on a separate server with enough power to handle this application. Second, they defined the priorities for the information that would be included in the scan:

▶ The purchasing department needs information on qualifications for an equivalent part. The scanned image should include enough to allow them to make that judgement.

▶ The receiving department needs to be able to check that the part is the correct one. This often requires showing an image of the physical dimensions of the part.

▶ The engineering department needs reference information (though this is lower priority, since they usually have this information readily available in any case).

Finally, there is a list of sources for these parts. The engineer will fill out the information gathered from the parts catalogs—each known manufacturer, along with the part number that manufacturer uses for this component, and any comments about the manufacturer or that part. These are all Rich Text fields.

The last fields on the form control notification. When a part document has been completed, it can be mailed automatically to the purchasing department and any other concerned people. This helps to account for the workflow piece of this puzzle. The notification message says "NOTICE: The above NMS part number has changed. Please check the NMS parts database ASAP."

There is a special version of the Component form called a Critical Component. Some components need special regulatory approval, so they cannot easily be substituted in a design, nor can they easily be supplied by a different manufacturer. This Critical Component form flags the parts differently, and is also noticeably different when viewed on screen. This warns people that making changes to this component is best done carefully.

Subassemblies are a collection of components formed into one logical, premanufactured unit. The *Bill of Materials* (BOM) is the list of all the parts required to build a subassembly—it is generated automatically by the component design software. Until this database arrived, finding the correct revision of the BOM for a given subassembly was often difficult. Now, the Subassembly form in the Notes database has a place to store the BOM. Since there's a new copy of the form made for every revision of the subassembly, there is also a new copy of the BOM, permanently associated with the revision level.

People will often enter information for several parts at once. To make it simpler to create a lot of part documents in one session, the form has buttons at the bottom that save the current document and create a new one of the specified type.

VIEWS

There are several views in the parts database. Engineers looking for particular components will often use the view By Component Type. This view shows only the Component documents, sorted by the Component Type field. This way, all of the similar components come together, so it's simple for someone looking for a certain component type to tell whether it already exists in the database.

The database is full-text indexed allowing people to search by fields not brought out into the views, such as manufacturer name.

The other major views, used more often by purchasing or manufacturing departments, are the view sorted by NMS Part Number, and the view sorted first by Part Type and then by Part Number.

There are also views By Author and By Date, which are almost always included in Notes databases. They can be useful for helping people to locate documents they worked on, when they don't necessarily remember everything about them.

◢ FACT SHEET

Natural MicroSystems Parts Database

Purpose: To track a list of electronic components and other parts used in a company's set of products.

Application Origin: Custom developed.

Application Development Time: Approximately 1 month in development, continuously improved with experience in the database and in the use of Notes.

Typical Size: 26 MB, 2,200 documents.

Typical Use: Engineers enter the parts during the design phase; purchasing staff select authorized vendors; the manufacturing department uses the database as a reference during product planning.

Forms: Various types of part forms—components, manuals, diskettes, and assemblies. Each form is customized to the needs of that particular part type; all parts have a unique corporate part number and description.

Views: Component view helps engineers to find parts in a particular class. Views by Part Number and Part Type help purchasing and manufacturing departments to track the information they need to ship a product.

Linking Multiple Stores Together: The Inventory Database

A chain of retail stores often starts as a single store. The store's success supports a second, and then a third. When the chain becomes dozens of stores, big computer systems may be used to centralize their inventory, ordering, communications, and so on. Until that point, when only a few stores or so are in operation, the stores face challenges such as how to communicate with each other, and how to know what inventory each store has on hand at the moment.

The issue of inventory can be a particularly crucial one for stores, since an unfilled order may send a customer directly to a competitor. With a small chain, it is likely that another store in the chain has the item the customer wants. This means that a store that has run short of an item will often call the others looking to see which store can help fill a customer's order. The more efficient this process is, the less critical it becomes that each store carry surplus items (which always come at a great cost).

Today's Shoes is a (hypothetical) small chain of a half-dozen independent shoe stores started by David Chopp, who still manages the original store. The stores buy inventory from a variety of manufacturers and distributors. Since they carry many product lines, keeping every model and size of every shoe in inventory is an impossible task. The stores commonly help each other out by filling holes in each other's inventory to fulfull a particular customer's need. In this chapter we follow Today's Shoes as they use Notes to facilitate communication between their stores, particularly in regard to inventory.

BUT I NEED A SIZE 10!

David Chopp is on the phone with Kate O'Connor. David manages the first location of Today's Shoes, and Kate O'Connor runs another Today's Shoes near by. David explains that he has a customer who wants a particular shoe in size 10, but he's out of that size. Does Kate have any in stock? Kate has David hold on while she checks the computer. Yes, she does. David asks her to put them aside so one of his workers can pick them up later. After hanging up, David explains to the customer that he can have the shoes the next day. The customer is satisfied, and the sale is saved.

After wishing the customer a good day, David has a moment to think about how often he makes sales in this manner. Today's Shoes carries over a dozen different manufacturers' product lines, and it's impossible to have every size of every line in stock. Even if his store were big enough, the inventory cost would be outrageous. So he and the other half-dozen Today's Shoes are constantly calling each other. This process works fairly well, except David feels it could be greatly improved.

One issue is simply the overhead involved in calling each store in turn to see if the store has the model and size the customer wants. The customer must wait while someone at the other end of the phone tracks down the shoes, and after waiting through half a dozen phone calls the answer could turn out that no store has the shoe in stock. David doesn't like keeping the customers waiting, nor does he appreciate the amount of time involved.

The other issue that bothers David is that of image. All of the Today's Shoes stores have computerized their inventory, and David likes the image of his store as a modern store. He likes to impress customers by going to the computer to see what's in stock. But since the computers at each store only support that store, he cannot use the computer to see what's in stock at the other stores. Therefore he must make "old-fashioned" phone calls in front of the customer to track down inventory. David would prefer a more modern method to solve the problem—fax, e-mail, satellite—anything to impress the customer.

David decides to call Kate back to discuss this with her. Kate agrees that some type of computerization could improve their stores' efficiency and image. Since neither knows exactly how to proceed, they decide to call in a consultant who can lay out their options.

DOES NOTES FIT, AND HOW?

Mike Weiss is the consultant David and Kate contact. Mike helped them originally set up their in-house computer system to track inventory and other things. David and Kate explain that they would like some way to link the stores electronically so each store can find out what the other store has for inventory.

Mike asks a few probing questions to find out exactly what they want and how much they are willing to invest. Do they want to completely centralize their computer operations, combining all the stores' inventory, point-of-sale, accounts receivable and payable, general ledger, payroll, and other functions into one computer system with remote links? This option could give the biggest payoff if the chain grows very large, but requires a large investment to purchase and set up equipment, transfer existing data and processes to the new system, retrain people, and so on. David and Kate explain that they are not looking for such a drastic infrastructure improvement at this time.

Mike then asks how accurate the cross-store inventory queries must be. He wants to know what the cost is if, on occassion, the computerized view of another store's inventory is wrong. Mike explains that if high accuracy is needed, the inventory will need to be centralized, and the point-of-sale system will need to interact with the centralized inventory. On the other hand, if the occasional mismatch is acceptable, a simpler and less expensive approach can be followed. David explains that he would prefer starting with as simple a mechanism as possible.

At this point, Mike begins thinking that Notes could be a good solution to Today's Shoes' problem. Notes is good at grouping data from multiple sites together when the high accuracy of transaction processing is not needed. Mike explains that installing a Notes server at each store might be the most cost-effective and flexible solution. He explains his idea:

"Each store has its own inventory computerized, but does not have access to the other stores' inventories. Each store could install a Notes server, and an automated process could periodically transfer the current inventory from the existing computer system, or *legacy system,* into Notes. The Notes servers would be set up to replicate frequently, so that within a couple of hours each Notes server would have all the stores' inventories. That way workers at each store can use their local Notes server to access every store's inventory."

David and Mike have talked about Notes before, and he likes the idea of bringing in Notes. David asks how the Notes servers would communicate, and Mike explains that they would use modems to transfer data over a normal business line, and that a new line might need to be purchased so the Notes communication does not interfere with other business communication. David then asks if each store needs a server, or if he could set up one server and have clients at each location dial in. Mike then explains the standard trade-offs between those two scenarios, and convinces David that the multiple-server approach makes sense. It will require fewer telephone lines, and will provide better scalability. The better scalability will be especially useful if, as David hopes, Today's Shoes grows to become a chain of dozens of stores. These tradeoffs are discussed in the sidebar, "Multiple Servers."

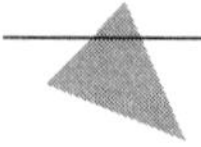

Multiple Servers

Notes is a client/server product, where the servers support users in accessing databases, sending and receiving mail, and handling the many administrative aspects of a Notes network. Because Notes has so many features geared toward handling a network of servers—that is, multiple servers, it is natural to wonder why you may need more than one, how many will you need, how do they get interconnected, and so on.

There are several reasons why a company might need more than one Notes server.

One big reason to get multiple Notes servers is to support many users. A Notes server can support somewhere between 50 and 100 simultaneous users, depending on the type of hardware the server is running on, the applications users are using, and other factors. If more users try to access the server than it can handle, the performance that users perceive will degrade—eventually to the point of making Notes unusable. At this point, another Notes server is required.

Another big reason to get multiple Notes servers is to support a geographically dispersed set of users. Imagine one group of users in New York and another in California. While one server may have enough capacity for all these users, where would you put it? If it is in New York, the users in California will have to dial long distance to reach it. If it is in California, the New York users have the same problem. No matter where you put it, you're looking at *huge* communication charges. To solve this, a Notes server would be put in New York and another would be put in California. This way all users could access a server locally (either via a local area network or a local phone call). The servers then periodically replicate with each other, limiting the long distance charges to the efficient interserver replication.

One final reason often found in large companies is the "We want our own server" reason. Often a department in a large company will decide to explore the potential of Notes by setting up their own Notes server, without looking first to see if they can share an existing one. This can result in many more servers being implemented than are actually required, at first. However, in the long run this is probably a good strategy, as it educates a larger pool of people in Notes administration, and ensures that there is extra capacity for the moment when Notes really starts to take off in the organization. The thing to watch out for here is having each department create its own "organizational certifier," since this always appears as the last part of each user's name and usually indicates the company the user works for. The best advice is to coordinate Notes deployments between departments to minimize downstream naming and security hassles.

Mike goes on to explain some of the other advantages of deploying Notes. In particular, he explains how Notes will support discussion databases and e-mail to help faciliate communication between the owners, managers, and other employees of Today's Shoes. David and Kate like the idea and ask Mike to put together a proposal.

LINKING THE LEGACY SYSTEM AND NOTES

Mike prepares his proposal for deploying Notes to Today's Shoes. For the most part everything is standard. Each site gets a Notes server. The Notes servers replicate on a hub-and-spoke system with frequent replications. (Mike will suggest every hour at first and then a study to see if the frequency should be changed.) The only real challenge is how to get the inventory out of the stores' existing computer system and into Notes.

Since Mike helped put in the first system, he knows that the system has the ability to export its inventory to flat files, simple data files that any program can easily interpret. He contacts the system vendor to find out how to schedule this export to occur every hour. Mike also knows that the existing system uses standard Windows networking, and so he knows Notes can access the flat file by mounting the legacy system's file system.

The last challenge is how to get the exported data into Notes. Mike is aware of a variety of solutions. He knows that the Notes API could be used to write a server *add-in task*. This add-in task could run on the Notes server every hour and read in the latest exported inventory data to a Notes database. Mike also knows there are off-the-shelf products such as InfoPump and Zmerge that can import data into Notes. Mike decides to contact a programmer he knows, and depending on the cost of developing a custom add-in task compared to the cost of buying and programming an off-the-shelf product, Mike will make the appropriate recommendation to David and Kate.

Mike then thinks about how to store the data in Notes and how to present it to users. Since the users are likely to be only part-time Notes users, he decides to keep the database as simple as possible. He designs a database with one form, the Shoe Model Inventory form. This form will indicate the store and the shoe manufacturer/model for which the form contains data. It will then contain the list of shoe sizes and number in stock for each size within that model.

He then designs a couple of views to make it easy to see whether another store has a particular shoe in stock. He designs a view called By Store, which categorizes the inventory by store. Within each store the view sorts the shoes by manufacturer/model. This means that a user can open the view, select the store, and then find the manufacturer/model a customer wants to see if that store has the desired size in stock.

He designs another view called By Manufacturer/Model, which categorizes the inventory by the shoes' manufacturer/models. Within each Manufacturer/Model, the view sorts the shoes by store. This means that a user can open the view, select the manufacturer/model a customer wants, and then see which store has the desired shoe in stock.

The By Manufacturer/Model view in the Inventory database

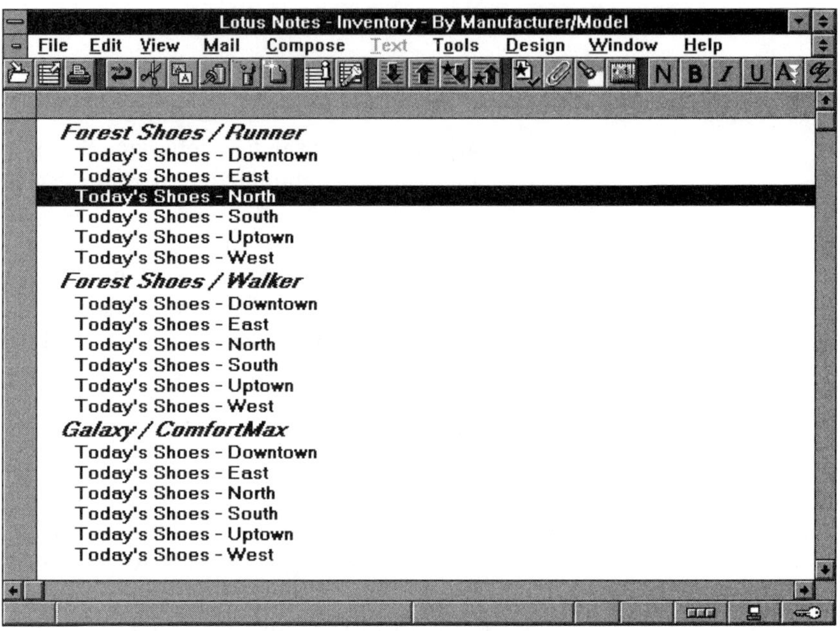

DEPLOYING THE INVENTORY DATABASE

Mike presents his proposal to David and Kate a couple of weeks later. His proposal includes:

▶ A Notes server at each site.

▶ A new phone line at each site for replication.

▶ The legacy system periodically exports its inventory to a flat file on a file system mounted by the Notes server.

▶ An off-the-shelf package imports this data to a Notes database called the Inventory database.

▶ The Inventory database provides two simple views to make it easy for workers to be trained to use it.

▶ Remote administrative support be provided on contract by Mike's firm.

Mike demonstrates a prototype Inventory database on a notebook computer he brings to the proposal meeting. David and Kate are impressed with the capabilities of the system and the reasonable cost and decide to go ahead with the proposal.

A few months later, the Notes servers and phone lines have been installed and the inventory of each store is stored in the Inventory database. The workers have been trained to locate a shoe by simply opening up the Inventory database in Notes and scaning all the stores' inventory to see which store has the shoe.

David enjoys the modern image the use of Notes brings to the store, and especially enjoys the lack of irritating phone calls to other stores while the customer waits to see if he can get them the shoes they want.

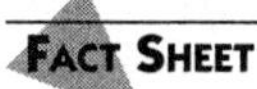

Fact Sheet

Inventory Database

Purpose: To link the inventories of more than one retail store to facilitate filling customer orders as efficiently as possible.

Application Origin: This application is an integration of legacy system data with a simple, custom Notes database.

Application Development Time: The Notes application is developed in a week. The legacy-system-to-Notes data transfer is developed in a week. Two weeks of integration and testing are done, and then a month trial is done to monitor and tune the system performance.

Typical Size: 5 MB for half a dozen stores.

Typical Use: Stores in a chain, where it is more important for one store to help another make a sale than to let that store lose the customer to another chain.

Forms: There is one form, the Shoe Model Inventory form. This form contains the store and the shoe manufacturer/model. The form also stores the number of shoes in stock for each size in the model.

Views: The By Store view categorizes the inventory by store and then sorts by the shoe's manufacturer/model. The By Manufacturer/Model view categorizes the inventory by manufacturer/model, and then sorts by the store the form pertains to.

Collecting Customer Feedback

The deployment of Notes-based applications inside a company becomes increasingly easy as the initial learning curve is overcome and as the company develops tools and procedures to support Notes-based applications. It is natural for a company that initially deployed Notes for a specific function to find that, over time, more and more functions are migrated to Notes.

Pretty Face is an example of such a company. Pretty Face is a large door-to-door cosmetics firm that has provided its sales force with notebook computers running Notes. The sales force uses Notes to enter orders, look up product information, exchange e-mail with co-workers, and support a variety of other functions. They are about to deploy another Notes application to support customer opinion surveys.

Customer opinion surveys are currently mailed directly to customers, some of whom will complete and return them. Pretty Face is looking for a way to get a higher volume of data back from these surveys, while reducing the overhead of processing the returned paper surveys. To meet these desires, they have decided to build the Customer Opinion application for use by their sales force.

LEARNING A NEW APPLICATION

Terry Rice has been a saleswoman for Pretty Face cosmetics since the days when they still used paper catalogs and order forms. While she had a hard time adjusting to using the computer and using Lotus Notes at first, she is now quite comfortable with switching between applications, using different views to find the information she needs, and finding various forms to fill out by looking in the Compose menu.

She has been called to a meeting by her local sales manager, Shirley Melnik, who is telling her salespeople about the new Customer Opinion application being deployed. Shirley explains that the old way of collecting customer opinions was done by mailing out survey forms and processing the handwritten responses. She points out some of the problems with doing surveys this way.

One problem is the low response rate. Only a fraction of the people who receive the surveys actually fill them out and return them. This is expensive because money is wasted printing and mailing surveys to people who just throw them in the garbage. This also makes it difficult to get a statistically significant amount of information back in order to make sound business decisions.

Another problem is the cost of handling completed surveys. Since customers fill them out by hand, they must be entered into the computer by Pretty Face staff before the data can be processed. This is not only expensive, but probably error-prone as the data entry staff tries to read the customer's handwriting.

Shirley explains that Pretty Face has decided to try a different approach to customer surveys. They have decided to have the sales force survey the customers directly and enter the customer responses into Notes forms. These forms will be automatically sent to headquarters every day during the salespeople's normal daily replication. She brings up Notes on her desktop computer and shows everybody the new Customer Opinion application.

Before Shirley gets too far, she is interrupted by a question. One of the salespeople wants to know if there are any incentives for doing this. "I'm pretty busy during the day, and so are my customers. Do we get anything for filling out these surveys? Can I give my customers a special deal for spending the time?" Shirley explains that the details of the incentives haven't been worked out yet, but that headquarters is going to do something. They will probably provide credit to the salespeople for completing the surveys, which they can use in turn to provide free or discounted products to their customers.

Shirley then points out the new icon on her workspace for the Customer Opinion application. She explains that the bulk of the application is located under the Compose menu, where all of the survey forms can be found. "When you have a customer willing to complete a survey, find the appropriate form under the Compose menu and fill it out. When you're done, the form will be automatically mailed to headquarters. It will stay in your mailbox like your other mail until the next time you replicate."

Shirley then goes on to explain the different types of surveys that can be found under the Compose menu. "There are three different types of surveys. Some are specific to a particular product, some are used for a type of product, and some are used for a product line.

"The Compose menu has a submenu for each product line. If headquarters has created a survey form for a particular product, you'll find it under the product line's submenu. For example, here you see the submenu for the To-day's Colors line of lipstick. Under this submenu, you see a few surveys for the lipsticks we carry by Today's Colors.

"Whenever possible, try to find one of these product-specific surveys to be filled out. They provide the most valuable data to headquarters. I expect that these forms will come with the highest incentives to you for filling them out.

"If you can't find a product-specific form to cover a product on which you would like to provide feedback, look at the Product Types submenu here in the Compose menu. Under the Product Types submenu you'll find surveys for types of products, like this one for Lipsticks or this one for Eye Liners.

"There is one last type of form, which is the Product Line form. If you cannot find a product-specific survey form, and the product you want to provide feedback on is not covered by the Product Types surveys, you can fill out a Product Line survey. As you saw before, each product line has a submenu in the Compose menu. In each of these submenus you'll find a generic Product Line survey you can fill out. It will contain questions about the product line in general and will provide places to answer questions about specific products in that product line."

Shirley then spent some time showing the salespeople how to compose the different types of forms. She showed them how, when they exit a form, they are asked if they want to mail it. They should generally say Yes, unless the form is incomplete. In that case, they can say No and come back to the form later. Shirley shows them the My Surveys view, which shows the surveys that the particular salesperson has filled out. She explains that if a survey must be saved in an incomplete state, this view can be used to find it. "Simply edit the form again, finish filling out the data, and then exit the form. This time when you are asked if you want to mail it, say Yes." Shirley completes a form, chooses to mail it, and then opens her local outgoing mail box to show every-one that the survey is there waiting to be sent to the server.

"There is one more thing I'll tell you and then we can call it quits," Shirley tells her salespeople. "There is a view called General Information that you should check out from time to time. It will contain instructions on filling out new forms that are put in the database. It will also contain information about the incentives that will be offered for filling out surveys. You will also receive mail when new incentives are announced, or when headquarters wants a par-ticular product or product line surveyed."

With that the meeting breaks up. Terry heads home and plugs her note-book computer into the phone line. She dials the server and find the server copy of the Customer Opinion application, which she then replicates to her notebook. In a little while, the replication is done and she is exploring her copy of the database, seeing which products already have survey forms. She sees a couple that she can use tomorrow when she visits Barbara Evans, one of her best clients.

MAY I ASK YOU A FEW QUESTIONS?

The next day, Terry tells Barbara about the new way that Pretty Face is handling the survey forms. Barbara says that she never bothered to fill out the surveys she received by mail, but would not mind chatting with Terry about some of the products she uses. Terry turns on her computer and goes into the Customer Opinion application. She tells Barbara that there is a survey form for the Today's Colors line of lipstick, which she uses. Terry composes a new survey form by finding the Today's Colors submenu and then the Lipstick form.

The first part of the form contains general questions about the customer. Terry knows most of the answers and fills them out quickly with a little help from Barbara. They ask how long the customer has been a Pretty Face customer, how old the customer is (roughly), approximately how much the customer spends a year on cosmetics, and so on. The next part of the survey is the questions specific to Today's Colors lipstick. Terry reads off the questions—covering details such as what color(s) Barbara likes and dislikes, how the lipstick feels when going on, how long it lasts, and enters Barbara's responses. There is room at the bottom for general comments, and Terry enters some of the things Barbara has said that don't fit into the other survey questions. When the form is complete Terry closes it, and answers Yes when asked if she wants the form to be mailed.

A product specific customer survey form in the Customer Opinion application

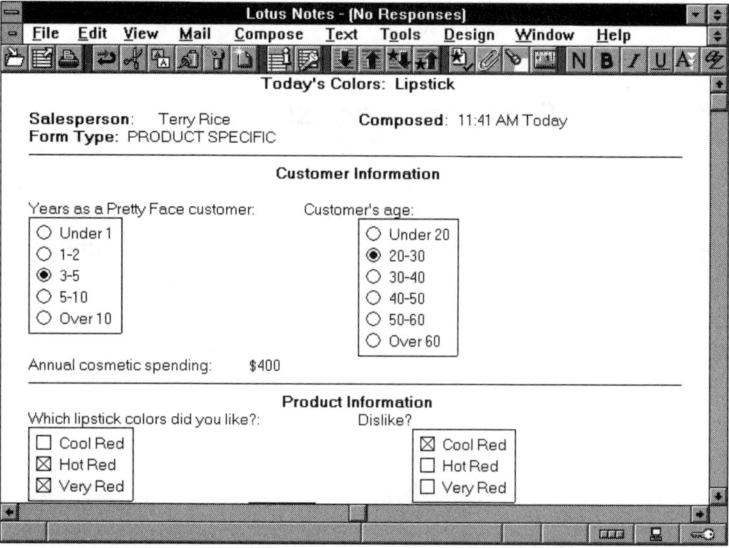

Terry then fills out a couple more surveys with Barbara. At the end of the meeting Terry gives Barbara some free products to thank her for her time. Terry looked in the General Information view of the database earlier and saw that to get people to use the database, headquarters is offering some free products for the first surveys each person fills out.

Later that day, when Terry is back home, she replicates with the server. Then she checks her mailbox to see if she has any mail. She reads and responds to her mail and then checks the general view of the Customer Opinion application. There is a new message there from headquarters about the surveys. She reads the message, which contains some additional instructions and a note about the new forms that have just been added to the database.

A couple of months later, a mail message is sent to all Pretty Face salespeople saying that headquarters wants to gather as much data as possible on a new line of cosmetics that they began distributing six months ago. They need to decide whether to continue with the line, and so they want as many survey forms completed as possible by the deadline three weeks later. The message also describes some of the incentives being offered for completed surveys, including a $250 bonus for the 10 people returning the most surveys. Terry switches to the Customer Opinion application and reviews the surveys in the new product line's submenu. She has many clients who have tried these products, and so she decides to go for the $250 bonus.

She spends the next couple of days working from home and making calls to her clients. She asks them if they need anything and if they'd answer a few questions about the new product line. In a couple of days she's got dozens of survey forms completed and mailed to the survey. Over the next couple of weeks she gathers many more.

CONGRATULATIONS!

At the next meeting with her local sales manager, Terry is congratulated by Shirley and awarded one of the $250 bonus checks for completing so many customer surveys for the new product line. Shirley thanks everyone for using the new Customer Opinion application and tells everyone that headquarters has been delighted with its use. She says there are more incentives coming soon, and that later in the year, headquarters is planning on doing a large, comprehensive survey of their customers—and there will be excellent incentives for participating.

Fact Sheet

Customer Opinion Application

Purpose: To provide a convenient way for a sales force to survey customers and provide feedback electronically.

Application Origin: Custom developed.

Application Development Time: The basic design of the database took one week. Each survey form takes a few days to develop and test.

Typical Size: Only forms completed by a specific salesperson are stored on the salesperson's computer. The typical size is less than 5 MB. The forms are mailed to a mail-in database for processing. That mail-in database will not get big because the forms are removed soon after they arrive.

Typical Use: Companies that place a high value on customer feedback and can motivate the sales force to complete customer feedback forms.

Forms: There are forms for specific products, forms for product lines, and forms for each general type of product. The forms contain sections for general customer information and sections for specific product feedback information.

Views: The General Information view is used to store information about the surveys like instructions and special incentives for completing them. The My Surveys view shows the surveys filled out by the user that are either completed or still being worked on.

Matching Buyers with Sellers: The Used Cars Database

Sometimes Notes is used in an application that might also use a standard relational database manager. Sometimes the key difference is whether people, programs, or both need access to the data. In situations where both people and programs need access, it might be prudent to use Notes. Once the user is trained in the Notes user interface, he will know how to use any particular application and to do things like full-text searches on the data.

Tom Bergin hit on the idea of providing a service where used car sellers and buyers can find each other. He knew he would need to store data about cars people were selling or looking to buy. He also knew that his staff would need to be able to search the data looking for matches and that he would need to write programs to search for matches. To meet all of these needs, Tom decided to implement the Used Cars application in Notes.

DESIGNING THE USED CARS DATABASE

Tom's idea was straightforward. He would offer a service where people could list used cars they wanted to sell or to buy. Both buyers and sellers could call in and find out whether there were any matches.

Tom would write a program to run continuously against the data, looking for matches between buyers and sellers. It would report matches back to the database.

When a buyer or seller called, one of Tom's staff could look in the database for computer-generated matches. If there weren't any, the employee could search by various views on the data or by full-text index search to see if any matches could be found.

Because his staff would need to be able to search the data, Tom chose to store the data in a Notes database. Notes provides an easy-to-use interface and has built-in, full-text index searching. He knew he could write a program using the Notes API or other tools.

To design the Used Cars database, Tom began thinking about the information he would have to store about a seller. He made a list of things like make, model, and year of the car, mileage, accident history, asking price, and overall condition of the car. He defined possible values for each item so that views could be sorted by the item easily, and searches could be easily performed. For example, for the accident history he decided to support the values No Accidents; Minor Fender-Bender—No Damage; Minor Fender-Bender—Minor Damage; and Major Accident. He also included fields where people could be descriptive. For example, in addition to the accident categories, he included an accident description field where someone could enter, "The car was in an accident, but only body work was needed. It was fully restored." Of course, Tom also included fields about the seller such as name and phone number. He even added a field indicating whether it is OK to give out the phone number.

Then Tom thought about the information he would need to store about buyers. In addition to the buyer's name and phone number, he would need to store things like price range, make, model, and year range. He decided to store a field indicating whether the buyer would accept a car that had been in a minor accident or a major accident. He included a minimum condition field, where a buyer could express the desire to buy cars that are in at least "good" condition.

When Tom had identified his data he built two forms in which to store it. To store data about a car being sold, he designed a Car Profile form. To store data about a buyer's desires, he designed a Car Wanted form.

Next Tom decided to design the views that his staff, as well as his programs, could use in searching for matches. His first concern was for his staff. When they have a buyer on the phone, he wants to make sure they can easily see whether there are any Car Profiles in the database meeting the buyer's criteria. When they have a seller on the phone, he wants to make sure his staff can easily see if any buyers have registered any Car Wanted forms that match the description of the buyer's car.

First Tom thinks about when a buyer calls. The buyer's first concern is probably price, so a view that categorizes cars by price range makes sense. However, instead of price, the buyer's primary concern might be the make and model, so Tom designs a view to categorize cars by make and model as well. Tom continues to design several more views grouping the Car Profiles in different ways.

Next Tom considers a typical seller's call. A seller is probably not interested in a list of 100 people looking for cars in his price range. The seller wants to know if there are a few buyers looking specifically for a car like his. Tom creates a couple of views that categorize on multiple categories, such as Make Wanted/Model Wanted/Price Range Wanted, or Make Wanted/Model

The By Price Range view in the Used Cars database

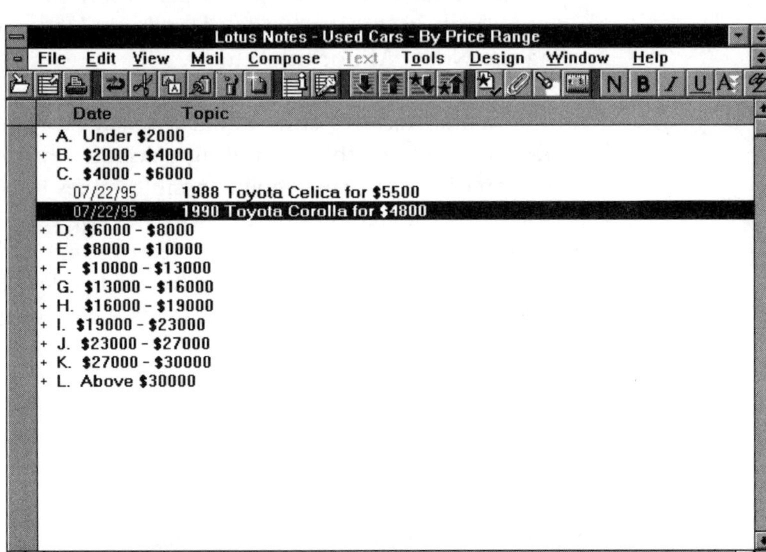

Wanted/Year Wanted, so his staff can locate close matches between buyer and seller.

Tom then thinks about the program he will write to find matches. He knows that when a match is found it will need to be stored somewhere. He decides to store the match back into the Used Cars database, so his staff will have only one place to go for any type of information. He then designs views to make it easy to find the matches. He designs a Matches By Seller view, which categorizes matches by the seller's name, and he designs a Matches By Buyer view, which categorizes matches by the buyer's name. When a seller or buyer calls, Tom's staff will then easily be able to find all the matches generated for that person. To store the match, Tom designs a Match form, with fields for the buyer's name, the seller's name, the date the match was found, a Match Score that he can use to rank how close the match is, and the ID numbers of the Car Profile and Car Wanted forms that generated the match.

DESIGNING THE MATCHING PROGRAM

After designing the view to store matches, Tom thinks more about the matching program itself. He makes a list of the program behaviors that he will have to build.

The first and most obvious feature is that it will need to find matches. To do this, he will write a program to loop through the Car Wanted forms. For each Car Wanted form, he will loop through the Car Profiles and evaluate how good or bad a match it is. He decides to implement a simple algorithm to start and make it fancier later if needed. Therefore, he designs the program to look at each Wanted field on the Car Wanted form and compare it against the data on the Car Profile form. If it matches exactly, he will give the match 1 point. If it clearly does not match, he will give the match −1 points. Otherwise he will ignore the field. He will add up these scores to compute a total match score. He will consider a Car Wanted form and a Car Profile form to "match" if the match score is above a threshold, say 3.

The second program feature is to store these matches back in the Used Cars database. Since he has designed a Match form for this purpose, the program will simply need to create a new Match form and populate the data.

The next feature is to avoid creating duplicate matches and to delete old matches. When the program generates a match, it must look to see whether the match already exists before creating a new one. This will avoid creating duplicate matches. Deleting old matches is a little trickier. Tom decides to implement a brute-force clean-up mechanism that can run after the match program completes a cycle. This clean-up will search through the Match forms and look for any that were created for Car Profile or Car Wanted IDs that no longer exist. If so, that Match form will be deleted.

Another feature Tom decides to build into the Matching program is to flag old listings. If a Car Profile or Car Wanted form is too old, say over two months old, the Matching program can flag it as an old form. A view can be used to see these old forms, possibly for the purpose of calling the buyer or seller and seeing if they wish to continue in the service. The program could also look for another age threshold, say four months, after which it can either delete the form or archive it to a second database.

PUTTING THE PIECES TOGETHER

After building the Used Car database and the Matching program, Tom is ready to get his service off the ground. He hires a couple of people to staff the phone, enter Car Wanted and Car Profile forms, look up matches, and perform other administrative tasks.

When he trains his staff, he spends considerable time explaining the use of full-text searching. He thinks that by searching for key words and phrases in the general comments that people give, his service may be able to provide better matching than the simple-minded criteria his matching program alone can implement. He emphasizes the ability to do wildcard searches, which will find whole words based on partial words, and the ability to use the NOT operator to exclude items that contain certain words.

Finally Tom is ready to unveil the service. He places a series of ads in newspapers and magazines and waits for the phone to start ringing off the hook. While things are slow at first, his service soon becomes successful. He finds he needs to hire more staff, particularly to staff the phone lines during off hours. Then he has another idea.

Since he does not have a car lot and he never sees his customers, why can't he advertise anywhere? With his 800 number, people won't know where he is located. He can match buyers with sellers anywhere. He then realizes he would not want to match a buyer in California with a seller in New York. He would need to upgrade his database and his Matching program to become geographically aware. For example, the views in the Used Car database would probably need to be categorized by state before anything else, so his staff would only look at forms in the buyer's or seller's local area. His forms would need to be upgraded to store the buyer's and seller's locations, which might be simply the state or might be more granular. His Matching program would need to match only within a geographic area.

Tom likes the idea and begins his modifications. He figures that in another year, he can expand his business far more than if he stayed in one area.

◤ Fact Sheet

Used Cars Database

Purpose: To enable a service to match buyers with sellers by storing data about used cars for sale and buyers looking for used cars.

Application Origin: The Used Car application is custom developed, as well as the Matching program.

Application Development Time: The initial version of the Notes database took a few days to implement, with incremental enhancements being done over the next few weeks. The Matching program took a week to develop a working prototype, with enhancements made for another week.

Typical Size: 10–50 MB, depending on how long data is allowed to remain in the database before being purged.

Typical Use: Used by "virtual used-car lots," where a service is supported to match buyers and sellers without the service provider actually needing a car lot.

Forms: The Car Profile form is used to store information about a car being listed as for sale. The Car Wanted form is used to store a buyer's preferences and criteria. The Match form is created by the Matching program to store the fact that the program has found a match between a buyer and a seller.

Views: There are a set of views to show information about Car Profiles. The By Price Range view categorizes the cars by their price range. The By Make/Model view categorizes the Car Profiles by their make and then by their model. There are a set of views to show information about Car Wanted forms. The Make/Model/Price Wanted view categorizes the Car Wanted forms by the make wanted, then the model wanted, and then the price range wanted. The Make/Model/Year Wanted view categorizes the Car Wanted forms by the make wanted, then the model wanted, and then the year wanted.

PART 4

Company-Wide Applications

Even at the level of a small group, Notes offers features and benefits that are tough for competitive products to match. At levels where an entire large organization begins to communicate freely, Notes has no competition at all.

The applications discussed in this chapter are ones where Notes is used as a platform for connecting widely disparate parts of an organization, not just group-to-group on an ongoing collaborative basis, but company-wide, where individuals and groups can associate anytime, in ways that might not follow the lines on an organization chart.

For example, the Help Desk and Customer Service applications make it possible for a support team to offer a whole new level of service. The Idea Management System developed by First National Bank allows anyone in the organization to have input into a continuous improvement process. Sales order and contact-management systems, which exist in other forms, attain a new level when combined with Notes. The flexible views and wide-area access provided by Notes allow the whole organization to participate in the sales process in a more informed manner, which keeps customers happier and improves sales. And Notes provides a platform for the simple distribution of "live books" that contain up-to-the-minute information about the company and its products.

When Notes is used in this fashion, it has truly become integrated into the corporate culture and business model.

The NewsEdge/ Notes Database

Desktop Data, Inc., is a Massachusetts-based company that provides a suite of news-monitoring tools to businesses. Their NewsEdge products accept real-time news feeds from all the major providers of such information, such as the *Wall Street Journal,* Reuters, Dow Jones News Service, the Federal Register, Associated Press, and many others. They then provide a wide variety of user interfaces to access that information.

In essence, a customized electronic newspaper is delivered to each reader's desktop. The set of stories that is delivered is determined by a *profile*—stories that match are delivered, stories that fail to match are ignored. A profile can be specified for a whole company, a group of people, or even an individual user. It contains a list of keywords and phrases that might occur in the story.

For example, a profile for an oceanographer might include "dolphin but not football"—this would include all stories with the word "dolphin" and exclude stories that mention the Miami Dolphins.

There are a number of different ways that Desktop Data can deliver this information to individuals, including e-mail and special purpose mail-reader applications. One of their most important user interface options is NewsEdge/ Notes, a tool that allows Notes users a wide range of ways to integrate news into Notes applications. Marni Hoyle, director of marketing for Desktop Data, says, "Notes provides a set of features that allow people to go beyond vanilla—there are things possible with Notes that are not possible with our other interfaces."

Application information and screen shots courtesy of Desktop Data, Inc.

The NewsEdge/Notes database

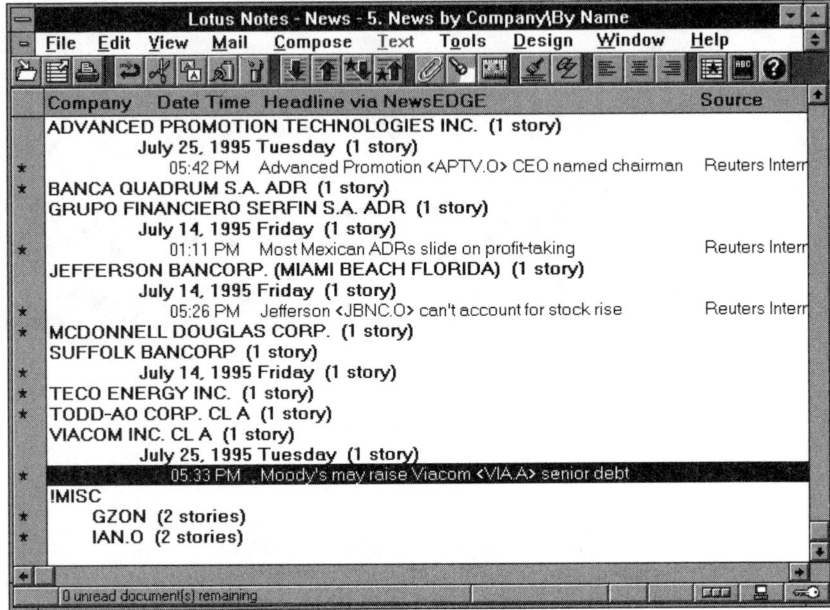

Some companies prefer to have news delivered to the electronic mailboxes of individual users. This is generally when the news is very limited in scope, such as news only about their company. Some organizations build a single news database in which all news is stored. This is useful as a reference, but may have too much volume for individuals to keep track of on a daily basis. Still others break the news up into chunks that are of interest to specific groups. These groups might then be expected to monitor the database more carefully.

HOW IT'S BUILT

NewsEdge/Notes is built around three basic types of Notes databases, which communicate with one another and with the NewsEdge Server to form the working application. The profiles are stored in one or more Profile databases, depending on the individual organization and the applications used. Each profile points to a Story database, in which all stories that match that profile are stored. In some cases, stories and profiles can share a single database. Every organization has exactly one Control database, which keeps track of all the profiles in the organization and provides a single point of reference for tracking the NewsEdge application.

PROFILES

A profile can apply to an individual user, a group of users, a particular database, or even an organization as a whole. Typically, the task of profile creation and management is given to a small number of trusted users. A profile describes three key things:

- ▶ The characteristics of news that someone may be interested in. For example, a profile may say the equivalent of "show me all articles that contain references to Lotus or Notes and do not contain references to automobiles (since those are likely to be about Lotus cars)." Of course, profiles can be much more complex, watching for dozens of keywords and news feeds and excluding news that is irrelevant.
- ▶ Where to find the news—which of the dozens of possible news feeds to watch. For example, you may specify that only the *New York Times* and *Wall Street Journal* should be followed.
- ▶ Where to deposit the news—the Notes database in which the stories get stored. This gives tremendous flexibility to the application. Some companies store all news in a single database, others will distribute it to individual mail files, and still others will organize it by topic in a number of different databases.

The NewsEdge Server takes news from its newsfeeds in *real time*. This means that news is processed as it is reported and comes over the newswires—it's delivered continually, not on a schedule.

Every word in every article is indexed and matched against all of the profiles in the organization. When a match occurs, the news is deposited into the database indicated by the profile.

These profiles are stored in one or more Profiles databases. A Profiles database contains Profile forms, which contain fields that define the following:

- ▶ Where to deposit the news (which server and database).
- ▶ A list of news sources. Each possible news source is marked as to whether it should be used as a source for this profile.
- ▶ The profile itself, which is a text field with a specific syntax. The profile specifies which words or phrases must be found in the stories, and which words must not be found. A sample profile might look like this:

```
Dolphins but not football
Tuna or fish but not sandwiches or food or casserole or recipe
Salmon but not clothing
```

- ▶ Buttons to help build the profile. So that people don't have to learn very much about the complex syntax of a profile specification, the profile

A profile being filled out

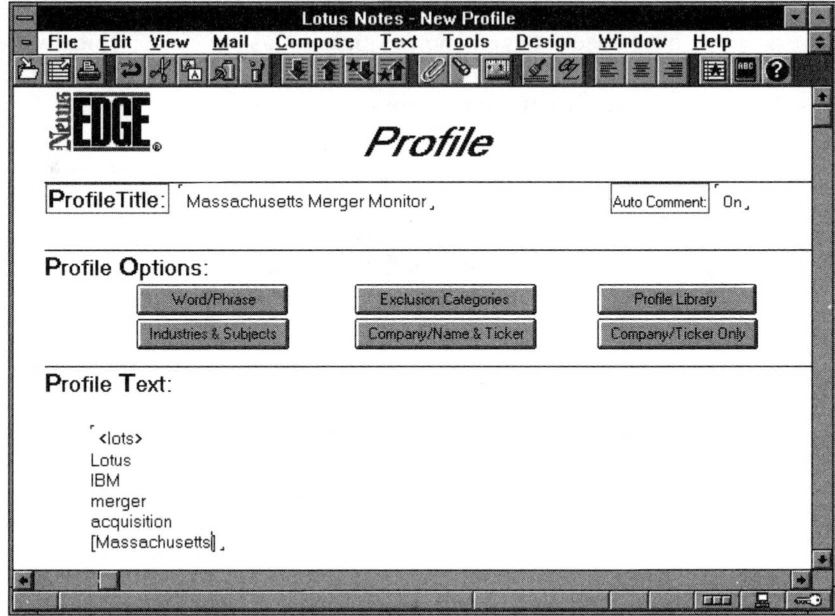

form contains buttons labeled "Company Name and Ticker," "Word/ Phrase," "Industries and Subjects," and so on. These provide lists of common items often found in profiles, and then insert them into the profile automatically.

Profiles can be filled out by individual users or by organizations, depending on their needs. There can be many databases throughout the organization that contain profiles.

THE CONTROL DATABASE

The Control database keeps track of the whole NewsEdge/Notes system. There is a single Control database per organization, which keeps a list of databases that contain profiles. It also stores statistics on the performance of the NewsEdge system, including errors found. It provides a single point of management for the entire system. The Control database contains one form for each profile database, plus forms for reporting errors and problems.

For performance reasons, the NewsEdge server stores its own copies of the profiles. When users change their News profiles, they are changed only in the

Notes databases that contain the profiles. Periodically (the rate is set by the system administrator), the NewsEdge server reads the Control database and uses it to scan the Profile databases looking for new, changed, or deleted profiles. These changes are then stored in the server and used for matching against the stories.

THE STORY DATABASES

When a story comes in on a newswire, it is formatted to match a standard NewsEdge story form. The story is broken down into its individual words, and each word in the story is matched against all of the stored profiles. One story can match many profiles.

Once a story is found to match a particular profile, it is inserted into the database specified by the profile. In some cases, the stories are put into the same database as the profiles; in other applications, it's more appropriate to store them elsewhere. Many different fields are filled in:

- ▶ The story text
- ▶ The headline
- ▶ A list of all the keywords that were matched from the profile
- ▶ A list of all the profiles that matched this story
- ▶ The date and time of the story
- ▶ The source of the story (the newsfeed)

This allows a wide range of different types of story databases. Because the news stories are stored with all of these different fields, it is then possible to build many different views for sorting the database in different ways. A Chronological view will always show the most recent stories at the top. A Headline view will show the stories with particular headlines grouped together. A Keyword view will usually group-related stories together.

One database can be used to store multiple profiles and the news that matches those profiles. This is most handy for creating industry-specific databases. One major corporation in the energy industry creates a database with specific profiles for all the different energy types, such as oil, gas, electric, solar power, and nuclear. Different views organize the news by date, by profile (which characterize the industry), by keyword, or by newsfeed.

By specifying a profile that only asks for information from one specific source (for example, ZiffWire, which contains news from the computer industry), a database can be built that further dissects that particular news source. Many computer software vendors use this application, which contains a view breaking the articles down by the magazine from which the story came. Another version of this same type of application simply stores stock quotes.

A popular type of story database is the Executive View. This summarizes stories of specific interest to the management in an organization. It includes industry-specific news, any news relating to the company and its major competitors, and key stories from major news sources. This application is often used as a painless way of introducing Notes to an organization. The users of such an application need do nothing more than click and read, and it's a good way to get people to see the power of Notes.

The true power of Notes comes in when news is added to another database, such as a sales management application. Salespeople use this application on a daily basis to manage their sales operations. Adding a news profile to this system specifying customer names and industry news can keep the sales team informed. It can also provide a powerful incentive to keep using the sales database effectively.

The NewsEdge product provides a useful set of information on its own, but combined with Notes it allows breaking news to be integrated into other applications in a way no other system can provide.

◢ FACT SHEET

NewsEdge/Notes Database

Purpose: Allows real-time access to breaking news from a variety of news sources.

Application Origin: Desktop Data, Inc., 1601 Trapelo Road, Waltham, MA 02154. Phone: (617) 672-2400.

Application Development Time: Most application development is done by NewsEdge; customization and integration is handled by the customer. Simple applications can be running in a few hours.

Typical Size: 20–100 MB, depending on the newsfeeds chosen, the number and complexity of the profiles, and the amount of time the information is retained. Above 100 MB becomes unwieldy. Typically, organizations reserve one or more servers just for news.

Typical Use: Management, sales, marketing—anyone needing access to current information available on newswires. News can be stored in its own databases, or integrated with other applications, such as a sales tracking database.

Forms: Profile forms determine which news is used and where it is placed. Story forms are placed into the news databases for each story that matches a profile.

Views: Views used depend on the particular database and its purpose. A particularly useful view is one organized first by profile (used to define the general topic) and then subcategorized by the keywords matched. Another is organized by news source and the date and time. Still another is categorized by stock market ticker symbol.

Help Desk

Gibraltar is a large (fictional) insurance company. A few years ago, Gibraltar's computer support organization was three or four people. This group focused on PC-related computing issues and complemented a larger organization of mainframe support personnel. At the time, this small group was able to support most of the company's PC computer needs. This assistance included software and hardware evaluation, purchasing, installation, general maintenance, and even providing some training to the company's PC users. As the number of PCs grew, so did the support organization. At one point Gibraltar's computer support staff consisted of about ten people—struggling to keep things functioning. In an effort to ensure that the systems were up and running, the computer support group had to cut back on user support. To fill this widening gap between the support organization and the user base, Gibraltar has decided to build a Help Desk—a system to track user's immediate and long-term needs, support staff activities, and problem histories. Carolyn Rojas, as a member of the computer support group, has been chosen to evaluate Help Desk systems and ensure that the system selected supports the needs of the Help Desk.

THE SEARCH

Help Desk support systems are not new, and there are many existing software packages that provide this type of functionality. These packages allow an organization to record phone calls, assign work items to various team members, monitor open and closed calls, and provide regular statistics on Help Desk performance. After evaluating a variety of options, Carolyn decides to develop her own system using Lotus Notes. Some of the key considerations are listed here:

▶ Gibraltar had already purchased and installed Notes. Many Help Desk systems are costly to install and implement. The fact that the company will not need to purchase additional software, if the support system is built in Notes, makes Notes a much more attractive option.

▶ Notes is used by end users, as well as the computer support group. This means that requests for help can be e-mailed, and that relevant Help Desk information can be distributed to end users in shared Notes databases.

▶ Notes has strong workflow and information-sharing capabilities. This facilitates the assignment of work items, and sharing of information amongst team members to resolve problems.

▶ All the help systems examined require some level of customization. Carolyn feels that she would rather spend the time developing a custom Notes application than learning a new environment.

In addition to the pluses, there were some negatives to creating the Help Desk in Notes:

▶ Notes does not support the sort of statistical analyses that most Help Desks use to measure their effectiveness. The ability to calculate a variety of numbers based on different sets of documents (e.g., for all closed calls, how long was each call open: for the last month–last 6 months?) is better suited to relational databases than Notes. That said, there are a number of external tools that can build these reports from Notes data (e.g., Forest & Trees, Notes ViP, and Visual Basic, with third-party add-ons).

▶ Notes relies on e-mail to send notifications, rather than messages that pop-up on the recipient's screen. Electronic mail will beep when it arrives, but it does not pop up on the user's screen. Once again, an external tool can be developed that performs this action, but this tool would again be a custom (non-Notes) software development, and might not be practical.

DESIGNING THE APPLICATION

There are a number of commercial vendors who sell "ready-made" Notes applications to support Help Desks. Unfortunately, all of these require some level of customization to be useful. Carolyn decides that with her reasonable understanding of Notes and the limited amount of time it takes to build a useful application, it is probably better to develop something herself initially. In the event that a more complete system is needed, the company can always turn to another system later. In addition, Gibraltar will at that point be better informed about critical features the Help Desk should have, and, therefore, better able to evaluate their systems.

In addition to commercial vendors of Help Desk systems, there are also a number of Help Desk templates that have been created over time by Lotus and other organizations that she believes could be a useful place to start. With later builds (versions/releases) of Notes V3, a sample Help Desk is actually included with the product. After talking to individuals at other organizations who are using Notes to support their Help Desks, Carolyn decides she has a good idea of what the Help Desk should contain.

First, the application will need a Call Tracking database. This database will be used to record all incoming calls, and any and all subsequent actions taken related to the call. This database will need forms to support taking calls, assigning calls to subject-matter experts, actions taken relating to a call, resolutions arrived at, and closing calls. The database will need to provide enough information for management to produce reports showing, among other things, how many calls were answered, the average duration of calls, and how many calls were left open.

In addition to the Call Tracking application, the Help Desk will also need a "knowledgebase" database. The purpose of this application will be to disseminate relevant information about the computer environment, and to capture helpful tips and tricks related to using company standard applications.

Finally, there needs to be some level of coordination with Gibraltar's change-management system (see the chapter on Change Management) to ensure that users are notified about impending changes to systems as soon as possible.

CREATING THE APPLICATIONS

In an effort to jump-start the Help Desk, Gibraltar contracts a consulting firm, Digital Doctors, which specializes in Help Desk management. Digital Doctors will supply Help Desk managers and workers until the company can hire and train their own personnel. Carolyn will be responsible for working with these people to ensure that the Help Desk system developed furthers the processes they define for Help Desk support.

Carolyn begins the development process by creating databases from the Help Desk design templates included with Notes. First, she renames all fields and views to names that seem more relevant to Gibraltar's needs. This takes a couple of hours. Next, she examines the fields contained in the forms to see which fields are relevant, which should be removed, and which can be renamed. Once she has started changing field names on the forms, the views in the database (which referred to the old field names) need to be updated. The process of updating the template takes about a day to complete. Once finished, Carolyn has a rudimentary call-tracking database, and a reasonable knowledgebase. She adds a few sample documents to ensure the database can be easily demonstrated.

Carolyn's next step is to schedule a meeting with the consultants. She wanted to ensure a prototype was available to demonstrate so that the feedback procured in the meeting was constructive and direct. In the meeting, she provides a general description of the type of information captured in each form, shows how the views can be used to list documents, and takes the attendees through each of the forms in the database. They provide comments throughout the demo, and at the end, indicate features they would need prior to actually using the application. A list of supported systems must be contained in the application (so Help Desk personnel can simply pick the system from a menu choice), also the application must support at least some level of task assignment related to a particular call. They also provide her with a list of call severities (ranging from unimportant to highly critical) and error conditions that should be included in the application (e.g., crashes, frozen, or slow).

After the meeting, she collects a list of supported systems (including hardware and software), and adds these lists to the application. Carolyn also adds in the systems supported, the list of call severities, and possible error conditions. These are relatively straightforward activities. It takes longer to figure out how to do notifications. She finally decides that the primary form, called Help Desk Call, will have a button called Assign To. When pressed, this button will allow the Help Desk person completing the form to select a person to whom the call will be assigned. This person will then receive an e-mail message with a subset of call information and a doclink back to the complete Call document. Once back at the original call, the assignee will not have the ability to edit the original Call report, but they can select a button that will allow them to respond to the call. In the response, they have the ability to reassign the call (in the event that someone else is better suited to handle the call or the call needs to be escalated—the exact reason needs to be provided); close the call (which requires they provide a description of the resolution); or provide an interim statement on the call (e.g., "This appears to be a bug in the software and I am waiting to hear back from the vendor."). Finally, a Help Desk person can go to an open call and click on a button to ask the assignee for more information on a particular call or a status update. This will be helpful in cases where a user disagrees with a call being closed, or a particular call is open for an inordinately long time. These changes take two days to implement, and another day to test. Ensuring that the mail-routing piece will work in all situations is the most difficult part of this activity.

Carolyn demonstrates the revised application to the consultants. Together they decide that the application can be placed on a server accessible to the Help Desk support personnel, and she can begin testing. Testing will require the active participation of a number of relevant personnel in the department to help take care of actual and mock calls. This will help to ensure that the application and the procedures developed meet the needs of the department and the organization as a whole.

TESTING AND REDESIGN

In some application environments, testing requires every aspect of the developed application to be tested. In Notes, only some features need to be tested. While it is typically self-evident whether forms and views are working, the Mail component of the application will need to be tested.

After some initial testing, it becomes clear that certain aspects of the application will need to change. For example, Carolyn initially assumed that the Call report would only need to be edited by the original author—all subsequent information would be kept in Response documents. As the Help Desk personnel begin adding calls to the database, it becomes clear that they need the ability to go back and update/change information in the original call. This is required in a number of situations: when the initial call does not provide complete information, when information is recorded inaccurately, and when the original author is unsure to whom the call should be assigned. The fact that calls need to be reopened means that other information should probably be moved back into the original Call report. For example, when a call gets reassigned, this is now handled in the original Call report (so that a person looking at open calls only needs to look at one document to determine who is responsible for a call). Each time a call is reassigned, a new mail message is automatically generated to the new responsible party. One final change—a button is added to the call report for Create Knowledgebase Document. Selecting this button allows the user to create a document in the Knowledgebase database. This will be used when the resolution to a call is relevant to a broader group of individuals than just the caller.

This period of reviews and design updates continues for approximately one month. At the end of this time, the rate of change in the application has diminished to a point that the consultants feel the application (and the Help Desk team) are ready to go online.

USING THE APPLICATION

The Call Tracking and Knowledgebase applications have already been deployed on Carolyn's group's production server. The Knowledgebase (which contains a few dozen documents) is now replicated to all servers in her company. An e-mail is sent to all employees providing the Help Desk phone number, e-mail address, the location of the Knowledgebase (the servers and directories where it can be found), and a brief overview of Help Desk responsibilities. The

Help Desk also places a more complete description of Help Desk policies and procedures in the Knowledgebase for reference.

Carolyn has decided to help staff the Help Desk for the first few days to ensure that the application meets the group's needs. For the first day, she helps answer phones. Her first real call (other than people calling to confirm that someone actually picks up the phone when they dial) is a person with an operating system or network problem—the cause of the problem is unclear from the information provided by the user. She opens a new Call report and types in the user's name, telephone number, and so on. All this information will be checked against her company's Name and Address book when the document is saved. If some information does not match, she will be prompted to either change the data or confirm the discrepancy. She categorizes the problem by selecting from her predefined lists. The user's problem is not critical (as it is intermittent and has not affected the user's ability to do work) and appears to be network related. Finally, after taking all the information, she assigns the problem to Jim, her group's networking person.

Later in the day, Carolyn sees that Jim has responded and closed the call. The network had been experiencing intermittent errors in the morning, which has since been rectified. Jim has called the user back, explained this to the user, and closed the call. The call had been open for less than two hours.

Calls by date in Help Desk Call Tracking database

	Priority	Status	Subject
05/05/95			
	Critical	Closed	File server is down
	Low	Closed	User question: How do I print
	Low	Closed	User Question: How do I save to floppy
	Medium	Closed	File server is down
	Critical	Closed	Print server is down
05/06/95			
	Low	Open	User Question: Do we have access to the Intern
	High	Closed	Server backup tape drive error
	Medium	Closed	User cannot access PPP gateway
	Medium	Closed	Replication failure
	Critical	Closed	File server is down
	High	Open	Power saver software disables network access
	Medium	Closed	Portable modem blown
	Low	Closed	User cannot access database catalog - Update
05/07/95			
	Medium	Closed	User hard disk failure
	Medium	Closed	User accidentally deleted a file
	Critical	Closed	Mainframe access is down
	High	Closed	User cannot replicate project database from ser
	Critical	Closed	Mail not routing properly - many delivery failures
05/08/95			
	Critical	Closed	Notes server down
	Medium	Closed	Printer won't feed from legal paper tray

Lotus Notes - Help Desk - Call Tracking - Calls by date

File Edit View Mail Compose Text Tools Design Window Help

Unfinished Business

While the application is up and running, a Help Desk system is never finished—there is always more data to be collected or another feature to be added. To that end, Carolyn has begun to maintain new feature requests for the application. She revisits the application at least once each quarter to implement the most desirable features:

- ▶ Reporting. Producing reports is one of the key measures of Help Desk success over time. Once the application was accepted, Carolyn could begin work on tools to draw the data out of Notes and statistically analyze the data. She selects one of the reporting tools mentioned earlier and develops the screens for management. The predefined screens themselves are saved as embedded objects in her documents so that management simply needs to double-click on these reports to execute them.
- ▶ Phone Notes. Notes has a companion product called Phone Notes, which allows application developers to define menus they can access by phone. This can be used to create Call reports automatically. For example, when the Help Desk is closed (its hours are 7:00 AM–9:00 PM E.S.T.), a user can call the Help Desk and pick menu choices that correspond to each field of the form. The application is less flexible than an agent taking information over the phone, but it is a useful way to automatically capture call information. In addition, in the event that a call is critical, it can send a message to the pager gateway (see next item) to page an on-call Help Desk agent. This ensures that the company has some level of 24-hour support without requiring on-site staff.
- ▶ Notes Pager Gateway. Another Notes companion product is the Notes Pager Gateway. The Pager Gateway takes standard Notes e-mail messages and sends the Subject field to a recipient's pager. This allows a Help Desk agent to send a page to relevant personnel to support-critical calls.

Fact Sheet

Help Desk

Purpose: To help the company better support partners and customers in getting product information.

Application Origin: Developed from Lotus-provided template.

Application Development Time: Approximately 2 man-months.

Typical Size: Varies directly with size of organization, number of help calls received, and duration calls are kept in the database. An organization of 1,500 with average usage of the Help Desk requires approximately 100 MB of space. This assumes a purge interval of 3 months.

Typical Use: Users call a Help Desk person who completes a Call Report for the call. The call is either answered directly or assigned to the appropriate Help Desk person. In the event the assignee cannot resolve the call, the call is escalated to one of the organizations responsible for the affected system.

Forms: Call Report, Resolution, and Comment.

Views: By caller, By assignee, By open calls, and By closed calls.

Streamlining the Sales Process

Prints And More prints posters, postcards, novelty diplomas, and a host of other printed items that are sold in retail stores. While they do print a quarterly color brochure of their products, which they ship to their customers and to purchased mailing lists, they have found their primary source of sales to be their sales force. These salespeople visit the retail stores and meet with the manager, owner, or whoever has purchasing responsibility, and display the company's products, describe what's available at discount, and bring in volume orders.

In order to differentiate themselves from their competition, Prints And More (a hypothetical firm) has strived to make their sales force as efficient as possible. This allows the salespeople to provide better information to their customers, which delights the customers and helps the salespeople maintain long-term, profitable relationships. This efficiency has been achieved by centralizing their information as much as possible by creatively using Lotus Notes.

I HAVE EVERYTHING RIGHT HERE

Gary Molnar is a seasoned salesman for Prints And More, having been with the company for ten years. He would not describe himself as a "computer person" and originally resisted the idea that he should carry around a computer to do his work.

When Gary first began selling for Prints And More, he had a fairly standard arrangement and was comfortable with it. He would stop in at the office every couple of days and pick up the latest brochures, find out what's been selling, what's discontinued, how his orders are doing, which orders are experiencing delays, and so on. On the road he would visit the stores he supplies and show off samples of his products. He would take orders on paper forms and phone them in, fax them in, or just wait until he was back in the office to deliver them. It worked fine.

Then the company handed out the notebook computers. He was told that to minimize costs, the salespeople were to enter orders on their computers, and then "dial in" to "upload" the orders to the new computer. This way people would not be needed at the office to key orders into the office computer. Order entry mistakes would be eliminated, orders would make it to the warehouse faster, and so on. Gary wasn't exactly enthusiastic, but the job was good, so he found himself in training for Lotus Notes.

At the training, he was shown two databases he needed to learn to access. One was the mailbox, where he could exchange e-mail with the other salespeople and office staff. The other database was the Prints And More application, which was where everything would happen. He learned how to create a new customer record, which has to happen before orders for that customer can be entered. He learned to enter orders. He learned to replicate his database with the company's server and then look to see what new things have shown up. He saw how product information was now located in the database and how he wouldn't need to carry brochures around anymore.

After becoming familiar with the database and how Notes works, Gary could see the value in the notebook computer. Everything he needed was right there in that one database. As he began using the application, he found he no longer needed to stop in at the office every couple of days. Now it's a lot if he visits once a week.

A DAY IN THE LIFE

This morning Gary is going to visit one of his best clients, JJ Gifts. JJ Gifts is a mall gift store that sells a wide variety of items, including posters, greeting cards, and the like. Before leaving home, Gary replicates with the server. He then spends half an hour reviewing the status of his accounts and products.

First he looks at the Order Status view to see how his current orders are doing. He first looks to see if any orders have been backordered and sees that there are none in that category. Then he looks to see which are In Process. These are the orders which are currently being filled and should be shipped soon. He sees a couple of orders there, as well as several listed as Shipped. One of the shipped orders is for a client who needed the materials right away, so he makes a note to call the client before leaving home to say the order is on its way. He sees that the order he entered yesterday before replicating, which was then in the Entered category, has been moved to the Received category.

He has learned to check this category to make sure that his orders have made it into the system.

After checking the status of his orders, he switches to the New/Discontinued Products view to see if any new products have been added to their product line. Since he is about to visit JJ Gifts, he hopes that there are some new products he can show off. He sees a new product titled 3D Solar System. He opens the document and reads the description as a stereogram poster of the solar system. There is also a picture of the poster showing how colorful and nicely printed it is. He scans the list price and the discount codes to see what they will sell for in the store and what he can charge JJ Gifts. The discounts are coded so he can show the picture and description to his customers without giving away too much information about Prints And More's internal pricing.

Having reviewed his orders and the new products, he switches off his notebook computer and heads for his car. He arrives at JJ Gifts for his appointment with Laura Crespo—the manager. Laura likes dealing with Gary. Not only are their meetings generally brief, but he always has all of her order status information at his fingertips. He is also always up on the latest products and can show them to her without a lot of fuss and bother.

At their meeting, Gary sits down next to Laura, as opposed to opposite her. He likes to invite his clients to look at the computer information with him. He finds that his company's efficiency impresses his clients and generates a great deal of trust that Gary is dealing openly and honestly. Gary opens his computer and goes into the Prints And More application.

He gets down to business. "OK Laura—let's take a glance at your current orders. I see we shipped you a large order last week. Did that arrive OK?"

Laura says that they did receive the order and everything was fine. Gary scans the database and sees no other orders for JJ Gifts and so he asks Laura if he can show her their latest poster. Laura agrees and he opens up the description of the 3D Solar System poster. Laura expresses interest in it and asks about the 3D posters in general. Are there any special deals going?

Gary switches to the Specials/Promotions view and scans the half dozen specials that are being offered. He spots one for 3Dimensional, the company he noticed produces the 3D Solar System poster. The special indicates that bulk orders of 100 or more 3Dimensional brand posters are being discounted by 15 percent. Laura asks Gary to enter an order for her for 100 assorted 3Dimensional posters, with 25 of them being the 3D Solar System.

Gary brings up the customer profile for JJ Gifts and pushes the button labeled "Enter an order." An order form pops up, and it already contains the name JJ Gifts, their customer number, the date, his name, and other information. Gary moves to the line where he can enter an order and enters 25 3D Solar System posters. He also enters 75 assorted posters from 3Dimensional. He asks Laura what else she needs.

The two of them spend a few more minutes scanning the products in the catalog embodied in the Prints And More application, and Gary enters a few more items in the order. When the order is done, Gary clicks the button labeled Save and the order form closes. Since Laura is one of his best clients, he takes a little extra time and asks to borrow the phone line. He plugs in the notebook and replicates the Prints And More application. He chooses only to send documents to make the replication time very short. After sending the order, he bids Laura good-bye.

Back in his car, Gary turns his notebook computer back on. When he was reviewing the promotions with Laura he noticed a special for new customers. He finds that document and opens it up. The promotion is for one third off a new customer's first order. He has been meaning to follow up on a lead for a new customer, so he decides to use this promotion as a way to "break the ice." He makes a call to Stewart Bigg, the manager of Bigg Things, and offers to come over and give him a great deal.

As they shake hands, Stewart offers, "Call me Stu." Gary thanks Stu for the opportunity to forge a relationship and describes Prints And More and their products. He asks if he can show Stu some samples of their product line, and when given the OK, he opens his computer.

"What's that for? Are you going to ask me a million questions before we really get started?" Stu asks. "Aren't we going to look at samples?"

While his computer comes on Gary explains that the catalog is in the computer. He quickly pops into the Prints And More application and switches to the Product view listing products by type. He shows Stu the types of products they sell, and Stu's eye is caught by the line of Novelty Diplomas. He asks to see some samples and Gary opens the category. A list of diplomas appears with titles like "Certified Nut," "Doctor of Laziness," and other goofy things. Gary opens up the first one to show Stu a picture of what the Certified Nut diploma looks like. As with a printed catalog, they can see exactly what is printed on it, how it is framed, and the list price. Gary quickly flips through a few other sample diplomas to show Stu what they are like.

Stu seems interested in the diplomas as an addition to what his store sells. Gary moves to the other types of products offered by Prints And More to give Stu a good flavor of their products. Gary also describes how the entire order entry and tracking process is computerized and how Gary will always be able to give Stu immediate answers to questions like "What is the status of my last order," "Did my order ship yesterday," and "I'd like to order some of these; are they in stock or back-ordered?" Stu seems impressed.

To close the sale and secure Stu as a client, Gary explains the promotion offering a first-order discount. Stu is sold and asks Gary to proceed with the paperwork. Gary quickly composes a Customer Information form and takes Stu's address, phone number, and so on. He then clicks the Enter an order button and opens an order form. Together they scan the product descriptions and enter orders. Gary clicks the "Tally" button to tell Stu how much the order

The Order Status view in the Prints And More application

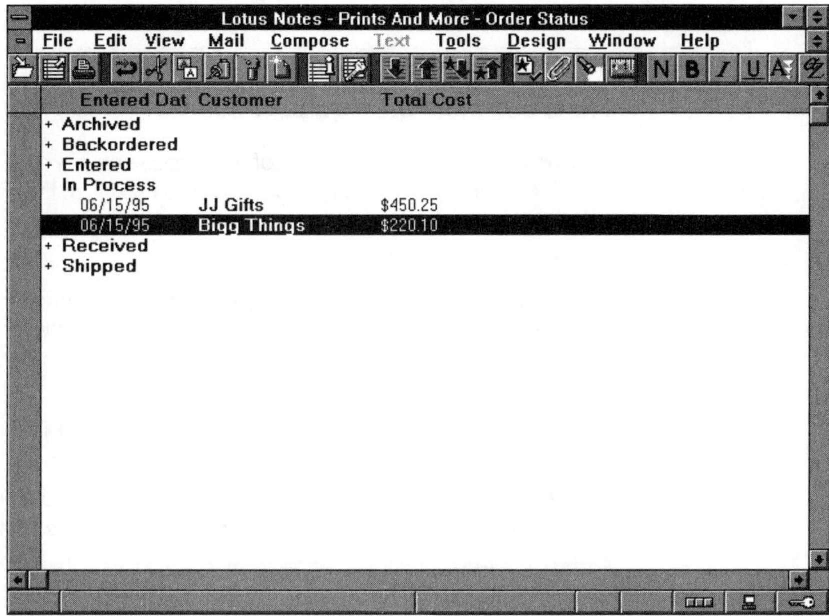

will cost before the discount, and quickly takes one third off to give him the final price.

Gary then closes up his notebook computer and thanks Stu for the business. Stu seems impressed with Gary and with Prints And More, and Gary has acquired another client.

At the End of the Day

Gary visits several more clients in the afternoon, taking nothing but his notebook computer with him. When he's back home, he plugs the computer into his phone line and replicates the day's business with the server while he changes into comfortable clothes. When the computer hangs up, he checks the database to see if there are any new developments. He also checks his mail.

In his mail there is a message from the office about the latest company financials. The company is having another excellent year and is planning on rolling out a new program to bring on many more salespeople in new territories. They are experimenting with bringing on salespeople who never need to check into the office at all, and therefore can support geographic areas that are not within driving distance of the office. While Gary would not have believed it possible five years ago, he can see how the Prints And More application in Notes could probably make this work.

◀ **FACT SHEET**

Prints and More Sales Application

Purpose: To integrate all aspects of a salesperson's needs, including product descriptions, customer profiles, order entry and status, and maximize the efficiency of both the sales force and the office processes.

Application Origin: Custom developed.

Application Development Time: The application template development time was approximately 3 months with incremental improvements afterwards. Populating the database at first took 3 months (scanning images, transferring customer data), and then requires incremental attention to keep the product catalog updated.

Typical Size: Depending on the number of products and customers, the database will range from 50–200 MB.

Typical Use: Used to support a sales force selling a product line that can be described/displayed using the multimedia capabilities of Notes (e.g., scanned images).

Forms: The Customer Information form is used to start a customer account. It assigns a customer number for order tracking and contains the billing and shipping addresses, phone numbers, contacts, and so on. The Order Form is used to enter an order for a customer. The Product Description form is used to describe a product, including a picture, the retail price, discount prices, and specials. The Promotions form is used to describe current promotions that are being offered by the supplier.

Views: The Customer List views are used to show the customers of Prints And More, with particular views to list customers alphabetically, by Salesperson and by Order Volume. The Order Status view is used to show the status of a salesperson's orders and is categorized by salesperson. The Products views are used to get information about the company's products, with particular views to list products by Type, by Brand, and by Cost. There is also a New/Discontinued Products view, which shows which new products have become available recently and that have been discontinued. The Specials/Promotions view shows special deals that are currently being offered that the salespeople can use as incentives to sell more products.

Canadian National Railway Employee Development System

In late spring of 1995, Canadian National Railway (CN) initiated an ambitious project to introduce technology to their front-line Supervisors. Under the direction of Gary Rennick, District Manager for Saskatchewan, the objective of the project was to provide their transportation supervisors with an "office in the field."

The idea was to automate a number of their existing functions onto portable computers that would enable them to carry out their duties in a more efficient manner. CN hired a consulting company, Changepoint Corporation, to help determine which functions could be automated and how best to do it.

The first application that was developed was the Employee Development System (EDS). This system enabled the transportation supervisors to monitor rule compliance by their train crews, a function they are required to do by federal regulators. Historically, this was a pen-and-paper operation. In the early 1990s, a mainframe-based rule monitoring system was developed, but it has proven difficult to use. Replacing it with a more user-friendly solution seemed to be the logical place to start.

As a secondary issue, in recent years CN had cut the workforce; they needed to be able to find ways to do more and better work in less time than it took to do it the old way. They needed to increase the operating efficiency and believed that technology was a key way to achieve this.

Changepoint is a consulting company that provides project management, custom application development, implementation, and training. They specialize in using Lotus Notes as an integration tool for smoothing the management of projects. Changepoint's task was building the application to help railway supervisors monitor and record rule compliance and provide the beginning stages of the office in the field.

Changepoint started with Notes. It seemed to be the right platform for storing and transporting the information around the company. However, taking observations in the field requires portability and extreme ease of use. Many of the people have had no computer experience at all, so they decided to use Fujitsu pen-based computers running Windows. They installed Notes on each machine, but felt that it would be more difficult to build an application using the Notes interface that would be easy enough to use on a pen-based computer. So they used HiTest Tools from Lotus to build a *front end* (a user interface) in Visual Basic that makes entering the data with a pen fast and easy.

Doug Watt, a consultant for Changepoint, was pleased with the HighTest tool set. "It gives us a lot more flexibility in the user interface. With a Notes interface, we may have had difficult data entry problems with the pens. With HighTest, it only took us about three weeks to get the first version of the application running. The pen interface is easy, with most of the data entry done through pick lists and checkoffs. And people think the pen-based computers are 'sexy'—they like using them."

PEN-BASED DATA ENTRY

The data entry application is built using Microsoft Visual Basic. The VB program is designed to let the user of a pen computer complete a whole series of observations quickly and easily. It uses a tabbed user interface (each page looks like a tabbed notebook divider), with plenty of pull-down lists to minimize the amount of typing or writing needed.

Each set of observations begins with the creation of a Header Info screen. The header is stored as a Main document in the Notes database. It contains information about the date, time, and location of the observations; who made them; and data on the train and train crew. For consistency and ease of use, all of this information is stored in pull-down list boxes so that the user can simply choose from the existing lists without having to spell the names correctly.

The Supervisor field shows the person making the observations. The District, Terminal, and Subdivision fields show where the observations are being made, down to the particular run of track. The two grids contain information about the particular train being used.

Some observations are made by riding on the train with the crew. Others are made in the train yard, and some are made in the field by watching trains pass such points as road crossings. The Observation Type field is where this is specified. The header also includes a list of the crew members being observed.

Once the header is complete, it is saved into the Notes database as a main document. The system is now ready to take down the observations.

The header for a series of observations

The Observation screen works as a sort of rule book. There are actually three different sets of rules that train crews need to follow. This screen allows the user to select one of the rule sets; it presents the list of rule titles as an outline.

Rules that have hidden subparts are marked with a large plus sign (+). Double-clicking on these rules will expand them to show the subparts, after which they will be marked with a large minus sign (−).

Clicking on a rule will show the text of the rule itself in the Description field and open up a place to mark the behavior of the crew with respect to that particular rule.

Each crew member gets a rating for each rule the supervisor chooses to observe. A rating of None records nothing in the database, a Satisfactory marking records adequate compliance with the rule, and Fail means that the supervisor has observed some behavior that is inappropriate. Marking Fail also brings up a dialog box with a choice of actions to be taken: No Action, Formal Investigation, or Interview (an informal discussion with the crew member). There are also places for free-form comments and a time and date stamp.

All observations are recorded as Responses to the Header document in the database.

The Observation screen

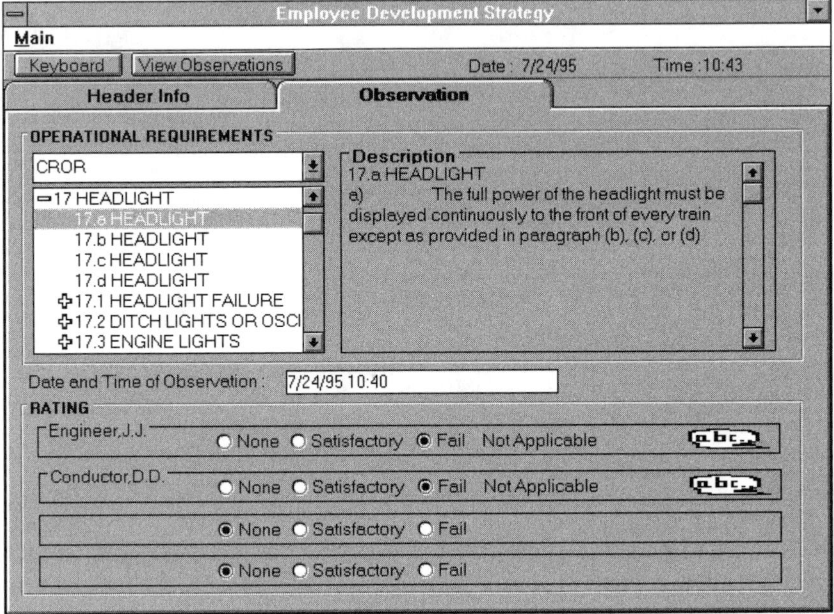

THE ANALYSIS

Once the data has been recorded in the field, the supervisor returns to the office and connects the pen-based computer to the network or connects to the server via modem and runs the synchronization program. This synchronization program is a one-button way to replicate the Notes database. It sends the observations to the central database and retrieves any changes that have been made to the rule book.

The central offices all use Notes directly to analyze the data. There is a large set of views designed to allow CN management to study the rules looking for trends and problems. Most of the views follow the same general template:

The By Crew Position view, for example, shows, for each different job on a train crew, all the failed and satisfactory observations broken down by employee. For failures, it also shows the action taken as a consequence of the failure. It shows the different positions as a percentage of all observations, and the percentage of times that the particular position had failures and successes.

The By Crew Position view

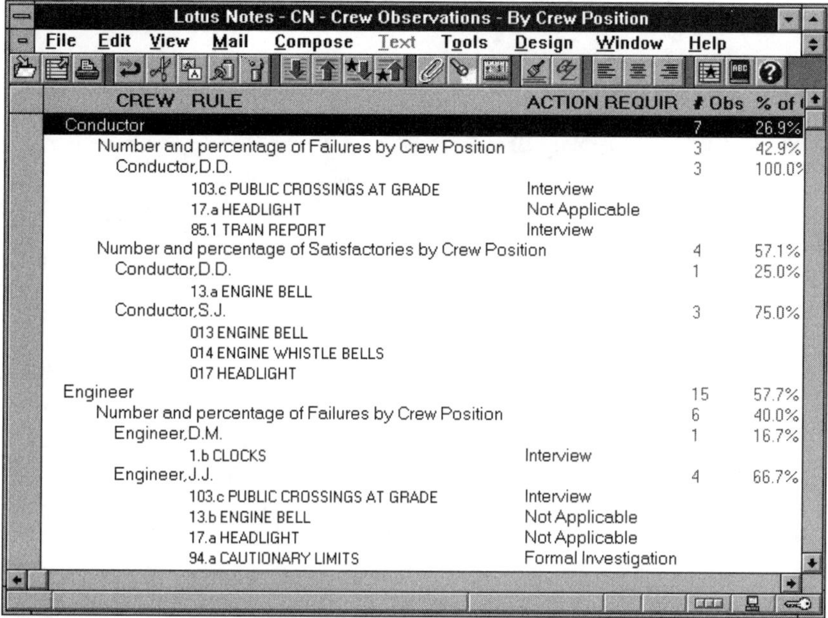

There is a view organized By District, and others By Employee, By Observation Type, By Subdivision, and By Season. These views can help to discover whether there are characteristic times or locations that tend to cause errors.

A view By Rule can show the rules that are most often broken, which may lead either to changes in the rules or enhanced enforcement.

CN has a view showing the Actions Taken in the case of unsatisfactory performance, and another By Supervisor. These views would help senior management to monitor the behavior of the supervisors themselves.

At this writing, the database has been in trial use for a few weeks with a limited number of supervisors. The supervisors are using the system and are quite pleased with it. They feel that it will help them do their jobs better.

FACT SHEET

Employee Development System

Purpose: To provide Canadian National Railway supervisory personnel with a convenient way of collecting observations on rule compliance by train crews, and to increase the operating efficiency through the introduction of advanced technology.

Application Origin: Developed for Canadian National Railway by Changepoint Corporation, a Canadian company consulting in project management, application development, implementation, and training. Contact: Changepoint Corporation, 1595 Sixteenth Avenue, Suite 702, Richmond Hill, Ontario, Canada L4B 3N9, Phone: (905) 886-7000

Application Development Time: 3 weeks from conception to first version.

Typical Size: CN expects the database to consume roughly 100 MB per year.

Typical Use: Supervisors in the field use pen-based laptop computers to record observations using a special data entry application built in Microsoft Visual Basic that stores data in a Notes database. The observations are then replicated across the organization and analyzed using a variety of Notes views.

Forms: There is a Header form used for each collection of observations, and an Observation form used for recording a single observation on a single employee. The observation forms are stored as responses to the header.

Views: A wide variety of views make it easy to analyze the data from almost any point of view. Included are views By Crew Position, By District, By Subdivision, and By Season, used to look for trends. Views By Employee and By Supervisor can identify personnel problems. Views By Rule, By Observation Type, and Actions Taken can be used to analyze the rules themselves.

Corporate Policy Manual

Many organizations distribute large manuals describing every aspect of corporate policies. These manuals typically contain information relevant to all employees including how and when salaries are paid, calculation of bonuses, a description of health care benefits, procedures to file a health care claim, and so on. These books are the responsibility of the human resources organization, which updates the information contained in the books regularly. At large companies, this book frequently is a three-ring binder issued to each employee when they join the company. Over the years, as information in the book is updated, the Human Resources department sends each employee an addendum or replacement section for the existing sections. Employees are expected to remove any outdated sections and replace them with the newer sections as they become available.

As an alternative to this, EcoTrail, Inc. (a fictional organization) has decided to move its corporate policy manual into Notes. EcoTrail is an environmental company that focuses on rearchitecting landfills to make the areas useful to the surrounding communities. By publishing its corporate policy manual in Notes, the company can eliminate the need to provide everyone with a paper manual and the need to send out updates as they become available. This will save the company real dollars. In addition, the manual will be more useful to employees. Employees will be able to use views to identify documents on the basis of subject. If a more complex search is required, the employee will be able to use the Notes full-text search engine. This provides the employee with powerful tools to identify documents with relevant information far more quickly and accurately than even a well-maintained index. Finally, if the database is replicated to servers throughout the company, changes to the contents of the database will replicate throughout the company in a

View By area in the Corporate Policies manual database

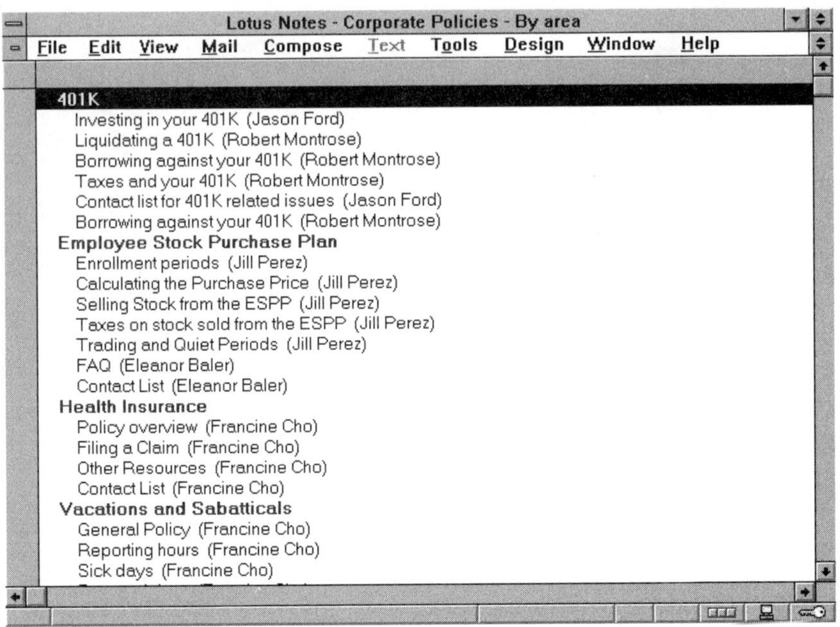

matter of hours. This ensures that the information contained in the database is up to date and more accurate than relying on individuals to update their Corporate Policies manual.

FIRST CUT

Jason Ford is the technology person in the Human Resources department. As such, he is assigned the task of developing the application. He has been using Notes as an end user for a while, and is anxious to try his hand at application development. Jason obtains a copy of the Notes application developer manual, and begins work on EcoTrail's policy manual database.

Jason decides that the easiest way to start this application is to modify one of the existing Notes templates. To that end, he examines the various template files provided with Notes. The template files are typically stored in the Notes data directory. To see the template files, select Open Database, from the File menu, pick a Notes server, type *.NTF into the filename box, and press Return. He decides the most likely candidate for the application is the Discussion template. The Discussion template appears to be the simplest, and therefore the most flexible.

Jason's first act is to create a new database from the template. Once this is done, he updates the forms to reflect his application's needs. This requires him to change the *static text* for the database's forms. Static text is a type of text in the form that is used to provide the end user with clues to the purpose of the form and the fields in the form. Jason's screen now looks somewhat different.

In addition to the Main document, Jason makes some other changes to the application. These include updating the Response document, and deleting the Response to Response document. This leaves a database with two forms: Main document, and Response. He intends to use the Main document to describe general categories (e.g., health benefits), and the Response document to talk about specific aspects of the general category (e.g., procedures to file a claim).

So far, Jason has not changed any of the field names in the documents. As a result, the views for the database are probably all right in their current form. As Jason adds data to the database, it may be necessary to reevaluate the views to see whether they could be better organized or if additional views might be necessary.

Jason's next activity is to populate the database with sample data. This provides people in his department with a real opportunity to evaluate the application. The simplest way of doing this is to collect electronic copies of a number

Before editing (standard Discussion template main form)

After editing form for Main document

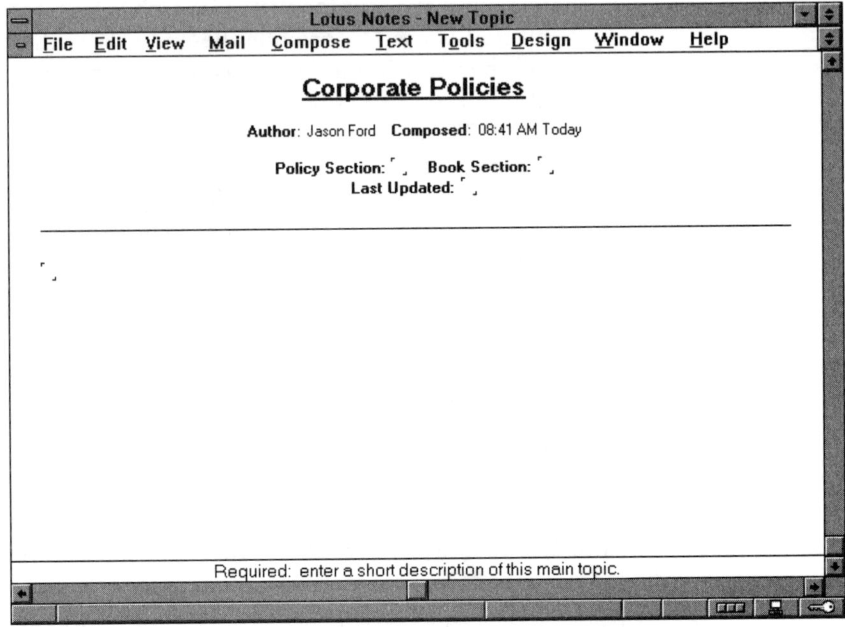

of sections of the old paper policy manual and cut and paste these into appropriately titled Notes documents. Jason decides to collect the documents regarding vacation time and health care benefits. These sections are well documented and typically garner the most questions from employees.

FEEDBACK

After populating the database with some sample data, Jason sets the default access control list to reader, posts the database to his organization's server, and enables the application for full-text search. To facilitate review of the application, Jason creates a Discussion database on the server for comment. He creates the new database from the standard Notes template and gives it the title Corporate Policy Discussion. He creates an initial document to help start the discussion (his document provides some background on the genesis of the Corporate Policy application), and the applications are ready for end users.

To make the users aware of the application, Jason sends out an e-mail. Jason's organization uses Notes Mail, so he can even send out a doclink to the actual database. A user receiving this e-mail just double-clicks on the doclink, and Notes automatically adds the appropriate icon to the user's desktop, and opens the database to the doclinked document. He creates an e-mail with a doclink to the first document in the Corporate Policy database, and another to the first document in the Discussion database. In the body of the e-mail, he provides users with a description of the purpose of the application, and the nature of the feedback he is expecting. Jason sends this e-mail out to the group and asks for a receipt upon delivery—selecting this option tells Notes to send a confirming e-mail message back to him when the e-mail is delivered to each user. The group has about twenty people, so, assuming the message is delivered to all, 20 delivery confirmations will be generated.

To get some idea of who has looked at the database, Jason enables User Activity in the Corporate Policy database. Enabling this feature causes Notes to record the number of documents each user of the database reads or writes to the database. By monitoring this over time, he will be able to track which users have used the database and which have not. Once the database is in production, it could be used to provide some feedback on the popularity of the database with employees.

Users start contributing to the Discussion database almost immediately. Much of the discussion is questions: When will the application be deployed? What other information could we post in the database? When will we stop production of the paper policy manual? Could we make the forms different colors; the current colors look the same on my laptop? He answers the questions he can, occasionally deferring answers to management. The majority of the questions/comments are related to process and content, rather than to the application itself. Jason's next step is to meet with management to review the application.

THE DATA...

The original policy manual was created with a word processor. While the manual was stored in a number of files (maintained by different people), the documents were quite large. In the prototype application, he simply cut and pasted entire word processing documents into Notes. Users suggested that this was cumbersome—it took Notes too long to read the documents. It would make more sense to break the large documents up into smaller documents, which are then stored in Notes.

When he presented this as part of his proposal to management, they indicated it would be desirable to review all data prior to publication to employees. Management asked a number of tough questions:

▶ Completeness: How will he ensure that all the information is available? Who will read through the original document and the new Notes documents to check this?

▶ Integrity: Does the new arrangement of documents make sense? Will end users be able to find the documents they need easily?

▶ Accuracy: Since this is essentially a new publication for the group, we should take the time to review all information submitted for publication.

▶ Updates: How will he update the information contained in the database? Should the updates be done in Notes? If so, what new procedures need to be put in place to support this?

All of his company's employees rely on the Corporate Policy manual for accurate information about health care, vacation, compensation, and so on. The information contained in this database *must* be accurate. The conclusion of the meeting is that development of the application should continue, but publication will be piecemeal—the paper policy manual will be converted to Notes section by section. Prior to final publication, each section will be subject to a comprehensive review by relevant personnel. While this will slow down the overall conversion from paper to electronic publication, it ensures that the data distributed is up to date, accurate, and comprehensive. This should help to ensure a positive reaction to the application among employees.

Additional issues raised by management included questions about how the manual would look printed (in the event a user wants to print relevant documents). Some of the formatting used in the word processor is lost in conversion to Notes. Users will want to print out relevant sections so it is important to ensure that the documents created in Notes take this into account. Another question surrounded the subject of new sections. Procedures need to be defined that allow the organization to add or subtract sections of the manual easily. Finally, the managers suggest that the Discussion database should be rolled out as part of the application to allow employees to make comments and suggestions about the database and to allow them to ask questions about content.

After the meeting, he develops a short project plan that identifies the order in which sections of the paper corporate policy manual will be converted to Notes. This plan calls for a conversion and review cycle of two months per section. This should allow ample time for conversion and review. The first step is to review the existing information in the database. Once this is complete, the Corporate Policy database and the Discussion database are posted to other servers around the company. A corporate e-mail is sent out with doclinks to the two databases explaining their purpose and providing a brief overview of the timelines defined in his project plan.

UNFINISHED BUSINESS

Employees might have questions that they feel are too private to post in the Discussion database. For those employees, it would make sense for Human Resources to provide an e-mail address to which employees can send more personal correspondence. This e-mail address could go to a central shared database, or to an individual who is then responsible for distributing the e-mail to the appropriate person within the group. Clearly, this information could be very sensitive—it would be critical to define policies and procedures to ensure that it is totally confidential.

FACT SHEET

Corporate Policy Database

Purpose: To manage and distribute corporate resources policies centrally.

Application Origin: Built from the Discussion template.

Application Development Time: 5 hours over 2 weeks.

Typical Size: Corporate policies do not tend to vary widely in size from organization to organization. Generally, about 5–10 MB.

Typical Use: The human resources department maintains documents describing various policies on compensation, health care, vacation, and so on. This application will store these policies and allow employees throughout the company electronic access to these documents.

Forms: Main and Response.

Views: By Area, By Document, All By Area, and All By Author.

Building an Electronic Forms Library

Every company uses forms in one way or another. Small companies might have just one or two for things like reporting time worked and logging miscellaneous expenses. Large companies can have dozens of forms that employees must fill out for one reason or another. Paper forms are generally used, but Notes can be used to minimize the overhead associated with paper forms while making life easier on the employees.

Don Chasin is the manager of the Notes Application Development Group, part of the Notes Support Department, at a large corporation. Being a Notes expert, and an employee of a large company, Don understands paper forms and Notes forms. In this chapter, Don applies his knowledge of Notes and his position as a manager to push his company to take advantage of the power of Notes.

MOVING TO ELECTRONIC FORMS

While filling out his weekly time report for the 213th time, Don considers the idea of using Notes to minimize the burden of paper forms. He thinks about the various aspects of paper forms that Notes should be able to improve. There is the process of ordering forms from a printer, receiving them, and storing them where employees can find them. As an employee, there is the constant searching for the right form and figuring out what to do with it especially when it requires multiple approvals. There is the process of receiving forms from employees, often handwritten and hard to read, and hand processing and filing the forms. Not to mention the process of dealing with lost paper forms!

Don then thinks about some of the advantages electronic forms have over paper. They never have to be ordered, printed, or physically stored (except on hard disk). They can be stored in a common, electronic repository to make them easily found for employees. They can provide online help about how to fill out particular fields, and what to do with them after completion. They can be programmed to route forms to the appropriate people or groups for approval automatically, with the final destination also programmed.

Further, electronic forms in Notes can take advantage of the special Notes security features like access control lists, field signatures, mail encryption, and digital signature to ensure that sensitive information is restricted to those required to have access. This can be especially important for forms containing financial and personal information.

Don decides to share his idea for converting his company's many paper forms to electronic Notes forms with his department head, Arnold Sherman. Arnold agrees that it's a great application of Notes. After further discussion, the two of them identify two main areas that require work if the application is going to succeed. One is the standard routine Don's group of application developers has become accustomed to: defining the application, developing a prototype, refining the prototype, putting together a deployment plan, and so on. The other is the more administrative task of identifying the current owners of the paper forms and their associated processes, and getting them to agree to use Notes electronic forms, indeed to get them to fund the Notes development in order to achieve cost savings when the paper forms are eliminated. Arnold's department head asks him to work on the logistics of implementing company-wide electronic forms. He says he'll talk to the other department heads about getting support for the project.

TAKING ADVANTAGE OF NOTES

Don calls his group together and suggests using Notes to replace many of the paper forms the company uses. A lively discussion ensues of the capabilities Notes provides to do this, as well as some of the hurdles the project is likely to encounter.

Sharon Nappi speaks up and explains about the Custom Mail Forms template that comes bundled with Notes. "Have you noticed that the Mail Compose menu has an item called Custom Forms? When you choose it you get a list of a few additional forms you can create as part of your mailbox. That is, in addition to the normal Memo, Response, and other forms, you get a new list. The forms that come with Notes are Fax Memo, Employee Performance Evaluation, Reply with History, and Weekly Time Record. These forms are just examples that come with Notes to get us started. The idea is that the forms are stored in this special template called FORMS.NTF, which is replicated to all servers and to all users using workstation-based mail. The menu item Customer Forms puts up a list of the forms defined in this template. That way, all we need to do is put the forms we want employees to have access to in the forms template."

Mike Valese picks up on Sharon's idea: "A key advantage of that is we won't need to create a new database and deal with getting it replicated to all the servers and then asking everyone to add it to their desktop. With the Forms template, we simply need to add forms to an existing template and make everyone aware of the special menu item that calls them up."

Don had not been aware of this feature of Notes, but he can see that it is very powerful. He asks his group about the fact that the forms seem to be completely tied to mail. Are all paper forms suitable for replacement by Notes Mail forms? What about forms that still need to be printed, signed, and mailed (old-fashioned, paper mail) or hand-delivered? Sharon responds. "That's a good point. Certainly the intent of the forms template is to tie electronic forms to mail. Most forms will be mail-enabled so that they are automatically routed to the appropriate person or group when the user saves the form. But the form doesn't have to be mail enabled. In this case, the form will be saved in the user's mailbox. The form can trigger printing, or the form can simply be saved, and the user can print it when paper is required. The alternative is to build a new database to store forms meant to be printed, but this raises the issue about everyone's forms being stored in the forms database. This may be OK, but requires special attention on security, and requires views to be built, access control lists to be monitored, and all that stuff."

Don agrees that the Forms template is the way to go, at least at first. He then engages his group in a discussion of some of the details of what electronic forms would be like, and the processes they would support. Sharon offers her thoughts:

"Implementing forms electronically gets us into the area of reengineering. Sure, there are simple cases where we are truly just replacing paper forms with electronic ones, which get filled out and printed. In this case, no reengineering is required. Users fill out forms, print them, and from that point on the form processing is the same as if they had started with a paper form. While there are definitely advantages to even this scenario, some of the real benefits will probably come in when the handling of the form moves from handling paper to handling electronic versions.

"For example, take the weekly time reports we fill out. We can certainly create the form in the Custom Mail Forms template, and that way everyone can fill one out electronically, print it, and give it to the secretaries. But what do the secretaries do with it? They check the forms to see if they need approval. If they need approval, they route the form to the employees supervisor and wait for it to come back signed. Then, the forms are mailed to the account department where people enter the information into a computer for further processing.

"The biggest benefits would come from reengineering the process so it is completely electronic. Employees could fill out a weekly time report, but instead of printing it, Notes could mail the form. It could be mailed to the secretary if there is no need for approval, and it could be mailed to the employee's supervisor if the form needs approval. The criteria for whether the form needs approval or not could be built right into the form.

"If a supervisor receives a form requiring approval, he or she can review it and click a button to approve. This will send the form to the secretary. When the secretary receives all the forms, they can be reviewed for correctness and then forwarded to the accounting department. Perhaps even the step of secretarial approval could be eliminated, and the forms could be mailed directly to the accounting department (after supervisory approval if needed).

"Finally, the accounting department could write a custom application to transfer the data to their accounting computers directly. This would eliminate the step of manually reentering the data from one system to another. The new process would be much more efficient than the current one."

Don summarizes the points he heard by defining three levels of sophistication that can be implemented in Notes when replacing paper forms with electronic forms:

1. Make forms available online to be filled out and printed. This eliminates the need to get forms printed in advance and makes them easy to update, readily available to all employees, and easy to fill out.
2. Basic mail-enabling to automate sending the form to the required destination. This provides additional benefits by not requiring the user to print the form and then address an envelope or hand-deliver it. The form automatically goes to the right place, and that place can be easily changed by changing the form (or the contents of the group the form is mailing to).
3. Reengineering the existing paperwork flow. This takes advantage of Notes security features, Notes' ability to route forms through multiple stops, and the ability to programmatically extract the Notes data for use in other systems. Significant cost and time savings can be achieved through the elimination of manual processes.

At this point, Don has enough data to report back to his department and show the support he's gathered for replacing the paper forms with Notes forms.

THE FIRST FORM

Arnold explains that the idea was met mostly with enthusiasm. Many of the department heads like the idea of replacing the existing paper forms with Notes versions. They suggest picking one and seeing how it goes. Don explains the built-in support Notes has provided with the Custom Mail Forms client feature and template, and that the main step is to simply create a new form in this existing template.

Don suggests starting with a form of the first variety—one that gets filled out and printed. Arnold agrees and suggests talking with the Purchasing department. He says they were particularly enthused about the idea of electronic forms. He makes a quick call and gets a contact name: Leslie Savas.

Back in his office, Don gives Leslie a call to discuss the trial. Leslie explains that they would love to turn their purchase orders into electronic forms, since they are constantly getting calls from people with questions like, "Where can I get a purchase order? Is the purchase order form I have the current one? What is the dollar limit where I need to get approval," and so on. She thinks making the form a Notes form would be great. Don tells her he will have one of his people contact her to get the purchase order implemented as an electronic form.

He then calls Sharon, who spoke up about the Custom Mail Forms idea in Don's group meeting, and asks her to work with Leslie to implement the purchase order form as a basic form. He asks her to build in as many helpful features as possible, since this form will be used as a test.

A couple of weeks later, Don attends a demo that Sharon and Leslie have organized. His department head is there, as well as the head of purchasing. Sharon is explaining the use of the form:

"I am now bringing up the Notes client. I am an employee looking to fill out a purchase order, so I access the custom forms via the Mail menu. I now see a list of forms including Purchase Order, which I choose.

"The empty purchase order appears on my screen. Notice the directions at the top of the form explaining that the form is to be filled out and printed. To print, there is a button at the bottom of the form. The instructions also explain that the form will automatically contain sections for approvals if the dollar amount exceeds the lower self-approval threshold.

"I am now proceeding to fill out the form. I enter my name, department number, and all that good stuff in the general information area. Notice if I try to save the form that an error message appears telling me I must enter my phone number. If I enter my phone number and try to save, the form will tell me what the next required field is.

"Notice the red box outlining the phrase 'Enter items being purchased here.' As I click on that text, see how a pop-up box appears, giving me information about how to fill out this portion of the form. These pop-ups have been included at every point were confusion might occur. This built-in help should eliminate most of the phone calls we get about filling out these forms.

"Now that I have entered a few items to be purchased, I'll print the form using the button at the bottom. When I do, the form is first automatically saved. In the process, the form calculates the total dollar amount of the purchase order. Since this dollar amount is less than $250 (which we programmed into the form), the form has displayed a message telling me I don't need to get this form approved—I can send it directly to purchasing.

The Custom Mail Forms dialog box

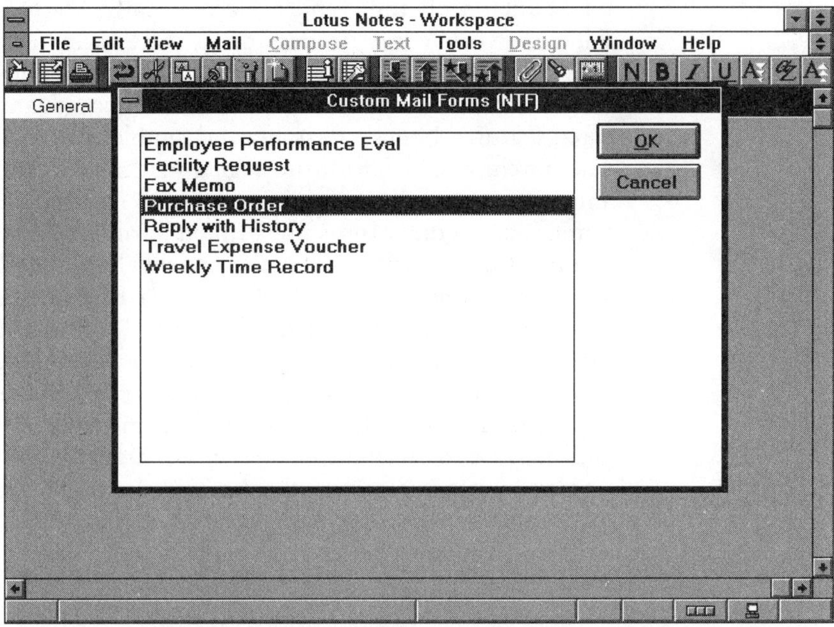

"You see now the form is being printed. It contains the address of Purchasing clearly marked at the top, and the message 'Total is under approval amount—send directly to Purchasing' has been printed. That's it. If you like the form, we can replicate it to the server and tomorrow everyone in the company will have access to it."

The department heads love it and instruct Don and Leslie to oversee the deployment of the form. They ask Leslie to select a department to help trial the form. If the trial goes well, then in another month or so the form will be made available to the entire company.

MANY FORMS LATER

A year later, many forms have been converted to Notes forms. The purchase order form was quite successful, and the employees appreciated the online help and clear instructions on when a form needed approval. The purchasing department also found it quite useful to be able to update the form by updating the form design in one database and replicating the changes out to all servers. This means that all users always have access to the recent form.

Seeing the usefulness of the electronic purchase order, other departments have added forms to the Custom Mail Forms template. Employees are now filling out weekly time reports electronically. Many facility requests like phone lines, network connections, and so forth can now be made electronically. Travel expense vouchers can be filled out online and printed.

Also, many of the departments are taking advantage of the more sophisticated features Notes offers beyond simple filling out and printing of forms. The purchase order form now gets mailed to a supervisor if its total dollar amount exceeds the self-approval limit. The form is then mailed directly to Purchasing so the form is not printed until it is received by purchasing. Notes security features ensure that the approval is made by a bonafide supervisor, and that no one modifies the form other than the person making the request and the approver (if needed). Since the form is sent by mail to Purchasing, there are no paper-mail delays to slow down the process.

The weekly time reports are also taking advantage of electronic routing and approvals, but are still sent to the department secretary for printing, approval, and mailing to Accounting. However, Don is working with Accounting on how to interface Notes to the Accounting system, and when that is achieved the forms will no longer need to be printed at all.

◢ **FACT SHEET**

Electronic Forms Database

Purpose: To eliminate the use of paper forms in an organization and obtain the benefits of electronic forms such as online help, centralized forms, and ease of updating forms.

Application Origin: Implemented with the built-in Custom Mail Forms template bundled with Notes, and the client feature that provides access to these forms via the Mail, Compose, Custom Forms menu selection.

Application Development Time: From a few weeks to a few months per form, depending on the sophistication of the work flow implemented.

Typical Size: 1–10 MB.

Typical Use: Used in medium and large companies where there are many paper forms that employees must deal with.

Forms: These will vary by company. Examples are weekly time reports, purchase orders, and facility orders. Any form that an employee must fill out and send somewhere is a likely candidate.

Views: There are no views in this application. When documents are saved, they are saved in the user's mailbox, and the mail views can be used to find the document.

Idea Management System: A Notes VIP Application

Marc Griseta is a Programmer/Analyst for the First National Bank of Chicago. In mid-1994, his division was targeted for a major reengineering initiative. He was chosen to be a member of a cross-functional team to examine the company's Product Development and Introduction (PDI) process.

The team members involved covered a wide range of groups involved in the development of products used to support the business. A key component of the reengineered process included the creation of a central repository of new product ideas and documentation associated with developing those products. The goal was to capture information from the people who work directly with customers regarding opportunities for new products and problems that can be fixed in existing ones. When it came time to create the system, Marc was chosen to develop what is now being called the Idea Management System (IMS).

RELATIONAL OR NOTES?

"We considered the various relational database management systems like Oracle and Paradox. We also considered Lotus Notes. At first, it seemed that they were split evenly—relational systems could do some things well, Notes could do other things well. After we prioritized our needs, we decided that the document management, full-text search, and replication features of Notes offered the better solution." Marc spent about six weeks learning about Notes and

Application information and screen shots courtesy of the First National Bank of Chicago. Application developed by Marc Griseta, Marily Berceau, and Ramninder Hansra.

developing a prototype of IMS based in Notes. Things were going fairly well, but there were a couple of problems.

One was a grouping problem. Ideas are generated at all levels of the organization—some of the ideas could become products in their own right, while others are not by themselves enough to constitute a product. However, when combined with other ideas, they might well form the outline for a product. So Marc wanted to allow people to create ideas as Main documents, and later on move them into Response documents of some other Main document.

"Trying to do that in native Notes gets pretty ugly," Marc said. As he put it, "The children come before the parent. We wanted to collect a whole lot of ideas, rearrange them, and attach them to a product. Notes doesn't do that very well."

The second problem was that they weren't happy with the Notes user interface for their application. Marc felt they couldn't manage the interaction very well using the Notes form-oriented structure. "We have a whole lot of questions we wanted to ask, but most of them are optional. We didn't want to just throw them all on a form and scare everyone away. Our user population was not currently using Notes and most of them were just getting PCs for the first time." He wanted to be able to create an application where anyone who had an idea, even those who don't normally use computers, could enter the idea into the system.

PERFECT TIMING

Shortly after the original prototype was completed, Notes/Visual Programmer (ViP) was released, and Marc was invited to a demonstration. Notes/ViP is a development tool from Lotus used for rapidly building Windows applications that make use of Notes data. It has a graphical user interface development tool (GUI builder), provides access to Notes data and relational data, and contains a report writer and a graphing tool. It uses the LotusScript language (which is a close cousin to Visual Basic), and provides a visual programming language that greatly speeds up the initial programming when building an application. Marc was interested.

"We were intrigued by ViP because it let us redefine the user interface of the project, while still letting us use all the features of Notes that were important to us. After the demonstration, we ordered an evaluation copy from Lotus. I think we were using it on the second day it was out."

He used the evaluation copy for about a month, at which time he was satisfied with its capabilities and excited by its potential. He committed to building IMS using a combination of Notes and Notes/ViP. Three months later, he delivered Phase 1 of the project.

Phase 1 allowed users to enter new ideas into the system, add comments to ideas, and view the idea documents and their comments, providing a substantial fraction of the features of the total system. Phase 2 followed three months later. It allowed the ideas to be grouped into concepts and linked to a parent document. It allowed reporting on and charting of the information in the IMS database.

A HIGHLY GRAPHICAL INTERFACE

Even Phase 1 was a highly graphical product. Because he was working with an relatively untrained user base, Marc wanted to make the product as accessible as possible. The opening screen is a graphical image of an office, showing a file cabinet (where the ideas are "stored"), a book to enter new ideas, and other miscellaneous office furnishings. Clicking on an item activates it.

For example, clicking on the file cabinet drawer "opens" the cabinet graphically, while the application is opening the Notes database. Once the file is opened, the documents display on a screen that looks like a folder. Tabs on the folder indicate different views of the data—different ways to sort the information.

"We really got very creative with this, because we wanted to make sure there would be no training required. We even put a few fun buttons on the

The opening screen of the Idea Management System

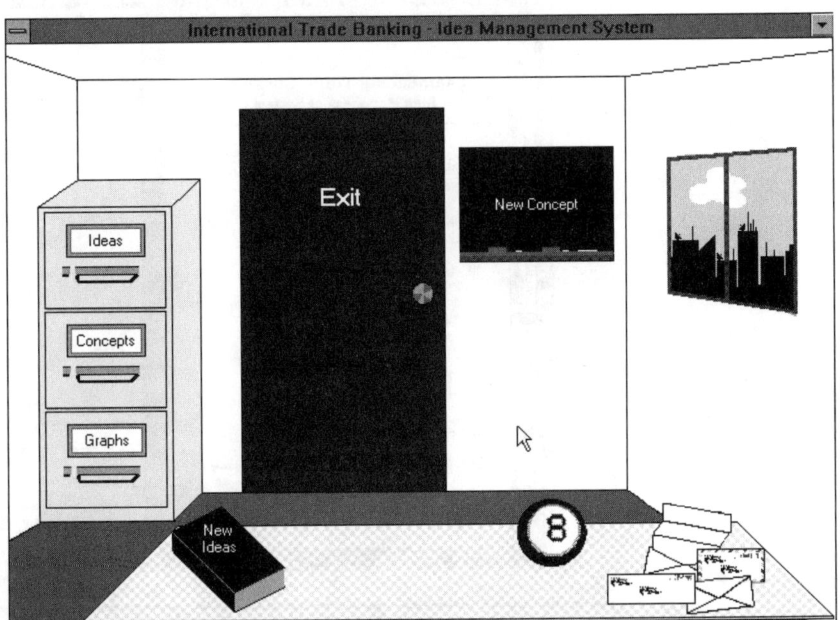

first screen, like the eight-ball—they don't do anything useful, but they're there to encourage people to try things out."

OPTIONAL FIELDS

There are only three fields that are absolutely required to enter an idea—a description of your idea, the department you work in, and a phone number where you can be contacted with questions. But there are a whole lot of optional fields to fill out time permitting.

"Our dilemma was to get the user to enter the required information and encourage them to complete the optional questions without making it seem like all of the questions were required. So we used the metaphor of a book. When you start filling things out, the introduction is the required fields. As soon as you start typing in the idea text, we turn on a bunch of tabs in the book and label them. If you're interested, if you have time, you can click on those and fill out more information. The user can at any time save an incomplete idea and come back to it later, or can submit the idea for review once the required fields are complete.

Entering an idea

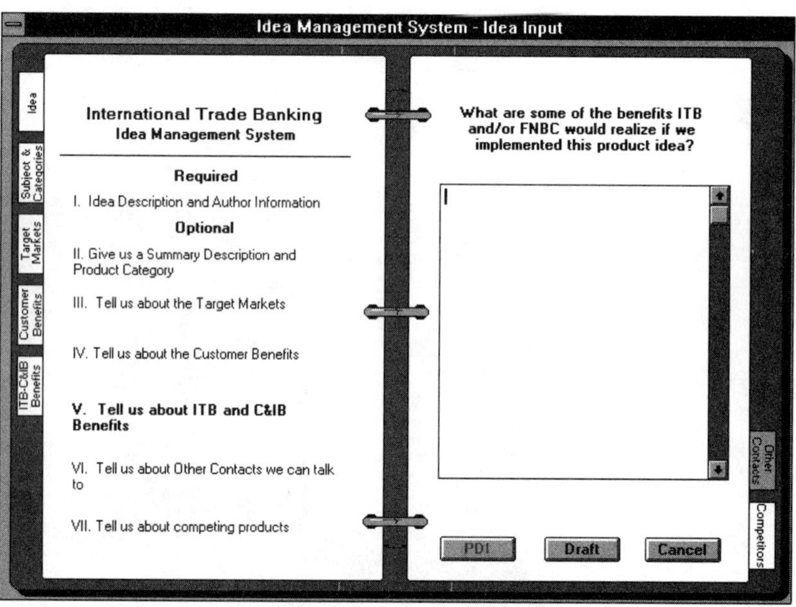

LESS TIME THAN ANTICIPATED

When Marc first began the project, he estimated that Phase 1 would take about four and a half months. He was able to deliver the product a month and a half early.

"There were two reasons we were able to deliver early," Marc explained. "First, because I was on the team of people who designed the processes, I knew what the system was supposed to do. Second, ViP and Notes are very easy to work with. I'd start with an idea, build a Notes view or form in ten minutes, build a ViP screen in another thirty minutes, and within an hour I had a working prototype. Looking back on it, I would estimate that I spent about 40 percent of my time on Phase 1 just tuning the graphics—nothing to do with the functionality, just tuning the look. Finishing ahead of schedule allowed my boss to commit early on Phase 2."

"The second phase was a bit more complex. I had reporting, tracking, charting, and regrouping ideas to do. Since I already had the graphics taken care of, I didn't spend as much time on the looks."

THE ROLLOUT

The application was first rolled out to about twenty people. Feedback was very positive. "Everyone was impressed," said Marc. "The people who have customer contact were very receptive. They found it very easy to use. We held a brief training course, and a week or so later they remembered how to use everything."

"Our biggest feature problem is a missing feature that we simply can't add because it isn't available in ViP—read/unread markers like you get in Notes views. The other difficulty we're having is in our corporate infrastructure. We would like to get IMS out to all of our offices, but most locations have yet to install Notes."

FUTURES

Marc actually made a demo of the product using Lotus ScreenCam (which is a tool for recording and playing back electronic movies of the action on a PC screen). This demonstration has been making the rounds of the company, and this application might be adopted by other groups who are also undergoing a reengineering process.

Marc was extremely pleased with the combination of ViP and Notes. "The development time was very quick with both products. ViP and Notes complement each other well."

FACT SHEET

Idea Management System

Purpose: To capture ideas generated at all levels of an organization so that they can be used to seed the development of new products.

Application Origin: Custom developed using a combination of Notes for data storage and Notes/ViP for the user interface and reporting.

Application Development Time: 7 man-months.

Typical Size: ViP runtime software, 5 MB; ViP application, 2.5 MB; Notes database, 1 MB.

Typical Use: Ideas are entered by anyone who has one; they often come from people whose primary job is customer relations, such as the sales staff. New ideas are reviewed; if they are clear and not the province of some other department, they are opened for full access. Other users can comment on and discuss the ideas.

Later on, the ideas can be categorized and classified into projects. The database tracks ideas, the status of the ideas, responses, projects, and project status, as well as support documents for the projects.

Forms: ViP manages the user interface; internally, the database has forms for ideas, projects, and comments.

Views: ViP makes use of many custom views to provide access to the database in various ways.

The Accounting Rules Database

Accounting firms, large companies, and companies in the financial services industries need to keep close track of changes to SEC and IRS rules and FASB pronouncements. FASB stands for Financial Accounting Standards Board. These and a few other government and independent agencies help define the Generally Accepted Accounting Principles (GAAP) employed by U.S companies. GAAP is a comprehensive set of standard accounting rules that corporations follow to ensure compliance with various tax and regulatory agencies (and to ensure good record keeping for themselves). GAAP takes into account all IRS and SEC regulations. The IRS's role (in this context) is to collect taxes from corporations in the most accurate and efficient manner possible. The SEC is responsible for monitoring companies that issue stock and bonds in the U.S. to ensure full and complete disclosure of relevant financial information and compliance with the law. This helps to ensure that markets in the U.S. remain fair and competitive. GAAP is used by accountants across the U.S. to ensure companies are collecting accurate financial information and recording it appropriately. Every corporation's annual report contains a letter by the company's auditors. The auditor's job is to ensure that the company's accounting records are consistent with GAAP. Changes to FASB rules (or GAAP) can dramatically affect a company's stated revenues or income. This typically happens when FASB issues a change to GAAP that affects ongoing operations. For example, recent changes to recording pension fund financial information required a number of large corporations to restate their financial earnings (significantly reducing the earlier released numbers).

Thayer Brothers is a relatively large investment bank (hypothetical) located in New York City. Thayer has 8,000 employees with offices in a number of US cities, London, Frankfurt, Tokyo, and Hong Kong. As an investment bank,

Thayer is responsible for helping corporations conclude financial transactions. These transactions might include issuing stocks or bonds, or acquiring another company. A number of years ago, Thayer Brothers hired Benjamin North to monitor FASB (pronouncments). Ensuring that the company is completely up to date on all FASB actions is critical to its business. Changes to GAAP can present opportunities for new business by making issuing stock more attractive, or undermine existing businesses by making acquisitions less attractive.

For the first few years of his tenure, Benjamin monitored the SEC, IRS, and FASB and distributed his reports (called the Financial Accounting Report or FAR for short) to the firm describing what changes in financial accounting practices were being contemplated and, more importantly, what changes were likely. Later, when the firm had acquired an e-mail system, he distributed these same reports through e-mail. Neither of these mechanisms was particularly effective. Typically, investment bankers would ignore, throw out, or delete Benjamin's Accounting Report unless it directly addressed an issue they were working on at the moment. Consequently, if an opportunity arose that might be affected by the FAR, bankers had no choice but to call Benjamin directly for help.

ENTER NOTES

Thayer had been running a pilot Notes installation for about six months and was looking for reasonable target applications. Maria Vasquez was one of the Notes application developers working in Thayer's computer support group. She was also aware of Benjamin North's reports. She suggested to her management that an application to store his reports might be a good way of getting bankers interested in Notes and would certainly be a better solution than sending the reports out through e-mail as he currently did. Maria's management liked the idea and approached Benjamin North about the concept.

Benjamin also was intrigued by the concept. While he realized his work was important to the firm, he continued to be frustrated that people would call him with questions that he had already answered in one of his reports. In addition, the ability to use a full-text index in all of his reports was particularly appealing. He agreed to sit down with Maria, and the two of them came up with a basic design for the application.

The database would have a form called FAR. This form would be used to "publish" Benjamin's reports on changes to GAAP. The form would include a field to record whether the FAR dealt with a change or an analysis. A change would be any amendments to GAAP motivated by the IRS, SEC, or

FASB. An analysis would be an assessment of enacted rules. The analysis might include how other firms are making or losing money on a particular rule. On Change documents, a status field would be included to record whether the change under discussion was contemplated, proposed, or in force. The FAR would also include fields for Industry (whether a rule affected a particular industry) and Category (which would be left up to Benjamin to define).

The database would also provide a forum for discussion. FARs could be viewed alone, or in the context of the discussion part of the database. Users would be allowed to create response documents to FARs or to create documents using the Main Topic form to ask Benjamin questions outside the context of particular FARs. The Main Topic form would include a button FYEO (For Your Eyes Only—bankers tend to fancy themselves as secret agents or commandos, so this reference would not be lost on them). By clicking FYEO, the document would be saved with a Reader field with Benjamin's and the author's names. A document with a Reader field cannot be viewed by anyone not named in the Reader field itself. Selecting FYEO ensures that only Benjamin and the authoring banker have access to this document. This is particularly important when secrecy is an issue (as it frequently is in banking). For example, if Larry works with high-technology companies and starts posting lots of questions to Benjamin about acquisitions, it might become clear that Larry is working on an acquisition for one of his high-technology customers. If a person knew who Larry's customers were, they just might be able to get into the stock market and make some money based on this knowledge—this is insider trading. As a result, the FYEO option is a critical component of the database. When Benjamin writes a response to an FYEO document, the Response is automatically FYEO. The FYEO button will also be included on all Response documents. This allows bankers to ask private questions in response to a public FAR.

The views in the database will show all documents By Topic, Date, Author, Industry, and Category. In addition, there will also be views of FARs only (that is, none of the Discussion documents will be visible) By Topic, Date, Industry, and Category.

DEVELOPMENT

Maria creates a new database from the standard Discussion template. She then adds the FAR form to the application. This form is very simple and takes less than an hour to complete. The next step is to create the views for the database. The database already has views By Date, Author, and Category, so Maria adds the views By Topic and Industry. In addition, she creates new views based on the Topic, Date, Industry, and Category views. Into these views she inserts a selection formula to ensure that only FAR documents are shown in these views. She names the views accordingly and saves them to the database.

Finally, Maria inserts the FYEO button into the Discussion forms (Main Topic, Response, and Response to Response). Maria adds a Reader field to each of the forms. This Reader field is hidden to the user. The FYEO button is the only way for a user to update the information contained in the Reader field. Normally, the reader field is blank. A blank Reader field means that all users of the database can see a document. Pressing the FYEO button inserts Benjamin's and the author's Notes names into the reader field. When the document is saved, only Benjamin and the original author will be able to Read it. When a user looks at a document in a view, there is typically no way for the user to tell whether the document has a reader field or not. As a result, Maria adds a column called FYEO to each view. If a document has a Reader field enabled (and therefore only the author and Benjamin can see the document), this column will contain the word "Secure." In this manner, bankers can confirm that the documents they have created cannot be viewed by other users. If a document they have created does not show up as Secure, they need to reopen the document and press the FYEO button.

DEPLOYMENT

The development process lasts only a few days. Once the application is completed, Maria talks to her manager about posting it to the company's New York server and getting bankers started using it. Most of the company's New York office has Notes. Her manager suggests having Benjamin send them an e-mail message announcing the availability of the new database to a few bankers (perhaps those who seem to ask the most questions). Maria discusses this with Benjamin, and they identify 20 bankers in the office to participate in the trial of the application. During this period, Benjamin will continue to send out his FARs by e-mail as well. The trial period will last two months during which time Maria and Benjamin expect to add more and more bankers to the system. At the end of the two month period, Benjamin would stop sending out his FARs to bankers located in New York.

Benjamin spends about a week identifying older FARs to include in the trial run of the application. He copies these reports, which are already in an electronic format, into new FAR documents to be posted into the database.

The results of the trial are very positive. The bankers find the system a far more effective mechanism to get information from FARs than either the paper or e-mail copies of the documents. A few suggestions are made to improve the database, but in general the structure defined by Maria and Benjamin remains intact. Unfortunately, as the popularity of the database increases so, too, do the shortcomings of Reader fields.

By Topic View in the Accounting Rules database

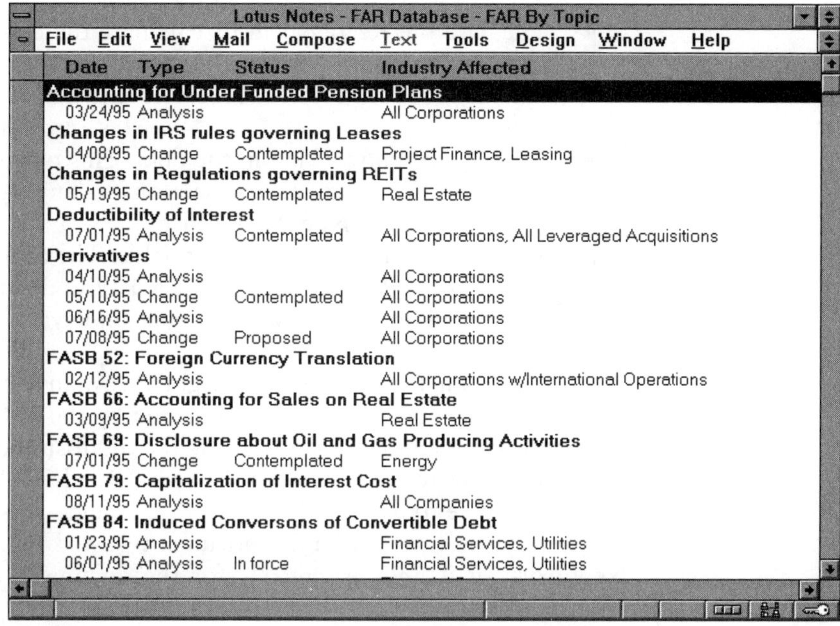

DISTRIBUTING SECURE INFORMATION

Once the application is accepted by the New York office, bankers in other parts of the U.S. start asking for access to the database. Being located in the field, the flow of information was always less than in New York. As a result, applications like the Accounting Rules database are even more valuable to people in the field. As the trial draws to a close, Maria works with her administrators to get the application replicated to the other Notes servers in the United States. This is done primarily as a stop-gap measure to get these offices some of the information in the database. Users located in these offices would not be able to use the FYEO feature of the application. This is because Notes servers (like users) need to be listed in a Reader field to be able to replicate a document. Maria had designed the FYEO feature to write only Benjamin's and the author's names to the Reader field. As a result, a user in one of the company's regional offices could complete an FYEO form, but this document would not replicate back to New York (as the New York server would not be listed in the Reader field on the document). Maria identifies a number of possible solutions to the problem, none of which were particularly satisfactory:

- ▶ Calculate the Reader field or calculate the contents of the Reader field based on the user's location. Users located in the field would need to add the groups ThayerLocalServers and ThayerHubServers to all documents.
- ▶ Leave FYEO unworking in the field. This option is not as unreasonable as it sounds. Almost all transactions of any significance are conducted in the company's New York office.
- ▶ Add server names to all Reader fields. The application could add server names to the Reader fields of every FYEO document created.
- ▶ Encrypt all documents with encryption keys.

Maria rules out the third option right away. Investment bankers deal with valuable information. They are monitored by the SEC to ensure their compliance with strict regulations governing the disclosure of private information. If server names were added to all document's Reader fields, all FYEO documents would replicate to all servers named in the field. This is highly undesirable. It is one thing to have an FYEO document posted on a highly secure server in New York. It is another entirely for the document to be flying all over the company's network and be posted on servers around the globe (even if the Reader fields prevent readers from seeing it). Maria knows bankers will not want to take that risk.

It is also fairly easy to rule out the fourth option. Encryption would scramble the text of the document so only a user with the correct key would be able to read the document. While this would ensure complete security, even if a document were replicated around the world, it would mean that each user of the database would need to have his own key (which they would need to create), and Benjamin would need everyone's key to ensure that he could read all documents. This would not be practical. In addition, encryption has the added drawback that if the users lose their keys, the encrypted information is lost as well.

The second option is distasteful because it will leave users confused as to what FYEO is and whether they have it or not, so Maria resolves to focus on the first suggested solution, calculate the Reader field. Luckily for Maria, the company has adopted a hierarchical naming scheme, which allocates the second level of the certificate to Location. As a result, if John Smith worked in the Chicago office, his name would be John Smith/Chicago/Thayer Brothers. Maria decides to use the user's name to determine the Reader field. If the user's name has anything but New York at the second level, the group's ThayerLocalServers and ThayerHubServers will be included in the Reader field. This has the drawback of tying her application directly to the company's naming structure. In the event that the Thayer Notes administrators decided to change how names are created, her application might not work correctly. Similarly, for users moving into or out of the New York office, the values calculated by the formula will be incorrect if they do not change their name. This will be a particular problem for users moving out of New York, as their documents will not include the additional groups, and therefore will not replicate back to New York.

UNFINISHED BUSINESS

Another issue related to reader fields and distributing the application is international users. Luckily for Maria, international uses the same hierarchical naming scheme. International also uses the same group names for replication (ThayerLocalServers and ThayerHubServers) so the application should work for international users. However, FASB (Standards Board), the IRS, and the SEC really only affect companies doing business in the U.S. Each country will have its own regulatory boards to determine accounting practices in that country. As a result, her application will be good for users needing information on U.S. rules, but does not address the needs of other countries around the world. This problem could be rectified either by updating the application to contain country-specific information, or by creating new copies of her application for each country.

One of the key components missing from the database is the source material used by Benjamin to write his analysis. It would be a powerful addition to the database to provide the user with a doclink to the original text of the FASB, IRS, or SEC rule being discussed. These documents are typically many pages in length, so this would likely need to be some kind of excerpts, or files stored on CD-ROM for retrieval. It is also possible that Benjamin's reports might have been prompted by an article in a journal. It would be useful to reference the article or include the full-text in the event that the text is available online.

FACT SHEET

Accounting Rules Database

Purpose: To provide bankers with a database of contemplated or enacted changes to GAAP (Generally Accepted Accounting Principles).

Application Origin: Developed from standard Discussion template.

Application Development Time: 2–3 man-weeks.

Typical Size: About 3–5 MB.

Forms: FAR, Main Topic, Response, and Response to Response.

Views: By Discussion, By Topic, By Date, By Author, By Industry, and By Category.

The Shotgun E-mails Database

Sharon Dungeness is the administrator for a large and successful Notes installation at Allied Communications Networks, a hypothetical, fast-growing firm that develops electronic communications systems. She has grown concerned about the disk space requirements for the corporate e-mail, which uses Notes Mail. With over a thousand users in the organization, every time someone sends out a company-wide (*shotgun*) message, something on the order of 3–5 MB of disk space is consumed on the company servers. It occurs to her that if all the shotgun messages were stored in a known place, people would not need to save them in their own Mail databases.

Furthermore, as the company has grown, it has become necessary to place tighter restrictions on who can send broadcast messages and on their content. When the company was smaller, e-mail use was more casual, and people would broadcast messages about softball games and Friday afternoon parties with no ill effects. But not everyone has realized that both the e-mail system and its users are growing less tolerant of trivia as the mail volume increases.

The last straw came last week when someone who lost a glove broadcast a message about it to the entire company, including a 100KB scanned image of the other glove. In a flash, 100 MB of disk space was consumed, and Sharon and the culprit were both inundated with complaints (consuming even *more* disk space). Although management made sure that the offender wouldn't repeat this incident any time soon, something more had to be done.

Sharon has been charged with finding a way to put a stop to this kind of activity without overly limiting the ability to reach the whole organization when necessary.

The first thing to do is limit people's ability to use the Shotgun mailing group. This turns out to be a bit tricky—Sharon has to ask someone on the Internet how to do it. Essentially, she uses a "cascaded" Name & Address book and restricts access to that secondary book. Once explained, it's fairly straightforward.

Although this stops the casual use of global e-mails, Sharon now needs to create a formal system that will allow them when necessary.

She first designs a way for people to request that an e-mail be sent. She uses the Forms Library database and creates a new form called Shotgun Request. The form has the following fields:

- ▶ To: is the standard address field. The form is always sent to a mail address called Shotgun Request, which is a mail address for a database Sharon will create called Shotgun Requests.
- ▶ From: Subject: and Body: are standard e-mail fields.
- ▶ Shotgun To: is a keyword field, implemented as a set of checkboxes. Sharon has organized the organizational mailing list into sublists for each of the major regions in the U.S. and internationally. Because not all e-mails need to go to the whole organization, this allows the sender to check which portions of the organization need to receive the mail.
- ▶ Send On: specifies the date and time the mail should be sent.
- ▶ Contact: contains information on who should be contacted with questions about the message.

Someone wishing to send a shotgun message will compose one from Custom Forms in the Mail menu. It will be mailed automatically to the Shotgun Requests database, which Sharon now has to create.

This database contains the same form used to compose the message, but it has an extra field, which is a Status field. An empty Status field marks the document as New. Other possible status values are Approved, Not Approved, Needs Revision, and Sent.

Most of the organization has no access to this database—only mail-in documents will be received. However, a few trusted people will have full editor access. For them, Sharon creates the following views:

- ▶ By Send Date: All received shotgun requests sorted by the date on which they should be sent, and subsorted by status.
- ▶ By Status: All requests sorted by status and subsorted by date.
- ▶ By Contact: All requests sorted by the contact name on the message.
- ▶ To Be Sent Soon: All requests with the status Approved and send date of tomorrow or earlier.

The administrators will read each new request and approve it, disapprove it, or request that the author make revisions. Once the request has been approved, it is eligible to be sent automatically.

Shotgun E-mail Request database viewed by Status

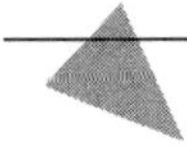

Sharon also creates a background macro that runs on the Notes server every hour and does three things:

▶ Composes and mails a Shotgun e-mail document. This is quite similar to the request form above, with a few key changes. The Shotgun To field becomes the To field, so that the mail will be sent to the selected groups. Also, the Contact information is incorporated into the Body field. She can't prevent Notes from marking the mail as sent from the shotgun server, but that seems acceptable. She could get around this limitation by some special-purpose programming in C, but decides not to bother for now.

▶ Copies the new document to the Shotgun Emails database.

▶ Marks the request document Sent.

The Shotgun E-mails database gives reader access to everyone. It simply shows a list of all sent shotgun messages sorted by date. It is also full-text indexed for easy reference.

Customizing Notes with Macros

Notes has a built-in macro programming language. It is used in a wide variety of places within Notes, including:

▶ Formulas for View columns. The columns in a view are not limited to displaying the value of a single field. The value displayed in a column can be composed of all or part of several fields. It can be the result of a value retrieved from some other database. It can be a translation from one format to another (numeric codes to English, for example).

▶ Formulas for form fields. Form fields may be *editable* (contain a value entered by a user), or they can be *computed* (the result of a calculation). Even when they're a value, there are several formulas associated with the field—there is a formula for the default value, one for translation (this can change the value before it is saved), and one for validation (checking to see if the value is allowed).

▶ Selection formulas. A view does not have to display all the documents in a database. A *selection formula* is used to determine which documents will be displayed in a given view.

▶ Buttons on forms. Notes allows a form to contain buttons. These buttons can contain macros that can help in the creation or processing of forms. Commonly used buttons include Previous and Next buttons to move around in the database, Reply and Send buttons when reading a Mail message, a Categorize button in a categorized database, or an Attach button to make attaching files to a document easier.

▶ Macros. Macros are stored with a database, and are used for performing repetitive tasks such as processing many documents at once. They can also be run automatically on documents added to the database, or run in the background as database maintenance tasks.

▶ SmartIcons. Common tasks can be coded into a formula (similar to a macro) and attached to a SmartIcon. Lotus provides several SmartIcons for things like running other Lotus products and mail integration. SmartIcons are great places for storing macros that aren't associated with a particular database; for example, a macro that paints a particular combination of colors and fonts.

Sharon builds and tests the database herself and then calls in the administrative team to roll out the database. She explains their tasks—read the database daily and approve or disapprove the messages. She tests the database with them and a small mailing list to make sure that they understand their tasks.

When she's got the databases built and tested with the small group of trusted administrators, Sharon kicks off the database with a shotgun memo to the whole organization. In it, she tells them that shotgun messages must now be approved by administration before being sent; how to find the database containing all shotguns; and that people should therefore not save Shotgun E-mail documents in their own mail folders for the long term. She was tempted to add something about lost gloves, but decided that she'd better keep that to herself.

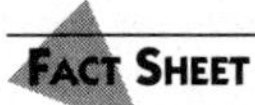

FACT SHEET

Shotgun E-mails Database

Purpose: To provide a measure of control over broadcast (shotgun) e-mail messages to large parts of the organization.

Application Origin: Custom-developed.

Application Development Time: 2–5 days.

Typical Size: 1–2 MB, depending on how long old messages are retained.

Typical Use: Larger organizations where e-mails broadcast to large populations are becoming a problem. There are two databases. One acts as a target for mailed requests, and only trusted administrators have access. Approved messages are mailed automatically from within this database. The other is an indexed repository of all broadcast messages, so that users can find old messages without having to store them in their own mail folders.

Forms: Shotgun Request (used to request that a shotgun message be sent out), Shotgun E-mail (used to send the actual message).

Views: The Shotgun E-mails database has one view, sorted by date. The Request database has views By Send Date, By Status, By Contact, and To Be Sent Today.

Naming Schemes: Merging Two Notes Installations

As the popularity of Notes increases, the likelihood that two separate Notes installations must communicate with each other increases. When two Notes installations merge, not only must basic communication be enabled, but a whole range of issues must be addressed.

SNS Consulting Group is a major environmental consulting firm (hypothetical) that provides its services nationwide. Its services include consulting for environmental issues like water and air pollution, testing of industrial output, and building conditions. To provide these services nationwide, SNS collaborates with hundreds of consulting and testing firms located throughout the nation.

SNS has merged with a smaller partner of theirs, East Coast Consulting. Both firms use Notes and now face the challenge of combining their Notes installations to work together as one network.

WHAT'S IN A NAME?

Evelyn Mancuso heads the group at SNS responsible for their Notes deployment. Her group not only sets up and maintains the users and servers, it also sets policy for server and database access control, naming, certificate expiration, and other issues associated with running a secure Notes installation.

Evelyn's group started as just a couple of people when SNS brought up their first server. Even with one server, Evelyn recognized the importance of getting their naming scheme right. She created a hierarchical organization with a root called /SNS. Since SNS has several locations, she created an organizational unit for each, resulting in /East/SNS, /West/SNS, and /South/SNS organizations.

Now her group is up to five people, and there are over a dozen Notes servers throughout the organization.

From time to time, Evelyn has had to connect her Notes network to other individuals and networks. Sometimes a consultant working with SNS needs temporary access to an SNS server. Sometimes SNS needs to establish a way to route e-mail between their own network and new partners' networks. Each of these tasks has been fairly painless. Creating temporary IDs for visiting consultants is no problem. Connecting to other networks is a little trickier and depends on how the other network is set up, in particular whether the other network is using flat or hierarchical naming (see the sidebar later in this chapter). In either case, getting a basic connection going is not very difficult.

Yet now Evelyn is facing a new challenge. As a result of the recent merger of SNS and East Coast Consulting, she has been asked to integrate their Notes installation with hers. She has been told to implement one policy across the board so that it is clear that SNS is one company.

The Notes installation at East Coast Consulting is based on the older flat security scheme. Evelyn tolerated this when SNS and East Coast Consulting were exchanging e-mail. Now that they are one company, she is going to have to make East Coast's Notes users change their Notes names to become SNS Notes names, and convert their network to hierarchical certificates. She decides to call East Coast's Notes network administrator, Ray Parker.

On the phone, Evelyn explains to Ray that they are to merge the two Notes installations into one that meets the naming and security policy of SNS. Ray is agreeable. He explains that when they started with Notes the natural choice was flat names, but that he's been meaning to upgrade to hierarchical. He's not quite sure how to do this, and Evelyn tells Ray that she will send him a hierarchical certifier called /ECC/SNS, which he can use to issue new names to his Notes users (and servers). Once the users and servers have been converted, his network will be able to fully access the SNS Notes network. (The difference between flat and hierarchical naming is discussed in the following sidebar.)

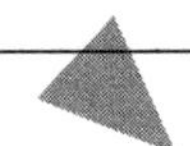

Flat Versus Hierarchical Naming—What's It All About?

In the world of Lotus Notes, everything has a name. In particular, users have names and servers have names. User names are usually based on the person's real name combined with additional information that identifies which company, department, or organization is running their Notes setup. Server names are made-up names (generally boring things like server3) that are also combined with additional information about company, department, or organization.

When Notes was introduced, it used a naming scheme called *flat naming*. In this scheme, names consist of two parts: the common name and the organization name. So, a typical name might be Barbara L. Miller/ABC Products or Server17/ABC Products.

There are a couple of weaknesses to this scheme that were fixed with the introduction of hierarchical naming in Notes release 3. One weakness is the inability to support big organizations where some people may have the same name. What if there were two Barbara L. Millers working at ABC Products? One of them would have to be named something like Barbara2 L. Miller/ABC Products, or some other awful choice.

Another weakness has to do with how Notes enforces security. The flat naming scheme bases its security on *flat certificates*. Without going into needless detail, suffice it to say that flat certificates lack some abilities that turn out to be extremely important for large Notes operations and for interconnecting Notes operations.

Therefore, in Release 3, a new naming scheme was introduced called *hierarchical naming*. In this scheme, names can have additional components beyond the common name and organization name. These additional components are called *organization units*, and they support names such as Barbara L. Miller/Sales/ABC Products, Barbara L. Miller/Research/ABC Products, and Server1/West Coast/ABC Products and Server1/East Coast/ABC Products.

You can see that hierarchical names get around the problem above where one of the Barbara's needed to be called Barbara2. With hierarchical naming, one Barbara can be identified as being in sales, while the other is in research. Or one could be identified on the East Coast while another could be on the West Coast. For very big installations, more organization units can be used, making names like Barbara L. Miller/Sales/Domestic/ABC Products and Barbara L. Miller/Sales/International/ABC Products. Hierarchical names can have up to four organization units, which supports a very large name space and means that people can always use their real name as their user name.

Hierarchical naming not only increases the name space, but it upgrades how Notes security works. Hierarchical naming uses a security scheme called *hierarchical certification,* which gets around the limitations of the earlier flat certification scheme. Hierarchical certification is designed to support large Notes installations and provide a truly workable way of enforcing security when interconnecting Notes installations. It also provides an excellent way of distributing some of the work of administering Notes names so that large organizations can decentralize some of the work.

When your organization is ready to jump into Notes, you will need to decide which of these two naming schemes to use, since Notes supports both. Here is some excellent advice: use hierarchical naming. Hierarchical naming is the more recent, better thought-out scheme with a lot of advantages over flat naming. It is aligned with accepted standards of naming, which will position you well for the future. Changing your choice of schemes is incredibly painful, so you want to make the right choice at first.

Notes will automatically default to hierarchical naming, so unless you really want to use flat, there is nothing special you need to do. Be very careful if you choose to override this default and implement flat names. It is extremely likely that in the future you will be forced to switch to hierarchical as you interconnect with other Notes installations. As with the Internet, the power and value of your Notes installation will increase dramatically when you interconnect with the rest of the world. Interconnected Notes networks will be based on hierarchical names.

A couple of final words on the subject: When you are ready to implement your naming scheme, take the time to do it well. Your organization will be living with the choices you make for a long time. If you are a large organization, you may want to hire some Notes consulting expertise to address some of the startup issues, including how to set up your naming scheme.

Evelyn tells Ray to give her a call in a couple of weeks once he's got a few servers and users converted. They will then start replicating the standard SNS databases like the Partners application, the Customers application, the Government/Industry Resources application, and so on.

OUT WITH THE OLD, IN WITH THE NEW

Later that day, Ray receives the /ECC/SNS certifier from Evelyn. He calls her on the phone and gets the password for the certifier. He then converts one of his servers that replicates with SNS from Server4/East Coast Consulting to Server4/ECC/SNS. He also updates several access control lists to recognize the new name. He then checks to see that the server is able to replicate with SNS. It is, so he spends the next couple of weeks converting more servers and some users to the new naming/security scheme.

He then gets back on the phone with Evelyn, and they discuss the progress. Evelyn has had her group identify a core replication server that Ray's servers can replicate with to get access to the main SNS databases. Evelyn gives the phone number for the core server to Ray, and Ray tells Evelyn the name of the server that will be replicating. Later, Ray and Evelyn make the necessary updates so Ray's server can replicate with the core replication hub.

Having joined the SNS naming and security scheme, and having access to a core SNS replication hub, Ray is now able to quickly convert his Notes users and servers to become full-fledged SNS Notes users. He replicates the Partners application, the Customer application, the Government/Industry Resources application, and several other SNS databases to his server, and begins to open up their access to the Notes users at East Coast Consulting (now SNS!).

A few weeks later, Ray and Evelyn are touching base again on the phone. Evelyn asks whether Ray is having any difficulty in the conversion, and Ray says things are going fine. Evelyn tells Ray that she wants to come to his site and provide training to his Notes users in the main SNS Notes databases, but that she doesn't want to come until everyone there has access. Ray estimates it will take another month to convert all of the users to the new naming tree and iron out the access control lists. They set up to meet six weeks out.

ONE HAPPY FAMILY

Six weeks later Evelyn finds herself on site at the former East Coast Consulting location. She will be providing training in the core SNS Notes databases to a group of East Coast people, who will in turn train the rest of the East Coast staff. She begins with the Partners application.

"This is one of our most important databases. It contains the full list of partners throughout the nation with whom we work. When we need environmental testing done, we search this database for the partner located geographically closest to the client. We also use these partners for local consulting because they tend to be expert in the local regulations. In the database you'll find views that list the partners alphabetically and by state.

"The next database is the Customer application. This is a standard customer database listing customer information like name, addresses and phone numbers. It also tracks the work we've done for customers so our consultants can review a client's history before getting involved in a new job.

"The Government/Industry Resources application contains documents and references to documents published by the government and by industries relevant to our consulting. You'll find views By subject, By agency/company, and By date. The database is full-text-indexed to help you find what you need."

Evelyn continues to discuss the other databases that the East Coast Consulting staff, now part of SNS, now has access to. Later, she meets with Ray to see how things are going.

Ray tells her that everything is fine, and that people are beginning to make use of the SNS resources. Some had complained about being locked out of databases after receiving their new names, but these problems were quickly ironed out and his network is once again running smoothly.

FACT SHEET

Merging Naming Systems

Purpose: To upgrade a separate Notes network implemented with flat naming to merge with a network implemented with hierarchical names.

Application Origin: The chapter mainly discusses hierarchical versus flat names, but also discusses a variety of applications used by a large consulting firm. These applications are custom-developed, and the development of these types of applications are discussed in other chapters.

Application Development Time: Converting from flat to hierarchical naming can take several weeks or more, as user and server IDs are converted, and access control lists are updated. Notes applications to support consulting firms, like the Partner application and the Government/Industry Resources application, can take weeks, sometimes months, to develop.

Typical Size: The size of consulting applications is discussed in other chapters.

Typical Use: The use of consulting applications is discussed in other chapters.

Forms: The design of consulting applications is discussed in other chapters.

Views: The design of consulting applications is discussed in other chapters.

The Secure Executive Decision Database

SkyWorks is a (hypothetical) producer of hardware and software to support CAD/CAM applications for Windows, Macintosh, and Unix computers. The company is based in San Francisco with offices across the United States. Almost everyone at the company (about 3,000 users) has Notes. Notes applications have been integrated into every aspect of the business, including sales, marketing, and development.

Recently, the CEO of the corporation, Amy Crelzer, was approached by the CEO of one of their competitors, Brent Elias of DynaCAD (a fictional company). Brent had a proposal—he wanted to investigate a merger between the two companies. It seemed to make sense—the companies had captured different segments of the market and had observed similar developing standards. Both companies were being solidly beaten by the leader in their market, Car-CAD. Brent added one complication to the deal—negotiations must begin immediately and the deal must be concluded as quickly as possible. The opportunity sounded intriguing, but Amy would need more information to make a better-informed decision on this issue.

FINDING A SOLUTION

Amy had used Notes for many years both to manage projects and communicate with her top managers. Amy naturally turned to Notes as a possible mechanism to get information. Unfortunately, the sensitivity of this subject meant that she could not post questions into a publicly accessible database. As a result, Amy had one of the company's Notes developers, Ron Brekman, brought in to create a database.

The requirements for the application were really quite simple: Amy needed a standard Notes Discussion database. The database would need to be replicated to the company's New York, Paris, and Hong Kong offices. Amy will be the only manager of this database (and any servers necessary—sometimes servers need to be managers to ensure that changes to the database replicate properly throughout the environment). She alone would be responsible for adding and deleting users from the database access control list (ACL). All data in the database would be encrypted with an encryption key called Dactyl. At no point did Amy tell Ron who would use the application, or what information would be contained therein.

DEVELOPING THE APPLICATION

Ron goes back to his office and creates a new database based on the design template for the Discussion database. In addition, he enables all forms in the database for encryption using the encryption key Dactyl. Amy or her administrative assistant will create this key to ensure that no one else has access to the data in the database. Ron then updates the access control list for the database to reflect the following changes: He sets the default access for the database to None and adds the groups SkyHubServers and SkyAdmins as managers. Then he adds Amy's Notes server, Amy's name, and, finally, his own name as managers. By listing Amy as a manager of the database, Ron ensures Amy can make changes to the database's ACL. Ron is required to list all the servers as managers of the database to ensure that Amy's changes to the ACL replicate throughout the environment. By listing Amy's server as manager, Ron ensures that the hub servers will accept any changes to the ACL emanating from Amy's server (as would be the case if Amy made changes to the ACL on her server). SkyWorks has a series of *hub servers,* which "manage" all replication and mail routing between SkyWorks servers. By dividing servers between *hubs* and *spokes* certain administrative activities (like communications and replication) are simplified. As the application will be replicated to a number of different offices, Ron needs to ensure that all the intermediary servers (the hubs) are listed in the ACL as managers. By listing the SkyHubServers as manager, Ron ensures that all ACL changes made by the hub servers will replicate to all servers (as might occur when Amy makes changes to the database on her server).

Once the process of developing the application, setting the ACL, and placing the database on the server are complete, Ron calls the head of Notes administration, Steve Shariman. He tells him that this is a high-priority item and needs to be replicated to the company's servers in New York, Paris, and Hong Kong as quickly as possible. Ron is not following standard procedures—standard procedures dictate that the database be placed in a database for the

Notes administrators to replicate when they have time. However, he gets the point across that this situation warrants an exception. Steve confirms that the database has SkyAdmins listed as manager, and hangs up the phone.

Steve has Notes running on his workstation. By listing SkyAdmins in the ACL, Ron has given Steve direct access to the database. Steve adds the database icon to his desktop and replicates the database to the appropriate hub server (one that replicates with Amy's server), the hub server that replicates with international offices (including Hong Kong and Paris), and the hub server that replicates with New York. Finally, he replicates copies of the database directly to the company's spoke servers in Hong Kong, Paris, and New York. Steve calls Ron to inform him that the database has been replicated to each of the locations required by Amy.

The company has set up their network so that users like Ron and Steve can have direct access to computers around the world. As a result, Ron can open the database on the servers in each of the target destinations. Ron adds a test document to the database on Amy's server. Each SkyHub replicates hourly with its spoke servers. This does not mean that every server should have this document in an hour. Much like a fire brigade handing buckets up and down a line, replication moves a document from one server to the next. It will take as many as three replication cycles for a document posted on Amy's San Francisco server to reach all of the destination servers.

Ron calls Amy to let her know that the application is on the server and has been replicated to each of the destinations she requested, but that they are still confirming replication works, and therefore, the ACL still shows himself and SkyAdmins as managers. Amy thanks Ron and asks him to call her back once replication is working.

Amy has her assistant write an e-mail message to a number of top corporate officers located in San Francisco, Paris, Hong Kong, and New York. She informs them that she would like their participation on a highly sensitive project with a company to be referred to as Dactyl (which is DynaCad). Each of the users will be expected to participate in the database to ensure that Amy is as fully informed as possible on all issues related to Dactyl. Amy's assistant provides a doclink to the database and sends the e-mail to all officers. In addition, she creates an encryption key called Dactyl and sends the encryption key to each of the designated company officers. This encryption key will be used by this team to ensure that only they can read the contents of the database. For each document sent out, Amy's assistant requests a Delivery Report and a Receipt Report. This ensures that she will get two receipts for each message: one when the message is delivered to the user, and a second when the message is actually read by the user.

A few hours later, Ron calls to indicate that the test document has replicated successfully, that he has removed himself and SkyAdmins as managers, and that the database is ready for use.

THE APPLICATION

Amy incorporates the secret key Dactyl into her ID file (a process of simply following the instructions Notes provides), and composes the first document in the database. In this document, Amy provides background on the situation. The document she is writing will be encrypted when she saves it in the database. This ensures that prying eyes cannot open the document and see its contents. Amy refrains from using DynaCad's name directly. There is always the chance that someone will leave the document up on their screen, or someone else will read the name over their shoulders. Amy's assistant is calling each of the participants in the discussion to inform them of the actual name of the company in question. After providing a brief overview of her meeting, Amy asks the question, "Why is Dactyl so interested in this merger?"

The first response to her memo is available only a few minutes after she posts it (when the CEO designates an item as a priority, the company listens. . .). The response suggests that there may be other companies looking to acquire Dactyl and they might be interested in arranging a deal before they are bought. Throughout the day, responses come in from the team of designated officers around the world. Amy continues to pose additional questions based on people's responses. At time the discussion almost appears real-time with questions and answers popping up rapidly. Typically, particularly with the overseas participants, questions and answers take a few hours to process.

Amy continues to add questions and collect information from the database for a week. In the meantime, she continues negotiations with Dactyl. It becomes clear based on the information possessed by the directors that Dactyl is in serious financial trouble. The company has lost a number of big accounts recently and the next version of their software is long overdue. It is also clear that Dactyl is being courted by some large software companies who might have an interest in entering the CAD/CAM business.

Dactyl does have a number of assets that SkyWorks would be interested in acquiring: a strong presence overseas and a superb support organization in the U.S. Amy starts to use the database to propose different strategies with the team. "How would we integrate Dactyl into our operations? Particularly, could our products be integrated?" The head of software development answers, "On the development front, we have long operated in similar operating environments and observed the same standards. It would be very difficult to integrate the two products—the level of effort should not be underestimated—but it is possible." Pierre Ellois from Paris posts, "Dactyl has 20 percent of the market in France and the best sales force in Europe. These would be immense assets to our operations in France."

As negotiations with Dactyl began, Amy posted Dactyl's proposals in the database for comment. The discussion participants were quick to dissect the

Main View in the Business Needs database

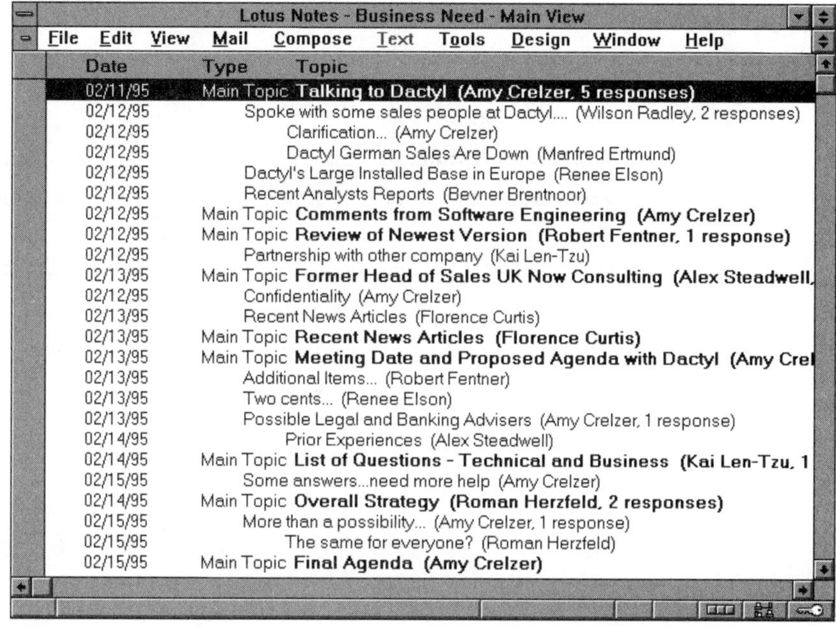

proposals, identifying the strong points and weak points of each. There was much contention over whether to integrate the two products or leave them as separate entities. In this manner, Amy was able to formulate a vision of how the merger might take place, the ultimate value of Dactyl to SkyWorks, and the terms necessary to ensure that the transaction was successful.

Dactyl agreed to extend its deadline to continue negotiations with Sky-Works. Amy felt confident that her final proposal was SkyWorks' best possible offer. This offer was best in the sense that it provided the highest per-share price SkyWorks felt it could reasonably pay for Dactyl, while ensuring a solid return on their investment. DynaCad ultimately accepted SkyWork's offer. The database was discontinued and deleted from each of the servers to which it had replicated. The application had helped Amy ensure she was at all times in possession of the most up to date accurate information available. It also helped to ensure that proposals and scenarios could be analyzed by the company's most important officers in a matter of hours. This contrasts with more traditional forms of communication which might take days or might not happen at all.

FACT SHEET

Business Needs Application

Purpose: To allow a team of geographically dispersed people to collaborate on a short-term project. The goal is to bring the team up to speed on issues and allow rapid response to new situations.

Application Origin: Developed from standard Discussion template.

Application Development Time: Created template and modified ACL only—less than 1 hour.

Typical Size: Short duration means typically small size, 1 MB or less.

Typical Use: Project team members post questions on breaking events.

Forms/Views: Those of the standard Discussion database.

The Survey Collection Application

It's time again for the employee satisfaction survey. Mary Chung works in the Human Resources department of a hypothetical rapidly growing, progressive health care conglomerate. Every year, Ahab Health Care surveys its employees in order to objectively measure the employees' morale, attitude, and knowledge of the corporate goals and objectives. The management tries to use this information to adjust its policies and goals.

Mary was responsible for collecting and tabulating the results last year, and she remembers how painful the process was. It took weeks to total and analyze the answers to each question. This time, she vows, it's going to be different—she is going to automate the task as much as possible.

A New Trick

It's a tough job. Mary has to find a way to meet the conflicting demands of privacy, accuracy, timeliness, and security. However, she has a new trick up her sleeve—this year, Notes was installed throughout the organization, and she thinks that Notes is probably up to the task.

This year's survey is bigger than ever. There are over 50 questions. Most of them are multiple choice, but several offer a place for fill-in-the-blanks answers. Although it's long, it will be a straightforward process to convert all of these survey questions into fields in a Notes form. Some of them will become "radio button" keyword fields, where the respondent will pick one out of several possible answers. Other questions that allow multiple selections will become checkbox fields. Still others will simply be blank text fields. It seems

A New Survey being filled out

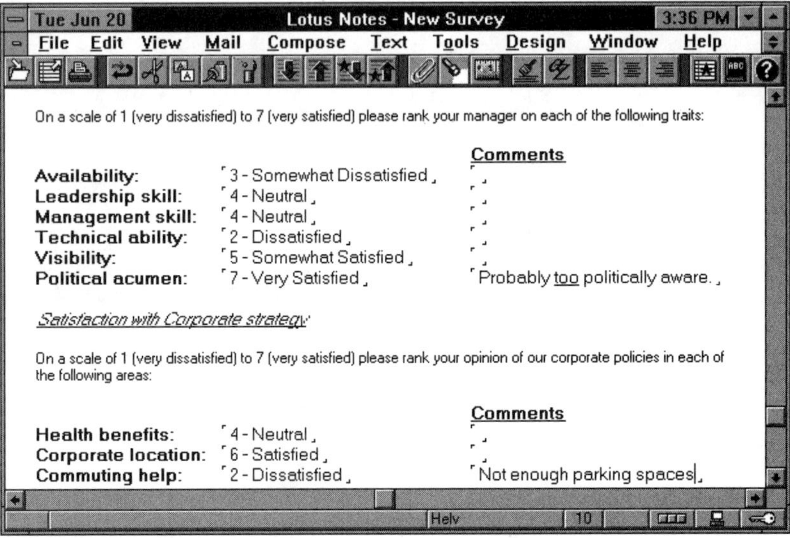

clear that a Notes form is a good way to distribute the survey; it will allow the respondents to fill it out quickly and easily.

OTHER WORRIES

There are other considerations, however:

▶ Security. No one but Mary, the administrator, should be able to see any of the survey data before it is time to analyze it. During the analysis phase, only the analysts should be allowed access, so that they can write their report.

▶ Privacy. Employees should feel comfortable that the survey will be completely anonymous—that no one will be able to trace survey results back to the individual. On the other hand, survey responses should be unique; an individual user should not be able to submit more than one survey.

▶ Timeliness. It should be possible to send out the survey and have all employees respond within a period of two weeks.

▶ Analysis. The analysts should be able to slice and dice the data in any way they choose. The data should be capable of being exported to other analysis tools.

Mary first considered the idea of building a database in which everyone would simply compose and fill out a survey form. The trouble with this, however, is that it violates the security provision above. It would be nearly impossible to create a database that simultaneously allows the users to compose documents and yet will prevent them from seeing the documents that others composed.

A MAIL-IN DATABASE

A much better solution is a mail-in database. A form is added to the file called FORMS.NTF, which places it on the Custom Forms menu in the Mail menu of every user. Each user will compose the form from within their own mail system and mail it directly to the survey database. Mary set up the ACL on the survey database so that only she has the ability to read it.

This handled the security element, but what about the privacy problem? Mary had to do a little work here, because, under normal circumstances, Notes automatically stamps mail forms with the author's name. She wanted to keep track of the people who've submitted surveys, because she didn't want them to submit a second one. On the other hand, she didn't want to keep track of it on the same form.

First, she created a second database that will store the name of each person submitting a survey. Then she wrote a macro in the Survey database that runs automatically when a survey is mailed in. This macro does the following:

▶ Looks up the name of the survey sender to make sure they haven't sent in a survey before. If they have, the second survey is deleted, and no more processing is done. She can't delete the first one, since no one keeps a record of which one it was.

▶ If the survey sender's name was not found, a new record for it is created and saved in the name database.

▶ The sender's name and any other identifying information is deleted from the survey record.

Mary believed that she had adequately dealt with both privacy and security. To collect the surveys within a specified time frame, she sent out an e-mail to every employee with instructions on how to compose and fill out a survey form. She made sure to emphasize the privacy features she implemented. The employees had two weeks from the date of the e-mail to fill out the survey and mail it back in. Mary sent out two reminders during the survey time to make sure that people remembered to fill it out.

At the end of the two weeks, Mary changed the access provisions around. She removed the Survey form from FORMS.NTF and removed the database from the Name and Address book (so that no one could mail to it anymore).

She also disabled the mail-in macro and changed the ACL to give access to the analysis team.

For analysis, Mary first began in Notes. She created views that showed the answers for different sections of the survey. She was able to use Notes' aggregation capabilities effectively—creating averages, totals, and percentages for the numbers as appropriate. These views were useful for achieving a general overview of the survey results. It was also a good way to find and read the individual survey forms that contained more detailed answers and commentary.

For more specific analysis, she created a big view that showed the key fields from all survey documents. She exported this view to a spreadsheet, from which the survey analysts could perform much more specific and sophisticated data reduction.

Notes definitely made this process easier than in previous years. It cut weeks off the preparation and survey collection time, and drastically reduced analysis costs by avoiding the process of data entry. In future years, it will be even simpler, since the basic infrastructure is now in place.

FACT SHEET

Survey Collection Database

Purpose: The anonymous collection of survey data from respondents using Notes.

Application Origin: Original design.

Application Development Time: 2 weeks, not including the time to design the survey questions.

Typical Size: Depends on number of survey respondents. A survey of 1,000 employees would consume approximately 5–10 MB.

Typical Use: One Survey form is added to FORMS.NTF. Survey participants fill out the form from the Mail Custom Forms menu. The forms are mailed to one database which acts as a mail repository. When a document is deposited into this database, a macro takes the name information and creates a record in a name tracking database, and then strips the survey form of all identifying information. The Repository database is then used for analysis by creating special views.

Forms: A survey form in FORMS.NTF and a name record in the Name Tracking database.

Views: Custom views are developed during the analysis phase that show aggregate numbers for the whole survey population. Another view is developed for use in exporting data to a spreadsheet.

Supporting a Landscaping Business

A large landscaping business, like any other large business, involves the coordination of large amounts of information. Suppliers must be tracked, and their current capabilities and prices must be readily available. Customers have complex requirements that need to be recorded over the life of the relationship to provide excellent customer service. The employees of the business must stay in contact with each other to be able to support customers, track the latest trends, and share expertise.

SCP Landscaping (a fictional company) has grown over the last 30 years into a very large, multisite landscaping business servicing customers in five states. Their individual sites have been run fairly autonomously. Suzanne C. Phillips, the founder and president of SCP Landscaping, chose to impose little centralized control over the individual sites to give each site maximum flexibility to react to the particular conditions and opportunities it faces.

Now, increased competition has motivated Suzanne to consider ways to combine the experience, expertise, and buying power of the combined business to lower costs and improve customer service. She hires an information management consultant who talks to her about Lotus Notes.

IDENTIFYING THE KEY INFORMATION TO BE SHARED

The information management consultant, Ed Margolis, asks to meet with Suzanne and a few members of her staff to discuss how information management systems could improve her business. He begins by asking what systems they currently use to track their information.

Suzanne's head of accounting, Amy Helsel, explains that they currently use information systems only for their accounting needs. They track accounts receivable, accounts payable, general ledger, and so on. Until a few years ago even much of this was done by the individual sites, but they found they could reduce cost by centralizing these responsibilities.

Ed then leads the group through a brainstorming exercise to think of all the other nonaccounting information the business has, but may be able to make better use of. The following items emerge:

> ▶ Customer Information. There is much information gathered about customers which is kept in filing cabinets. This information includes before and after photographs of the customer's property, their preferences, sketches and drawings of the customer's property, how the customer found out about SCP Landscaping, ideas for future work that the customer expressed an interest in but did not have done, and so on.
>
> ▶ Supplier Information. Each site deals directly with suppliers to negotiate prices and other terms. Some suppliers are local, while others are national. In addition to prices, there is much information about such things as how to use the suppliers materials (tips, tricks, rules of thumb), suppliers and products to avoid, contact names and phone numbers, and product brochures.
>
> ▶ General Information and Tools. There is much expertise, literature, and tools embodied in the collective experience of the business. There are experiences working with various materials, flowers, trees, and so on that have been recorded. There are reports and brochures that people have collected. There are software tools such as time and labor estimators that people have found useful.

Ed suggests that if this information could be captured in such a way that all employees have easy access to it that the business could leverage the information into competitive advantage. He outlines several requirements that such a system should meet. The system should be flexible enough to store a variety of types of information, such as plain text, scanned drawings and photographs, computer-created drawings, and binary attachments to store software. The system should be easy for all employees to use with a little training. And the system should support a variety of access methods so that field personnel at customer sites—not just workstations located at the individual sites or headquarters can access the information easily.

Ed outlines a plan where each site and headquarters would have a Notes Server to support the local personnel. These servers would call each other to replicate data being entered at each site. Notes clients would be installed at each site to provide access to the Notes databases, and field personnel would be equipped with notebook computers so they can access and enter information while on the road and at customer sites.

Suzanne and the group like the idea and ask Ed to put together a demonstration so they can better understand the capabilities of Lotus Notes and how their business can use it.

THE POWER OF A PROTOTYPE

Ed knows the power that a prototype can have. It can crystallize the capabilities of a system and open a user's imagination to further possibilities in a way that discussion and reports cannot. He therefore agrees to Suzanne's request and schedules another meeting in a few weeks to view a demonstration of Notes and of particular applications of Notes that might be useful to their business.

Ed begins by listing the ways he thinks SCP Landscaping can use Notes and taking a guess at how these uses break down into Notes databases. He begins with the major classes of information identified at the meeting with Suzanne.

He begins with the customer information. It is clear that each customer should have a standard profile where information such as name, contact names, phone numbers, and other standard information can be stored. This will likely be a form called Customer Profile. Then there is information about customer's premises, like the size and shape of their grounds, the type of soil, the size and shape of current structures and landscaping features. This information may be descriptive text, but will also include photographs and sketches. Clearly, Notes' Rich Text capabilities will be required. Ed figures that a form called Description of Customer Grounds could be used. It would contain a field called Customer to link the form to the customer it describes.

Ed brings up Notes on his PC and begins to create what is becoming the Customer Information database. He creates the Customer Profile and Description of Customer Grounds forms. He then creates a view called Main View, which categorizes the forms by customer so the Grounds Description forms will be grouped with the Customer Profile form (and any other forms he invents). He realizes that there could be multiple Description of Customer Grounds forms and other forms associated with a customer. To lend more structure, he adds another field to each form called Form Type. He then categorizes by form after categorizing by customer in the Main View.

Looking back at his Notes, Ed sees that SCP Landscaping would also like to track the work done for each customer, "after" photographs of the work done, and ideas for future work that the customer expressed. He creates another form called Work Done and one called Customer Desires and Ideas to track this information.

Ed knows that the Customer Information application will need to be expanded to meet more requirements from SCP Landscaping, especially once the database is in use. But for now, the prototype he has built will be enough to communicate the capabilities of Notes. He moves on to the next major category of information: Supplier Information.

While it might be possible to store the supplier information in the same database as the customer information, Ed creates a new database called Supplier Information. This will be easier for Suzanne and others to understand, and will probably be easier for new Notes users at SCP Landscaping to understand. In the database he starts, as he did with the Customer Information database, with a profile form. This Supplier Profile will store standard information like the supplier's name, phone number, and fax number.

Ed then looks at the specific types of information SCP Landscaping wishes to track about suppliers. The main information is the supplier's product/price list. Ed creates a form to store this information called Product and Price List. SCP also discussed additional information that seemed to fall into two categories: additional information like brochures and other information created by suppliers, plus product reviews, hints, warnings, and other information created by SCP personnel. To support these two types of information, Ed creates a form called Supplier Provided Information and User Comments, Reviews, Etc. He also makes sure that all forms have a field to store product name(s) to make it easy for users to find relevant material independent of the supplier.

Ed then looks at the third type of information SCP Landscaping identified—general information and tools. This information is not associated with particular customers or suppliers, and is likely to be of value to various personnel at the different sites. This information includes government and industry reports, employee reports, and software utilities. Ed creates a third database called General Information and Tools to store these items. Since there is no ready index or key that users could use to find this information (unlike the other databases where the user generally knows the customer, supplier, or product of interest), Ed includes a standard text (not Rich Text) field on each form for users to enter a description of the document. This description can be displayed in views, and will ensure that the user supplies good keywords to support full-text searching.

At this point Ed has enough to show Suzanne and the folks at SCP Landscaping. He transfers the databases to his notebook computer so he can bring them to SCP for the scheduled demonstration.

MOVING FORWARD TO IMPLEMENTATION

At the demonstration, Ed walks Suzanne and her staff through the basic capabilities of Notes such as using views, composing forms, and accessing different databases. Once they understand Ed moves on to the three custom databases he has created.

Suzanne is impressed at the easy-to-understand layout of the three databases: one for customer information, one for supplier information, and one for general information. She and her staff grasp the way the three applications function. Ed demonstrates how scanned images can be placed inside the forms, and how software utilities can be attached and launched. He also demonstrates importing text from ASCII files, which some suppliers provide. He uses the full-text search engine to pull out general information about a particular topic. He makes sure everyone understands how easy it is for the field personnel to add information about customers, like their desires for future jobs. He also shows how users can enter their tips and tricks and how they can look up other tips and tricks people have entered.

Since the staff at SCP is not quite sure how their people will upload and download information, Ed connects his notebook to a phone line and dials into a server he set up before the demonstration. He makes a call to the server and replicates the databases he has been demonstrating. He then opens them up again and shows them the new documents that were just received. He also opens the databases on the server to show how the information they entered during the demonstration is now on the server for the next user to get.

Suzanne consults with her staff and they agree that Notes looks like a great solution. Suzanne meets with Ed to discuss pricing, training, and rollout issues. They decide to proceed.

The Main View in the Customer Information database

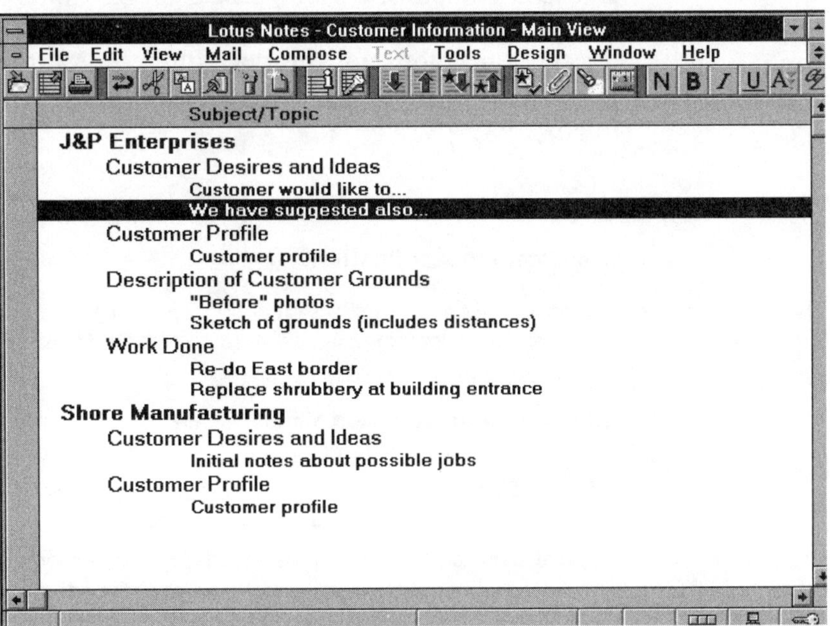

THE LANDSCAPING APPLICATION IN FULL SWING

Six months later, SCP Landscaping's Notes application is in full swing. All employees have their Notes user IDs, and the field personnel have notebook computers. One such person, Michele Dobrin, is visiting a large customer to discuss the status of a job they just finished, and to see if the customer wants any more work done now. She meets with Richard Gunning.

Michele sits down at the customer's office and turns her computer on. She goes into the Customer Information database and finds the information about the customer. She pulls up the before and after photographs and reviews them with Richard to see if he is satisfied. She then calls up the notes about other jobs that the customer has expressed interest in. Richard seems keen about one particular job, the installation of additional trees along the customer's west border. He wants to know approximately what it would cost to plant a row of trees for noise insulation, and how soon it could be done.

Michele brings up the sketches of his property to see how long the border is. She then goes into the General Information and Tools database to use the tool that estimates how many trees are needed for noise insulation and what types of trees are recommended. She then goes into the Supplier Information database and uses the view By Product to see which suppliers provide trees. She then quickly finds a couple of prices and gives the estimate to Richard. Richard is impressed with Michele's ability to do so much so fast and asks her to send over a formal quote with exact dates for his approval. Michele creates a new form for this new job in the Customer Information database and logs her Notes about Richard's preferences so she can produce the formal quote later in the office.

FACT SHEET

Landscaping Application

Purpose: To centralize the customer, supplier, and general information embodied in individual sites of a landscaping business to reduce cost and improve customer service.

Application Origin: Custom developed.

Application Development Time: There are three fairly straightforward applications. Development time is roughly 3 weeks.

Typical Size: 20–50 MB per database, depending on how much binary information (scanned photos, software utilities) are included.

Typical Use: Landscaping businesses (though easily modified for other businesses) where there are multiple sites that wish to use Notes to track their own information and share information with other sites.

Forms: Each application has its own forms. The Customer Information application has the Customer Profile, Description of Customer Grounds, Work Done, and Customer Desires and Ideas forms. The Supplier Information application has the Supplier Profile, Supplier Provided

Information, and User Comments, Reviews, Etc. form. The General Information and Tools application has a form to store any type of information with fields to help locate desired information via full-text searching.

Views: The Customer Information application has a Main View that categorizes information by customer and then by form type. The Supplier Information application has a By Supplier view to group information by supplier and a By Product view to help find suppliers for a particular product. The General Information and Tools view has a Main View from which users can do full-text searches to identify the desired data.

Research Collaboration: The Idea Discussion Database

Cochran Research (a fictional company) has 12 employees and is based in New York City. Cochran analyzes stocks and provides reports on economic indicators, market analysis, and particular companies. These reports are read by executives throughout the financial services industry. While the company's staff is too small to have a person dedicated to computer-related issues, Janet McPhee has taken on the mantle of managing the company's computer resources. This job fell to Janet primarily by chance, as she had had little experience with computers before joining Cochran. Janet attempts to keep in touch with developments in the computer industry by reading some of the major computer magazines on a regular basis. As a result, she had heard about Notes prior to her first experience with the product. She was invited to attend a seminar on Notes being offered by a Lotus business partner, RAD Consulting. At the seminar, the business partner demonstrated a variety of the features Notes had to offer, including a number of demo applications that they had built for clients. Janet was intrigued with Notes. It appeared that it might be able to help them manage some of their internal production processes much better than their current systems. At the conclusion of the seminar, Janet spoke to the business partner. They arranged to meet the next week to discuss how RAD Consulting might be able to help Cochran.

MEETING THE BUSINESS PARTNER

Janet met with two people from RAD. The purpose of the meeting was to explore how Lotus Notes might be able to help Cochran improve its work processes. During the meeting, Janet provided RAD with an overview of her company and their primary business processes. Much of the discussion focused on the editing and publishing processes. The RAD consultants proposed a number of ideas and suggested that a pilot application might help the organization evaluate Notes. They expressed interest in making a formal proposal to Cochran Research. Janet expressed interest in the pilot and indicated she would be glad to take the proposal to the owner of the company, Ed Cochran.

A few days later, the RAD Consultants provided Janet with a proposal for a pilot Notes application to help the company in the idea-generation/editing/publishing process. The proposal included the purchase of a Notes server, client software for each of the company's employees, and consulting services to build the application. Janet took the proposal to Ed Cochran, who expressed sincere misgivings. The company had already invested in a small network and computers for everyone. The new installation seemed to be more hassle than it was worth. Janet outlined some of the key benefits of Notes, suggested that he speak directly with RAD, and arranged the meeting. As preparation for the meeting, RAD quickly put together a prototype Notes application to demonstrate some of the key features. The application highlighted a number of the reasons Cochran could benefit from using Notes. Janet knew that this would be a difficult meeting. Ed Cochran was particularly suspicious of the "technology du jour" mentality that pervades so much of the financial industry. If an application couldn't demonstrate a concrete benefit to his organization, he wouldn't buy it.

Much to Janet's surprise, the meeting went smoothly. Ed was actually impressed with Notes and with the RAD consultants. They demonstrated a reasonable understanding of Cochran's current business and technical needs. Furthermore, the consultants presented an application that could really help the organization out. Ed rationalized that Notes might even justify the cost of the network they had installed. It was agreed, after a short negotiation on price, that Ed would sign the contract the following week and RAD could begin work.

DEVELOPING THE APPLICATION

RAD's first act was to purchase and install a Notes server for Cochran. RAD also helped Janet create the company certifier and create IDs for all the users in the company. They provided her with some basic guidelines for managing certificates and ID files (she responded that "security isn't that important to us here"). The process of installing the server software and creating the IDs took the better part of a day. Next, RAD went around to each workstation to install and configure Notes client software. This proved more difficult—many of the users had changed the configuration of their workstations to suit their own needs (one person had completely deleted the network software from her machine). This also included installing software on the company's three laptop computers. Installing the client software took approximately two days to complete.

RAD started work to turn the prototype they had demonstrated to Ed Cochran into a full-blown application. This required frequent meetings with Janet and other Cochran employees. The purpose of these meetings was to review design documents written by RAD and to confirm that various features of the application met organizational needs. The development process lasted approximately two weeks. RAD began testing the application with Janet and a couple of other computer-knowledgeable employees. This led to a few additional changes to the application. This process of review and testing lasted another week. At the end of that week, the application was ready for general deployment, and the database icon was added to everyone's Notes desktop.

RAD then provided a customized training session for the entire organization. The purpose of this training was to introduce Cochran's employees to Notes and to their particular Notes application. The course focused on providing an overview of Notes, an understanding of the basics of the Notes interface (the desktop, forms, and views) and the structure of their application.

THE APPLICATION

The application built by RAD is actually three different databases: Idea Discussion, Drafts/Editing, and Production. The three databases together provide Cochran with a comprehensive set of tools to manage the production of research. The Idea Discussion database provides Cochran employees with a forum to discuss ideas for new topics (as well as items of general interest to the company). The Drafts/Editing database allows the organization to take an idea from inception to completion. The Production database helps authors through the process of publishing research.

The Idea Discussion database is, for the most part, a standard Notes Discussion database. RAD made a few minor modifications to forms to support Cochran's processes. For example, RAD added a button to each form in the database. The button is used to create a new document in the Drafts/Editing database based on the current active document. The purpose of this button is to provide an efficient, easy to use link between the two databases. This button would be used whenever a topic should be moved from the idea phase into the production phase. The Idea Discussion database contains all the standard views included in the Notes Discussion database template.

The Drafts/Editing database is the core of the application. This database is used to take an idea from its initial inception (an idea posted from the Idea Discussion database) to a completed piece of research that is ready for publication. Each topic is created as a main document in the database. The author of the main document fills in the topic of the concept (e.g., prices will fall), the source of the concept (e.g., because markets have gone up too much), an expected delivery date (optional), the analyst to whom the piece is assigned, and the status of the document. The expected delivery date only needs to be pro-

Main View in the Idea Discussion database

```
Lotus Notes - Idea Discussion - ID Main View

File  Edit  View  Mail  Compose  Text  Tools  Design  Window  Help

   Date        Type      Topic
   08/01/95     Idea      Deteriorating Dollar  (Janet McPhee, 4 responses)
   08/05/95               Good idea - more information on FED position (Ed Cochran, 1 response)
   08/08/95                  Recent analysts reports... (Jay Fowler)
   08/05/95               Our last report on this topic (Nancy Carlucci)
   08/06/95               My two cents... (Reggie Harmon)
   08/08/95     Idea      Current Economic Indicators and The Election  (Scott Franc
   08/08/95               Make this a definite (Ed Cochran)
   08/08/95     Idea      Article in one of the rags...  (Janet McPhee, 3 responses)
   08/11/95               Effect of technology on indicators (Terry Walton, 2 responses)
   08/12/95                  Similar tripe in other magazines (Nancy Carlucci)
   08/12/95                  I saw it too... (Sam Friar)
   08/12/95     Idea      Overseas investors inflating bond market (Ed Cochran, 1 re
   08/14/95               Move this one over to Drafts... (Reggie Harmon)
   08/14/95     Idea      Property markets in Tokyo, New York, London  (Allerton Sm
   08/16/95               Continuing decline in Tokyo (Janet McPhee, 1 response)
   08/17/95                  Affect on Japanese banks (Nancy Carlucci)
   08/17/95               Dutch and German ownership of US properties (Jay Fowler)
   08/17/95               Movement in Eastern European land values (Beverly Garfield)
   08/20/95     Idea      Insurance Industry Fallout  (Terry Walton, 4 responses)
   08/21/95               Disaster du jour (Ed Cochran)
   08/22/95               Overexpansion (Janet McPhee, 1 response)
   08/23/95                  Not true for all companies (Sam Friar)
   08/23/95               Recovering from storms (Hawaii, Florida, etc.) (Sam Friar)
   08/24/95     Idea      Elaborate and add to drafts  (Ed Cochran)
```

vided if the piece of research will be done by a set target date—some research may be lower in priority and therefore not have a defined completion date.

Once the Main document has been completed, the analyst responsible will create a Response document (called Documents), containing a first draft of the document. The document itself will be written in Microsoft Word and will be attached to the Notes document. The analyst should also attach any supporting files that he or she might use in the analysis (like a spreadsheet analysis). Other analysts will then have an opportunity to comment on the document in a document called Response. The analyst is also responsible for updating the status field in the Main document. There are buttons on the Document's form that allow the analyst to set the status of the Status field in the main document. Successive values for status include Submitted For Comment, Final Edits, and Awaiting Approval.

Each week, Ed Cochran calls a meeting of the senior analysts to discuss that research to be published in the coming weeks. During this time, the group consults the list of all documents that are in the Drafts/Editing database with a completion date in the next two weeks, or a status of either Final Edits or Awaiting Approval. From this list, a set of analyses is selected to be completed in the next two weeks. Completion date typically drives this process, but if the organization finds itself with too little or too much material for a given period, it uses status to add or drop from the list.

The Completion Date on all selected materials is updated to reflect a completion date in the next two weeks. For those items not selected with Completion Dates that fall within the next two weeks, two weeks are added to the completion dates. This ensures that they will be reviewed again at the next meeting. Those documents that are due in the next two weeks go through a semistructured review process. The analyst is responsible for ensuring that the status of their document is set to Submitted for Comment at least one week before the completion date. A macro is run to ensure that this criteria is met. If the macro encounters a document that does not match this criteria, an error message is generated to Ed. Each topic is assigned to two reviewers who review and comment on the analyst's work. Once the status of the document is set to Submitted for Comment, the reviewers are responsible for submitting comments to the analyst. As long as the document does not need to be completely rewritten, the status of the document is set to Final Edits. Once the analyst has incorporated the reviewers' comments, the status of the document is set to Awaiting Approval.

Ed Cochran has the final say on all pieces to be published. Awaiting Approval means that Ed needs to approve the document. Ed requires two days advance notice prior to the completion date to review and make comments on research. RAD installed a section on each document that only Ed can edit. In this section (by clicking a button), he can input his approval or rejection of a piece of analysis. In the event the analysis is rejected, Ed makes comments to the analyst about which changes need to be made for the document to meet with his approval.

The views in the Drafts/Editing database include Completion Date, Analyst, Status, and Topic. In addition, Ed asks RAD to add another view to the database called Next Two Weeks, which is a listing of all topics that have completion dates falling in the next two weeks.

The Production database is essentially a repository of all works to be published by the company. The Production database has a Main document (including the word processing file and any supporting files) and a Response document, where any amended files can be posted. Amended files are the files actually used by the printing company for the printing process. Occasionally, the printers require changes to be made to the documents to meet their printing software's requirements. These amended documents are posted as attachments to Response documents in the database.

The production database has views By Published Date, By Analyst, and By Title.

UNFINISHED BUSINESS

Cochran's needs are fairly simple. The organization is small, so structure and formality are not critical for the application to succeed. The significant benefit of the application to the group is that all analyses are stored in a central location (which is automatically backed up to tape each night). Furthermore, Notes has helped to simplify the editing process. The group might look into an improved workflow process to review and approve analysis, or it might consider restructuring some of the forms to more closely match their needs, but these changes are simply not critical for an organization of their size. What is important is that the key features of the application strongly support the organization's work flow and provides personnel with an opportunity to do their job more efficiently than they could before Notes.

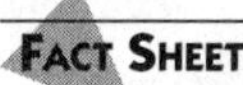

FACT SHEET

Research Collaboration Application

Purpose: To help a periodical capture and refine ideas into articles.

Application Origin: Actually a series of applications, developed by consultants from similar models.

Application Development Time: 3 man-weeks to complete development (consultant was basing work on other similar applications).

Typical Size: Total can be quite large when attachments are included; total for all three could reach 50–60 MB over the course of a year for a small team.

Typical Use: Team members submit ideas for new articles; ideas are discussed and good ideas are moved into the drafts area; drafts are rewritten until final copy is available; final copy is submitted to publishers. Final copy is also stored in its own database.

Forms/Views:
   Idea Discussion
     Forms
       Main Topic, Response, Response to Response
     Views
       Main View, By Author, By Category

   Drafts/Editing
     Forms
       Main Document—Topic, Documents, Response
     Views
       By Completion Date, By Next Two Weeks, By Analyst, By Status, By Topic, By Creation Date

   Production
     Forms
       Main, Response, Response to Response
     Views
       By Publishing Date, By Analyst, By Title, By Topic, By Creation Date

Corporate Process Manual

In a fast-growing company, the corporate culture is vitally important to the way it does business. This comprises everything from the dress code (or lack of one) to the way products are developed and sold. Paradoxically, in a small business, almost no one has time to pass on that culture to new employees. Only the most forward-looking companies invest time in formally training their employees on the corporate culture. However, many companies are investing some effort in at least writing down their processes and procedures. The idea is that anyone who needs to can consult "The Book" to find out how things should be done. One big issue to be dealt with, however, is how to distribute and update this book. Notes provides an excellent solution.

DOCUMENTING THE DEVELOPMENT PROCESS

PhiComp (name changed for confidentiality) is just such a company. Two years ago, worried about the quality of their development process, corporate management created a team to examine the development process, with special attention to new product development. The team was comprised of members of all the departments involved in that process—Engineering, Quality, Manufacturing, and Marketing. Their task was to examine and document the existing development process and make recommendations for improving it.

After several months of meetings and effort, the team produced a 200-page document containing everything anyone would want to know about developing new products at PhiComp, along with recommendations for improving it. It was a masterpiece. Management hailed the document as a major achievement, accepted most of the recommendations, and gave a copy of the document to all the managers.

Unfortunately, there were some problems. First of all, there weren't enough copies to go around. Some of the people who most needed it didn't have copies (though copies were made available to anyone else who wanted one). Furthermore, the document was static. If part of the process wasn't working, it was extremely difficult to modify the document to take the fixes into account. In order to change the document, it was necessary to go around to every copy and insert the change pages manually. Finally, since the original committee broke up, there was no strategy for discussing future changes to the document.

Fortunately, it's not all bad news. In early 1995, PhiComp began to implement Notes.

NOTES AS A PUBLISHING MEDIUM

Notes provides a wonderful tool for publishing information that is up to date and easily accessible to whomever needs it. The people responsible for maintaining the information only have to keep it in one place, and the people who need to use it always know where to go for the latest version.

Albert Laurel, a manager at PhiComp, decided that Notes would be a great place to store the development process document. While a simple discussion database might cover the minimum of needs, he believed that it was possible to do quite a bit more. He designed a view that could act as a live table of contents for the book.

The structure of such a database is quite simple, although the details are tuned to the needs of the particular document. Only one form is necessary. At PhiComp, this form is titled Section. The sections are collected into larger Chapters (a Chapter is simply a category in the database).

Each section of the book was entered into one of these Notes documents and given a section number. Multiple sections were marked with the same chapter name and chapter number.

To make navigation through the book easier, the form has several buttons on it. Previous and Next buttons move through the database page by page. The Print button will print the current page, and Find activates the full-text search mechanism. The buttons are marked Hide when printed in the design form so they don't show up when printing.

The view simply categorizes these documents first by chapter, then by section. The outline starts out collapsed, so that people can see the flow of the whole book when they start out.

Once he had the database up and working, Albert stayed late for a couple of nights moving documents into it. He made his life easier by programming a couple of SmartIcons to access things like common font formats.

Part of a Section

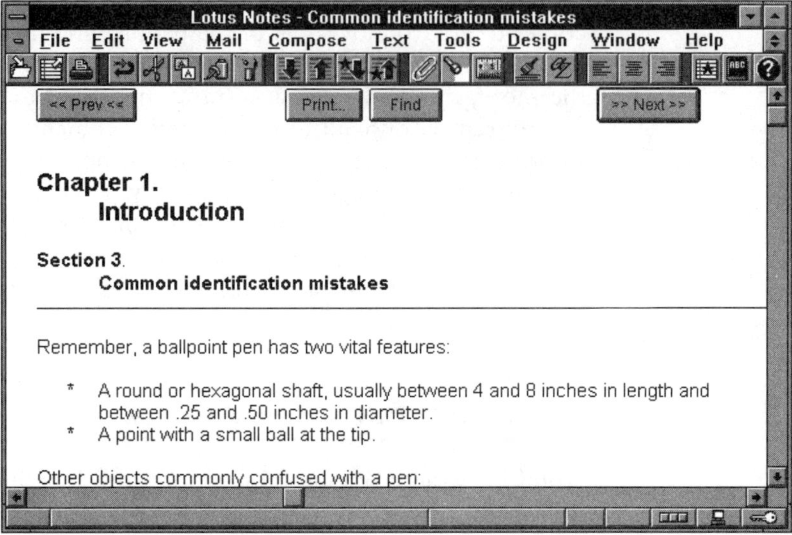

Part of the outline of a book

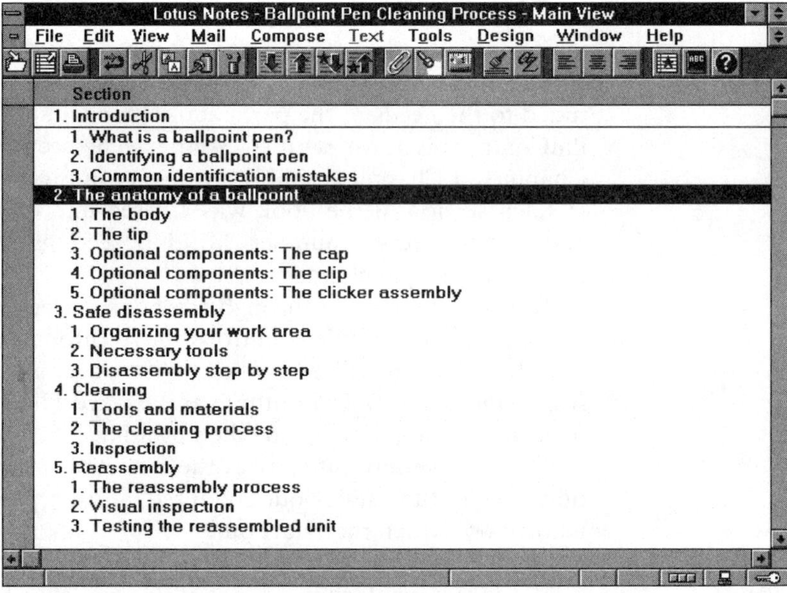

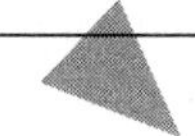

SmartIcons

SmartIcons are a feature of every Lotus application. The SmartIcon bar is a collection of buttons that gives you one-click access to almost any standard task in the system.

SmartIcons are easily customized. With SmartIcons it is possible to

▶ Move the icon bar to any edge of the screen or leave it as a floating window you can put anywhere you like.

▶ Keep multiple sets of icons for different tasks. In Notes, clicking the small SmartIcon button at the lower-right side of the Notes window will show a list of all the icon sets. Choosing one will change the icon set on the icon bar.

▶ Customize any one of the icon sets or create new sets of icons to meet specific needs.

▶ Create custom icons (both the pictures and the functions) and add them to any icon set. In Notes, these are programmed with the Notes macro language.

SmartIcons are commonly used for such tasks as opening a Mail file with one click, setting standard fonts or colors, attaching files, or opening a frequently used database. They let the Notes environment be tuned to the specific needs of a particular user.

ONSCREEN READING

There are some special considerations to be made when planning a document for electronic reading. It's hard to read large quantities of text on screen. Sections should, in general, be kept fairly small—usually no more than two or three printed pages. Good use of subheadings and inline images will help to break up the text. It's also a good idea to leave some white space between paragraphs for readability.

In order to make the process of moving documents into the database simpler, Albert first modified the style sheets for the original documents to add some white space around headings. He also added additional headings and occasional paragraph boundaries where he felt that there was too much text. He then copied each major section of the document to its own document in the Notes database, including the graphics.

The result has been a success. PhiComp employees now have a single point of reference for their development processes. Changes are much easier to make, and people always have an up-to-date copy available.

These kinds of databases are usually small enough that people can copy them to a laptop computer if they need to make regular reference to them, or read them off the server while connected. They can easily be kept up to date as processes and business needs change.

◀ Fact Sheet

Corporate Process Manual

Purpose: The storage of business processes or other reference information as an electronic book.

Application Origin: Custom developed.

Application Development Time: 2–4 hours, plus time to transfer the documents into the database.

Typical Size: 3–10 MB.

Typical Use: Whoever writes a process manual adapts this database and imports the documents. Others who use the process use this database as a guide. Typically, full-text search is enabled to allow people to find particular items more quickly.

Forms: Section is used to store a single section of the process. Sections are organized into chapters by a Chapter field on the form.

Views: Table of Contents—the Table of Contents is organized by Chapter and Section. The date of the most recent update is included so that people can easily identify changes.

Building a Training Signup Application

Since Notes excels at managing documents and automating work flows, big-company administrative processes are obvious targets for Notes applications. One such process, that of administering the registration of training classes, is targeted by Alice DaPron for re-engineering using Notes.

Alice runs the classes her company offers to its employees, and with budgets being cut left and right, she needs to find a way to minimize the overhead of scheduling employees in courses and of disseminating information about new courses. Since everyone in her company uses Notes, she looks into how Notes could make her work more efficient. She contacts the Notes development team and brainstorms some ideas. At the end of the conversation, she's decided to focus on providing a way to let people browse up-to-date course listings, get other related information, and even sign-up for courses without requiring assistance. This should reduce the number of people it takes to run the Education department, while providing excellent service to prospective students. Alice decides to call the new Notes database the Training Signup application. She tells the developers she will work up how she thinks the database should behave, and promises to get back to them in a few days.

How Will Users Use It?

Sitting quietly in her office, Alice imagines being an employee looking for information about courses. In this role, she immediately pictures opening the application and seeing a list of courses grouped by subject so she can see if any courses she likes are offered. When she finds a course she is interested in, she imagines clicking on it and seeing all the relevant information: when and where the course is offered, who is teaching it, and a detailed enough description to be able to decide whether or not she is interested. (Alice jots down on her pad, "Need a form to store class information and a view of courses categorized by subject.") She even selects a few of the courses and clicks the Print button to get a printed listing of exactly those courses she feels she might sign up for.

Next Alice imagines choosing a particular course to sign up for. She imagines filling out a form in the Training Signup database where she can enter the course number and date she wishes to take it. The form also prompts her to enter information like her name, address, phone number, and department number. She saves the form and closes the database.

Now, as a user, what would the next step be? Ahhh. . . the confirmation. Alice imagines getting an e-mail within a day or two confirming that a slot for her in the class has been officially reserved. She jots down on her pad, "Need a signup form. Should have a button to send confirmation back to employee when a member of her staff confirms the reservation."

Alice then imagines that a week before the class date she gets another e-mail reminding her of the course. She makes a note to ask the developers if the database can automatically do that.

Alice sits back in her chair and thinks about what she's got so far. People can access the database and get a listing of courses by subject. They can get detailed information about particular courses and can sign up by filling out a form. Her staff can easily send a confirmation back by pushing a button on the signup form when they assign a slot to the student. While just that much alone would reduce her overhead (no more printed publications, fewer telephone support staff, etc.), she continues to imagine being a user and to think about what other features would add value to the application.

First Alice thinks of additional ways to view the available courses. As a prospective student, she imagines wanting to take a course sometime in the next couple of weeks. What she would want is a listing of the courses that are being offered during the next couple of weeks—preferably restricted to those with empty slots. She makes a note to create a view to show this listing.

She then thinks about another way to view courses—by the person giving the course. Often a course will be taught by different people at different times, and a student may prefer one teacher over another. As a student, Alice can imagine wanting to see which other courses are being taught by a teacher she particularly liked from a previous training class. She makes a note to create a view of courses categorized by the person teaching them.

Alice starts to feel those creative juices flowing as she gets even more ideas. She imagines how useful it would be to put information about the various teaching facilities into the database so people won't have to call her staff so often. She could put in directions to each location, the description of the facilities offered at each location, and even information about taxis, limos, and public transportation that can be used to reach the facility. She jots down that

The Offered Soon view of the Training Signup application

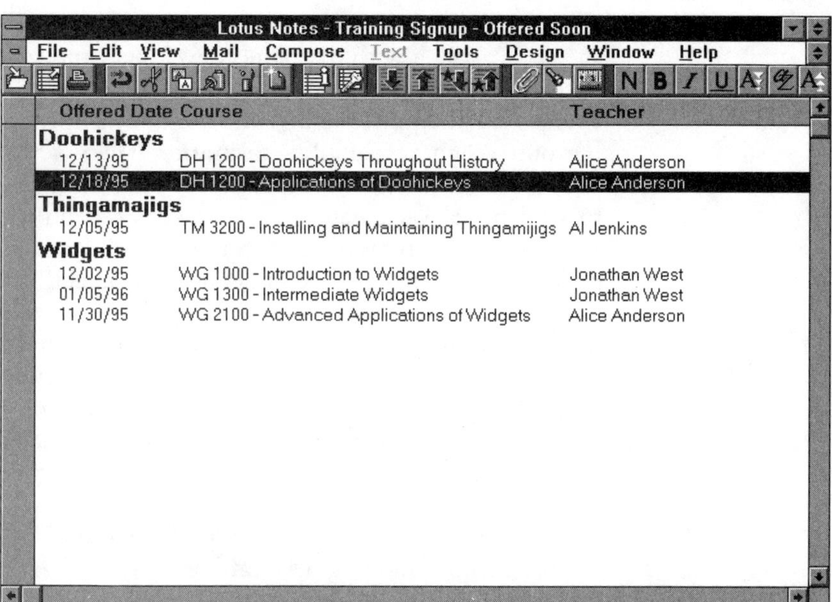

she'll need a form to store location information, and a view that lists the locations.

While she is thinking about additional information to help students, Alice thinks of adding a form to store teacher profiles. Each teacher could have a profile describing what they do, the subjects they teach, their interests, their experience, how to contact them, and so on. Students could scan the list before taking a class to help select a class, and could use it afterwards if they need to contact the teacher. That's another form for teacher profiles and another view to list them.

It then occurs to Alice that a resource she's never quite been able to make use of is student reviews. Often after taking a course, employees will call her department to express opinions on the quality of the course. Occasionally she uses the information in selecting courses and teachers, but the information never directly reaches other employees, except through word of mouth. Alice imagines letting employees enter comments about courses and teachers directly in the database so others can scan them at their leisure. She knows this could easily be implemented by letting employees create Response documents to the course descriptions and teacher profiles, so she decides to discuss the idea with others in her department.

MAKING IT HAPPEN

At this point, Alice thinks she has plenty of ideas to get the database going, so she gets in touch with the Notes developers and together they lay out the database. The developers see no problems with any of the requests: forms to store course, teacher, and facility information; a form to let users sign up with a button to send an e-mail confirmation back; views to display courses by subject, by teacher, and by date; and the automatic reminder feature to send mail to students a week before their class is scheduled. The developers predict it will take them about a week or two to build and test the database, with some additional help from Alice in defining the exact layout of the forms.

The developers then ask who will need access to the database. Alice explains that all employees register for training through her department, so the database must be usable company-wide. The developers start describing some of the complications of replicating company-wide such as the problem of different Notes communities and administrative headaches. It becomes clear that it might take a while to get the database out to everyone. Alice had hoped to have the application up and running in just a few weeks.

The developers suggest enabling the database as a mail-in database (see the sidebar "Mail-Enabling a Database" in this chapter). They explain that users could use mail to send sign-up forms to the database, and that Alice could send out a mass mailing containing an empty database with the signup form in it. Alice thinks to herself that she would still have to send paper catalogs to these people, but at least they could sign up electronically, and get automatic confirmation and reminders. She decides to use this solution until she can get the database fully replicated so all employees have access.

Mail-Enabling a Database

Notes supports a feature that can turn a database into a mail-in database. This means that people can use Notes Mail to send documents to the database. What does this mean? Let's answer that by seeing how it works.

The crux of the feature is the creation of a Mail-in Database document in the Name & Address Book of the server where the database resides. The mail-in database document contains two key pieces of information: the filename of the database to be mail-enabled and the mail address to be used when sending mail to the database.

Once this document is created, mail sent to the address listed in the mail-in database document will be deposited into the database.

This provides a nifty way to get input from people without hassling with access issues like Cross-certification. As long as someone can send mail, they can deposit documents in a mail-in database.

Mail-in databases can be used to gather any kind of data: requests for information, comments and suggestions on any topic, and so on. The database can also contain a *mail-in macro,* which provides the ability to run a macro whenever a new document arrives. This means databases can be built that automatically process incoming documents. The database might even send an e-mail out in return, thereby turning the mail-in database into an automated response system.

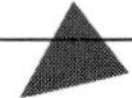

After a couple of weeks, the developers have the Training Signup application ready. They put it on Alice's department's server and replicate it to a few others. Alice sends out a shotgun mail message to all employees containing information about the new database and how to use it, and also containing the mini-database with the signup form. She also has her staff working to load up the database with the current course offerings, teacher profiles, and information about the facilities. Within the first couple of weeks, she receives dozens of signup forms, lots of kudos about the database, and suggestions for improvements.

FACT SHEET

Training Signup Database

Purpose: To reduce the overhead involved in providing course information to prospective students and to facilitate the signup and course reminder process.

Application Origin: Custom developed for this application.

Application Development Time: 2 weeks, with involvement from the training department on form layout.

Typical Size: 5–20 MB

Typical Use: Large corporations that offer an extensive training program.

Forms: The Course Description form stores the course name, number, subject keywords, dates offered, and a detailed description of the course contents. The Teacher Profile stores information about the teachers that do the training. The Location Information form stores information about training locations, the facilities offered there, directions to the location, etc. These three forms are used by the training department's staff. The Training Signup form is used by employees to request a slot in a course on a particular date.

Views: Several views show various listings of courses. The By Subject view shows courses categorized by subject keywords chosen to make searching easy. The By Teacher view groups courses by who the teacher is. The Offered Soon view shows courses with available slots being offered over the next few weeks. There are also views to display the other information in the database. The Teacher Profile view lists the teacher profiles, and the Location Profile view lists the location profiles.

Large Capital Expenditures: Expense Approvals Database

Metric, Inc. is a (hypothetical) manufacturer of scales and thermometers located in the midwest. Metric has around 2,000 employees, most of whom work in the company's manufacturing facilities. Metric considers technology a strategic asset and is usually on the cutting edge. The company purchased Notes in 1992 and has deployed the product to hundreds of employees. The company has used Notes to support or manage many of its business processes. One of the more successful applications has been to help the organization manage the approvals process for large expenditures (at Metric, any purchase or service over $50,000).

Metric was founded by the Saltzman family in 1912. All major business decisions were made by the patriarch of the family, Eli Saltzman. If a new piece of equipment needed to be purchased or a building needed to be built, Eli would evaluate the needs of the business and purchase whatever was necessary or beneficial. Over the years, the Saltzman family retained a small percentage of the company's stock, but their participation in day-to-day business decisions gradually declined. By the 1980s, decisions concerning large capital expenditures had become highly structured and rigid—one might go so far as to say "bureaucratic." To get a new piece of equipment required the approval of many review panels and, ultimately, the Capital Expenditure Review Committee (CERC). The CERC had six members, and required at least four to approve a proposal before it could be accepted. The review process alone for major expenditures took months.

Soon after the company installed its first Notes server, one forward-thinking member of the CERC had an idea for a Notes application: the company could use Notes to streamline the CERC process. This person, Andrew Thompson, knew that Notes was good at collecting and sharing information. The product provided an easy-to-use interface and could duplicate paper forms to a point where even computer-shy executives might use it. The CERC process, a process of completing an application (or "proposal") and seeing that proposal reviewed by a number of panels until it finally made it onto the CERC's agenda, lent itself directly to a Notes application. If they could integrate Notes into this process, he felt they might be able to reduce the length of the review process and ensure that the process was conducted more completely.

Andrew brought this idea to Jack Bloom, the employee who had been responsible for installing and managing the company's first Notes server. Andrew and Jack worked out a preliminary design for the application, which was then circulated to the various members of the CERC for review. The application would have five forms: Proposal, Response, Response to Response, CERC Agenda, and CERC Minutes. The Proposal form would be the main form in the database. This form would contain all information related to a particular proposal and would closely match the current paper form used for this purpose. The Response and Response to Response forms were included to allow people to comment on Proposal documents. The views included By Author, By Date, By Status, By Cost, By Proposal Number, and By Business Unit.

Andrew and Jack's proposal was reviewed at a meeting of the CERC. The other team members on the CERC were intrigued. Notes had only been deployed

Main View in the Expense Approvals database

Date	Type	Topic
03/01/95	Proposal	**Upgrade Plant Safety Systems (Alvin Trevor, 6 responses)**
03/03/95		More detail on expenditures... (Jill Remmer, 1 response)
03/05/95		Additional Details... (Alvin Trevor)
03/04/95		How does this relate to John Albertson's proposal? (Rob Taubman, 1 resp...
03/05/95		Mine addresses factory floor issues... (Alvin Trevor)
03/04/95		Relationship to other operations (Sarah Broadgate)
03/05/95		Does this proposal comply with federal standards? (Erin Flanagan)
03/04/95	Proposal	**WAN Connection For US Offices (Carl Wriston, 2 response...**
03/05/95		Technical Analysis of Feasibility (Sarah Broadgate)
03/07/95		Questions for consultants... (Ben Forrester)
03/09/95	Proposal	**Additional Delivery Trucks (Kerry Grier, 3 responses)**
03/08/95		What is the status of the current fleet? (Morris Kent)
03/09/95		Shipping in bulk... (Randy Parsons)
03/11/95		Other alternatives... (Larry Watkins)
03/10/95	Proposal	**Building Extension (Donna Savage, 8 responses)**
03/10/95		What bids have been obtained? (Jill Remmer, 1 response)
03/12/95		Currently out for bid... (Donna Savage)
03/11/95		Where are blueprints? (Randy Parsons)
03/12/95		Questions concerning construction materials... (Fred Trent, 1 response)
03/13/95		Other options (Donna Savage)
03/15/95		New plants vs. expansion... (Mel Wexler, 1 response)
03/16/95		Results of our analysis... (Donna Savage)
03/16/95		Impact of construction on productivity (Jerome Weller)
03/12/95	Proposal	**Management Consultant Analysis of Production (Evan Herr...**

to a few dozen people, but if this application could be made to work, it would justify deploying it to all CERC team members, as well as any of the review boards that preceded the CERC in the expenditure review process. The rollout to CERC members was particularly appealing to Jack, as the CERC was made up of the company's most senior executives. Jack was given the go-ahead at the meeting to pursue development of the application.

Jack developed the first version of the application in Version 2 of Notes. As a result, many of the bells-and-whistles features that would eventually find their way into the application did not exist in the first version. These included buttons, macros, and signatures for approvals. The work flow of the application was to be as follows: the author of a proposal for capital expenditures would complete a Proposal form in the database. This Proposal form would include a brief overview of the item(s) or service(s) being purchased, the purpose of the purchase (including a business justification for the expenditure), the amount of the purchase, the vendors involved in the purchase, prior business experiences with this vendor, references to related proposals (whether this purchase was part of a larger project or prior similar purchases), a utilization plan (how and where the purchased goods or services would be used), and the status of the proposal. Only the overview, purpose, and amount were required inputs. Documentation written to support the application indicated that the CERC would be much more likely to approve proposals where the author had provided the committee with a complete description of the proposal and any relevant background information.

Once a proposal had been added to the database, its status would be set to either Draft or Available for Comment. A status of Draft would indicate that the proposal was incomplete and needed more information. Available for Comment would indicate that the users of the database should feel free to comment on the content of the proposal, or ask questions of the author. The Available for Comment phase would provide the author with an opportunity to get feedback on the proposal without submitting it directly to the CERC. This would serve the dual purpose of providing the author with time to address shortcomings of the proposal and alerting the CERC that this proposal might soon be coming their way. Once the author felt confident of the proposal, the proposal's status would be set to Submitted. Submitted indicates that the proposal should be added to the next CERC agenda for review. The CERC secretary would take all the Submitted proposals for a given week and place them in the CERC Agenda. Next to each proposal listed in the Agenda the secretary would include a doclink back to the corresponding Proposal document. Prior to the CERC meeting, each of its members would be expected to review the proposals listed in the agenda. In the meeting, the CERC would allow time for a quick discussion of the proposal followed by a vote. The vote would be recorded in the CERC Minutes form in the database. Each proposal could be approved or rejected. Typically, rejected proposals would include some level of discussion as to why the proposal was rejected. In some cases, this might lead to a new proposal by the original author with amendments suggested by the committee (like a more complete business justification for a proposal). The secretary would record the meeting minutes and go back to the original Proposal document to update its status based on the vote of the CERC.

The primary objective of this application was to reduce the CERC meeting to an approval/rejection process rather than a review of each proposal. A secondary objective was to reduce or eliminate many of the review processes that used to precede the CERC. The objective of most of these reviews was to ensure that a proposal was complete and ready for review by the CERC.

CHANGED PROCESSES

The net result of the conversion of the CERC's processes to Notes was to reduce the length of the approval process from months to a few weeks. The many levels of reviews necessary to get a proposal approved were virtually eliminated (some remain to ensure that business units check the validity of the proposals prior to submission to the CERC). By providing the organization with a history of past-approved/rejected proposals, the database helped authors improve the quality of their proposals and allowed CERC team members to become more informed decision-makers. This application and others have helped Metric become a more responsive organization both to its customers and its suppliers.

Over time, the application was updated to reflect suggestions or changes in process. At some point in the process, authors began submitting a spreadsheet analyzing costs and benefits with their proposals. The spreadsheet was embedded into the Notes document (so it could be seen by a Notes user) and sent as an attachment (so it could be detached and examined in the spreadsheet application). When expenditures proposals were made that were identical to prior (approved) proposals, authors began using doclinks to refer CERC people to those prior proposals.

UPGRADE TO VERSION 3

When it became available, the application was upgraded to Version (V3) of Notes. By the time V3 was deployed at the company, the application had been in use for a number of years. The fact that the organization had a relatively mature Notes installation meant that the rollout of V3 progressed quite slowly. Everyone wanted to ensure that the upgrade proceeded without disrupting the services that Notes provided. Once the rollout had occurred, Jack and Andrew got together to review the CERC application. Jack had been to a couple of Notes V3 classes to help him understand the new features available in the product. They produced a document describing every contemplated change to the application and an assessment of how it would affect the application. The application had become so important to the CERC process, that it was highly undesirable to have the application down or information inaccessible for even a short period of time. To address this issue, the document provided a test plan to ensure that each new feature would not affect functionality.

Simple changes to the application included the addition of buttons and pop-up help to the forms. Buttons would be implemented to help users navigate the documents in the database (e.g., forward/backward through documents in a view). Other buttons would help the user compose a new document (a Response) to the current document. Pop-up help would be used for all fields in the Proposal form. Included in each pop-up would be a short sample entry for the field. This would help authors to understand exactly what was expected for each field.

Finally, Jack and Andrew proposed to do away with the CERC meetings entirely and move the approval process into Notes. The addition of "signed sections" in Notes would now allow this. The proposal allowed each member of the CERC to open the database and click a button to approve a section of the document. Jack and Andrew's proposal was not completely accepted—the organization was not prepared to accept getting rid of the CERC meetings outright. However, the group did agree to conduct a trial whereby the new mechanism would be tested to see if it might be made to work.

The new process would require at least four approvals by CERC members to be accepted. Every proposal would have six sections (one for each CERC team member). These sections would appear at the bottom of the document, and be inaccessible to proposal authors. Each section would have two buttons, one to accept a proposal and the other to reject the proposal. Once a proposal's status was changed to Pending, the CERC members could examine the proposal and make their decision. Each CERC member would go to their own section of the document and make their decision. Any document with four approvals was considered accepted. Any CERC member who voted to reject a proposal would need to substantiate the rejection. Once a document had four approvals (or three rejections), a message would be automatically sent to the proposal author indicating the result of the CERC vote.

The new work flow was tested by the team for two weeks (two CERC meetings were eliminated). The initial tests of the new application were so successful that the CERC agreed to continue using the Notes database in meetings for all but the largest proposals (over $100,000).

UNFINISHED BUSINESS

CERC members can currently edit a document at the same time. For example, while one member is reviewing a proposal, another could open the same document issue an approval, and save the document. If the first user now tried to save his document, he would get a message indicating that someone else had saved a copy of the same document. To get around this problem, the application would need to employ mail routing of each proposal. This would send the document to each one of the CERC members sequentially. When the last member voted on the proposal, the proposal would be sent back to the CERC database. Jack thought that one of the problems with this option is that since all approvals are routed sequentially to each CERC member's mail files, the entire process might bog down if someone did not read their mail for a while.

Another area that might be examined is the use of sections. While sections allow multiple signatures on a single document, they cannot prevent a user from tampering with a document. For example, if a malicious author got hold of a proposal he had submitted, he could actually delete one of the signatures (like a rejection by a CERC member). The author would not be able to change the vote, but could delete it outright. This sort of tampering could undermine the usefulness of sections, depending on the application's needs.

Metric also might consider linking the approvals directly to the Purchasing department's accounting computers. In this way, the authorization to purchase the commodity or service could be implemented almost instantly.

Finally, Metric could consider measuring the success or failure of various expenditures over time. For example, for those proposals submitted with a business case study in an attached spreadsheet, it would be interesting to see how closely profits and losses matched up with the original projections. This would certainly be a difficult quantity to measure (as many other factors might be involved in the success or failure of an expenditure), but insofar as the quantity is measurable, it might be desirable to do so.

Fact Sheet

Expense Approvals Database

Purpose: To provide the Capital Expenditure Review Committee with the opportunity to collect information on and manage the approval process for requests for large capital expenditures.

Application Origin: Developed from scratch in Version 2 of Notes.

Application Development Time: 2 man/weeks for initial version.

Typical Size: 10–15 MB (the company archives the old information).

Typical Use: An organization needing to acquire new equipment totaling over $50,000 completes a Proposal form; this form is then reviewed by the CERC in the database; finally, the Proposal is voted on, and the result is posted to the database.

Forms: Proposal, Response, Response to Response, CERC Agenda, and CERC Minutes.

Views: By Author, By Date, By Status, By Cost, By Proposal Number, and By Business Unit.

Supporting Guests in a Secure Fashion

Notes is built on an infrastructure of public/private key technology. This makes Notes an extremely secure platform for storing sensitive corporate data. This was a key factor in HTC's decision to standardize on Notes for their corporate desktops.

HTC is a (hypothetical) manufacturer of components and systems for high-reliability computer systems. HTC encompasses a large research and development organization for the development and exploitation of new technologies. This often involves working with partners and consultants who come on site to work hand in hand with their own staff.

Currently, supporting on-site visitors means creating Notes user IDs for these visitors and granting them access to the same systems the HTC personnel uses. Because there are security risks in doing this, HTC decides to provide "guest" accounts in a better way.

IT WORKS NOW, BUT...

"As you know, when we set up our Notes network we explicitly deployed organizational certifiers so we could distribute the administration of user and server IDs to the various divisions. R&D creates their own servers and sets up their own users. The same for product management and marketing, administration, manufacturing, and so on. This has worked well, since we haven't had to be involved every time the divisions wanted to bring up new servers and users. The divisions have even been able to cross-certify with our partners to provide secure collaboration."

Ruth Derhey is opening the meeting of the Guest Account subteam she has formed to study how HTC supports providing Notes access to visitors. Ruth heads the Notes administration department at HTC. This department is responsible for setting standards on setting up Notes, maintaining the overall naming tree and security model, and providing backbone replication servers to support collaboration between geographically separated Notes networks.

"I recently received a call from Leon Mann, who, as you know, heads the R&D division. He told me that quite frequently R&D must work with visitors who come on-site to support his projects. Like the other divisions, they create user IDs for the visitors so they can use e-mail and access the Notes applications the particular project is using.

"He pointed out the obvious risks in doing this. Once the visitor has access to the company Notes servers, only database access control lists (ACL) restrict what the visitor can see. Of course, all databases are supposed to set the default access level to No Access, but that is not always the case. He also pointed out that most servers do not explicitly grant access to an 'allow access' group, and so a visitor who receives a Notes ID has automatic access to many of our Notes servers."

Carl Gould, a member of Ruth's team, offers his thoughts. "Another problem I see we have is how to handle when the visitor leaves the project. Since the divisions have set up their own domains, the visitor may still have access to other divisions' servers, even if they put the visitor's name in their local Deny Access list, which will prevent the visitor from being able to access their servers."

Ruth replies, "Exactly. I think we should develop a better company-wide way to support these guest accounts. Let's get some thoughts on the table."

The subteam spends half an hour or so discussing possibilities. One suggestion is to provide a service where the divisions can call and report an ID as no longer valid. Then Ruth's team could add the name to all Deny Access lists in the company. A tool could be developed that would add a name to all the groups, thus solving the problem of older IDs still being able to access HTC Notes servers. The team feels this solution is inadequate in that it does not address the issue of visitors accessing databases they shouldn't while they are on-site. It also leaves open the issue of visitors being able to access other divisions Notes servers while they are onsite.

Another suggestion is made to purchase one of the available ACL monitoring products available and use it to ensure that no database provides a default access level other than No Access. This, combined with the previous suggestion about administering all deny access groups, could provide a high level of security. This suggestion is considered a viable solution, but the team has some reservations. They are not sure they want to be so closely involved in the administration of each division's servers. The organization units were specifically set up to help decentralize the administration of Notes networks in HTC. There is also the cost of buying and/or developing the required tools.

Carl then speaks up again. "I've been giving this problem a lot of thought and I suggest we set up a second name tree. This second name tree would be used to create guest servers and guest user IDs. We then replicate databases that guests need to access to the guest server. This way no guest would ever have direct access to one of our existing Notes servers."

The team asks Carl to elaborate on how the naming would work and how the security model works to grant the appropriate access where necessary and to restrict access where it is not needed.

"OK, follow me now. We currently have one big name tree called /HTC. All servers and users are created under this name tree, and that's why all users and servers can access all servers. In order to provide a bigger 'name space' to avoid the problem of two John Smiths and to let each division administer its own server and user IDs, we deployed organization units. That is, R&D has an organization unit (or OU), called /RD/HTC. All of their server and user names end in /RD/HTC, like Server1/RD/HTC and Leon Mann/RD/HTC. Similarly, there is /PMM/HTC for the product management and marketing division, and /ADMIN/HTC for our Notes administration department.

Any user with an ID created by any of these OUs will have /HTC as the root. That is why Leon Mann/RD/HTC can access a server called Server1/PMM/HTC. The IDs have a common parent, in this case /HTC. In order to create guest user IDs that cannot access our servers, we need a different root. I suggest we create the /HTCGUEST organization. Then users will be called things like John Smith/HTCGUEST. These IDs will only be able to access servers we create under the same tree, like GuestServer1/HTCGUEST."

The team sees how this separate name tree with its own server and users will prevent guests from accessing the regular HTC Notes servers. But does data get replicated to these servers? How do HTC employees get access to these servers to manage the databases placed there?

"Here's where things get a little confusing, since there is an asymmetric relationship we need to establish. Basically, we will want all /HTC servers and users to be able to access, or be authenticated by, the /HTCGUEST servers. However, we only want the /HTCGUEST servers to be able to access, or be authenticated by, the existing /HTC servers. Here's how we will do it.

"To let all /HTC servers and users access the guest servers, we will use the /HTCGUEST certifier and Cross-certify the /HTC safe ID. This Cross-certificate will go on all guest servers. This will cause the guest servers to authenticate all /HTC servers and users—all /HTC servers will be able to replicate to the guest servers, and all HTC employees will be able to access the guest servers to administer databases they might place there. By the way, we might not want all employees to be able to do this, so we may enforce an Allow Access group on these servers to restrict access.

Now, we need to do a Cross-certification in the other direction so /HTC servers will authenticate the guest servers, but so the /HTC servers will *not* authenticate the guest users. To do this, we will use the /HTC certifier and Cross-certify each guest server's safe ID. In effect, we will grant permission to /HTC servers on a guest-server-by-guest-server basis. This Cross-certificate will need to be placed in each Notes domain that wishes to replicate databases to the guest servers."

The team takes a few minutes to let this sink in. The proposal seems solid, but the team wants to know how some of the details work. One team member asks, "Doesn't this still have the problem of guests accessing databases where the default is not No Access?"

Carl responds, "Yes and no. It makes the problem smaller. Since the only databases guests will be able to access are those on the guest servers, we need to watch the ACLs only on those databases. This proposal will require our department to perform some administrative duties for these guest servers. Obviously we will need to set them up, and we will need to create user IDs when the divisions request them. I think checking the default access level on the guest databases could be done manually by us, at least at first. If we find ourselves with too many servers and databases to check manually we can purchase one of the off-the-shelf ACL monitors we discussed earlier.

"Another administrative duty we will have to take on is placing users in the Deny Access list of the Guest domain (we'll put all the guest servers in one domain to make administration easier) when the divisions let us know an ID is no longer valid. We will also need to create groups for employees to use to administer the ACLs of their databases replicated on the guest servers. We can make employees owners of their own groups so we don't have to maintain these groups on an ongoing basis.

"By the way, another advantage of centralizing the responsibility of creating guest user IDs is that we can enforce near-term expiration dates. That way even if the divisions forget to notify us that a guest has left, the IDs will expire shortly anyway."

The team agrees that the proposal is sound. Ruth asks about the difficulty of administering the guest servers and databases. In particular, she wants to know how databases get replicated to the guest servers. Carl responds.

"I suggest we handle it like we handle any other replication we support through our administrative servers. We currently let the divisions replicate through our servers to link the separate networks. They either send us the database in the mail for installation on one of our servers, or call us to pull it from their servers to our servers. It's pretty simple, and I doubt we couldn't handle the extra load of the guest databases. If the load gets too high, we may want to consider providing a Request form via the FORMS.NTF mechanism to streamline requests for replicating databases to the guest servers."

Ruth agrees that her team can handle the load of the guest databases. She asks Carl to document the proposal, including the details of the Cross-certification and the new name tree, the new administrative tasks required, and the schedule to roll out the first server and be prepared to create the first guest ID.

Ruth then calls Leon Mann back to explain what her team has decided to do. Leon likes the solution and thinks that the effort will be well worth the extra security. He offers to test the new system once it is up and running and Ruth agrees to contact him at that point.

TESTING FOR LEAKS

A month later, Carl is ready to test out the new system. He has created the new name tree and set up a server called GuestServer1/HTCGUESTS. He has placed the Cross-certificate from /HTCGUESTS to /HTC in the N&A Book on GuestServer1. He has placed the Cross-certificate from /HTC to GuestServer1/HTCGUESTS in the N&A books of the administrative servers and has replicated a test database from one of his administrative servers to GuestServer1. He lets Ruth know he's ready.

Ruth calls Leon and lets him know that GuestServer1 is up and ready. Leon tells Ruth he'll ask around in his division for a test project. A couple of days later, he gets back to Ruth and says that he has identified a project just getting underway that needs to support guest accounts. He asks Ruth to have her administrator get in touch with Janet Heely, who is leading the project. After their call, Ruth lets Carl know to proceed by calling Janet.

Carl calls Janet and finds out that she has just created a database on her server called Project Oak, which will need to be accessed by a guest consultant working with her. Carl asks the consultant's name, which is Helen Sessa. Carl explains that he will create an account called Helen Sessa/HTCGUESTS, and that Janet should add this name to the database with Reader, Author, or Editor permissions, whichever is appropriate. Since the R&D servers are on the same network as the guest servers, Carl explains that Janet's server and the guest server will be able to replicate directly. He instructs her to add the name GuestServer1/HTCGUESTS to the ACL with Manager access to support the replication. He asks her to send the database to him via e-mail so he can install it on the guest server. He says he will e-mail the user ID for Helen Sessa as soon as he has created it.

By the next day Carl and Janet have exchanged e-mail. The database is installed on the guest server and is replicating with Janet's local server. Janet has the new user ID for Helen. Carl asks Janet to sit with Helen and try a few experiments to see if Helen can access any of the regular HTC notes servers, and to confirm that she can access the new database on the guest server.

Later that day Janet meets with Helen in Helen's temporary office. Janet brings Helen's user ID on a floppy. Helen says that Notes has been installed on her PC and that she was told to wait for her ID before running it. Together Janet and Helen run Notes on her PC for the first time and, when prompted, indicate that Helen's user ID was provided to her on a floppy. A couple of minutes later they have confirmed that Helen can access GuestServer1 and can open

Information about a user ID including expiration date

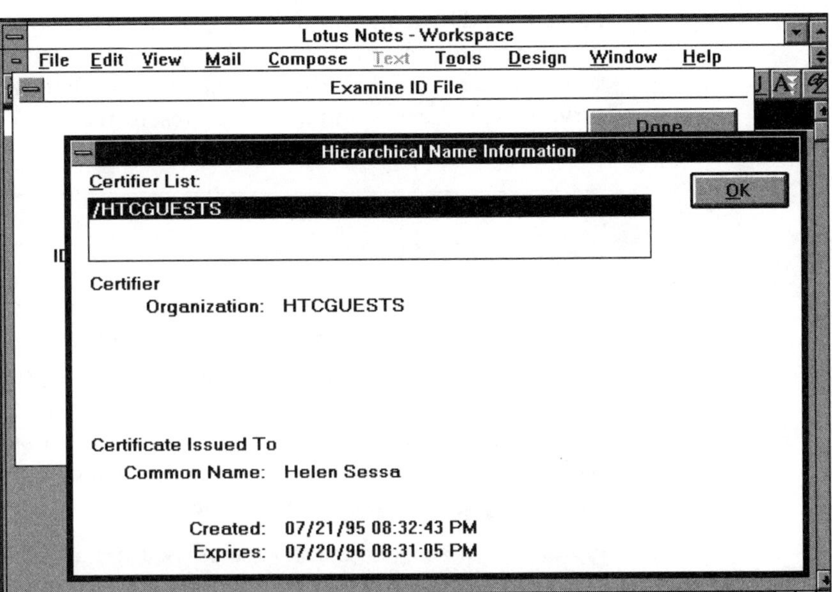

the Project Oak database. Janet then tries to access her regular Notes server and receives an error message about not having the right Cross-certificates to access the server.

Back in her office Janet calls Carl and lets him know that everything seems to be working as expected. Her guest has access to the guest server and the database they replicated to it. She is now able to work with the consultant without worrying about the other resources the consultant has access to. Carl thanks her and writes a note to Ruth, letting her know that everything is running fine.

MAKING IT AIRTIGHT

Ruth calls another meeting of the subteam that formed and executed the proposal to support the guest accounts in a secure fashion. She asks Carl to report on the status of the project.

"The guest server is working fine, and at the present, one server seems like it will do the trick. We've created a few dozen guest accounts and everything is running smoothly."

Ruth then asks the team what actions should take place to close any existing security holes that may be associated with past guest IDs created in the /HTC name tree. The team suggests forming a task force with the various divisions' Notes administrators to convert any current visitors to the new guest ID and server system and put their names in the Deny Access groups of all Notes servers. Ruth agrees and asks the present team to coordinate the effort.

FACT SHEET

Guest Security System

Purpose: To provide guests access to corporate data in a secure way which limits their access to any data other than that they are required to have.

Application Origin: Not applicable. This is a method by which to implement the secure guest accounts.

Application Development Time: Implementing the system involves setting up a separate name tree and a separate server. Implementation time is a few days to a week or two.

Typical Size: Not applicable.

Typical Use: Used by organizations large enough to support the overhead of an extra server for guest accounts.

Forms: Not applicable.

Views: Not applicable.

Odds and Ends

In this chapter, we review a series of smaller applications that have been used to good effect in corporations but do not warrant an entire chapter on their own. While each of these applications covers a unique topic, they are all very similar in design and could all be classified as "helper" applications. As such, they might warrant grouping in a particular directory on your company's Notes server. It might also be useful to provide users with a Discussion database in the same directory to provide an opportunity to discuss the content of the databases in that directory.

CLASSIFIEDS

Many organizations have created a database to allow employees to post and access classified ads. Typically there is a single form, which is used to post requests or offers to sell. A user opens the form and selects Buy or Sell. Selecting Buy indicates that the author is looking to acquire something. Selecting Sell indicates that the author wants to sell something. The author then needs to put in a contact name and number. This is the name and telephone number of the person selling the item or looking to buy an item. Next, the author chooses the type of item, such as a car, apartment/house, furniture, stereo, or computer. Another field allows the author to describe more completely the item they are looking to buy or sell. Another field captures the selling price or desired purchase price. Finally, there is a field to allow the author to scan an image of the object they are buying or selling. This is particularly helpful when the object is a car or house. This type of application can provide such views as By Item Type, By Author, and By Price. Below that, the view typically shows a

Classifieds By Type view in the Classifieds database

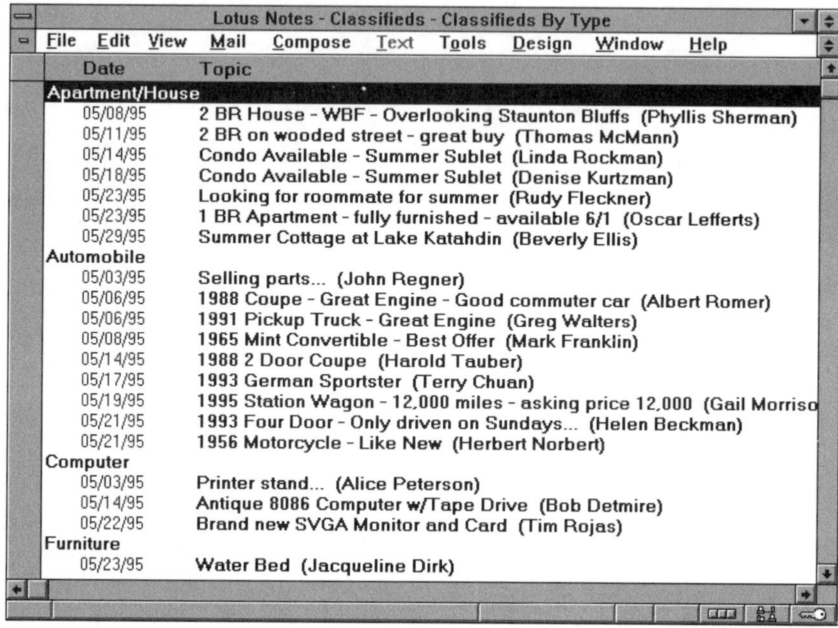

description of the item to be bought or sold. Some organizations might consider allowing employees to post requests for employment opportunities. While this might be acceptable if an employee is looking for someone to mow their lawn, it would be highly inappropriate if an employee were offering or looking for other professional opportunities. As a result, most organizations do not allow posting of services in a classifieds database.

There are some pros and cons to creating this type of application. On the one hand, it provides responsible employees with an opportunity to buy and sell goods in a convenient manner. An employer could argue that it might actually get more work out of people, since they would not need to be working through a newspaper or broker to buy and sell goods. However, there is a real cost to these databases. The application takes up disk space and, if replicated widely, takes up network bandwidth as well. One way of mitigating the storage issue is to purge documents more than a certain number of days old. As classified ads typically have a time value (the older they are the less likely they are to be valid), this should not be a problem. Regardless, users of the application will most likely access the application during working hours. If the buyer and seller both work for the company, it is also likely that the employees would use company resources like e-mail or telephone to communicate and would do so on company time.

Classified Ads Database

Purpose: To provide employees with a place to post and read classified ads.

Application Origin: Derived from standard Discussion template.

Application Development Time: A few hours.

Typical Size: Depends on number of postings and number of bitmaps—database of 150 documents (with few bitmaps) is about 2–3 MB; ensure that documents over 30 days old are deleted.

Forms: Classified.

Views: By Type, By Author, and By Amount.

UTILITIES

Another application that many organizations find useful is a database of standard utilities. These are programs or files that are generally useful to employees. It is expected that the users posting these utilities will have investigated any software copyright issues prior to posting a program. This can be completely explained in the About page of the database. Once again, the design of the database is quite simple. There is one form, which allows an author to post a file. The database can be a Discussion database with all forms but Main Topic removed from the database. It would be helpful to add a list of categories to classify each file (e.g., network drivers or file utilities), and force each author to classify her files. An author would compose a Main Topic, fill in the topic for the form, select an appropriate category for the form, attach the file to the form, and save the document. The views in the database could be kept from the Discussion database: By Author, By Category, and Main.

This database is somewhat less frivolous than the classifieds. It can be a critical mechanism to distribute important files. For a user who needs an updated network driver or the latest version of a virus-scanning software, this can be a life saver. Examples of files that might be included in this database include screen savers, compression software, company specific utilities, file viewers, and standard configuration files (e.g., WIN.INI). Typically these types of files are relatively small and the database, as a result, does not get too large. This type of application can be a real asset to a distributed organization that uses Notes.

Utilities By Type view in the Utilities database

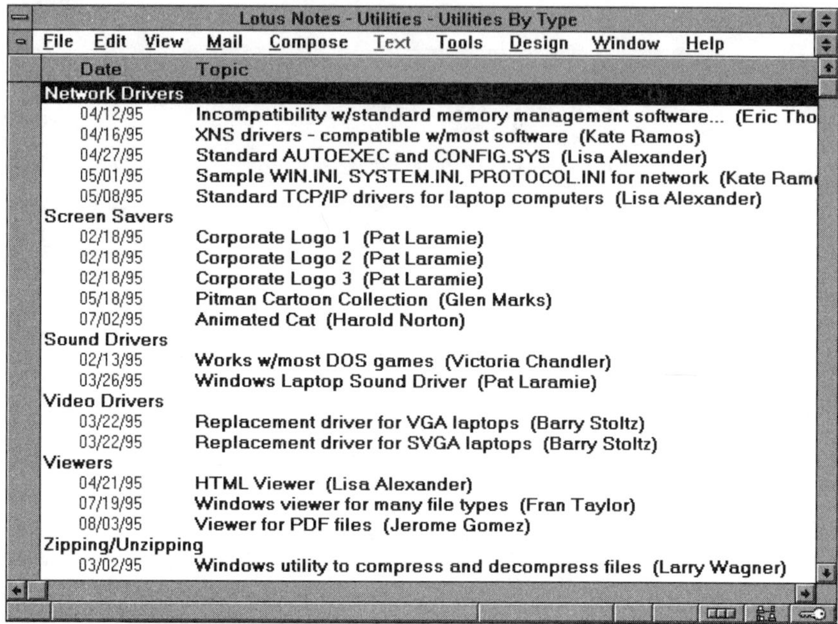

FACT SHEET

Utilities Database

Purpose: To allow users around a company to share useful software utilities and drivers.

Application Origin: Derived from standard Discussion template.

Application Development Time: A few hours.

Typical Size: Depends on the number of documents and size of attachments—generally a few megabytes in size.

Forms: Utility.

Views: By Type, By File Name, and By Author.

GRAPHICS

The Graphics database is a place for users to post their favorite bitmaps or icons. End users can use the .BMPs as backgrounds for their desktops. Notes application developers (and other developers) can use the icons for their Notes databases (and other applications). The database could be built from the standard Notes Discussion database by deleting all but the Main Topic form. Users would be able to post documents by filling in the topic, category (user-defined in this case), and body of the form. The body would contain a file attachment or an *embedded graphic*. Embedded graphics are created by importing the file (Notes will recognize a limited number of graphics types) or bringing the graphic up in a different application and copying/pasting it into Notes.

Unfortunately, graphics can take up large amounts of disk space, and unlike classified ads, graphics can be good forever. As a result, there is no easy way to delete unused documents from the database. An organization should carefully weigh the costs of maintaining a graphics application before adding one to its environment.

Graphics By Subject view in the Graphics Database

Date	Topic
Animals	
02/06/95	Fish in a pond – BMPs (Sam Hortens)
04/01/95	Lions in Africa – BMP (Albert Treadwell)
04/09/95	Snakes – GIFs (Peter Biltman)
05/16/95	Large Dinosaurs – BMPs (Ezra Hammer)
06/02/95	Cats, cats and more cats – BMPs (Harry Irtzwell)
07/10/95	Hi Res Frog – GIFs (Alice Cranwell)
09/14/95	Deer on a mountain – BMPs (Jane Tarley)
09/14/95	Bear on a mountain – BMPs (Jane Tarley)
Cartoons	
03/22/95	Elephant – TIF (Syd Vernon)
04/09/95	More icons – ICOs (Terry Williams)
06/02/95	Assorted Cartoon Icons – ICOs (Norman McMurtry)
06/13/95	Perly the Dodo – BMPs (Jeremy Vaner)
Computer	
02/19/95	Computer Icons – ICOs (Dave Young)
03/08/95	Collosus – BMPs (Walter Erskine)
03/24/95	Various computer types – ICOs (Nora Thomas)
04/30/95	CPU manufacturing – BMPs (Kenneth Treadwell)
05/03/95	Inside of a mainframe – BMPs (Kevin Brackman)
09/04/95	Common Computer Types – ICOs (Phil Henny)
Landscape	
01/31/95	NYC Skyline – BMPs (Laurie Merriweather)
02/11/95	Large mountain – BMPs (Roberta Young)

FACT SHEET

Graphics Database

Purpose: To allow users to share interesting bitmaps, screen savers, icons, viewers, etc.

Application Origin: Derived from standard Discussion template.

Application Development Time: A few hours.

Typical Size: Depends on the number and size of postings; database can get quite large: BMP files average around 300–400 K each.

Forms: Graphic.

Views: By Type, By Size, and By Author.

POWER USERS FORUM

The Power Users Forum provides application developers, power users, and end users with an opportunity to exchange information on technical topics. The structure of the database can be a standard Notes Discussion, or the ap-

Tips view in the Power Users Forum database

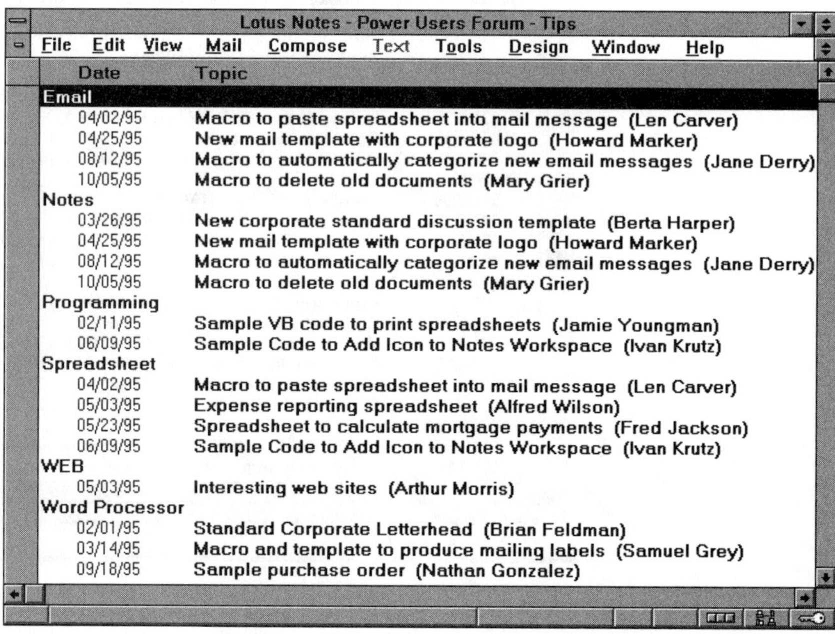

plication design may be more targeted. For example, it is possible to set up views by Application (e.g., Lotus Notes, Novell Word Perfect, or Microsoft Excel). In this application, there might be a single form called Tips & Tricks. With this form, users could share useful code samples, solutions to problems, macros, and the like which they have come across which have helped them do their jobs more effectively. Typically the documents contained in this forum are related to more complicated problems in these applications. It is important to ensure that this application is full-text search indexed to give users the maximum flexibility in finding relevant information.

FACT SHEET

Power Users Forum

Purpose: To allow application developers, power users, and end users with highly technical questions a place to exchange and share ideas.

Application Origin: Derived from standard Discussion Template.

Application Development Time: A few hours.

Typical Size: Typically quite small (less than 5 MB); size will vary depending on the size of the attachments.

Forms: Tips & Tricks, Main Topic, Response, and Response to Response.

Views: By Tip, All By Date, All By Author, and All By Category.

OneSource Information Applications

OneSource Information Services, Inc., located in Cambridge, Massachusetts, provides a variety of business-related information products. They distribute financial and market data along with business background information on public and private companies around the world. OneSource customers are basically buying information about their competitors, their customers, and their prospects. OneSource products include such items as SEC filings for public companies, *Ward's Business Directory, The Investext Reports,* and *American Banker.*

Originally, OneSource distributed this information on CD-ROMs using their own custom user interface, and they still do that. Lately, however, they found it useful and profitable to deliver the information using Notes.

Jimmy Becker, vice president and general manager of OneSource, keeps a list of the reasons his company decided to use Notes to deliver their product. First is the "instantly familiar" user interface—if an organization has already rolled out Notes, users will be comfortable adding more applications to their existing desktops.

Also important is the way Notes databases are used—the information is instantly accessible (because the databases are stored on a local network), searchable (by using the full-text search capabilities), browsable (users can choose between the different views to examine the databases in any of a vari-

---

Application information and screen shots courtesy of OneSource Information Services, Inc.

ety of different ways), and scalable (it can work in organizations from 10 to 10,000 users).

Finally, information stored in Notes can be easily integrated with other Notes databases to form a more powerful total solution, and retrieval of the information can be automated through information agents. Both of these features are particularly important to OneSource, which uses them to provide a competitive advantage.

OneSource has three major product areas with respect to Notes:

▶ OneSource Databases, which comprise an electronic library of business and financial databases delivered as complete Notes databases.

▶ OneSource Monitor software, an "information agent" that collects data from multiple sources and creates a single integrated Notes database with all the information.

▶ The Company Watch service, a way for customers to receive a broad range of information on a specific set of companies. Company Watch information is delivered into a Notes database.

THE ONESOURCE DATABASES

OneSource provides more than a dozen different Notes databases with valuable information. A subscriber to one of the OneSource databases would receive a CD-ROM monthly. A complete Notes database is stored on this CD. The database views have already been precalculated, and the full-text index has been built and stored. These two operations are by far the most time-consuming processes in Notes. The end result is a large database with excellent performance for its size.

Many of the OneSource databases are just large collections of one particular data item. Each of these databases has a single form, designed to accommodate the needs of the particular database and information.

For example, in the PROMT database (a collection of news abstracts and full-text articles covering U.S. businesses), the form contains the title of the database, the source of the article (magazine and page number), the body of the article, and index information.

OneSource has taken care to store the data on the forms in such a way that it's easily reusable. For example, when tabular data is included, it is formatted in such a way that it can be cut and pasted easily into spreadsheets or graphics packages.

A sample form in the PROMT database

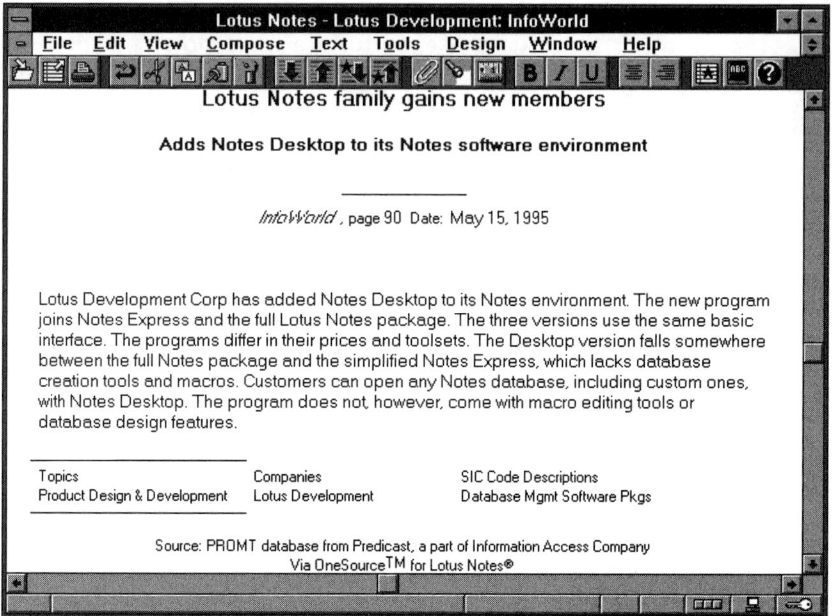

THE VIEW FROM HERE

The OneSource databases really shine when it comes to the range of views available. Each database has been indexed in all reasonable ways to provide views that let users browse the information in whatever order seems appropriate at the time. For example, the Disclosure database (which contains public filings by public companies) includes a wide variety of interesting views:

▶ Area Code By Revenue. This finds companies in a particular region, sorted by corporate size.

▶ State By Revenue, City By Revenue. These views are particularly useful for tax planners or anyone looking for the largest employers in a particular area.

▶ Forbes Rank. By Assets, By Market Value, By Profits, and By Sales. These four views show the Forbes-ranked companies, according to the different ranking methods.

▶ Revenue. All companies sorted strictly by size.

▶ SIC Code, By Revenue. The *SIC* (Standard Industry Classification) code classifies companies into product lines. Companies with the same SIC code are likely to be competitors. This is a good way to analyze the structure of the market.

▶ Directors. This shows all of the people listed in the database as corporate directors. Expanding the list for an individual shows all of the companies that employ that person as a corporate director.

▶ Tables By Company, Ratios. This view shows all of the commonly used "ratios" that investors use when analyzing businesses.

▶ Company Name. This shows all companies in the database sorted by company name.

▶ Ticker. This shows the businesses organized by stock ticker symbol.

One of the big features of the OneSource databases is that all of these views come precalculated. One of the most time-consuming events in the life of a Notes database is calculating views, particularly new views. OneSource has taken care of this in advance. The end result is excellent performance, even for views with 100,000 items, such as the PROMT news article database.

The Disclosure Profiles database viewed by City, By Revenue

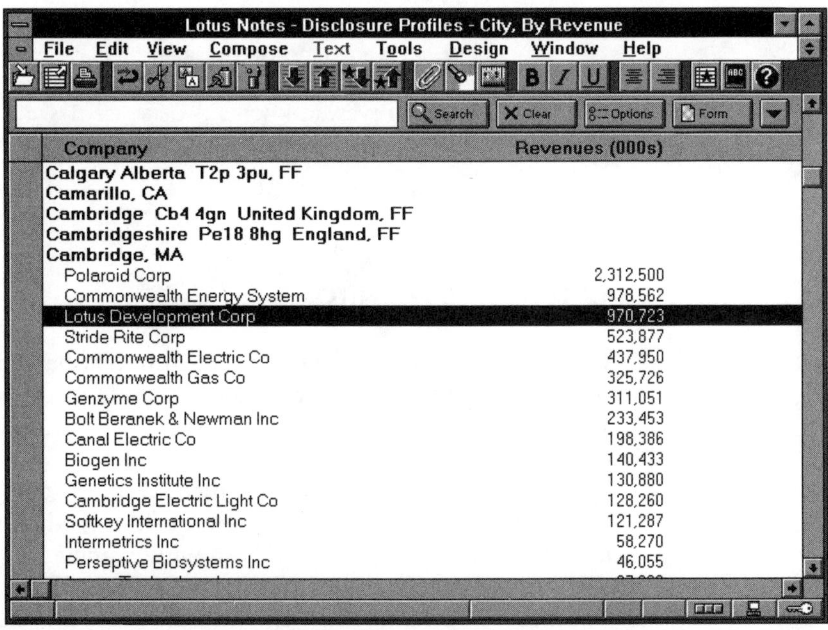

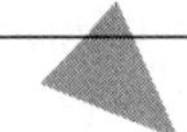

View Indexing

A Notes database consists of three major pieces:

- ▶ The actual Notes documents themselves. Each document contains a list of fields, but has no inherent "form" or field layout.
- ▶ The forms used to display the documents.
- ▶ The views. A view is a list of some or all of the documents in the database, organized into some useful order.

While forms don't often change, and documents change one at a time, a view could potentially change every time a document gets added to the database or even just due to the passage of time (for example, a view that shows the last 30 days of customer contacts).

Also, views take up space in the database. Depending on the size of the documents and the complexity of the view, a view might potentially take up more space than the documents themselves.

Notes calculates views whenever necessary, which is usually whenever someone is using it. When someone switches to a new view, Notes must first calculate (index) the view. If only a couple of documents have changed since the view was last used, this doesn't take long. If there have been many changes, or this is the first time a view is being used, it might take anywhere from a few seconds to a minute or longer. A database designer can control how views are reindexed, specifying that a view should only be reindexed on demand (when the user presses F9) or that views should be recalculated no more than every few hours. A database designer can also specify how quickly view indexes will be deleted when they're not used.

OneSource Monitor

OneSource offers nearly a dozen different databases in Notes format. Many of their customers subscribe to more than one of them, and probably also subscribe to some sort of online news service, such as NewsEdge (see the chapter called " The NewsEdge/Notes Database").

OneSource provides a tool, called Monitor, that helps people to navigate this sea of information. The first part of the product is a simple, but clever, use of Notes forms. This is a database with a single form that does nothing more than provide one-button access to all the NewsEdge databases on the system. But this one-form database is nicely designed, and definitely improves the ease of use of the whole system.

The second part is much more sophisticated, but just as clever. Monitor is an "information agent" that reads databases from OneSource, third-party

The OneSource database navigator

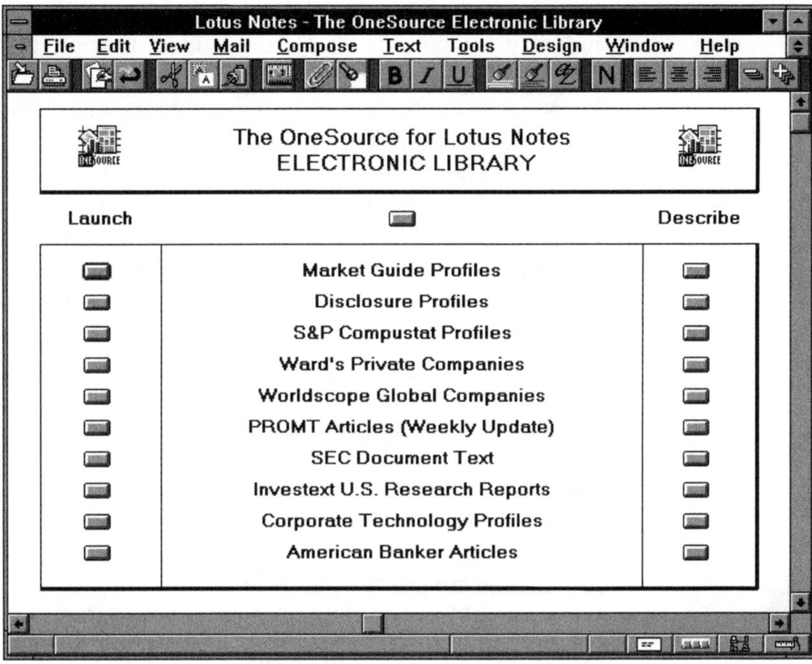

news providers, and customers' internal Notes databases. It filters out information from key companies and topics, integrates them into a single Notes database, and then monitors that information for future changes and posts the updates.

Monitor is set up by first telling it which databases it can use. Next, it needs a list of the items to keep track of. There are two parts to the Monitor product—Topic Monitor and Company Monitor. Monitor uses Notes forms to maintain lists of the search criteria. For example, such a list might include industry segments and topics, names of competitors and suppliers, and key accounts and prospects.

Monitor then uses the full-text indexing features of Notes to search all the databases for information matching these criteria. It integrates the results into a single database reserved for containing Monitor data.

Over time, Monitor keeps watching these databases for new and changed information pertaining to the chosen items. It will then update the Monitor database.

As a result, users of Monitor need only look in one place for all the Notes-based information they need.

COMPANY WATCH

Some organizations need to keep track of only a few competitors or a small industry. OneSource also has a product that might appeal to them. OneSource Company Watch lets the customer choose between 12 and 100 companies to keep track of. OneSource will then create a custom database with all the information in their system about these companies.

In fact, OneSource simply creates a custom Monitor database for that customer, and lets Monitor keep track of things automatically. They then replicate the resulting database to the customer's site.

Company Watch can be a cost-effective alternative for organizations on a budget or with limited needs.

FACT SHEET

OneSource Databases

Purpose: To deliver large quantities of business and financial information that enable business professionals to make faster, better-informed decisions. To allow this information to be easily accessed, integrated, and analyzed.

Application Origin: OneSource Information Services, Inc., 150 Cambridge Park Drive, Cambridge, MA 02140. 1-800-554-5501 (US), or +44(0)1483 241212 (Europe).

Application Development Time: None to end user.

Typical Size: 100–500 MB.

Typical Use: Background research information on industries, competitors, customers, and prospects. Often purchased and managed by corporate research groups.

Forms: Typically one form per database, organized in the most useful way for the particular information found.

Views: Many preindexed views per database, sorted in as many different ways as are useful to researchers.

PART 5

Intercompany Applications

Notes is only now beginning to reach the kind of critical mass that makes it relatively easy for companies to use it to communicate with others outside the organization, but this application has lots of potential.

There are significant issues regarding security, once the decision has been made to break down the barrier to the outside world. Notes has the ability to handle these security worries, and the benefits will usually be worth the effort.

This section is more "blue sky" than the others. The applications described here are designed more to show what Notes could do, rather than what it actually does today. There are a few more potential and actual problems indicated. However, this should not be taken as an indictment of Notes—on the contrary, it demonstrates the power of the tools, and shows that it needs to be managed well to avoid potential problems.

Over the next couple of years, as Notes spreads through the marketplace, we expect to see many more applications like these rolled out in real companies. The companies that take the risks will reap the benefits.

Providing Product Support to Customers with Notes

Companies that rely heavily on commercial software for their mission-critical applications are finding that excellent customer support from their software vendor is absolutely essential. The ongoing administration and support of software applications can far outweigh the up-front cost of the software, and high-quality support from the vendor can help minimize these costs.

Tim O'Conner is a product manager of an expensive software product. One of the areas in which he chooses to differentiate himself from his competition is in the area of customer support. Therefore, he has programs in place to distribute manuals and other reference material, product upgrade announcements, software patches, utilities, and other support items to his customers. Currently he uses standard package-delivery services to distribute these materials. But, now that he's become well versed in the capabilities of Notes, he begins to think of other options.

USING NOTES TO BE MORE COMPETITIVE

Tim realizes that many of his customers have Notes up and running, and others are planning on installing it as well. This means that a customer's users and servers could dial into his Notes servers, providing a Notes connection between he and his customers. Further, this opens up the possibility of receiving information back from customers and even letting customers exchange information with each other. Tim calls his Notes administrator, Dale Gondell to discuss the idea.

Dale explains that to support this application, the company might need to bring up an additional server to provide enough capacity. Also, a couple of phone lines and modems will be needed to support the customer dialing into the new server by modem. As a product manager, Tim understands that if the project succeeds, the extra few thousand dollars required to support the extra server and phone lines will be more than made up for by the increase in customer satisfaction. Tim continues to pursue the idea.

Dale also explains that Notes does not, by default, let just anyone dial into a server. Good thing too, since that would make security impossible and would mean that no sensitive information could be stored on Notes. A method is required to support customers gaining access to the new Notes server. Tim and Dale discuss a couple of possibilities.

One idea is to distribute a user ID that customers could "switch to" when they wish to connect to the new server. This has the advantage of being easy to implement for Tim's company, and easy to use by the customers' end users. However, it is an option available only to individual end users, and each end user must have a modem. Furthermore, Notes servers cannot automatically switch IDs, meaning that the scheme will not support connections between the customers' servers and Tim's new server.

The other idea they discuss is to use Cross-certification, so that the customers' servers and Tim's new server will "trust" each other. This process involves the company and each customer exchanging a file and performing an administrative procedure (Cross-certification) on that file. While this is certainly more cumbersome to implement than the previous idea, it will support server-to-server replication. So Tim's customers provide servers on which Tim can replicate the support database, meaning that the customers' users will be able to interact with the support application on their own networks.

Tim decides that using Cross-certification will be worth the headache, and he asks the administrator to work out the details of what the company will need to do, and what the customers will need to do to support Notes connections. Dale says she'll get back to Tim later.

EXPLORING THE POSSIBILITIES

Now that Tim has thought about how to connect his customers to his Notes servers, he thinks about the application itself. In what ways will Notes enhance customer support? He tries to put himself in his customers' shoes as he comes up with the following ideas:

▶ The manuals and technical reference material Tim distributes with his product could he put into the Notes application database. That way, his customers would always know where the materials are.
▶ As the materials get updated, the new versions will automatically replicate out to customers whenever their servers dial into Tim's server. This way his customers can be assured they have the latest versions of the support materials.

▶ Tim can now use Notes mail to send product announcements, upgrade announcements, and other timely information directly to his users.

▶ Since Tim knows he can attach software directly to Notes documents, he realizes he can use the Notes application to store patches and bug fixes so that his customers can easily download them.

▶ Tim can store demo versions of all of his products and product upgrades so customers can easily download them and try them out.

As Tim's mind shifts into high gear, he expands the possibilities even more:

▶ Tim knows that many users have written their own utilities to enhance the use of his product. Some have even posted these utilities on the Internet so others can enjoy them. Tim imagines gathering them up and putting them in the Notes customer support application so all customers have easy access to them.

▶ Tim begins to think about the two-way nature of Notes communication, realizing he can use this as a method of gathering comments and suggestions from his users—this feature is a must!

▶ Further, the Notes application could be used to support a user self-help forum. By letting users post comments, questions, and responses in the database, Tim's server can serve as a central replication hub joining the users into a user community.

Before Tim's excitement carries him too far, he decides to contact his Notes developers to see what can be developed in what time frame. He finds that an experienced developer could build all of the features above in about a month or so, including several weeks to test all the features and ensure that the database performs well when it is populated with a fair amount of data.

Tim writes a project plan for implementing the customer support application. He incorporates the feedback he received from Dale and from his developers to develop estimates of the cost and schedule for the project. Tim presents his idea to the powers that be and. . . (time passes).

Using the Application

A couple of months later the application has been up for a few weeks and Tim accesses it to see how it turned out. The developers built two databases. One provides users Reader access and contains reference materials, software patches, and so on. The other gives users Author access and supports the user-group discussion idea.

First Tim explores the main support database containing the reference materials and patches. He chooses the Reference Materials view and is pleased to see a list of the manuals, technical reports, and other reference materials listed in a categorized view, where the documents are grouped by the product they relate to. He opens the reference manual for one of the products and sees the document contains the full text and picture of the original, paper version. (Note that converting documentation to electronic format can be a time-consuming task, and may take months on its own if there is a large number of documents to be converted.)

Next Tim switches to the Product Announcements view. Here he sees documents sorted by date, with the most recent listed first. There are documents containing press releases and other announcements of new products the company has launched recently. There are also upgrade announcements. He even sees that a demo of one of his products has been file-attached directly to its product announcement.

He then switches to the Fixes and Utilities view. Here Tim again sees documents categorized by the product they relate to. Under each product is a variety of documents containing file attached bug fixes and utilities. He opens up one of the documents whose title indicates it is a shareware utility a customer wrote. In the document he sees a few paragraphs of text the utility author wrote describing the function of the utility and how to use it. Also, he sees an icon, which is the utility as a file attachment. At the bottom he sees there is some text stating that "If you would like to contribute a utility to this database, please use the user-group database." He decides to see what the other database contains.

Reference materials view in the External Customer Support application

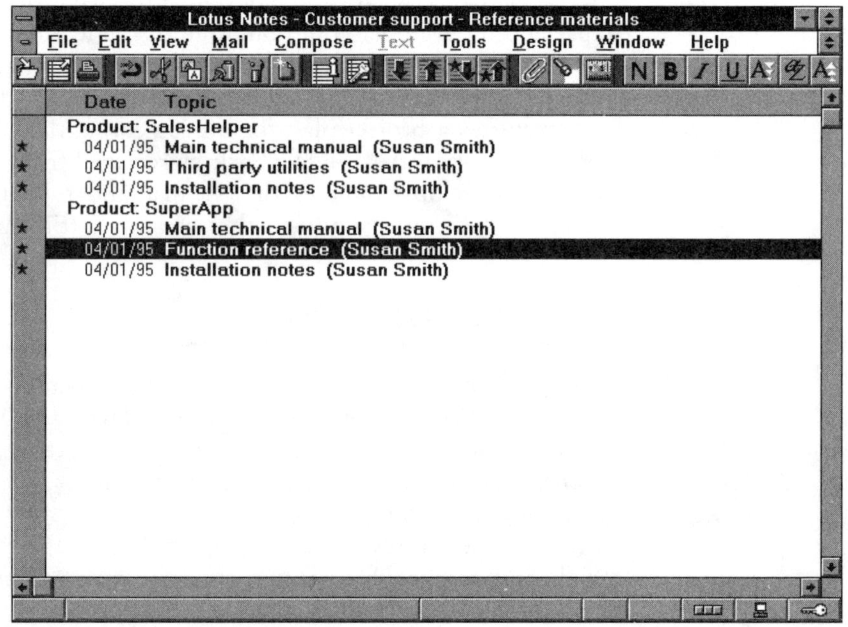

Tim opens the other database comprising the customer support application—the "user-group database." It opens into the Main view, and he recognizes it as a simple Notes Discussion database. He sees that users from various customers, as well as people at his company are participating in discussions about various aspects of his products. In many instances users from one customer can help answer questions posed by users from another customer. Tim knows that not all companies are willing to support this type of communication among their customers, but is optimistic that the advantages of providing better customer support outweigh the risks.

In the Compose menu Tim sees that in addition to the standard Discussion database forms (Main Topic, Response, and Response to Response) there are a couple of additional forms. One is titled Submit a Utility. When he chooses to compose one of these forms, he sees a document appear with instructions on how to submit a utility to his company for inclusion in the main support database. This is a mail-enabled form, and when a user attaches a utility and saves the form, the form is mailed to personnel at Tim's company to be tested (mainly for viruses) and possibly included in the main support database. If included, they will have access to the new utility the next time customers replicate with his server.

Another additional form is titled Submit a Comment or Suggestion, and when used, it produces a document with various questions about the user's experiences with the products, including places for them to write-in lengthy comments. This form is also mail-enabled, and sends the user's comment/suggestion to the appropriate personnel at Tim's company.

Tim exits the Customer Support application, pleased that he has added real value to his company's product line. As time goes on, the databases will only become more valuable as more and more information is added, both by personnel at Tim's company and by his customers.

FACT SHEET

External Customer Support

Purpose: To provide excellent customer support for the products in a product line, including online reference materials, easy access product announcements, bug fixes, utilities, etc. Also to allow customers to form their own user-group in which they can help each other use the products better.

Application Origin: Two databases: The main support database is a custom development, and the user-groups database is derived from the Discussion template with two extra forms added.

Application Development Time: 40–80 staff hours including testing.

Typical Size: Main support database, 10–100 MB—250–1000 documents. User-group database, 1–10 MB—100–1000 documents.

Typical Use: Companies whose customers are likely to have Notes installations in order to provide customer support.

Forms: The main support database contains forms for Reference, Announcement, and Software used to support manuals and technical reference material, product announcements, and bug fixes/utilities respectively. The user-group database has the forms of a Discussion database (Main Topic, Response, and Response to Response), as well as two additional forms to support sending mail containing either software submissions or comments/suggestions.

Views: The main support database contains a view called Reference Materials to list manuals and technical support documents, Product Announcements to list new product and upgrade announcements, and Fixes and Utilities to list documents containing software bug fixes and other utilities. The user-group database contains the standard views of a discussion database (Main View, By Author, and By Category).

Providing Automated Technical Support to the World at Large

Providing technical support is always challenging. The support information must be centralized. Personnel must be trained. People needing support, either internal or external, must be provided a way to get to the information.

The typical solution is to provide a Help Desk staffed with trained people who answer phone calls, look up the appropriate information, and read the answers to the caller. This is exactly the solution that Techno Corporation, a hypothetical computer component and system mail-order house, uses to provide support to its large customer base.

Since providing a staff of trained personnel taking phone calls is expensive, Techno is looking for ways to make technical support more efficient. In this chapter, Techno explores the idea of fully automating technical support so customers can access the information they need without talking to a Techno employee.

YOU ARE CALLER 15—PLEASE HOLD!

Ellen Cavise heads the technical support department at Techno. The tech support department is large, including a staff of 25 people who just answer phone calls. Even so, her department has trouble keeping up with all the requests for tech support.

Ellen would love to increase her staff to supply more responsive tech support to Techno's customers, but in fact, she has been asked to reduce her costs, not increase them.

Ellen calls Dan Katz into her office to discuss what they might do to reduce their costs while still providing the same level—or better—of technical support to their customers. Dan has been the lead engineer in charge of implementing and supporting the systems that Ellen's department uses. These systems track the known problems that customers are likely to face and possible solutions.

Ellen asks Dan about the state of the tech support systems and if they are providing adequate support for the support staff. Dan explains that the system they use is fairly rudimentary. In particular, he says, it is not always easy for agents to get to the information they need through the simple keyword search and index facility it offers. He would like to see the department implement a new system with some better capabilities.

"What kind of capabilities?" Ellen asks. Dan explains that the most important capability would be the ability to do a full-text search of all the tech support documentation. This would allow the tech support staff to enter queries like "SCSI and Techno-4K and boot and not JG" to locate documents that relate to problems booting a Techno-4K system with SCSI adapters, and that do not discuss problems with JG brand hard drives. This would make it much faster for the support staff to get to the right information to help solve the customers' problems.

Another useful capability would be the ability to store pictures of things in addition to text descriptions. An agent should be able to pull up a picture of a component or system to help the customer work through a problem. Now the agent must find pictures and sketches by locating the appropriate manual and searching through it.

Dan then tells Ellen that he has been talking to Harry Trott, who has been leading the Lotus Notes rollout inside Techno. "From talking to Harry, it sounds like Notes might be a good replacement for the existing tech support system. It has great full-text-search capabilities, supports Rich Text for pictures and diagrams, and has a lot of other nice features."

Ellen understands that full-text search and Rich Text would be nice additions to the support system. But she also wonders if there isn't something more they can do to make a big change in how they support customers. She asks Dan if he's used fax-back services. "Oh, sure. I've requested information about software I was interested in from those systems. I called the phone number and a computer answered and asked me to enter in the code of the software product I was interested in. I entered the code and it asked me for my fax number. It then hung up, and a little while later the information was sent to my fax machine."

Dan paused to think for a moment about whether they could use a system like that for tech support. "I see what you're getting at, Ellen. The system was completely automated so I didn't have to use up a person's time to get what I needed. But it seems to me that getting technical support is a lot harder than getting basic product information. How would the user enter their request? We can't have them going through menu after menu like 'Press 1 if it is a hard disk problem, press 2 if it is a monitor problem' and so forth.

The customer would hang up long before they got to the information they need. But maybe. . ."

Ellen urges Dan to continue. "But maybe the phone isn't the right interface. Maybe we should think about e-mail instead. Almost everyone has e-mail these days, and if we hook up to the Internet, then we can have our system automatically exchange e-mail with customers. If the customer didn't need the information immediately they could send an e-mail message to our new system with keywords to indicate what they need. The system could look up the appropriate information and e-mail it back. If we could get the turnaround time to under 30 minutes, we'd often be about as quick as trying to get through today on the phone during a busy period."

Ellen is excited by this possibility. She knows that if the system worked, not only could it reduce the number of people she needs answering phones, but it could provide a clear competitive edge over her competition. It makes sense to her that many of the people calling for support are computer-savvy enough to use such an e-mail interface. She asks Dan to look into the feasibility of implementing the automated support system.

IT'S NOT EXACTLY EASY, BUT. . .

Back in his office, Dan calls Harry and sets up an appointment to discuss the idea of replacing the existing tech support system with one based on Notes, and the idea of building an automated, e-mail-based tech support system.

At their meeting, Dan tells Harry that Ellen seems to appreciate the advantages a Notes-based system would have in terms of full-text searching and the ability to store and use rich-text, but, what she is really excited about is the automated e-mail system. Dan outlines his idea of users sending requests that get processed automatically and returned with the appropriate information. He asks Harry whether Notes supports these types of things.

Harry thinks about the problem for a couple of minutes. "It seems to me that there are two types of challenges here: the technology and the usability issues.

"Technologically speaking, I think this can be done. We have already set up a gateway to the Internet for e-mail, so it will not be hard to build applications that receive e-mail requests from the Internet and respond to them via e-mail back to the Internet. To process the requests will probably require the development of an external application written to the Notes API or that uses a third-party API or other tool like a VBX."

Dan interrupts, "API? VBX?"

Harry explains, "The Notes API is a programming interface so application developers can write programs that interact with Notes. VBXs are plug-in tools that can make writing these programs even easier. The point is that I don't think the built-in programmability of Notes will be enough. The program we would want to build would have to be able to do a few things. It would need to be able to detect when a new e-mail message has arrived and start acting on it. It would need to be able to strip out the request from the rest of the message. It would then need to invoke a Notes full-text search using the request from the e-mail. Based on the results of the search, it would send a message back to the user. The message might be 'Sorry, your search returned no documents.' It might be 'Sorry, your search returned too many documents.' If only a few documents were returned, the program could read them and format them into an e-mail (probably losing any graphics and special formatting, since it's Internet e-mail) and send them back.

"Also, the program would have to be built with some monitoring capabilities so we know if it's serving requests in a timely fashion, and if it's sending back information or just a lot of 'Sorry. . .' messages. Finally, if the program detected that it was getting behind in its requests, it might forward the requests to people for handling."

Dan understands that it is technically feasible, but that it also sounds like a fair amount of work. Dan asks Harry if he can build a prototype to demonstrate technical feasibility and Harry agrees that, given a few weeks, he could put one together. Dan then asks Harry about the usability issue he mentioned before.

"Oh yes. It's not clear to me that people will be able to use this system effectively via e-mail. With Notes, a user can type in a full-text search and within a few moments can see the results. If it's too many or too few, or not the right information, the user can refine the search or enter a whole new one. Several iterations can take place in a minute or two, and the user can get used to how to enter searches that result in retrieval of meaningful data.

"Via e-mail, the turnaround time between submitting a request and getting the information may be anywhere from 10 minutes to over an hour. This may not be fast enough to satisfy customers. Furthermore, without training, users may not be able to figure out how to send effective search requests. They may be continually frustrated by those 'Sorry. . .' messages."

Dan understands and suggests a couple of measures they could take to give the idea its best chance. "In our 'Sorry' messages we should send back a list of sample search strings so users can see what kinds of things they can do. Perhaps the system could track who is sending requests, and if someone sends a request two or three times in a day, then the request could be sent to a person. Maybe if the subject line of the e-mail says 'help' we can send them a detailed explanation of how the searches work and advice on how to form good searches."

Harry thinks these are all good ideas and that they will be required to make the system as usable as possible. The next issue they discuss is that of security around the tech support database. Dan is concerned that since users can now retrieve documents from the tech support database that anyone with access to the database can make documents publicly accessible. If not properly guarded, this could result in proprietary information accidentally being made accessible to the public. Or in the case of a malicious user, all sorts of material might be returned to customer searches that could be embarrassing to the company.

Harry explains that Notes comes with excellent security features that can put tight controls on who has access to the Tech Support database. He explains that a wide audience can be given Reader access so they can have access to the information without the ability to change it or create new documents. Only certain people will be given Author or Editor access, which will give them the ability to create new documents and update the information currently in the database.

Harry and Dan finish their conversation by discussing migration from the current system to a Notes-based system. As with any system conversion, migration issues include how to move information from the existing system to the new one, how to train people on the new system, how to manage the cutover, and how to take advantage of the new system instead of simply reimplementing the old one with new technology. They part company with Harry agreeing to build the automated e-mail system prototype and Dan agreeing to report the results of their conversation to Ellen.

Is It Worth the Risk?

Dan meets again with Ellen to discuss the results of his conversation with Harry and to decide how to proceed. He explains that in a few weeks, Harry should have a prototype of the automated e-mail system. He also explains Harry's concerns about usability and whether people will actually use the system.

Since it sounds like upgrading to a Notes-based technical support system makes sense, Ellen instructs Dan to proceed with the implementation of the Notes-based system. She asks Dan to put together a project plan for staffing and resource requirements and a schedule for implementing and cutting over to the new system. She is confident that this is a good move and will make her department more efficient (thereby justifying the short-term expenditures).

Ellen is also excited about the automated e-mail system and is anxious to give it a try. She finishes her meeting with Dan and asks him to set up a demonstration of the prototype when it is ready.

A few weeks later, Dan and Ellen visit Harry in his office to view the prototype. Dan composes an e-mail message addressed to TECHINFO@TECHNO.COM. In the body of the mail message he types REQUEST SCSI AND ADAPTER AND IRQ. He sends the mail.

After sending the mail he turns and explains the prototype to Ellen and Dan. "I wanted to send the mail first and then talk, since it will generally take a few minutes for the response to come back. I have set up a small sample Technical Support database with a few dozen documents. I have also developed a program

Sample Internet e-mail message requesting technical support

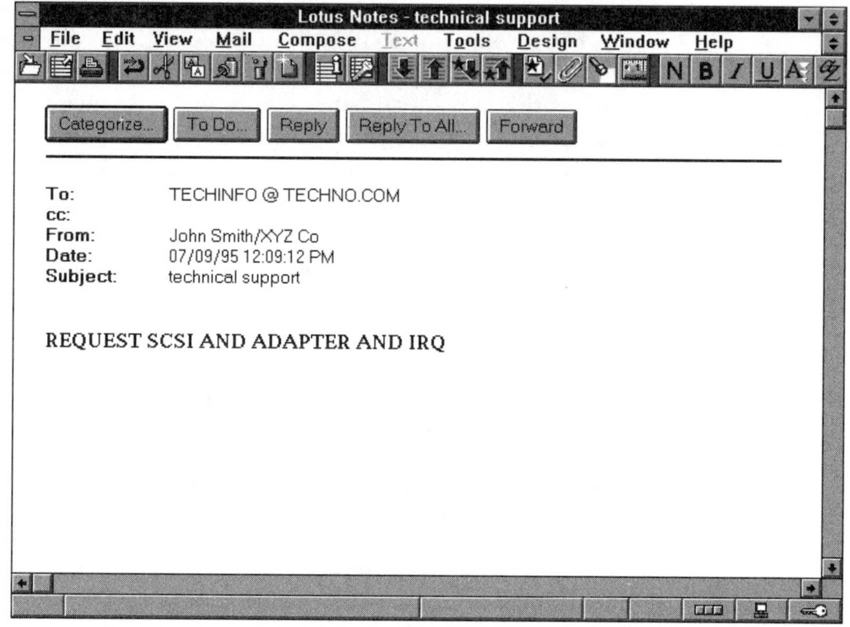

running on my PC here that, every 60 seconds, looks to see if the TECHINFO account has received any new mail. If it has, it looks for a line starting with REQUEST, and if it finds one, uses the rest of the line as the full-text search string. It searches the sample technical support database using Notes' full-text search capability and returns the results if one to three documents are found. If none are found, a message to that effect is sent back. If more than three are found a different error message is sent back.

"While building the prototype, it occurred to me that if more than three are found, perhaps we might send back a list of titles that were found so the user can see whether search is on the right track. If we continue to work on the prototype, I will add that as an enhancement.

"Let me check my mailbox now to see if we've received any new mail. As you see, here is a new message from 'Techno Technical Support Server.' I'll open it up, and now you see a message that the search found one document titled 'IRQ conflicts with certain SCSI adapters,' followed by the text of the article."

Ellen is impressed. She asks Dan to keep working with Harry on improving the prototype. Ideally she'd like to be able to try it internally to get some feedback about the usability of the system. She also asks Dan and Harry to evaluate the resources needed to build a field-grade version. Given what she has seen, and the fact that they will be converting the technical support system to a Notes-based system, Ellen feels it is worth the risk to proceed with the idea.

Back in her office, Ellen and Dan discuss the automated e-mail system. Ellen comments on the ugly plain text that came back. She asks Dan if there is any way to send back documents with formatting and pictures and such.

"Harry and I discussed this a little. Right now we are using basic Internet mail, and that supports only the plain text you saw. But if the system became popular, we might include a faxing option. With this option, the user could specify a fax number to send the requested documents to. We would need a 'fax gateway' from Notes, but then we could send fully formatted documents with pictures.

"Another idea is to publish our database to the World Wide Web, which is a graphical-user-interface based way of accessing the Internet. Our users could access our information on the Web and view it, fully formatted. We could provide a form where users would enter their search string, and then we could display a list of found documents. The user could then click on a found document to view it. As with the e-mail interface, we would probably want to limit the search results to a few documents to avoid our competitors from being able to easily download our database for their own use."

Ellen commends Dan for his work on the new tech support system and the automated e-mail support idea. They agree to push the automated e-mail support idea to the field.

Fact Sheet

Tech Support Database

Purpose: To reduce the costs of providing technical support and gain competitive advantage by offering better service.

Application Origin: Custom developed.

Application Development Time: A prototype was developed in a few weeks. The development required is the e-mail server, and approximate development time is 2 months for a dedicated programmer.

Typical Size: Not applicable. The system taps the technical support database which can be quite large. The automated e-mail support application itself requires approximately 1 MB of disk space.

Typical Use: Used by companies with a large technical support cost looking to reduce the cost and provide an alternative to the telephone for technical support.

Forms: Not applicable.

Views: Not applicable.

Shared Specifications Database

A True Story

This is a story with no happy ending. It tells of an attempt to use Notes that failed. Kayex (this name, like all names in this chapter, has been changed) is a Massachusetts-based company that develops multimedia software for specialized markets. At the time of this incident, they had been using Notes for a few months.

In early 1994, they were approached by Chapter Zero, a California company that specialized in software marketing, who asked them to participate in a large-scale, multi-year, joint development project for multimedia software. Chapter Zero was beginning to use Notes in one group of the company.

Also participating was Longhorn Corporation, a Texas-based company with particular expertise in the subject matter of the multimedia package. They had never used Notes. Chapter Zero hired a private consultant, Linda Houlihan, as a project manager, giving her the primary task of ensuring that the project vision was clearly defined and executed. She too had never used Notes.

Since this was a far-reaching, long-term project that was envisioned as defining an entire marketplace, the whole team gathered in Texas for a two-day brainstorming session. One of the biggest points of discussion was the simple matter of communication: how do you get three different companies spread over at least four different sites communicating about the design of a multimedia project in an efficient fashion?

COMMUNICATIONS STRATEGIES

The people from Chapter Zero (who, after all, were paying the bills) were inclined to continue exactly what had already begun to happen—people would talk to each other over the phone and send faxes back and forth when documents needed to change hands.

Others explained that to date, most communications had been point-to-point between Chapter Zero and the other companies, and of a relatively low volume. As the project heated up, everyone would need to talk with everyone else, and the volume of communications would rise significantly. During the design phase, literally thousands of pages of multimedia storyboards would need to be developed, communicated, and commented on.

Someone from Longhorn software suggested that everyone could dial into their network and simply share files as if everyone were on the same LAN. Kevin, a developer from Kayex, explained that since the Longhorn network was restricted to Macintosh computers, only Mac users (about half the team) would be able to share the information. Furthermore, as the volume of documents rose, there would be significant problems relating to the naming and tracking of documents. In particular, even with a carefully defined protocol for naming documents, there would be conflicts between documents with the same name but different contents, duplicated documents with different names, and multiple people editing the same document at the same time.

Furthermore, Kevin said, the telecommunications costs would be astronomical, as people dialed in to Texas from around the country to connect to the LAN. Each individual user would need access to a modem, and the Longhorn LAN would have to have enough modems to allow multiple people to dial in simultaneously.

Kevin then explained that Lotus Notes could address all of these issues:

- ▶ Geographic separation. Notes could replicate documents automatically between servers. Since each site, rather than each user, does the replication, and replication is very efficient, telecommunications costs would be drastically reduced. Kevin calculated a cost savings of thousands of dollars a year.
- ▶ Document ownership. Notes security would allow this to be as rigid or flexible as needed. The database design could allow for people to comment on existing documents without modifying the originals, or it could give them direct edit access if that were desired.
- ▶ Duplication. Since Notes documents are stored on the server, only one copy exists at any given site. Replication ensures that the copies are kept synchronized across the various sites.
- ▶ Accidental overwriting. Notes replication detects and flags this problem automatically.

THE WORRIES

Kevin sat back, sure that he'd made a convincing case for using Notes. But in fact, people were not convinced. Longhorn was very worried about the difficulty of setting up and managing a Notes network internally. They had a solely Macintosh-based network that they felt worked for them, and didn't see that it would be all that different to add everyone else to it. Furthermore, installing and operating a Notes server would require that they acquire and operate an OS/2 server, which they didn't have the expertise to do.

Chapter Zero and Linda Houlihan were concerned about the cost of acquiring and installing Notes for all the participants. At Chapter Zero, the group working on this project was not the same group that had installed Notes already.

Finally, although Kayex was using Notes, there was some concern that if everyone else were to adopt it, Kayex would end up providing lots of expensive support for the Notes installation across all of these companies.

Kevin tried, too strenuously, to talk people past these problems. But he overplayed his hand, and ended up getting labeled as a Notes zealot.

Linda saw that there were three different groups with three different agendas, and decided that for the time being, the whole team would continue to work with faxes, phones, and e-mail over the Internet. However she also asked Kevin to work up a plan for using Notes to address the problem, including costs of installation and operation.

Everyone who worked at Kayex had a Notes installation, and Kayex already had its own Notes server with a modem connected, so nothing new needed to be done there.

Longhorn did not have Notes installed, nor (since they had a network based exclusively around the Macintosh) did they have a server on which it could be installed. There were about six users there, so installing a server was the only practical solution. Unfortunately, because of the network they used, it would also have been necessary for them to install a new network operating system. This was turning out to be an expensive problem for them. Furthermore, Longhorn's people had never had the need to work with people outside their own company, and were not yet convinced that they actually would encounter the kinds of problems that Notes was designed to solve.

Chapter Zero was actually implementing a Notes pilot on a different project, but their MIS department was not particularly inclined to handle two new and different installations at one time. However, they were willing to set up a single Notes workstation at Longhorn that anyone there could use.

THE TEST

Linda felt that here might be an inexpensive way to test whether Notes could work. She convinced Longhorn and Chapter Zero to each install a single Notes workstation; she did the same on her own machine. She asked Kevin to create a discussion database that could be used as a starter for project discussions and storage of project documents. He had already done so, and Kayex was already using it internally.

The database was a fairly standard Notes Discussion database (as discussed in "The Discussion Database"), with an extra field that was used to categorize the documents into specific project areas. A categorized view helped to organize the discussion.

Kevin issued three new Notes IDs. A Notes ID is a File that uniquely identifies a particular Notes User. He created one for Longhorn, one for Chapter Zero, and one for Linda. He then added the three new users to the ACL, and helped them to get connected and replicate the database.

Kevin had taken every electronic document he had access to and loaded them all into the Notes database. Whenever an e-mail came in, he also moved it into the database. He also attempted to start some discussions by using the Notes database rather than phone calls and faxes. Unfortunately, since anyone outside Kayex who wanted access had to get up and go to a different machine, this database was less than a roaring success. Some activity took place, mostly to placate Kevin, who was trying very hard—perhaps too hard—to get this project to succeed. He felt strongly that there was no good alternative to using Notes, and that significant problems would occur if it weren't used.

THE (UNSATISFYING) CONCLUSION

After many faxes and phone calls, plus a few e-mails, and with very little help from the Notes database, the team managed to produce a rough prototype of the concept for review by Chapter Zero. After a couple of weeks of frustrating silence, Chapter Zero announced that the project had been cancelled for lack of long-term funding by their parent corporation. It's safe to say that everyone was disappointed at this conclusion.

With respect to Notes, it was not at all clear that the project would ever have made good use of Notes. There was significant resistance from several parties to the concept and costs. In large part this was due to the fact that they had never had the experience of trying to collaborate at a distance, and so they had no good idea of the problems that were inherent in that process.

Kevin might have been wiser to have put off the Notes discussion until after the prototype was completed and accepted using other communications methods. Many of the problems he was trying to anticipate would probably have already occurred on a small scale. Had the project continued, he might then have found an audience more receptive to change.

▶ FACT SHEET

Shared Specifications Discussion Database

Purpose: To allow multiple organizations to collaborate and discuss a joint development project.

Application Origin: Standard Notes Discussion database, with a Categories field added.

Application Development Time: 1–2 days.

Typical Size: 2–20 MB, depending on the project.

Typical Use: Managers, developers, marketing for discussion of the project and its specifications.

Forms: Main Topic, Response, and Response to Response.

Views: Categorized By Author, and Main View (by Date).

Knowledgebase

Freedonia Refrigerators (a fictional company) has decided to create a Knowledgebase about their company's products. The CIO of the company calls a meeting of all his managers. In the meeting, he assigns the task of creating the database to Len Faun. Len heads the Information Systems group for the company. Upon getting this assignment, Len runs back to his department thinking, "Time for a department meeting!" The next morning is reserved on most people's calendars for development—"Perfect! Everyone will be free!" He sends out an e-mail to the department requiring everyone's presence at the meeting the next morning.

Len opens the meeting by stating, "Management has tasked us with creating a Knowledgebase for the company's products and I couldn't agree with them more. It's our job to be proactive and come up with something cutting edge. Any suggestions?"

Charlie asks, "What's a knowledgebase?"

"Well what do you think it is?" Faun asks. Charlie responds with a blank stare.

After a rather painful pause, Alice breaks the silence. "Generally speaking, Knowledgebase is a term that describes a database used to store all of the known information about a particular subject. In our case, a Knowledgebase would probably be targeted at our partners and customers. The Knowledgebase would seek to get customers and partners better informed about who we are as a company, how our current products can help them in their businesses, and what future directions we might be taking. The Knowledgebase might include product specifications, a list of authorized dealers, known problems with products, and marketing materials."

"Exactly," Len says. "Alice, as you have given us this comprehensive overview of this Knowledgebase, how would you suggest we build it?"

"Well, I personally would suggest using Lotus Notes. Notes provides a relatively simple interface to retrieve information. Views (which are lists of documents) can be organized according to the nature of the subject the Knowledgebase describes. Users can either scan views for relevant information or use Notes' full-text search engine to build complicated queries to retrieve specific pieces of information."

"Just what I was thinking," Len responds. "Alice, you start work on this Notes thing as quickly as possible. I'll report this up to management. When do you think we can have this thing done?"

"That depends—the design of the database can probably be completed in a relatively short amount of time. Lotus actually provides a Knowledgebase in Notes that we can use as a model. However, we will need at least one person to provide content for the database. This person will need to be an expert in our products, have some understanding of the needs of our customers and partners, and be able to commit at least 50 percent of their time to adding to and maintaining this database—into the foreseeable future. Another area that I can't work is distribution of the completed database. Once the database has been completed, the application will need to be distributed internally and to partners and customers. We need someone to plan and implement the deployment of the completed Knowledgebase."

Len begins to worry that this could be more complicated than he had originally thought. "Well, is there anyone you have in mind?"

"I do know that Bob in the Customer Service Center has the right skills to manage the content, however he might not have the time. As far as the deployment is concerned, I would suggest Jane as an appropriate person. She has a good understanding of Notes administration and has worked to connect our Notes environment with some of our partners in the past," says Alice.

"Well, you get started on the Knowledgebase, Jane get started on the deployment stuff, and I'll see what I can do about getting Bob to work on this project. Please submit project plans to me in the next couple of days," Len says. The meeting breaks up, and Len goes back to his office to relax—what a taxing day!

Len calls the head of Customer Service. He describes how important the project is to management, and that it is critical to their success with customers—that this really is a "fourth-and-goal" situation, that the "game is tied and its bottom of the ninth," and that we really have to "take the ball and run with it" to succeed on this one. Finally, Bob's manager succumbs to Len's arguments and agrees to let Bob work on the project.

Len schedules a meeting for the following week with Alice, Jane, and Bob. Together they have come up with a rough project plan. Overall, the development should take about two weeks. This includes time to develop a prototype, review the prototype, and add some sample data to the database.

Bob estimates that it will take about three weeks to locate and add enough data to the application to make it generally useful. While the company has lots of electronic files that can be imported into Notes, some retyping of older documents will be necessary. At three weeks Bob believes the database will have enough data to provide real value to customers and partners. He will need to continue the process of gathering information for weeks thereafter. Once the information has been collected, his job will gradually move from collecting information to ensuring that the data in the database is accurate, and adding new relevant information as it becomes available.

Jane has developed a phased deployment plan to roll the application out. The application will initially be distributed to ten customers and partners who already have connections to Freedonia's Notes environment. These customers and partners will be the simplest to deploy and the most likely to take an active interest in the data. After this, the company will allow up to ten additional customers and partners per month to connect. Jane believes this can be supported without affecting existing systems and services. Jane points out that some companies have actually provided copies of Notes to their customers and partners to distribute data. This has been seen as cost effective because it draws the customers and partners closer together. However, Jane feels that the Knowledgebase is not enough in and of itself to warrant the cost of purchasing a Notes license for customers and partners.

As the presentation goes on, Len feels a weight lift from his shoulders. "These people appear to understand the problem," he thinks. "Well, well, well," he says aloud, "Sounds like we have this one licked."

"I think so," Alice says, "but there are some security concerns." Len feels the uneasiness returning. "We are providing our customers and partners with an electronic database full of information on our products and our services. This could be of immense value to our competitors. We can set the access control lists on the databases to prevent copying the database, but once they have it on their server, the access control list is only a minor hindrance. Any Notes-knowledgeable person can get by the access control list. I suggest we want our customers to sign some type of agreement not to redistribute this data, or be liable for any damages that might result from their distribution of the data."

"Exactly what I was thinking. I'll take this up immediately with senior management. In fact, we'll discuss this over lunch." Over lunch, management agrees to involve the company's lawyers to write up a contract. The lawyers' first reaction is to shut down the project, but, with some patience and understanding, they are led to draw up a contract with the requisite terms.

COMPLETING THE APPLICATION

A few weeks later (long after Len had forgotten about the project), Bob, Alice, and Jane invite him to a meeting to demonstrate the application they intend to deploy. They have been sending Len e-mails to keep him posted on developments, but he has been too busy to read them. Alice begins the meeting by demonstrating the application's forms and views. The forms allow input of a variety of different types of information. The main form is called In Depth Info. This form is used by the customer support organization to provide detailed information on the purpose and use of various product features. Other forms are for press releases, new product announcements, white papers and the like. The views allow the user to sort data by Product, Date, Topic, Author, and Document Type.

Alice's demonstration takes Len through two scenarios of how an end user of the application might get an answer to a question. The first example involves the customer looking for an answer to a specific problem with one of the company's products. In this case, the user opens the view By Product Type, opens the category for the particular product, and identifies the In Depth Info documents related to the issues he or she has with the product.

In the second scenario, the user wants more information on a problem he or she has been having across a number of products. In this case, the user opens the database and performs a full-text search on the database. A screenful of documents is returned, and the user can check the documents to see if they relate to his or her problems.

"Good work team," Len says. "I think this application is ready to go. I think it would also be a good idea for me to demonstrate this personally to se-

By Topic view in Knowledgebase

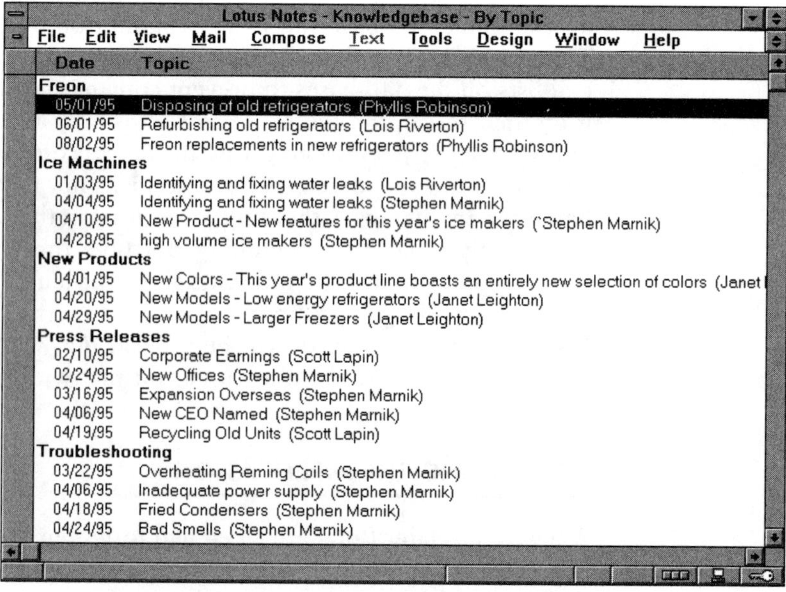

nior management. This is a good example for them to see of how well we work as a team."

UNFINISHED BUSINESS

A few days later, Len gets an e-mail containing Alice's resignation. She has decided to open a consulting business around Lotus Notes. "That's the problem with employees today—no loyalty," he thinks. In her e-mail, she has suggested some changes he might want to consider that could help the Knowledgebase application. Len deletes the memo without reading it. Fortunately, we have preserved some of the suggestions here:

- ▶ Multiple Language Support. Freedonia is in business in a number of countries. It would probably make sense to provide documents in more than one language.
- ▶ More Granular Security. A "More Granular" system is one with more subdivsions than the current system. For example, if our security system is based on groups (that is groups are the basic unit of distinction in our system), a more granular security system would be based on users. The application should be able to contain information that is not distributed outside of the company. In this way, the database could become the repository for much technical knowledge in the organization. Similarly, there are some pieces of information that should be shared with partners, but not with customers. It is possible to create this type of security using Reader Fields. Alice tried to warn Len that Reader fields can be very complicated to implement correctly. She suggested a consultant who could help out with this problem.
- ▶ Eliminate Redundant Information. Finally, this database has some significant overlaps with existing databases used in the Support, Sales, and Marketing organizations. It would make sense to have someone analyze the applications in use in these departments to determine which should be the primary source of information.

◢ **FACT SHEET**

Knowledgebase

Purpose: To help the company better support partners and customers in getting product information.

Application Origin: Developed from the Discussion Database template.

Application Development Time: Over 3 weeks.

Typical Size: Over time, the database will grow to be in the tens of megabytes. A large Knowledgebase may exceed 50 MB.

Typical Use: Customers, business partners, and employees looking for more information on products and the corporation can find relevant information in the database. Typically, customers with questions or problems related to a particular product consult the knowledgebase. This is often more productive than calling the company directly.

Forms: In Depth Info, Press Releases, New Products, White Papers, and General Information.

Views: By Product, By Date, By Topic, By Author, By Announcement, By Category, and By Document type.

Supporting the Development of Multimedia Applications

"You just can't find good help these days." It's true that finding someone who brings the required expertise to a team is hard. Finding someone with expertise and a good solid work ethic is nearly impossible. Forcing a potential hire to move to where headquarters is located can easily dissuade someone from taking a job. Therefore, it is extremely valuable to enable people to work from wherever they are located.

NFX (a fictional company) discovered this several years back. NFX is in the business of multimedia. In particular, NFX develops multimedia software applications such as prototypes, demonstrations, kiosks, and computer-based training courses. These applications incorporate the work of programmers with that of graphic artists, musicians, and other specialists. In order to employ the varied talent required to produce these applications, NFX uses Notes as the infrastructure that ties together employees and consultants located at headquarters, remote locations, other business, and even people's homes.

Roger Purnell is a salesman with NFX who supports the VBC Inc. account. He is about to start a new project to build a computer-based training application.

MAKE IT EXCITING, BUT COST EFFECTIVE

Before driving to the headquarters of VBC Inc., Roger turns on his notebook computer and brings up Notes. As a salesman for NFX, Roger uses Notes for his everyday work. Since he is about to start a new project, he creates a new database from the Project template provided by the NFX Notes support group. He titles his database VBC Inc./Training, since he knows that the application is a computer-based training project. After his meeting at VBC, Roger will mail the database to the Notes support group to get it replicated to their server, so he can begin involving other people in the project.

For now, Roger fills in some basic information in the VBC Inc./Training database. He copies the Customer Information document out of one of his other project databases for VBC and pastes it into the new database. He then composes a Project Overview form and writes what he knows about the project so far, which is that it will involve computer-based training. Roger will fill in more data later in his meeting with Stan Caslow.

Stan works in VBC's Technical Education department. He is currently assigned to decrease the cost of the training program for customer support positions. Since the customer support jobs experience very high turnover, the need for customer support training is practically constant. This requires a fair amount of time from trainers, which equates to a high training cost, which VBC would like to reduce. Furthermore, new customer support personnel must wait for the next training course, and in the meantime they might be starting their support functions without adequate training.

Stan contacted Roger to see whether NFX could put together a training aid to reduce the cost of training and allow new support personnel to begin their training whenever they want. Roger is visiting Stan today to discuss some ideas.

At the meeting, Roger asks Stan to describe the existing training. Stan explains that training consists of a mix of lectures and hands-on experimentation. Customer support involves answering customer questions over the phone, as well as visiting customer sites. There is a computer system used by the customer support staff as a database of known problems and situations, with recommended actions. The computer system also provides other functions like logging customer complaints, tracking "open" complaints, and producing reports about how well customer troubles are being resolved.

Stan continues to explain that they have tried videotaping the lectures to play for new support personnel, but that this was abandoned because it did not work out well. "The tapes were, well, boring. The students wouldn't really pay attention. And there were no exercises and no chance for students to ask questions. We had to provide as much assistance to the students using the videotapes as we did the old way, so we threw out the tapes."

Roger explains that a computer-based training application would be a good solution to his problem. "With a multimedia computer-based training application, the student is totally engaged in the material. Graphics, sound effects, and music are used to keep the application interesting as well as to reinforce the points being made by the application. The application itself can be very interactive, so the student learns how to use the real system while going through the application. Furthermore, the student can go at his/her own pace, and can back up or get more help on topics."

Stan agrees that this could be a good solution. He asks Roger to put together a demonstration of the idea so he can sell it to his management. Roger asks if he can sit in on part of a training session to get the flavor of the application. Stan obliges and brings Roger down to a classroom where a training session is underway. Roger watches for an hour and then shakes hands with Stan and departs.

In the car, Roger brings Notes up on his notebook computer and logs his observations and thoughts about the training application. He enters it into the Project Overview form he created earlier. He takes special care to describe the computer system functions as best he can, so they can be mimicked in the demonstration prototype he will have built. He then heads into the office and mails the database to the Notes support group to be replicated to the NFX server.

GATHERING THE TEAM

After sending off the VBC Inc./Training database for replication, Roger contacts Lisa Kovach, a project manager with whom Roger has worked on VBC projects before. He asks Lisa if she can handle putting together the demonstration prototype for the training application. Lisa says she'll look at the material in the database once it's available on the server and get back to Roger. Roger makes a note to himself to update the access control list (ACL) of the new database to give Lisa Manager rights. If Lisa is going to be the project manager, she'll need to be able to give other people access to the database, so she must be a Manager.

The next day Lisa calls Roger on the phone. "I've looked over the material you put in the database. It looks like a fairly straightforward job. I see you stressed the graphics/sound aspect of it as much as the simulation of their computer system."

Roger responds, "Yeah, the client said their attempt at creating training tapes produced something that was boring. I want this to be anything other than boring!"

Lisa told Roger she understands and will make sure to get a sound effects person involved to really liven up the application. She asks Roger if a month is OK. Roger says he thinks that is fine, but will check with Stan. He will also tell Stan that she might call to get more details about the training material.

Lisa immediately begins to gather her team to put together the demonstration. She opens the database containing the list of current employees and contractors available to work on projects. She sees that Lois Taddeo, an application programmer Lisa has worked with in the past, has converted from a part-time consultant to a full-time employee. She calls Lois to see if she is available for the project. She is, so Lisa makes a note to call Lois' supervisor and clear the project. She adds Lois to the ACL of the VBC Inc./Training database so Lois can begin looking over the materials.

Lisa then identifies George Vitek as a graphic artist to work on creating artwork and diagrams for the application. George is a part-time consultant who works out of state. Since he does a fair amount of work for NFX, George runs Notes and can dial into the NFX server. Lisa calls him and asks him to check out the materials in the database and start thinking about a style to use for the graphics in the training application. George says OK, and when he gets off the phone with Lisa, he calls into the server and replicates the database down to his home-office PC.

Lisa then identifies Jeremy Cain as a musician/sound effects expert who she thinks can add a lot to the project. Jeremy is also a consultant who works out of state. Since everyone uses Notes, it is easy for different members of the project team to work together. She contacts Jeremy and asks him to check out the materials also.

DEVELOPING THE DEMONSTRATION PROTOTYPE

Lisa gives her people a couple of days to think about the training application. She then checks into the database to see if people have started working. In the General Information view, she sees that Lois, George, and Jeremy have started a discussion about how to build the application. They pick their favorite multimedia authoring tool and agree to start developing some samples. As the application programmer, Lois describes how she expects the application to start, what kind of intro it could have, and how the application will flow. George agrees to develop some artwork for the opening screens as well as a general style for each training screen. Jeremy describes some ideas for sound effects and asks for comments from the others.

Lisa responds to some of the comments her team has put into the database. She likes the direction they're going and would like to see the initial artwork, sound effects, and application framework in a week. When she checks the next day she sees that the others have agreed to the time frame.

A week later, Lisa checks in to see the progress her team has made. She opens the Application Components view to see the actual code, artwork, and music/sound effects her team has produced. She sees in the category labeled Application Software that Lois has created a document titled Training Demonstration/Prototype. She opens the document and sees a file attachment and some text. The text describes the file attachment as containing the very first shell of an application so that George and Jeremy know what they're working into. She launches the file attachment and sees a skeleton program with no artwork, music, or sound effects. It does, however, have a layout of buttons to let the user navigate through the training, pause, request more help, and so on.

In another category, Artwork, she sees several documents authored by George. One is titled Splash Screen and contains the very first piece of artwork the application will display. Another is titled Logos and contains the VBC logo in various sizes and color schemes. Another, titled Standard Background, is a soft marble background to be used throughout the application.

Lisa composes a Response to the Standard Background document in which she writes, "This is a very classy background scheme, but I wonder if we couldn't use something a little more colorful and snazzy?" George will see this Response the next time he replicates the database and can incorporate her comments into his artwork.

Another category, Music, contains a couple of documents created by Jeremy. One, titled Opening Theme, contains a file attachment with some music. It also contains a note saying, "Here are a few measures of a theme we might use in this application. Let me know what you think." Lisa launches it and listens. It's great and she writes a Response saying so. Another document titled Background Music contains a few file attachments of some different possible background themes to play during the training.

The final category in the view is labeled Sound Effects and contains several documents by Jeremy. One is titled For a Right Answer. Another is titled For a Wrong Answer. Another is titled For Three Wrong Answers in a Row. These contain short sound effects Jeremy thinks could help keep the application interesting. He asks for comments to see if they are too "wild" for a corporate training application. Lisa listens to them and lets Jeremy know that they seem right on target to her and to go with them for the demonstration.

The Application Components view in the VBC Inc. / Training application

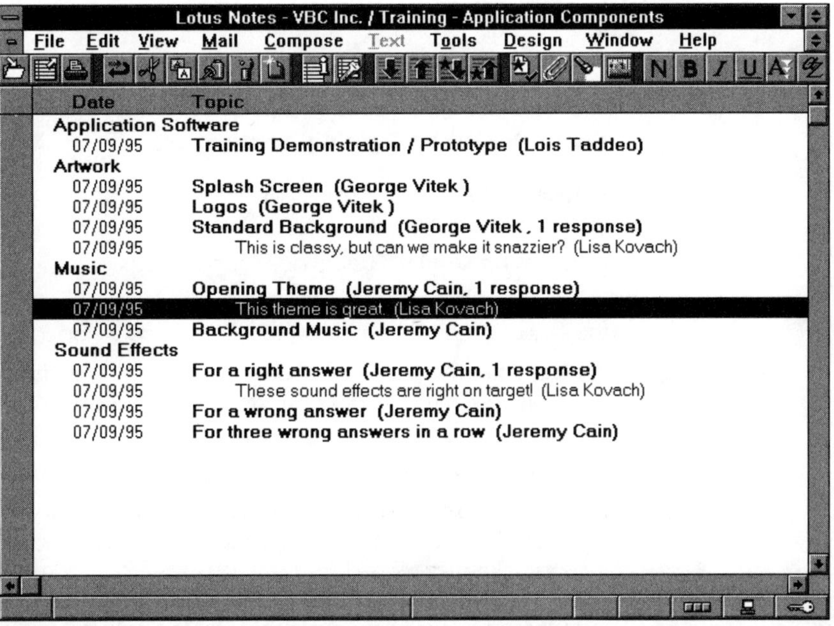

Lisa can see that the team is making progress. Every few days, she checks in to see how things are going and to run the latest version of the application contained in the database. As the end of the month-long development period draws near, she is pleased to see how well the prototype has taken shape.

LOOKS GREAT—LET'S DO IT!

Lisa sets up a meeting with Roger and Stan to show off the demonstration prototype and plan out their next steps. The day of the meeting she replicates the database to her notebook computer so she has the latest version of the demonstration. She brings her notebook computer with her to VBC, where she meets Roger. Together they go into Stan's office and view the demonstration.

Stan is impressed with the sparkle of the prototype and with the programming job done to simulate their support system. He makes some comments about how the final version should look and asks for a formal estimate of the total price and schedule for the job. He also asks for another meeting where he can show the demonstration off to his management to get approval for the project.

Lisa and Roger agree to work out the bid and set up the next meeting. Afterward, Lisa enters her congratulations into the database about the good work her team did including Stan's comments. Later she replicates the database to the server so the team can access her note.

FACT SHEET

Computer-Based Training Application

Purpose: To support a multimedia development team in working together while being geographically separate.

Application Origin: Custom developed.

Application Development Time: Each project is contained in its own database based on the Project template. The Project template was developed in a few weeks.

Typical Size: The size of these databases can be quite large since they contain application code, artwork, music, and sound effects. A 50-MB database would not be surprising.

Typical Use: On projects where it is hard to obtain local expertise, or where the part-time services of experts are often needed, as in the case of sound effects and artwork.

Forms: The Project Overview form is used to describe the project being proposed. It contains fields such as Target Platform, Hardware Limitations, Approximate Cost, and Approximate Development Schedule. The Customer Information form contains general information about the customer, including name, address, phone numbers, contacts, description of their industry and particular products/services. The Application Component form is used to store code, artwork, music, sound effects, or other material used in the application being developed. The Response and Response to Response forms are used to capture comments about other's submissions.

Views: The General Information view contains such information as the customer information, the project overview, the project schedule, and bids. The Application Components view lists the Application Component forms and their Response and Response to Response forms.

Designing a Product Jointly with Suppliers

Designing a new product is a challenging process. These challenges are heightened when the people involved are not located at the same site. A Discussion database can be used to support people working together on a design, and Notes replication features can be used to bring geographically dispersed groups together.

Beth Hughes is the product manager of a new product her company plans to produce. To get the product out on time and under budget, her team rapidly has to develop requirements for components of the product. This could best be accomplished by working directly with a team of people from one of her suppliers. Beth's team is located in New York and her supplier's team is in California. Her goal is to develop a complete set of requirements in six weeks. She plans to meet this objective by creating a Notes database in which the two teams share ideas and discuss proposed requirements. She plans to call it the New Component Requirements database.

MAKING THE NOTES CONNECTION

The first issue Beth faces is how users in New York and California can work on the same database. One option is to place the database on her Notes server in New York and have the California users dial in to modems connected to the server. This would require each user on the supplier team to dial in individually. Each team member would incur long distance phone charges each time they accessed the database. If five users in California needed to access the database, that would be five long-distance calls.

Another option is to install a dedicated line between her LAN and the supplier's LAN, forming a WAN between the two organizations. Users on both teams could now access the data on her Notes server in New York directly. While this would allow all users to share information instantaneously, it would be very expensive and time consuming to install.

To handle these challenges, Notes provides a feature called *replication* which solves most of the problems with the other two options. Beth can place a replica copy of the database on her own server in New York, and another replica copy on the supplier's server in California. The Notes administrators can then schedule replication between the two servers whereby they will call each other using modems and a regular phone line. Each time they replicate, all changes to the database that have occurred since the last replication will be exchanged. At the end of the replication, the two copies of the database have the same information. Notes is very efficient at replication, and in general these phone calls will be fairly short (depending on the amount of activity that has taken place in the databases since the last replication).

The servers can be scheduled to replicate every hour, which means that there will be a maximum delay of one hour between the time something is entered into the database in one location, and when it is be replicated to the other location.

Having solved the problem of how to provide access to the database to all users at a reasonable cost with minimal delay, Beth can turn to the next issue—security. How will she know her competitors aren't dialing into the server to copy the requirements? The answer to this lies in Notes' built-in security features.

When Beth's server receives a call from another server or a user, it will force the other computer to *authenticate* itself. Only those servers belonging to organizations she has *certified* will pass the authentication test. For more information, see the sidebar "How Do I Know You Are Really You?"

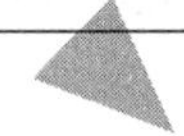

How Do I Know You Are Really You?

Notes provides a robust security model based on RSA public-key technology. This powerful security system is one of the key features that differentiates Notes from other groupware applications. What follows is a simplified discussion of the Notes security model. For more information on Notes security, see the Notes administrator's manual.

Anytime a user attempts to connect to a server, the server attempts to *authenticate* the user. Authentication is a test that seeks to verify that a user is who they say they are. This test relies on certificates. Each user in Notes has an ID file. Each ID file needs to be stamped with a certificate by an administrator to get access to a server. When you attempt to connect to your server (either through your LAN or by dialing in), your computer gives the server your *public key* (which is part of your ID file) and your certificate. The server takes this information and matches your certificate against a set of certificates it knows and trusts. If your certificate proves to be valid (that is, it passes certain mathematical tests that prove it was not forged), the server sends back a random number encrypted with your public key. Your machine decrypts it using your private key and sends it back. If you send back the correct unencrypted number, you must have the correct private key (as this is the only key that will be able to decrypt the number). The server can then assume that you are really who you say you are. These same rules apply when two servers communicate in Notes. Each server attempts to authenticate the other server by validating certificates and the fact that the other server has the correct private key.

Another security issue is granting the appropriate access levels to each user or group of users in the database. Beth can tackle this problem by setting Access Control Lists for the database.

Ready for Use

The New Component Requirements database is now ready for action. A good way to kick off the database is by entering a few of the well-known requirements. Beth can assign a category to each document to start building up the list of categories that the requirements would fall into. She can even initiate a couple of discussions to provide users with examples of the type of dialog she'd like to see, so Beth creates some Main documents and some corresponding Responses. Now the members of her team have access to the requirements and questions she has answered, and within an hour, so will the members of the supplier's team.

Because all the members of both teams use the database, individuals can contribute ideas, questions, or requirements without needing to address those comments to anyone in particular—all postings are seen by all team members, and anyone can respond. By storing each of the postings, the database allows users to have online discussions of ideas or proposals. Team members can trace back the origin of ideas and the logic of how they got transformed into requirements. Beth's team will be able to use the database to provide one another with feedback and to ensure requirements address the overall needs of their team's project. The supplier's team will be able to use the database to increase their understanding of Beth's team's needs, to develop ideas proposed by her team, and to provide pointed feedback on proposed requirements. As the weeks go by, Beth can watch the progress of the requirements by monitoring open and closed issues, which categories are fleshed out and which are weak, and so on.

Jill Gibson leads the supplier's planning team in California. She will also head the team to actually develop the component once the requirements are complete. Jill's first contact with the Notes database is in helping Beth get the database replicated to her server in California. She has provided Beth with the name and telephone number of her Notes administrator. The two administrators will work together to exchange certificates, get a replica copy of the database on Jill's server, and schedule the replication.

At the completion of this process, Jill gets an e-mail from her administrator indicating that the database is up and available on her server. She adds the database to her desktop and opens it. At this point, the database contains only the documents Beth put there to initiate the discussion. Jill realizes that she will have to set an example to her team members to show them that participating in the discussion is important to the success of the project. She responds to each of Beth's comments and sends some e-mails to her team members asking them to respond also.

Notes can be set up to show the number of unread documents in each database. When someone adds or changes a document, the unread count will increase. Beth can use this as a signal to check the database for new information. Since all documents are labeled with the author's name, she can easily track the use of the database.

The By Category view in the New Component Requirements database

As the database grows, Jill sees a number of comments from one of Beth's teammates that she perceives as unreasonable requests. Knowing how easy it is to misinterpret electronic communications she posts responses asking for clarification of a number of points. Once she receives clarification, she is able to propose some alternatives that are more readily achieved given other project constraints. This sort of response is critical to ensuring that the two teams continue to move forward in identifying requirements.

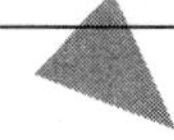

Notes Etiquette

With face-to-face communications, there are many nonverbal clues that help us understand the other person's perceptions and motivations. We use these clues to help us clarify differences and similarities in our views and objectives. Understanding these is critical to successful business ventures. The lack of these clues significantly complicates electronic communications. Misinterpretation and invalid assumptions of others' views are common. To ensure successful communications, the following rules may be helpful:

▶ Communicate your ideas clearly and completely. It is common for people to leave out what they perceive as being obvious when this is anything but obvious to the reader.

▶ Reread all postings prior to submission. By rereading your writing and taking the point of view of an ignorant reader, you can better understand how your posting will be interpreted.

▶ Never make assumptions about a writer's intentions. It is common (particularly when a writer has not followed the first two rules) to make assumptions about a writer's intentions. This can lead to significant misinterpretation and rapid escalation of problems.

THE FINAL PRODUCT

At the end of the six-week design period, Beth can archive the database and print a copy of the requirements. She can create a private view of the database containing only the final requirements without the questions, comments, or discussion. This will enable her to print a clean copy of the requirements. The result is a set of requirements that are understood and can readily be fulfilled by her supplier in California.

FACT SHEET

New Component Requirements Database

Purpose: To support two organizations, e.g., a customer and a supplier, in jointly discussing requirements for a new product. The organizations are in different companies and are located in different parts of the world.

Application Origin: Derived from the Discussion template bundled with Notes.

Application Development Time: 36 hours over 2 weeks—all customization work done by the database owner.

Typical Size: 2–5 MB, 200–500 documents.

Typical Use: A product team in the customer's organization would use the application to develop requirements by entering requirements, comments, and questions into the database. The product team in the supplier's organization can oversee the evolution of the requirements, and can to participate in the discussion, answer questions, and pose alternatives. Servers at the customer's and supplier's locations will replicate the discussion database frequently (e.g., every hour to every day, depending on needs) so that both product teams have timely access to the current state of requirements, and can support rapid issue resolution. When the product teams reach consensus, the requirements can be frozen and printed to constitute a formal agreement.

Forms: The Main Topic form is used to enter a requirement. The Response form is used to enter comments or pose questions about particular requirements. The Response to Response form supports discussion about a comment or question.

Views: The By Category view is the most frequently used view. It provides a listing of requirements grouped by category, where the categories are created on the fly by users entering requirements. This provides a logical grouping of requirements so users can easily understand the contents of the database. The By Author view is used by a user reviewing their own requirements or looking for a requirement written by a particular person. The Main View is used less often, and provides a chronological view of the requirements, showing the most recently entered requirements last.

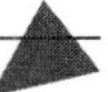

Electronic Publishing in Notes: The News-letter Database

Irish Software (IS) is a (hypothetical) software company that develops database systems for large multinational companies. In an effort to serve its customers better, IS has decided to provide a newsletter to keep the customers up to date on company and product news. The newsletter will be published twice a month, and will contain announcements, descriptions of new products, new alliances and partnerships, and a case-study section, where examples of how the IS products are being used by specific customers will be provided. Management hopes that providing this information directly to customers will help forge closer ties between IS and its customers. Providing the newsletter electronically offers a number of benefits to customers. An electronic newsletter can be updated rapidly to reflect new announcements or changes to existing information. Electronic information can be more readily shared among co-workers. It can be searched, copied, pasted, and printed with ease. Anna Phillips works in the marketing organization and has been assigned the task of developing this electronic newsletter.

IS's marketing group already "publishes" a number of different types of information (see the "Knowledgebase" chapter). It will be important that the newsletter relies on the existing resources as much as possible. Unfortunately, each one of the existing publications is produced in a different manner. For example, IS's Knowledgebase is developed in Notes, the company's product catalog is stored in a Unix-based desktop publishing system, and corporate presentations are done on a Macintosh.

It will also be important to clarify the relationship between the Knowledgebase and the Newsletter. In some organizations, these databases can be merged. At IS, the content is generally distinct (some overlap is conceivable), and the two databases have different audiences (the Knowledgebase targets technical personnel; the Newsletter targets business managers). These reasons justify keeping the applications separate.

CHOOSING A PLATFORM

Anna's first step is to identify a target platform in which to publish this information. What follows is a list of some of the alternatives with a brief description of the pros and cons of each:

- ▶ Electronic Mail. One option would be to send copies of new documents to a list of electronic mail addresses. This option is flexible, in that any user who can receive Internet mail can get documents. However, it would be difficult to embed graphics (as they would need to be encoded differently for each mail system), the delivered mail message would be in a user's mail file and therefore not readily accessible to other users, it would consume large amounts of disk space, and it would be difficult to issue updates to sections of the newsletter.
- ▶ World Wide Web (WWW). When combined with a graphical browsing tool like Mosaic or Netscape, the WWW is a powerful and economical tool to publish electronic information. Benefits include low setup and operating costs, its widespread acceptance as an intercorporate communication standard, its support for a variety of data types, and its general ease of use. Drawbacks include restrictive document formatting, lack of tools (e.g., full-text search, Discussion databases, tools to create and maintain documents), questionable reliability, and lack of security.
- ▶ Commercial Online Services. A number of large companies provide electronic information to their customers through one of the commercial on-line services (Compuserve, AOL, Prodigy, and Delphi). These services are typically costly and complicated to establish and maintain. However, these services are available throughout the U.S. and in many foreign countries.
- ▶ Lotus Notes. Notes provides powerful tools for building applications and identifying relevant information (e.g., full-text search). It is available on multiple platforms and provides support for numerous data types including OLE objects, text, sound, and video. Unfortunately, Notes can be complex to install and maintain (which would be a problem for those customers who do not have Notes already), and the process of connecting customers requires significant effort (though once a connection is made, it is simple to maintain).

For a number of reasons, Anna decides Notes should be the target platform for initial development. In addition to the reasons mentioned above, Notes was chosen because her company already has a mature Notes installation and has connections to a number of customers. This has the effect of reducing some of the negative aspects of creating the newsletter in Notes mentioned above, and making the initial investment (in time, training, and equipment) minimal.

The Application and the Published Document

Anna bases the application on the Discussion template provided with Notes. She deletes the Response document form and creates one Main Document form. This form has a Category field—she provides the following categories: Newsletter, Product Information, Case Study, Tool, and Miscellaneous. It also has a Rich Text field for the body of each document and some administrative fields, including Author Name, Creation Date, and some Revision History information.

Users will be expected to "categorize" (by selecting one of the provided categories in the category field) each document added to the database. These categories will be used to distinguish different document types in views.

The basic views provided in the Notes discussion template prove adequate for the first iteration of the newsletter application. Anna updates field names to include the new field names she has created and creates a number of documents to ensure that the views categorize the documents correctly.

She still has to solve the problem of multiple sources of information. There are a number of potential sources of information from different platforms. One option is to have each organization publish their information directly into Notes. While Lotus has attempted to provide tools to streamline this process, it would still require significant work on the part of the publishing organization to publish information twice (once in the native format and again in Notes). A more desirable option would be to provide the data in an electronic publishing tool format.

Electronic publishing tools like Common Ground or Acrobat take data created on any one of a number of platforms and applications and save it to a proprietary format. This new file will look similar and print identically, regardless of the user's operating environment (Macintosh or Windows). As long as the recipient has the software to read the file, they can see a document exactly as it was created, regardless of the platform or application used by the author to create the document. Notes has the ability to display embedded files (including files created by electronic publishing tools). If files are embedded in this manner, the recipient only needs the reader to manipulate (e.g., zoom in, zoom out, copy or paste) the embedded file. Since the electronic publishing readers are typically free, the reader can be attached to a document (using the Tool form) and distributed to recipients.

Once the application prototype is complete, Anna reviews it with other Notes developers. This review leads to a number of technical and aesthetic suggestions. She obtains sample data from some of the target publishing groups, and writes a brief newsletter to showcase the application. Next, she schedules a meeting with the managers of the marketing department for a more formal review of the application. Suggestions are made regarding target customers, rollout dates, expected content and the like. She incorporates their suggestions and starts work on a rollout plan. The total development time has been about two weeks.

THE DEPLOYMENT

The deployment targets a large group of prominent customers to help evaluate the application. Each of these clients is contacted in hopes of finding other customers interested in participating in the evaluation. The large number of companies is gradually reduced to a more manageable number (under ten). The criteria used include the level of interest they exhibit in the application, their relationship with IS, whether they have Notes, and whether they are currently connected to IS's Notes environment. She provides the list of companies to the Notes administrator. This helps the administrators ensure that each company can replicate the newsletter a short time after the initial document is complete.

Anna begins working with other individuals from the Marketing department to identify topics to discuss in the newsletters. Enough topics are identified to fill up a few months' worth of newsletters. Assignments are distributed to group members. Much of the data will come from existing sources. Each assignment indicates where the data is available, and an expected format for the data. A week later, the first issue is complete. She adds the documents to the database, posts the database to a local server, sets up the access control list (individually listing servers and users from each of the trial customers), setting the default access to No Access, and notifies her administrator that she should replicate the data to the target customers.

The trial period lasts two months. This duration allows the target customers to evaluate a number of newsletter publications, allowing them to make more precise comments. Near the end of the trial period, an electronic survey form is sent to relevant parties at each of the participating companies. In general, comments suggest that both the format and content is relevant. Suggestions are also made to provide more information about certain topics and less about others. It is also strongly suggested that a Comment form should be provided to allow customers to comment on either the content or structure of the application.

At the conclusion of the trial period, a letter is sent out to customers indicating general availability of the newsletter. The default access control for the database is changed from No Access to Reader. This allows customers who are already connected to her Notes server the ability to replicate the database to their local Notes server immediately. Customers who are not already connected are handled on a first-come–first-serve basis.

By Date view in the company Newsletter database

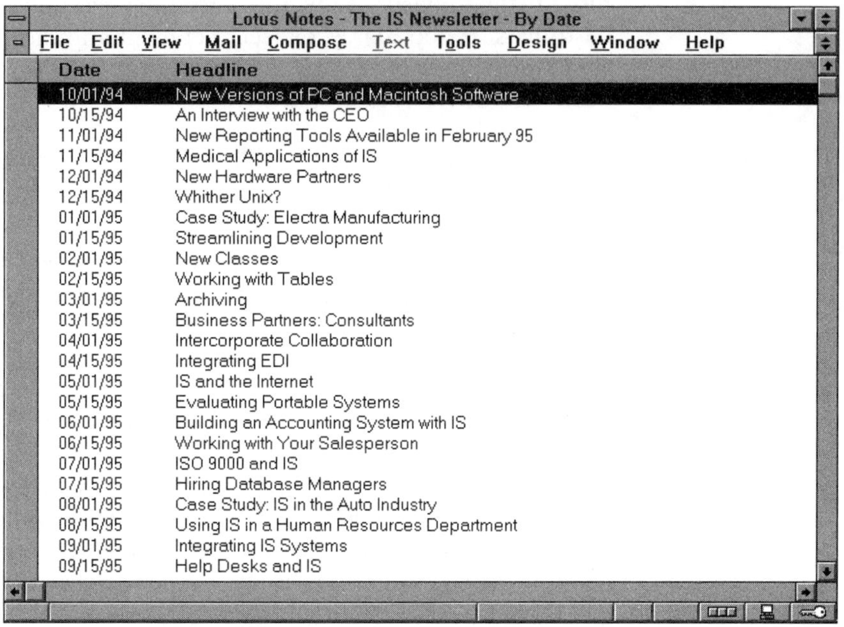

UNFINISHED BUSINESS

Over time it becomes clear that publishing the newsletter is more than a full-time job. Content must be checked for relevance and accuracy by a number of people before being distributed. In addition, some customers have questioned the value of the newsletter. Usage of the application on their servers remains light. Discussions ensue in Marketing, and it is decided that the newsletter should be "repackaged" as part of a suite of information applications including the company's Knowledgebase and a Discussion database to be shared with major accounts. The newsletter will then be one of a suite of applications that new customers will get when they connect to the company's Notes environment. The general consensus is that the newsletter will be more sympathetically received as part of a larger package of information about IS. This larger package might include other types of reference materials, product updates, utilities, and more.

 **FACT SHEET**

Newsletter Database

Purpose: To distribute a corporate newsletter to an organization's customers. This newsletter might complement other Notes databases provided to customers to keep them informed about the company and its products.

Application Origin: Derived from the Discussion template.

Application Development Time: Approximately 16 hours.

Typical Size: Under 5 MB.

Typical Use: The company regularly produces a newsletter which is posted to the database. The database is replicated to all customers, who can thereby keep informed about developments at the company.

Forms: Newsletter and Comment.

Views: By Topic and By Date.

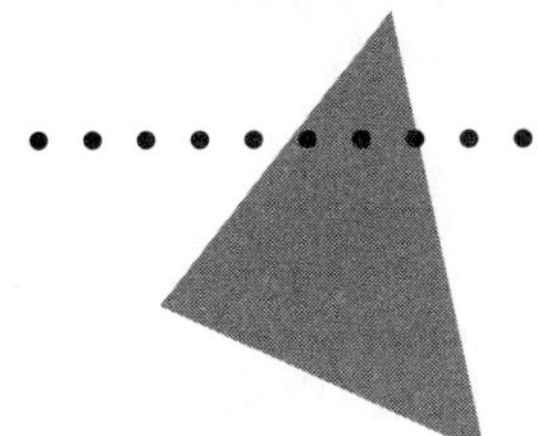

Index

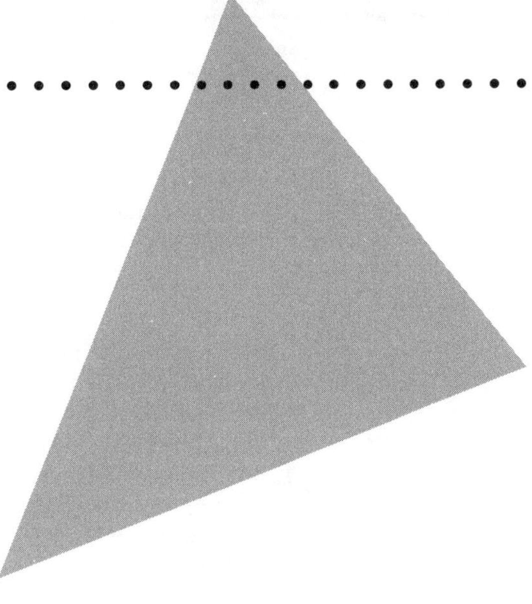

describing, 79
indexing, 330
private, 145
selecting which documents displayed,
   265
shared, 145
types, 145

W
WANs (wide area networks), 74
Windows
   applications that use Notes data, 250
   help system, 9
Workstation-based mail, 24
Writing Request for Proposals (RFPs),
      109–110
Z
Zmerge, 191